Into the
VIETNAMESE KITCHEN

Into the
VIETNAMESE KITCHEN

Treasured Foodways, Modern Flavors

ANDREA QUYNHGIAO NGUYEN

FOREWORD BY BRUCE COST

PHOTOGRAPHY BY LEIGH BEISCH

TEN SPEED PRESS
www.tenspeed.com

To my parents, Tuyet Thi Nguyen and Hoang Quoc Nguyen, and my husband, Rory.

Ten Speed Press
PO Box 7123
Berkeley, California 94707
www.tenspeed.com

Distributed in Australia by Simon and Schuster Australia, in Canada by Ten Speed Press Canada, in New Zealand by Southern Publishers Group, in South Africa by Real Books, and in the United Kingdom and Europe by Publishers Group UK.

Cover design by Toni Tajima
Text design by Ed Anderson
Typesetting by Katy Brown
Food styling by Karen Shinto
Prop styling by Sara Slavin
Photography assistance by Angelica Cao
Styling assistance by Katie Christ

Frontispiece: Yellow rock sugar

Library of Congress Cataloging-in-Publication Data

Nguyen, Andrea Quynhgiao.
   Into the Vietnamese kitchen : treasured foodways, modern flavors
   / Andrea Quynhgiao Nguyen ; foreword by Bruce Cost ;
photography by Leigh Beisch.
      p. cm.
   Includes bibliographical references and index.
   ISBN-13: 978-1-58008-665-3
   ISBN-10: 1-58008-665-9
   1. Cookery, Vietnamese. 2. Food habits—Vietnam.   I. Title.
TX724.5.V5N47 2006
641.59597—dc22
                                        2006012158

Printed in China
First printing, 2006

1 2 3 4 5 6 7 8 9 10 – 10 09 08 07 06

CONTENTS

ACKNOWLEDGMENTS

I have wanted to write a Vietnamese cookbook since I was ten years old. When I was offered the opportunity to do just that, I discovered both how much and how little I knew. Many people assisted me along the way, and I am indebted to all of them for their guidance and support.

First and foremost, I want to thank Mẹ and Bố, who sparked and then fueled my interest in food, cooking, and Vietnamese traditions. How lucky I am to have parents who are also passionate food experts. As I wrote, they tirelessly answered my questions, shared their knowledge and discoveries, helped with translations, and reviewed the manuscript. When they did not know the answers, they tapped their network of Vietnamese retirees.

A number of recipes and cooking tips were shared by family members and friends over the years. These contributions are recognized in the recipe introductions.

Special thanks to Susan Littwin for believing in this project from its inception. She helped me polish the proposal and guided me with her wisdom as a seasoned author.

I am equally grateful to recipe testers Sue Holt, Victor Fong, Al Meyers, Maki Tsuzuki, and Mike Crane. Their steadfast dedication and enthusiasm kept me on track and buoyed me when my spirits flagged.

I was also blessed by the insights of Asian food expert Bruce Cost. Our lengthy e-mail exchanges helped me to solve a variety of vexing issues.

Most Vietnamese immigrants in the United States do not become food writers. Asian parents prefer that their children follow practical and profitable career paths. My parents were no different, but they also instilled in me a love and appreciation for the culinary arts. I started out in banking and went on to a handful of other careers, but this one has been the most fun and the most rewarding. I would have never pursued this book project had it not been for the following individuals: Colman Andrews, who invited me to write for *Saveur* magazine and saw the potential in this endeavor; Russ Parsons and Leslie Brenner, who accepted my ideas and edited my work for the *Los Angeles Times*; and Carolyn Jung, who started me writing for the *San Jose Mercury News* and encouraged me to continue writing. These journalists, along with their colleagues, helped me hone my writing skills and steered me in the right direction. Although our interactions were sometimes fleeting, I owe each one of them a great deal.

Generous thanks are owed to Mishka Michon for her early enthusiastic support of this book. At the University of Southern California, Professor Michael Preston mentored me with his practical and sage advice.

These pages would not have materialized without the folks at Ten Speed Press, in particular, Philip Wood, Lorena Jones, Kathy Hashimoto, and Aaron Wehner, my enthusiastic and thoughtful editor. They all believed that I had something valuable to say. My words benefited from the professional excellence of copy editor Sharon Silva and proofreader Desne Ahlers; photographer Leigh Beisch, assisted by Angelica Cao; food stylist Karen Shinto, assisted by Katie Christ; prop stylist Sara Slavin (and the generous loan of props by Sue Fisher King); designers Ed Anderson, Toni Tajima, and Katy Brown; and indexer Ken DellaPenta.

A zillion thank-yous to William Rubel and Sonia Bañuelos for cracking open the door.

My dear husband, Rory O'Brien, has always been and continues to be my number one fan. He has suffered, celebrated, critiqued, and smiled through this entire journey. His patience, understanding, and love are amazing.

Finally, generous thanks go to Internet visitors like Karl Nguyen who have perused the content of vietworldkitchen.com and e-mailed comments. Their insights and feedback inform and improve my work.

FOREWORD

Andrea Nguyen has taken a big step forward on behalf of Vietnamese cooking. She has written a cookbook that you can use and enjoy, layered with details—practical, historical, and personal—that foster a deeper understanding of this ancient cuisine.

You need only turn to her recipe for *phở bò*, Vietnam's famed beef noodle soup, to appreciate her achievement. She wants you to love this soup, but in order for you to do so, she insists that you must make it right, a process that begins (and ends) with the broth. This requires using high-quality marrow bones, to impart a rich beef flavor, and a little yellow rock sugar (also used in the wonderful braised pork and duck dishes of eastern China), to lend complexity that mere granulated sugar lacks. When Andrea introduces a recipe by writing, "Traditional cooks use extra lard or oil to give the shrimp, which are still in the shell, an appetizing sheen," she is giving the reader an important option: follow her recipe, which is delicious, or seek even greater insight into the cuisine by rendering your own pork fat and sourcing head-on, or even live, shrimp.

I have gotten to know Andrea over the past couple of years, mostly through lengthy correspondence about arcane aspects of Asian food and cooking. She has taken me shopping and eating in Little Saigon in Westminster, California, and she directed several of my top chefs in Chicago in the preparation of an array of classic dishes from this book. I felt a kinship with her in her search here for a whole catfish, *with skin*, because the gelatin is necessary to give proper body to her caramel sauce. Her technique of cooking shrimp in a little water and salt until dry, and then mincing them as a garnish for steamed rice pancakes, was new to me. Capturing the essence of their flavor, the method transformed the shrimp into a terrific seasoning.

Andrea's book is timely because Vietnam is rapidly becoming a tourist destination for Americans after years of isolation following the Vietnam War. I had the opportunity to travel in Vietnam last summer with my teenage son, Ben, eating and visiting markets. What struck us (and this is true elsewhere in Asia) is that the freshness of the ingredients drives the cuisine, as Andrea so often reminds us. When entering a seafood restaurant on the coast south of Nha Trang, rather than looking at a menu, our first task was to peruse tanks of swimming fish and crustaceans both familiar and unfamiliar, such as mantis shrimp and slipper lobsters. After deliberating with the restaurant staff over how each should be cooked, our table was loaded with the tastiest possible sea creatures and an array of delicious dipping sauces and fresh herbs. Andrea's book vividly evoked this memory for me, and should I care to re-create the feast, she equips me with the necessary recipes and insights.

Andrea brings an extra measure of intelligence to this volume, and she is an uncommonly good writer, encouraging readers to share in her vision and learn what she knows. She is an engaging ambassador for the wonderful cooking of Vietnam.

Bruce Cost
Chicago, May 2006

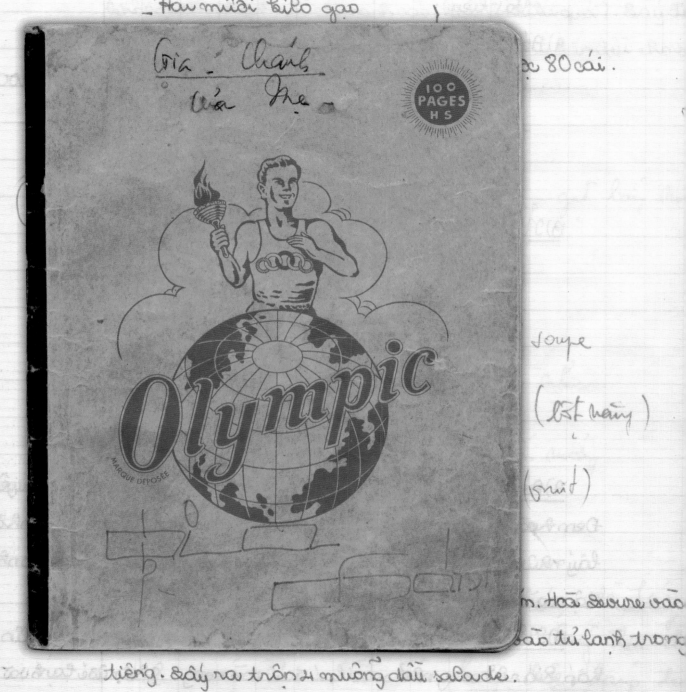

INTRODUCTION

We heard the plane coming in low and I was scared. Mom grabbed me, pulling me underneath the staircase as a bomb exploded nearby. I shrieked, believing the end was near. It was April 8, 1975, and though I was only six years old, I knew that the stalemate between North and South Vietnam was about to end. All I could do was cling to my mother's legs and cry.

"Hush child. Calm down. What will you do in the time of real war?" my mother said in a steely voice. For her, this was not the time to panic. Instead, it was just a minor incident in a bad situation that was soon going to worsen. When the noise subsided, Mom went about restoring calm, first inventorying the kitchen to make sure nothing had broken.

Indeed, events were coming to a head. The dry season was ending, the humidity was rising, and the air was thick with worry and fear. North Vietnamese forces were advancing quickly toward Saigon. On April 21, South Vietnam President Nguyen Van Thieu announced his resignation.

My dad locked the door to our house for the last time on April 23. That morning the seven of us crammed into the family

Left: My mother's orange recipe notebook
Top right: My parents and me at Vung Tau beach, circa 1972

Peugeot sedan and drove away. We resisted the urge to take a last look back at the house for fear of drawing suspicion, and instead focused on the road that stretched before us.

What lay ahead—the unknown—scared us all. In a photo of my mom and us five kids taken just before we left (shown on page 2), everyone except my sister Ha, who is displaying a characteristic smirk, looks grim. But the alternative to escaping was worse: stay in Saigon and wait for the Viet Cong to take over our home and send our father, a former military governor in the administration of President Ngo Dinh Diem, into a reeducation camp.

In truth, my parents had been planning a sea escape for months. My father, who had been carefully monitoring political developments and international negotiations, knew that it was just a matter of time before South Vietnam would fall. Using money pooled with four other families, a cargo boat had been purchased, renovated, and equipped. Because life jackets could not be bought in Vietnam, my mother sewed one for each of us, with our names in bold lettering for easy identification in case we were lost at sea. All of my parents' clandestine planning came to a halt, however, when the government decided to prohibit any unofficial boat from leaving the harbor.

1

Frustrated but determined, Dad made his rounds of the city, asking the few remaining foreigners for assistance. But no one could help him. Without strong overseas connections, he was told, there were few options for escaping. At the same time, others seeking to leave were calling on my father, but there was nothing he could do for them.

On April 22, my father's sister told him that she had made a connection with a former colleague, a U.S. State Department officer with whom she had worked eight years earlier. On the eve of South Vietnam's collapse, this man, along with a friend, had reentered the country to bring out as many people as they could. He had told Aunt Hue to pack and meet him at the Notre Dame Cathedral in central Saigon on the morning of April 23 at ten o'clock. Aunt Hue offered to take my two oldest sisters with her and promised to find a way to sponsor the rest of us after she got to America. Dad refused her offer. The entire family must go, he said.

My parents decided to take all of us to the cathedral. That way, if Aunt Hue's contact permitted us to leave, we would all be ready. Our housekeeper, whom we called Older Sister Thien, waited at home to hear from us. When Aunt Hue emerged from the cathedral and gave Dad a firm nod, we knew it was a go. As

---

A photo taken just before we left Vietnam; clockwise from top left: Ha, Chi, Linh, Dang, my mother, and me

it turned out, the men also agreed to help additional members of my father's family and Older Sister Thien to leave the country. On hearing the good news, Mom sent word to our housekeeper and my father's brothers.

We drove from the cathedral to an empty office building, where we rendezvoused with the two men. The afternoon hours were spent creating documents to get us into Tan Son Nhat airport and out of the country. In the evening, we successfully passed through the government checkpoint at the airport and knew that we were safely on our way. Seven days later, Saigon fell to the communist North.

My parents had purposefully packed light to avoid suspicion, bringing along only their most precious yet practical belongings. Two small, black leather suitcases held identification papers and a change of clothes for each of us. My mother squeezed her best jewelry, a couple of important photos, a bottle of water, two packets of dried instant noodles, and a small orange notebook filled with her handwritten recipes into her handbag. She decided she needed the recipes so that she and Older Sister Thien could open a restaurant in America. Surely, she thought, all the Vietnamese refugees heading for the States would want a bit of home to chew and savor. She guarded her handbag at all times, and the notebook traveled with us from Saigon to Guam to Hawaii and finally to California.

But as soon as we arrived at the Camp Pendleton refugee resettlement facilities (a U.S. Marine base in Southern California), Older Sister Thien thanked my parents and informed them that she had no intention of remaining their employee. She was in the land of opportunity and wanted her liberty. They could do nothing but wish her well.

Eager to get out of the resettlement camp, my father contacted one of the few Americans he knew. Surprisingly, Robert Beals lived only thirty minutes away from the base. Within days, he was made our official sponsor, and we found ourselves at his seaside Laguna Niguel home, eating our first home-cooked American dinner and experiencing many new things.

Our family (on the right, minus my mother) with some relatives and an American reporter at Camp Pendleton in May 1975

Mom now laughs at how astounded she was when Mrs. Beals served her water straight from the tap. In Vietnam, you had to boil water before drinking it because tap water was unreliable. Out of courtesy, my mother drank the water and was relieved to find out it was potable. My siblings and I ate dinner off of TV trays, all the while gazing at a large color television set. Everything seemed like an amazing luxury.

Mr. Beals, who knew my dad as a successful entrepreneur in Vietnam, checked us into an apartment hotel at Dana Point Harbor, a scenic destination for boating, fishing, and vacationing. We welcomed the real pillows and mattresses after living in tents and sleeping on cots at Camp Pendleton. But our new refugee status meant that we couldn't afford the hotel for long. It was quickly eating up the savings we had carried with us from Saigon.

After a week, we checked out and started a new life in the nearby beach town of San Clemente. Dad figured that if San Clemente was good enough for former President Richard Nixon it was good enough for us. We moved into a four-bedroom apartment and immediately went in search of the nearest supermarket to assess what was available. Since we didn't have a car, the seven of us—my dad in front, of course—walked through the streets of San Clemente to an Albertsons supermarket. Curious locals stopped and welcomed us along the way.

At the market, I was amazed to find meats sealed up neatly in Styrofoam and plastic wrap. Much to my parents' chagrin, I poked at each package as we walked down the aisle. I wanted to see if the resilient fleshy objects resembled what I identified as meat on my frequent visits with Older Sister Thien to Saigon's outdoor markets. After all, we used to purchase food with life still in it!

On our way from meats to produce, we passed through the dairy section. Butter, milk, and cheese were displayed among unfamiliar items, such as sour cream and half-and-half. It was clear that the American cow had replaced our beloved water buffalo. Waiting for us in the produce section were beautifully arranged and polished fruits and vegetables. My parents were delighted with the abundance and variety of produce that had been either expensive or unavailable in Vietnam. America gave us the opportunity to eat grapes to our heart's content and cook zucchini for the first time.

As new immigrants, we could not budget a lot of money for groceries. Since the restaurant idea had fizzled, Mom applied her French sewing skills to start a home tailoring business that catered to well-heeled women. She spent long hours in a workshop set up in one of the bedrooms. In addition to other jobs, my father taught ESL classes at the local junior high school. My three older sisters, Chi, Linh, and Ha, pitched in with the cooking, sewing, and cleaning. My brother, Dang, and I were too young to do much.

Times were tough, but our family always enjoyed satisfying meals. At first, we made do on what we could afford to spend and what was locally available. That meant Americanizing Vietnamese food. Mom and Dad hunted down substitutes for key ingredients, such as fish sauce, that were unknown in supermarkets. But as diligent as they were, the food wasn't the same because we had to rely on unremarkable rice and soy sauce.

Once we bought our first car, a used Mercury Comet, Chinatown in Los Angeles provided many of the items Mom needed. The trip was always a daylong event, so we usually filled the trunk with food to make the journey worthwhile. Other destinations included piers in Long Beach and San Diego, where we would load up on inexpensive fresh fish that my mother simmered in caramel sauce for traditional *kho*.

Whenever we heard of old friends opening markets or managing restaurants, we would stop by to show our support. Our former Saigon neighbors, the Hop family, started two grocery stores that we frequented for years. My parents' Chinese Vietnamese friend Ly Siu Coong was the accountant and eventually the manager at Tai Hong, a Chinatown restaurant where I fell in love with dim sum breakfasts. To show his esteem for my parents, whom he had known for years in Vietnam, Mr. Coong always made sure that our table received fresh-from-the-oven *char siu bao*. When broken in half, the golden *bao* exhaled fragrant vapors of rice wine.

By the early 1980s, the Vietnamese population in Orange County, California, had reached a critical mass. Businesses such as the well-stocked (but now defunct) Maikong market started to draw refugees to Bolsa Avenue in the sleepy suburb of Westminster. Families like ours came in search of food and experiences to remind them of their homeland. Because we lived only forty minutes south of what would become Little Saigon, we frequented the bakeries, grocery stores, and cafés and brought home fresh herbs, high-quality fish sauces, and good rice. These trips made being Vietnamese in America—and eventually Vietnamese Americans—a reality.

PRESERVING HERITAGE THROUGH FOOD

Displacement often leads people to seek solace and comfort in simple pleasures that give them a sense of stability. My parents, in their forties when they fled their homeland, placed great importance on maintaining Vietnamese culture in our family. In many ways, they subscribed to ideas imparted by Jean Anthelme Brillat-Savarin, the nineteenth-century French gastronomic philosopher, who said, "Tell me what you eat: I will tell you what you are." Mom and Dad believed that food was a practical and easy way for us to experience and express our ethnic identity.

As a result, we rarely ate out and bought few processed foods. Most nights, my mom and sisters prepared a homey meal of a quick soup, meat dish, vegetable dish, and rice. Recipes from the orange notebook guided us in making such classics as *chả giò*, crisp rolls filled with crab and shrimp. Re-creating specialty foods traditionally prepared by Vietnamese professional cooks was harder. New techniques and American ingredients had to be used. For example, after consulting with friends and family members, Mom and Dad realized that they could make great *bánh cuốn* (steamed rice paper rolls filled with pork, shrimp, and mushroom) in a nonstick skillet, instead of laboriously steaming them on fabric stretched over boiling water. Their New World batter featured cake flour, tapioca starch, and cornstarch instead of rice flour. Suddenly my father, who rarely cooked anything for us in Vietnam, was in the kitchen making *bánh cuốn* on Saturday mornings. Preparing and consuming good Vietnamese food reminded him of home and helped lessen the burden of starting anew in America.

Traditional eating practices were always followed at the table. We dined together as a family, my father receiving the first and best parts of each dish. Instead of using paper napkins that would be thrown away at the end of the meal, we shared wet hand towels that were washed after each meal. Even though we used cheap plastic chopsticks decorated with a colorful dragon design (a failed attempt to look like carved ivory), my mother wanted each pair placed perfectly straight at every setting, with its fanciful motif facing upward. She had left her real ivory chopsticks in Vietnam, but she wasn't about to abandon the civility that they evoked. Every night, she made sure the table was set correctly before dinner could be served.

Growing up with such strict rules on food and dining, I struggled, yet obeyed. At the time, such customs seemed contrary to the casual, practical, and consumer-oriented philosophies of modern America. Looking back, however, I realize that Mom's rigorous demands gave greater meaning to eating and food. A meal wasn't only about filling our bellies, but also about weaving elegance, refinement, and tradition into what was otherwise a modest situation.

Ultimately my parents were successful in educating us about our heritage through food. Most of what I know about Vietnamese culture and history evolved from exploring the country's culinary traditions. The number of Vietnamese living in America has grown tremendously in recent decades, making this enjoyable task easier now than it was in 1975. Between 1990 and 2000, the U.S. population of Vietnamese Americans nearly doubled to 1.1 million. The 1994 lifting of the U.S. trade embargo on Vietnam and the subsequent signing of trade agreements have increased the variety of foods available. More and more, Asian markets are carrying items that proudly bear the words "product of Vietnam." Major supermarket chains are stocking lemongrass, fish sauce, and jasmine rice. The rising interests in Asian food and travel have fueled people's desires to eat *phở* (noodle soup) and *gỏi cuốn* (salad rolls).

This book is designed to help you explore the breadth of Vietnamese cuisine. The recipes and anecdotes offer both cooking instructions and cultural insights into the lives of the Vietnamese, their history, and their spirit. Discussions on how traditions have been preserved and transformed in modern Vietnamese kitchens will ground your understanding of the repertoire, give you confidence to prepare delicious foods, and inspire you to innovate.

Remember that little orange notebook that my mother carried when she left Vietnam in 1975? Then, it was the means for our family to preserve its heritage. When I began writing this book, my mother gifted the notebook to me, explaining that she no longer needed it because she now uses a large recipe-card box. So consider this book a new, expanded version of that notebook. I present it to you from the heart and soul of our family kitchen.

THE ROOTS OF VIETNAMESE COOKING

The cuisine of Vietnam, with its refreshing flavors, varied textures, and vibrant colors, intrigues, beguiles, and charms. Its cooking techniques and ingredients are relatively simple, yet the sum of the parts is often greater than the whole. Blending East Asia and Southeast Asia with a touch of the West, Vietnamese food is captivating but also eludes easy description.

In what other cuisine do you find baguette sandwiches stuffed with banana leaf–scented cold cuts, garlicky liver pâté, cucumber, pickled daikon and carrot, cilantro, and chiles? Vietnamese cooking is filled with countless other equally interesting juxtapositions. Vegetables range from asparagus, lettuce, and potatoes to water spinach. Fermented seasonings include fish sauce, shrimp sauce, and soy sauce. Black pepper, white pepper, chiles, ginger, and galangal lend heat. Tartness comes from limes, tamarind, and vinegar. Food is eaten with chopsticks, hands, and, on occasion, knife and fork.

Making sense of the cuisine requires examining the country's legends, history, and geography, factors that shaped the culture and circumstances in which Vietnam's large, rich culinary repertoire was created.

LEGENDS AND LEGITIMACY

Throughout its history, Vietnam has had to defend itself repeatedly against foreign aggressors. It is no coincidence that the lore surrounding the country's beginning reflects a strong desire for independence—a core value that permeates Vietnamese culture. According to legend, the country was founded by Hung Vuong, the first king of the Hong Bang dynasty that ruled over the kingdom of Van Lang in the Red River Delta (in the vicinity of Hanoi) from 2879 to 258 BC. Only eighteen Hung kings reportedly served during the dynasty, which means that their combined reigns lasted over twenty-six hundred years, an unlikely total. These kings are said to have descended from Lac Long Quan, a prince of the sea who civilized the Vietnamese people by teaching them to cultivate rice. When a monarch from the north (presumably China) claimed the people's land, they called on Lac Long Quan to rise from the sea and save them. He kidnapped Au Co, the wife of the intruder, and then drove the aggressor away. Lac Long Quan and Au Co gave birth to Hung Vuong, thereby becoming the progenitors of the Vietnamese people.

Lac Long Quan's role in Vietnamese mythology also underscores the cultural significance of rice and the sea. Indeed, for some Vietnamese, a bowl of rice seasoned with fish sauce constitutes a meal. Also, the invention of round sticky rice cakes (*bánh dầy*) and square sticky rice cakes (*bánh chưng*), two classic rice-based foods (the latter a traditional part of the New Year celebration), is believed to date to the Hong Bang dynasty.

These seemingly far-fetched myths are partially supported by archaeological findings. Although Vietnam has been inhabited since the Paleolithic period, scientists link the start of its civilization to 2000 to 1400 BC in present-day Vinh Phu Province, northwest of Hanoi. Around the twelfth century BC, wet rice cultivation was being practiced in the flood plains of the Ma and Red rivers, and by the sixth century BC, an elaborate canal-and-dike system was in use for irrigating rice fields. A similar system was also at the center of the Dong Son culture, a civilization known for its elaborate ornamental bronze drums, many of which have sea motifs. Vietnamese scholars place the legendary Hung kings in this Dong Son period.

COLONIZATION AND EXPANSION

Vietnam's access to the sea and commercial trade ports made controlling its territory particularly attractive. For that reason, people rightfully feared foreign intrusion. Their sovereignty was always being threatened, particularly by their powerful neighbor, China.

The longest period of Chinese domination lasted a millennium, from 111 BC to AD 939, during which the Vietnamese adopted a Confucian bureaucratic, family, and social structure; added Chinese words to their vocabulary; began creating a written form of Vietnamese based on Chinese characters; and intermarried. But when the opportunity arose, they revolted. By the time they gained independence in the tenth century, they had become expert survival artists. Through this strategy of accommodation, acculturation, and rebellion, their culture evolved by selectively absorbing new ideas and reinterpreting them in unique Vietnamese ways.

Understandably, Chinese culinary influences run deep in Vietnam. It is the only Southeast Asian culture where people eat primarily with chopsticks. In the kitchen, authentic Chinese foods coexist with riffs on Chinese classics. For example, a cook may perfectly replicate Chinese moon cakes, yet fill steamed *bao* with a Vietnamese-style mixture of meats, vegetables, and boiled egg. Stir-fries will be lighter in flavor and less saucy than their Chinese counterparts. Vietnamese cooks are in awe of Chinese cooking, but they also look to it for ideas that they can adapt and make their own.

Following independence from China, the Vietnamese spent nine centuries fighting off repeated Chinese, Mongolian, and European incursions, while pushing southward in search of more land to farm rice. (Tenth-century Vietnam was only the northern half of its modern borders.) By the end of the seventeenth century, the Vietnamese had subdued the fierce Chams in the central region and conquered Khmer territory in the southern Mekong River Delta. In 1802, Emperor Gia Long unified Vietnam in its present S shape. He strategically located the capital in the middle of the country at Hue, where it remained until 1945.

When Vietnam absorbed Cham and Khmer territory, it added their Hindu-influenced Southeast Asian cultures to its already Chinese-oriented society. These new regions were part of the international maritime trade route, which meant they also had extensive contact with outsiders. Roman coins, along with Greek, Indian, and Persian artifacts, have been found at Oc Eo archaeological sites in the lower Mekong River Delta. Hoi An, a coastal town south of Danang, was once an important port with Chinese, Japanese, Dutch, and Indian residents. Vietnamese kings employed some Chinese principles in establishing control over their realm, but they also knew there was a limit to the amount of Middle Kingdom mores people would tolerate. By weaving Southeast Asian with East Asian traditions, Vietnamese culture became more distinctive. That's why the Vietnamese pantry includes coconut milk, curry powder, five-spice powder, and oyster sauce.

The arrival of European missionaries and merchants in the sixteenth century and the subsequent years of French colonization (1883 to 1954) brought pressure to Westernize. The Vietnamese applied their old survival tactics, augmenting their vocabulary with some pidgin French and switching to a romanized form of their language. They added Western ideas to their cuisine and created a more unique repertoire. Such Vietnamese sweets as éclairs, agar-agar gelatin desserts, almond cookies, and ice creams made from bases thickened with tapioca starch or cornstarch reflect the Vietnamese skill at adaptation.

However, the French imprint on the Vietnamese table pales when compared with Chinese and Southeast Asian influences. The foreignness of French techniques and the high prices of such nonnative ingredients as butter restricted French cooking to the well-off. But resourceful Vietnamese cooks, left with only a carcass after the colonialists carved off their beef steaks, used the scraps to create popular dishes like *bò kho*, a beef stew made with star anise and lemongrass, and *phở bò*, the fragrant beef and rice noodle soup that is the national dish. These foods are the measure of the French culinary legacy.

FAMINE AND FEASTING

French colonization and war took their toll on Vietnam during much of the twentieth century. In 1940, Japan sent troops into Vietnam to rule alongside the German-controlled Vichy French colonial government. Gross mismanagement by the Japanese and French authorities, Allied bombing of the roads and railways used for shipping food from south to north, and a terrible 1944 northern rice harvest contributed to the famine that killed hundreds of thousands of northerners (some estimates run to two million) in 1945. After Japan's defeat, France tried to reassert its power over Vietnam, but the horrific famine had eroded their legitimacy. In September 1945, Ho Chi Minh proclaimed the Democratic Republic of Vietnam, citing the famine among the major failures of the French colonial government. The resulting war, which lasted until 1954, ended French rule and split the country into two entities, North and South Vietnam.

Food options were extremely limited for anyone living in communist North Vietnam. In her memoir *Ao Dai: My War, My Country, My Vietnam*, Xuan Phuong details the daily struggles in post-1954 Hanoi: meager rations, persistent hunger,

long lines to buy rice. In South Vietnam, residents fared better because of more open economic policies and richer farmlands.

It wasn't long after the French left Vietnam that American involvement in the country escalated. With the goal of stopping the spread of communism throughout Southeast Asia, U.S. military advisers began working directly with South Vietnamese officials to prevent the northerners from reunifying the country. From the early 1960s to the cease-fire in 1973, millions of American soldiers were sent to fight the Vietnam War. Despite the intense contact with America, the war had practically no impact on Vietnamese cooking, except for the resulting diaspora that introduced the cuisine to countries around the world.

After reunification of North and South Vietnam in 1975, living conditions declined. Disastrous economic and agricultural policies cut crop production, and Vietnam flirted with famine in the 1980s. One of my father's brothers, Bac Lai, lived in Saigon during those years. When he reunited with our family, he spent hours recounting to us how little food was available in those days and how he and his family were forced to subsist on home-grown vegetables and a mixture of rice and other grains.

To overcome the food shortages, the communist government enacted free-market reforms in 1986, which spurred agricultural, economic, and gastronomic revival. Dining out and a love of food were no longer frowned on as bourgeois expressions by party hardliners. Restaurants sprang up and people began to enjoy food again. Newspapers printed rhapsodic articles on traditional favorites such as *bún thang* (Hanoi noodle soup). Conspicuous consumption of exotic foods rose in the cities, while religious festivals and celebrations involving feasting returned to the villages. The reforms also enabled Vietnam to become one of the world's leading rice exporters, an indicator of the country's resiliency. The country was slowly emerging from its years of war and deprivation.

A PROUD AND DISTINCTIVE CUISINE

Today, culinary pride in Vietnamese cuisine rides high, both inside and outside the country, on national and regional levels. For example, a Vietnamese will declare *phở* the world's best noodle soup when surrounded by other nationalities. But assemble a group of Vietnamese in a room and the tone is different. Northerners, staunch traditionalists who actually created the soup, will argue that their beef noodle soup is both the original and the tastiest. Strong-willed people from the central region will at first demur and then counter that *bún bò Huế*, a chile-and-lemongrass-seasoned beef and rice noodle soup from the former imperial capital, is equally good. Freewheeling southerners will boast that terrific bowls of both soups are served up in Saigon, along with specialties from all over the country and the world.

Friendly competition aside, the three regions do share the cuisine's main characteristics. First and foremost, rice is the chief food. Cultivated mostly in the Red River and Mekong River deltas, it is fashioned in countless delicious ways. (Some describe the country's S shape as two baskets of rice suspended from the ends of a bamboo shoulder pole.) Aquatic animals, whether caught from the sea, river, or rice paddy, are the major protein source, plus fish sauce flavors most dishes. Bittersweet caramel sauce, another distinctive ingredient, is widely used to impart savory depth and rich color to foods. Finally, everyone in the country eats lots of fragrant raw herbs and wraps morsels of grilled or fried food in herb leaves, lettuce, and rice paper.

But the three regions also exhibit noticeable culinary differences. Physically and culturally closer to China, northern food leans toward the kitchens of the Middle Kingdom. For example, generous amounts of black pepper and ginger (not chiles) often heat things up. In the Hanoi area, Vietnam's birthplace, diners favor straightforward approaches to food, with flavors that are pure but not lacking in complexity. In the drizzly cold winters, people welcome seasonal treats like *bánh khúc*, hot sticky rice dumplings filled with mung bean and caramelized shallot. Along with fish sauce, northern cooks like to season foods with shrimp sauce, a briny condiment that is also favored by central cooks. Additionally, both regions like pungent galangal, which is popular in Cambodia, Laos, and Thailand.

The narrow central region is not blessed with much arable land, and though its winters are dreary, they are not as cold as those in the north. Central food tends to be gutsy, earthy, and spicy, such as the already mentioned *bún bò Huế* and crunchy *bánh khoái*, rice-based crepes filled with pork, shrimp, egg, and vegetables. Hue, the capital for nearly 150 years, is known for its complex imperial cuisine beautifully presented in tiny portions for greater variety. While modern re-creations of imperial banquets may have a dozen dishes, Emperor Tu Duc, who reigned from 1848 to 1883, is reputed to have regularly sat down to fifty different dishes prepared by fifty cooks and served by fifty servants. Even today, central food often appears small and dainty.

In the hot, fertile south, an entrepreneurial spirit prevails. Economically and agriculturally richer than the rest of the country, southerners prepare food with great flourish. Everything is larger, more embellished, and sensuous. For example, the southern spin on the central region's traditional *bánh khoái* is nearly twice as big. Enriched with coconut milk, shaded yellow by turmeric, and filled with lots of ingredients, the chewy, crispy crepe also goes by the more alluring name *bánh xèo*, or "sizzling crepe." Southern Vietnamese food also tends to be sweet and garlicky in comparison to what lies north. Curries, an Indian legacy, and coconuts, which thrive in the heat, are often featured. Since most Vietnamese émigrés are from the south, Vietnamese food abroad has generally been filtered through the southern palate.

With people of Vietnamese ancestry living all over the world and many others discovering the cuisine of Vietnam, Vietnamese foodways are certain to change. The country's history and culture have always been shaped by a frontier spirit, and its cuisine has never fit neatly in a box. Vietnamese cooks are forever innovating, discovering new flavors and ideas, and then making them their own. Indeed, it is common to hear a Vietnamese say, "Let me tell you about a new dish I invented!"

USING THIS BOOK

As you use the recipes that follow, remember that Vietnamese cooking doesn't have many rules. Instead, you need to keep only these few guidelines and suggestions in mind.

Harmonize and Personalize Flavors

In Viet cooking, balancing the sweet, salty, sour, and spicy flavors allows a dish to strike multiple notes. The proportions of seasonings in a recipe are meant to lead you toward an understanding of how to paint with a Vietnamese flavor palette. Feel free to adjust for more (or less) fish sauce, lime juice, sugar, or chiles. As master of your own kitchen, it is your right to fine-tune the final flavors according to your ingredients and taste preferences.

Intuit and Measure Ingredients

Traditional Vietnamese cooking measurements are impressionistic. People measure by the rice bowl, handful, and odd-sized spoon. While that approach has its charm and pushes you to cook intuitively, it provides little practical guidance for anyone unfamiliar with the cuisine and culture. These recipes rely on standard American measurements. However, too much precision can limit the art and pleasure of cooking, which is why in some instances I call for a "small onion" or a "chubby piece of ginger."

Gauge Portions

If a recipe yield indicates a specific number of servings, such as "serves 4," it will satisfy that number of adults with a moderate appetite. Recipe yields expressed as a range, such as "serves 4 to 6," will satisfy adults with moderate appetites, in case of the smaller number, and moderate-light appetites, in case of the larger. A recipe that "serves 4 to 6 with 2 or 3 other dishes" is part of a traditional meal in which all the foods, typically a soup, meat, vegetable, and plain rice, are served at once. Depending on your guests' appetites, pair the dish with others to round out the menu, expanding it with a starter, noodle dish, or another meat and/or vegetable. Because plain rice is central to Vietnamese cuisine, it never counts as a dish.

What Is Viet?

For Vietnamese people, the term *Viet* connotes nationalism and resistance to foreign domination. Used by Vietnamese speakers to describe anything Vietnamese (like Thai for Thailand), Viet was originally the Chinese term for the various peoples living on the southern fringes of the Han Empire. In the second century BC, the Red River Delta region was part of the maverick kingdom of Nam Viet (Southern Viet; Nan Yue in Mandarin) that fought Han rule. Under Chinese and French control, Viet was absent from names applied to Vietnamese territory. The term reemerged during periods of independence to express Vietnamese self-determination. Thus the nation's names have included Dai Co Viet, Dai Viet, Nam Viet, and the modern Viet Nam (Vietnam). Given the term's significance, Viet and Vietnamese are used interchangeably in this book.

KITCHEN ESSENTIALS: INGREDIENTS AND EQUIPMENT

The earliest Vietnamese refugees in America started with little in their kitchens to re-create the flavors of their homeland. Today, of course, all the ingredients you need to make and serve delicious Vietnamese are generally available. And in the end, you don't need much, just a few staple ingredients and everyday pieces of equipment. If you already prepare other Asian food, you are likely to have most of what you need and know where to find the rest.

FISH SAUCE AND RICE

Fish sauce (*nước mắm*) is a keystone of Vietnamese cooking. The amber red, salty liquid is sprinkled straight onto hot rice, mixed with other ingredients for dipping sauces, and used in cooking to add depth of flavor. When a dish needs that extra something, a shot of fish sauce is often the solution. In the kitchen, it is normally kept in its original large bottle for easy access. More elegance is required at the table, where a small bottle of fish sauce is always part of the assemblage of soy sauce, chiles, salt, pepper, and toothpicks.

Clockwise from bottom left: star anise, annatto seeds, cinnamon, oyster sauce, fish sauce, chile sauce, and curry powder

Without *nước mắm*, Vietnamese food would be lackluster. If fish sauce seems alien to you, take a whiff of dried porcini mushrooms and then sniff the condiment. The aromas are remarkably similar, and, like good aged cheese, fish sauce smells stronger than it actually tastes. In food, the condiment is transformative. It unifies complex flavors and provides a distinctive finish. Some people say it is full of umami, the Japanese term for a savory or meaty taste.

Fish sauce is the liquid that results from salting and fermenting fish, an ancient and practical way of preserving seasonally abundant supplies of protein. To make it, fresh fish (usually anchovies, but other types of fish or shellfish may be used) are packed in layers of salt in large earthenware jugs, wooden casks, or concrete vats. Bamboo racks and rocks are placed on top to keep the fish from floating as their juices are drawn out during fermentation.

Left in a hot, sunny place for months or even more than a year, the fish break down and turn into liquid. High in B vitamins and protein, the fluid is removed via a spigot at the bottom of the salting container, or by siphoning. This first extraction, called *nước mắm cốt* (or *nước mắm nhĩ*), is the most prized. Slightly oily, richly flavored, and deeply hued, it was traditionally reserved for dipping sauces and special occasions. To get more use from the same fish, salted water is added to them, and after a shorter second fermentation period, a lesser-quality condiment is collected for everyday use.

Today, it is virtually impossible to purchase unadulterated *nước mắm cốt*. To keep their condiments competitively priced, fish sauce producers dilute the different extractions with water and add salt and sugar to yield the desired flavor balance. Some manufacturers also include sodium benzoate, a preservative, or hydrolyzed wheat protein, a flavor enhancer that is basically proteins chemically broken apart into amino acids.

None of this means that what is available nowadays is bad. In fact, Viet cooks, like many others for whom fish sauce is a staple, have been using diluted *nước mắm* for decades to prepare first-rate food. It is now the accepted standard.

Traditional cooks like my mom go through *nước mắm* quickly, which is why they frugally keep high- and lower-grade fish sauces on hand. The former is used at the table and for making dipping sauces and the latter is for cooking. I exclusively use high-grade fish sauce (a dilution of the first extraction) because at under $3.50 per bottle, it doesn't break my budget and it helps me make consistently tasty food.

Keep in mind that fish sauce is also used in other Asian cuisines, primarily in Thai and Filipino cooking, where it tends to have a saltier, heavier flavor. Thailand is the source of most of the fish sauces sold in the United States. Some of them are made in a more delicate so-called Vietnamese style. Fine examples are Viet Huong's Three Crabs and Flying Lion's Phu Quoc brands, which always deliver great flavor, aroma, and color. When shopping for good fish sauce, remember the following:

- Premium fish sauce is reddish brown and clear. Avoid dark, inky liquids that are overly salty and flat tasting. Good fish sauce is fragrant and pleasant tasting.
- Price matters. The goods ones typically come in glass bottles, rather than plastic, and cost more.
- Labels contain clues to quality. *Cốt*, *nhỉ*, or *thượng hạng* signals a premium product made with the first extraction of liquid from the salted fish. Phu Quoc and Phan Thiet are two places famous for the production of fish sauce in Vietnam. Some Thai products use these place names, but the sauces

aren't made there. Finally, *cá cơm* are anchovies native to the waters surrounding the island of Phu Quoc. Fish sauce made from these light-fleshed fish is considered prime.
- If you are at a complete loss, ask a fellow shopper and/or select a mid- to high-priced bottle.
- Fish sauce bottles are rarely well sealed. Transport and store them upright.

Although not widely available, excellent *nước mắm* is being exported from Vietnam to the United States. Keep an eye out at Vietnamese grocery stores. If you travel to Vietnam, visit artisanal producers in Phu Quoc and Phan Thiet to see fish sauce being made in traditional wooden casks and earthenware jugs. It is unforgettable. My father, to whom fish sauce is like liquid gold, fondly remembers how his mother annually prepared fish sauce in a fifty-gallon earthenware jug to ensure a year's supply for the family. Later, Dad served as provincial governor of Phan Thiet, where he was able to enjoy fine *nước mắm* from small producers. For him, nothing he tries now can match the versions he experienced in those days.

As the distinguished late food historian Alan Davidson wrote in *Seafood of South-East Asia*, "Looking to the future of Vietnamese cookery . . . one thing may be prophesied with confidence. The nuoc mam or fish sauce of Vietnam has been supreme in the region and is likely to remain so. It comes in various qualities. The best has no rival."

Fish sauce is required to prepare Vietnamese foods, and rice is needed to appreciate them fully. The grains absorb other flavors and provide textural contrasts. Rice is the foundation of the Vietnamese diet.

In its raw state, rice is called *gạo*. When boiled in a pot, it becomes *cơm*, and when cooked in a steamer, it is known as *xôi*. Several kinds of rice are used in the Viet kitchen, including long-grain rice (*gạo tẻ*), broken long-grain rice (*gạo tấm*), short- and long-grain sticky rice (*gạo nếp*), short-grain brown sticky rice (*gạo nếp lứt*), and long-grain black sticky rice (*gạo nếp than*).

TIPS ON USING FISH SAUCE

- The degree of saltiness in *nước mắm* varies from brand to brand. In developing and testing these recipes, my testers and I exclusively used Viet Huong's Three Crabs for consistency purposes. While the additional use of salt in the recipes should equalize major differences between brands, feel free to make any adjustments to create flavors that suit your palate.

- If you rarely use fish sauce, refrigerate the bottle. Otherwise, store it in a cool spot in the cupboard. If crystals form, discard the bottle and buy a new one.

- For table use, pour fish sauce into a recycled small glass bottle. For example, the type that bitters comes in has a plastic insert that is perfect for dispensing small dashes of *nước mắm*.

The recipes in this book focus on long-grain rice and sticky rice because these are the most frequently eaten types. What differentiates them is the amount of multibranched starch molecules, or amylopectin, in the grains. Long-grain rice has less of it, and sticky rice is nearly all amylopectin. Boiled long-grain rice, which cooks up chewy-firm and fluffy, typically accompanies food at mealtime. Sticky rice may be cooked and served the same way, but it is more often steamed into *xôi* dishes for breakfast or snacking. Although I have not included recipes for the other types, it is interesting to know how they are commonly used: Broken rice, which is simply uneven bits of long-grain rice, is used for certain specialty rice dishes. Both white and brown sticky rice are sometimes fermented into a sweet "drunken" rice snack, while black sticky rice is fermented into a rice wine beverage or soaked and steamed for a sweet treat.

When shopping for long-grain rice, look for long, pointy whole grains with a slight sheen. Fragrant jasmine rice is generally preferred nowadays, but you may enjoy another variety. (Never use parboiled or converted rice, or basmati rice, which is too dry for Viet food.) Find a brand you like and stick with it, and then never hesitate to switch if the quality degrades.

Most Chinese and Southeast Asian markets carry several brands of long-grain rice, to satisfy their fickle and finicky clientele. At this writing, my favorite brand is Golden Phoenix jasmine rice. If you find yourself standing clueless in front of a wall of rice bags, ask another shopper or someone who works at the market for his or her opinion. Expect to buy at least five pounds of long-grain rice at an Asian market. That may sound like a lot, though you will find you use it up fairly quickly. Health-food stores, specialty grocers, and supermarkets sell good-quality jasmine rice in smaller quantities but at higher prices. You will find cooking tips for long-grain rice beginning on page 238.

Sticky rice, also called sweet rice or glutinous rice, is sold at Asian markets alongside long-grain rice. To avoid confusion, remember that raw sticky rice is opaque, while long-grain rice is translucent. Once cooked, however, the reverse is true: sticky rice becomes translucent and regular long-grain rice turns opaque. As noted earlier, Viet cooks traditionally steam long-grain sticky rice. However, the long-grain sticky rice sold in the United States toughens quickly after it is removed from the steamer and doesn't reheat well. It is best suited for boiling in a pot, and is what is used for traditional *bánh chưng* (Tet sticky rice cakes), which are boiled for seven hours. Short-grain sticky rice steams up beautifully and holds its softness well, which is why I specify its use in *xôi* recipes. It also cooks up well in a pot.

Look for short-grain sticky rice at Chinese, Japanese, and Vietnamese markets. Koda Farms and Hakubai are two excellent brands. Long-grain sticky rice is available at Chinese, Thai, and Vietnamese markets. Three Ladies and Golden Phoenix are popular, consistently good brands.

SECONDARY INGREDIENTS: MORE HELPFUL STAPLES

Here are the other ingredients I frequently reach for when cooking Vietnamese food. The list is not exhaustive, but rather includes the basics, minus the common items most kitchens have, that you will need to make the recipes in this book. Don't load up your kitchen with all these products before you dive into the recipes. Instead, add them gradually as you discover new favorite dishes.

In the Vietnamese language, there can be different regional names for the same thing. This is particularly challenging for anyone who is new to the cuisine. If it is any consolation, Vietnamese people regularly get confused, too! For ease, I've included terms that are more commonly used in speech and on food labels, which is particularly helpful when you are trying to find an ingredient. If there are two terms separated by a slash, the first term is used by southern and central Viet speakers, and the second by northerners. For more details on Vietnamese ingredients, see the Guide to Ingredients on page 325. Recipes for the asterisked items are included in the Basics chapter.

IN THE REFRIGERATOR
Dried shrimp *tôm khô*
Fine shrimp sauce *mắm ruốc/mắm tôm*
Fresh ginger *gừng*
Hoisin sauce *tương hòi xìn*
Limes *chanh*
Oyster sauce *dầu hào*
Scallions *hành lá/hành hoa*

IN THE FREEZER
Banana leaves *lá chuối*
Chicken stock* *nước lèo gà/nước dùng gà*
Chiles *ớt*
Galangal (in pieces) *riềng*
Ground, steamed mung beans* *đậu xanh*
Tamarind liquid* *nước me*
Toasted sesame seeds *mè rang/vừng rang*
Trimmed lemongrass *xả*
Unsalted roasted peanuts *đậu phụng rang/đậu lạc rang*

IN THE PANTRY
Flours and Starches
Cornstarch *bột bắp*
Glutinous rice flour *bột gạo nếp*
Rice flour *bột gạo tẻ*
Tapioca starch *bột năng*

Condiments, Sauces, and Wine
Caramel sauce* *nước mầu/nước hàng*
Maggi Seasoning sauce *Maggi*
Sesame oil (Japanese) *dầu mè*
Shaoxing rice wine *rượu đế/rượu trắng*
Soy sauce (Chinese light and dark) *nước tương/xì dầu*
Vinegar (distilled white and Japanese rice) *giấm*

Dried Mushrooms, Noodles, and Rice
Cellophane noodles *bún tàu/miến*
Flat rice noodles (narrow, medium, and wide) *bánh phở*
Sticky rice *gạo nếp*
Rice paper (8½-inch rounds) *bánh tráng*
Round rice noodles *bún*
Shiitake mushrooms *nấm đông cô/nấm hương*
Wood ear mushrooms *nấm mèo/mộc nhĩ*

Canned Goods
Chicken broth *nước lèo gà/nước dùng gà*
Coconut milk *nước cốt dừa*
Straw mushrooms *nấm rơm*

Spices and Seasonings
Annatto seeds *hạt điều*
Chinese five-spice powder *bột ngũ vị hương*
Cinnamon (ground and sticks) *bột quế* and *quế chi*, respectively
Curry powder *bột cà-ri*
Dried red chile flakes *ớt khô*
Ground turmeric *bột nghệ*
Star anise *đại hồi/hồi hương* or *tai hồi*
Whole cloves *đinh hương*

Finally, I do not cook with monosodium glutamate (MSG), a staple for many Asian cooks. My mom routinely uses the flavor enhancer, but I believe that you don't need it if you have fresh, quality ingredients. Indeed, you can't avoid the white crystalline powder. Certain prepared ingredients contain MSG, which is a commercial concentrated form of glutamic acid, a naturally occurring amino acid and thus a building block of protein. In fact, glutamic acid is found in many common foods, including mushrooms, ripe tomatoes, fish sauce, soy sauce, seaweed, and Parmesan cheese.

According to food science expert Harold McGee, most tasty amino acids are to some degree sweet or bitter. Perhaps that is why *bột ngọt*, the Viet term for MSG, literally means "sweet powder." The recipes here don't include MSG, but I assume that any cooks inclined to use it will know how to include it.

HERB PRIMER

At the Vietnamese table, raw fresh herbs are usually eaten as an accompaniment to foods, a custom that distinguishes Vietnam from its Asian neighbors. Whole sprigs are arranged on platters heaped with soft lettuce leaves, cucumber slices, and other garnishes. You help yourself, pinching or tearing off individual leaves from the stems and adding them to your bowl of food or incorporating them into a hand roll. This allows you to vary each morsel as you please. When herbs are used in cooking, they are generally added at the end to finish the flavoring of the dish.

Fresh herbs not only contribute to the flavor of the cuisine, but also deliver certain health benefits. Many herbs aid digestion and some are folk remedies for fever, headaches, and nausea. When you combine them with chiles, spices, and aromatics such ginger, galangal, and turmeric, all of which boast their own health benefits, you have a potent phytochemical mix.

Viet herbs are collectively known as *rau thơm*, or "fragrant vegetable." Although the formal (dictionary) name of many herbs begins with *rau* (vegetable), people mostly omit it in everyday speech. The few exceptions, such as *rau răm*, are listed below with *rau* attached. Since an herb may have several names in Vietnamese, I have included only the most popular ones. The Viet name presented in each heading is the one most frequently used at Asian markets in the United States.

While all these herbs may be found at Vietnamese markets, not everyone has that kind of easy access. Indeed, certain herbs pair particularly well with certain dishes, but don't fret if you can't get a particular herb. You can start off with fresh cilantro and mint like many early Vietnamese immigrants did and expand from there.

The list is divided into Easy to Find, the most commonly used herbs, and Harder to Find, herbs definitely worth exploring if you come across them. I have also included phonetic pronunciations to aid in shopping, as well as gardening tips to encourage you to grow the herbs yourself, just as many Vietnamese do.

EASY TO FIND

Cilantro - *Coriandrum sativum* - *Ngò* (N-gaw)
An everyday herb in the Viet kitchen, cilantro is used to garnish foods, to add a bright flavor to a finished dish, and to round out the ubiquitous plate of lettuces and herbs eaten alongside many fried and grilled foods. Both the mature broad leaves and the tender tiny tops are eaten. Fresh cilantro is easily purchased, and seeds and plants are also readily available. Cilantro plants bolt (go to seed) quickly, so eat them up or regularly pinch back the new growth. (Alternate names: Chinese parsley, coriander, and *mùi*.)

Dill - *Anethum graveolens* - *Thì là* (Tee lah)
One of the few herbs not eaten raw in Vietnam, dill is added during cooking and to finish a dish. The feathery tops are chopped and mixed into a fine beef paste that is boiled and served as a cold cut and is used in Hanoi-style grilled catfish with turmeric. Middle Eastern and farmers' markets are great sources for beautiful bunches at reasonable prices. (Alternate name: *Thìa là*.)

Mint - *Mentha spicata, Mentha x. gracilis* - *Húng* (Hoong), *Húng cay* (Hoong kay)

Thank goodness mint is one of the primary herbs eaten in Vietnam because it is easy to grow and buy. The mint available here isn't exactly the same variety as what you get in Vietnam, but the taste is basically the same. At Vietnamese American markets, you'll find two mints, one called *húng* (*Mentha spicata*), which is just like supermarket mint, and another called *húng cay* (*Mentha x. gracilis*), which has roundish leaves and red stems. Both have sweet spearmint qualities, but the latter often has a slight bite, hence its Vietnamese name, which means spicy mint. Most people enjoy milder *húng,* but you can use either variety. (Alternate names: spearmint, *húng lũi,* and *húng láng.*)

Red perilla - *Perilla frutescens* - *Tía tô* (Tee-ah toh)

This herb is one of the most unusual in the Viet culinary palette. Green on top and purple-garnet underneath, the leaves are beautiful, and the flavor, a mix of cinnamon, mint, and lemon, is a perfect finish for such bold foods as mock turtle stew (*thịt heo nấu giả ba ba*). They are also eaten with sizzling crepes (*bánh xèo*). In Vietnam, the leaves are sometimes purple on both sides. When growing this annual, let it flower and go to seed, saving the seeds or sprinkling them in the soil for the future. A close relative is Japanese *hojiso,* a type of *shiso.* (Alternate names: purple perilla, beefsteak, and *shiso.*)

Thai basil - *Ocimum basilicum* var. - *Húng quế* (Hoong quay)

This is the basil commonly served with bowls of *phở* (beef noodle soup) in the United States. It's also traditionally enjoyed with *dồi lòng heo* (pork blood sausages), its strong clove scent providing the perfect contrast to the pungent richness of the sausages. The literal translation of *húng quế* is "cinnamon mint," but the herb is botanically basil. Siam Queen is a great variety to grow. (Alternate names: Thai basil, anise basil, *húng chó,* and *hương thái.*)

Clockwise from top left: wild betel leaf, rice paddy herb, red perilla, Thai basil, fish mint, Vietnamese coriander, culantro, sorrel, two varieties of mint (húng *on the left,* húng cay *on the right), and Vietnamese balm (center)*

Vietnamese coriander - *Polygonum odoratum* - *Rau răm* (Rau rahm)

A truly special Southeast Asian herb, *rau răm* is heady and peppery, with hints of cilantro. It is one of my favorite herbs, so I grow it to ensure a fresh supply of the small, spear-shaped leaves. The hardy perennial tends to spread, so plant it in a pot and pinch it back to prevent the pinkish stems from becoming leggy. Propagate new plants by putting freshly cut stems into water; when a fair number of roots have grown, put the stems in soil. (Alternate name: hot mint.)

HARDER TO FIND

Culantro - *Eryngium foetidum* - *Ngò gai* (N-gaw gai)

When the garnish plate for *phở* contains thorn-edged leaves of culantro, you know you are being treated well. Stronger tasting and earthier than true cilantro, it is expensive because it grows slowly. Each leaf emanates from the center of the plant, and there are no stems from which multiple leaves may flourish. A native of tropical America, it is used in Southeast Asian, Latin American, and Caribbean foods. Cilantro is a fine substitute. (Alternate names: Mexican coriander, thorny coriander, saw-leaf herb, saw-tooth herb, stinkweed, *mùi tàu,* and *ngò tàu.*)

Fish mint - *Houttuynia cordata* - *Diếp cá* (Zeep kah)

The spade-shaped leaves of this herb have a slightly sour, fishy flavor. Some people love the tanginess, while others are put off by the unusual taste. For that reason, fish mint is not commonly found at the Viet table. I enjoy it with boldly flavored grilled meat, such as skewered beef with lemongrass (page 28). Look for it at Vietnamese markets. A variegated relative is often planted as a decorative ground cover. If you grow fish mint, remember that it is hardy and can be invasive. (Alternate names: vap ca and *dấp cá.*)

Rice paddy herb - *Limnophila aromatica* - *Rau om* (Rau awm)

Tasting lightly of both citrus and cumin, this herb is typically used to finish sour fish soup (page 66). However, because it is often difficult to find nice fresh stems at Viet markets, I often

FINDING AND STORING HERBS

Finding Herbs

The most reliable places to shop for Vietnamese herbs are Viet markets, Chinese markets catering to Viet customers, and farmers' markets in areas with good-sized Viet communities. Select the freshest, perkiest bunches possible.

If you regularly eat herbs, grow them yourself. In the summer, check for starter plants at Viet markets, or look for itinerant vendors with plants for sale in areas with a concentration of Vietnamese shops. Mail-order seed companies also sell starter plants and/or seeds for some of the herbs. Check Resources (page 335) for details. Use the botanical name when purchasing, since Vietnamese and English names can vary. For detailed gardening tips, consult Carole Saville's *Exotic Herbs*.

Storing Herbs

I prefer what is sometimes called a florist's approach to storing store-bought herbs. Take each bunch and trim off the bottom, leaving an inch or two of stem. Remove any twist ties or rubber bands holding the stems together and place stand them in a jar, glass, or plastic container partially filled with water. Try to keep the leaves from touching the water (you may need to remove some of the lowest leaves on the stems), or they will spoil more quickly. Loosely cover the container with a plastic bag (a clear one will let you see what is inside) and refrigerate it. Change the water every three or four days, and your herbs will stay perky for a good two weeks. This works especially well for cilantro, which tends to get slimy in the crisper.

If your refrigerator space is limited, put the herb bunch, along with a paper towel to absorb excess moisture, in a plastic bag and store in the crisper. If you are a gardener, stand your just-harvested herbs in a container of water and keep it on the counter for a beautiful and useful bouquet.

substitute ground cumin. The delicate stems and small leaves are beautiful, but propagating these moisture-loving plants is challenging. (Alternate names: *bà om, rau ngổ, ngò om*.)

Sorrel - *Rumex acetosa* - *Rau chua* (Rau chu-ah)
Sorrel made its way into the Vietnamese fresh herb assortment in America. The reasons for its addition aren't clear, although some people like its pleasant tartness as a nonfishy alternative to fish mint. Because it is a foreign adaptation, it doesn't have a Vietnamese name, and is known simply as *rau chua*, or "sour herb." Enjoy it as you would any of the raw herbs used to add a bright flavor to food. Because sorrel is popular in western European cooking, seeds are widely available. However, it is prolific. *R. acetosa* is the well-known garden sorrel, not true French sorrel.

Vietnamese balm - *Elsholtzia ciliata* - *Kinh giới* (Kin zoy)
One of my favorite herbs, Vietnamese balm has an unparalleled lemongrasslike quality. Speckled with purple on the back side, the delicate saw-edged, slightly fuzzy green leaves are tasty raw, great with grilled meats, and are what pull together a banana blossom salad (page 52). If you grow this annual, let it go to seed and save the seeds—or sprinkle them over the soil—for next year's crop. Watch out for snails; they like this herb. Vietnamese balm can also be propagated by rooting freshly cut stems in water. (Alternate names: Vietnamese mint and *giả tô*.)

Wild betel leaf - *Piper sarmentosum* - *Lá lốt* (Lah loht)
Shiny and wet looking on top but matte underneath, these heart-shaped leaves are dear because you don't get many for your money. They are often rolled around a bit of seasoned ground beef and grilled on skewers, a dish that is part of the traditional seven-course beef feast. The raw leaves have little fragrance, but when exposed to heat, they release an unusual sweet, spicy scent. Because perfectly fresh leaves are hard to find and their usage is highly specialized and limited, I rarely cook with them. Don't confuse *lá lốt* with the thicker type of betel leaf that is wrapped around slaked lime and areca nut and chewed. (Alternate name: pepper leaf.)

EQUIPMENT

You probably have most of the equipment you need to prepare Vietnamese food. When we first arrived in America, all we had—and needed—were a few nonstick eight-, ten-, and twelve-inch skillets and some deep saucepans. My mom bought an aluminum *Chinese steamer* as soon as she could, however, because a Vietnamese kitchen isn't complete without one. In fact, when my sisters left home for college, my parents sent each of them off with a steamer. Steamers are used for cooking many dishes, such as *xôi* (sticky rice), and for reheating food in a flash.

Metal steamers come with a pan for holding the water, two trays, and a lid. They are sold at most Asian markets and housewares shops. I prefer stainless-steel steamers because they are long lasting, easy to clean, and have heat-resistant plastic handles. Some come with handy see-through glass lids that allow you to monitor the cooking. (Traditional bamboo steamers are attractive but are prone to mildew, scorching, and falling apart.)

When selecting a steamer, look for one with trays about twelve inches wide (excluding the handles), large enough to accommodate a whole fish or a big batch of *bao*, reducing overall cooking time. Also consider the size of the holes in the tray bottoms. Food can fall through the holes if they are too big, while if the holes are too small, not enough steam will reach the food. Ideally, one tray will have largish holes measuring about ⅓ inch, and the other tray will have holes half the size. The larger-holed tray is perfect for steaming foods like whole duck legs, while the smaller-holed tray is great for sticky rice and mung beans. (If both trays have large holes, line the tray bottoms with parchment paper or banana leaf when steaming rice or other small foods, to avoid losing them to the steamer pan.)

Some cooks create a steamer with just chopsticks and a wok: Crisscross two wooden chopsticks inside the wok, add water to reach almost to the chopsticks, bring the water to a boil, balance the dish of food on the chopsticks, and cover the wok with a lid. I find this method cumbersome, however, and think that thirty to forty dollars isn't too much to spend on a piece of crucial kitchen equipment.

Because making Vietnamese food requires a lot of chopping, it is important to have reliable *sharp knives*. A chef's knife, paring knife, and heavy cleaver are essential. Keep them sharp with a steel or electric knife sharpener and occasionally

WOK TIPS

Seasoning and Maintenance

Take good care of a wok and it will return the favor at your table. Every new carbon-steel wok requires seasoning before use. Start the process by washing both sides of the wok in hot, soapy water to remove the protective coating of machine oil from the factory. Dry the wok thoroughly. Turn on the exhaust fan and heat the wok over high heat until hot but not smoking. Add a tablespoon of oil, such canola or corn oil, and evenly rub it all over the interior with a wad of paper towel. Rotate and tilt the wok from side to side for a couple of minutes to expose the entire surface to the heat. Turn off the heat, wipe excess oil from the wok, and let it cool completely. Repeat the entire process (heat, rub with more oil, rotate, and cool) two or three times to finish the seasoning. A newly seasoned wok will usually have a black, burned-looking area in the center. Use it often (daily or several times a week) to develop a rich, dark patina.

Once the wok is seasoned, don't use soap on it. After stir-frying, immediately rinse the wok with hot water, gently scrubbing with a sponge or soft-bristled brush to remove excess food or oil (traditional bamboo wok brushes tend to scrape away some of the patina). If you used the wok for deep-frying, let the oil cool first and pour it out before washing. When necessary, scour away stubborn bits with salt. Follow every washing with a thorough drying over medium-low heat. While it is still hot, use a paper towel to smear a bit of oil on the interior surface.

Don't be afraid to reseason the wok if the original metal becomes exposed or gets rusty. Woks used for boiling or steaming will need reseasoning.

Cooking in a Wok

To achieve great wok-searing action and flavor, always heat the wok until hot (a bead of water should vaporize within a second or two of contact) before adding oil for stir-frying; when deep-frying, there is no need to preheat the wok before adding oil. If the oil gets too hot and smokes, remove the wok briefly from the burner and lower the heat. Don't stir-fry too much food at once. An overloaded wok lowers the temperature and the ingredients cook too slowly to acquire that inimitable stir-fry taste.

have them professionally sharpened. Good knives make cooking easier and faster. Besides, I've had too many accidents from using dull knives. Other time-savers that most people nowadays have are a *food processor, electric mini-chopper*, and *spice grinder* (or electric coffee grinder reserved for cooking).

USEFUL ADDITIONS

While you can stir-fry in a heavy-duty twelve-inch skillet, it is more fun and efficient to use a *wok*. Many gas stoves now come with high-output booster burners that are perfect for wok cooking. The curved walls of a wok also make it great for deep-frying, as less oil is required. An inexpensive fourteen-inch, flat-bottomed wok made of carbon steel is most practical. Nonstick woks don't handle high heat well, and electric woks don't heat hot enough. See page 21 for more information on seasoning, maintaining, and cooking in a wok.

A *mortar and pestle* are good for breaking down food fibers or mixing ingredients without risking total pulverization. While many options are available, I often reach for a small marble mortar (4½ inches wide at the top) for most needs; they are available at cookware stores. Larger mortars made of granite, handy for pounding meat pastes (*giò*), are sold at Chinese,

Vietnamese, and Thai markets and Asian restaurant-supply and housewares shops.

A *mandoline*, with its razor-sharp blades, yields beautiful shredded and sliced vegetables for Vietnamese salads and pickles. Options include the true French mandoline, an expensive but impressive hunk of metal (about $150), the OXO Good Grips version (about $70), and the inexpensive Japanese Benriner slicer (about $35). They are available at cookware stores, Asian restaurant-supply shops, and Japanese markets or by mail order. In the absence of a mandoline, use a food processor or sharp knife.

And if rice becomes a major part of your diet, an *electric rice cooker* is wonderful to have. It cooks rice to perfection, occupies little counter space, and frees up a burner on your stove. Like other modern appliances, rice cookers are now available in different colors to match your kitchen, and can perform miraculous tasks, such as keeping your rice warm for hours. Of course, these improvements are reflected in high prices. My mother used a basic black-and-white National brand rice cooker daily for over fifteen years before it finally broke down. Rice cookers are now widely available because of the popularity of Asian cooking. On the other hand, a heavy-bottomed saucepan also makes good rice.

TABLEWARE AND
DINING GUIDELINES

Vietnamese cuisine represents many culinary crossroads, so setting the table can be tricky. Before a meal, inventory the menu to figure out what is needed at each place setting. In general, set out a plate, a rice bowl, and a small dipping-sauce dish for each person. Salad plates are great for most meals, since diners help themselves to only small portions at a time. If bulky foods or dishes that require wrapping are involved, use dinner plates instead. Dinner plates placed under big bowls of soup are pretty as chargers and useful for bones and the like. Of course, Western-style dishes require Western-sized dishware. Feel free to mix things up as needed to help diners manage their food.

The primary eating utensils at the Viet table are chopsticks. (China, Japan, Korea, and Vietnam are the official chopstick-wielding countries.) Place a pair, along with a Chinese or Western soup spoon, on the right side of each plate. Add a knife and fork if the menu requires them. Although traditionalists like my parents use damp hand towels for wiping their hands and mouths, you may set out either paper or cloth napkins.

Everyday Vietnamese meals are enjoyed family style and all the dishes are served at once. It is somewhat of a free-for-all, with people helping themselves, picking up food from serving plates with chopsticks, and asking others to serve or pass dishes to them. Each person is responsible for a nearby dish and must be ready to serve or hand it over graciously when asked.

If you have prepared an elaborate menu for a special occasion, serve the starter and soup first as separate courses. Follow with the dishes that make up the main part of the meal, and let the table become laden with food. Invite guests to serve themselves and remind them to return to the starter or soup, if any remains.

Most Vietnamese foods are best eaten from the rice bowl (which doubles as a soup bowl at everyday meals). It is fine to pick up the bowl and move food from it to your mouth with chopsticks. Spoon the rice into it (not onto your plate) and, if you like, top it with a small amount of one of the dishes for flavor. Contrary to Western custom, the plate plays a secondary role at the Viet table.

1. GIFTS TO THE MOUTH

Whether it is a midday sandwich, an appetizer that opens a sumptuous meal, or a salad for a special event, the broad range of Vietnamese snacks and little plates reflects the culture's penchant for small, varied bites. Survey all the goodies for sale at any Viet deli and you will agree that the Vietnamese love to snack.

Vietnamese often refer to snacking as *ăn quà*, literally "eating" (*ăn*) a "gift" (*quà*), a term that conveys the pleasure connected with consuming delectable morsels of food. But they also say *ăn quà sáng*, *ăn quà trưa*, and *ăn quà tối*, for eating breakfast, lunch, and dinner, respectively, thus the act of giving gifts to the mouth occurs throughout the day.

Snacking comes in several guises. First, there is the ubiquitous street-food snacking that goes on all day. When my mom was growing up in the northern town of Hai Duong, she could tell time by the recognizable calls of the hawkers who strolled by her family's house on their daily routes. They each sang a clever song to identify the wares that dangled from the ends of their bamboo poles (*quang gánh*). Noodle soups, crispy baguettes, and steamed *bao* were some of the early morning items. Those vendors faded away as the midmorning hours brought new sellers hawking creamy rice soup and other foods. Their bipedal businesses disappeared during lunchtime, when most Vietnamese preferred a sit-down meal at home or in a restaurant to eating small bites on the street. Around three or four o'clock, the afternoon vendors arrived with different savory and sweet snacks to tide people over until dinner.

A complete kitchen dangled from the pole balanced on each vendor's shoulders. For example, if you hankered for a morning bowl of *phở* (beef noodle soup), you would flag down the appropriate hawker and present your bowl, or use one of the hawker's bowls. The vendor would stop, put down the pole, and set up shop. Out came the implements: the dry components—noodles, meat, and various aromatics—were usually hung from one end of the pole, while the hot broth was hung from the other. It is not clear how things were kept piping hot, but every bowl was freshly prepared and customized to each customer's preferences. It was like having an itinerant open kitchen come to your doorstep.

In 1954, when Vietnam was split into North and South under the Geneva Accords, my parents' families migrated south to avoid communism. In more modern Saigon, customs were different. The street hawkers had abandoned the rural use of *quang gánh* for carts with wheels that could be pushed or pedaled like a bicycle. Instead of coming to you, most of the vendors occupied key street corners in high-traffic areas, or had stalls in open markets. Only a few maintained a regular route past our house. The progress and prosperity of big-city living meant that if you wanted a snack, you had to go looking for it. The legion of street hawkers competed for everyone's business, keeping prices low and creating a festive atmosphere as vendors tried to lure customers to their specialties. "Dear sister, no one makes a finer sandwich than I . . . Uncle, try my food and you'll keep coming back for more!" You'll still find this charming competitiveness in Vietnam today.

A second category of snacking is known as *nhậu*, slang for a type of partying traditionally reserved for men that usually

continued

RECIPES

involves boisterous conversation lubricated by savory snacks, such as stuffed squid, and alcohol, namely beer. These lively sessions typically occur in the afternoon at someone's home or at a café or restaurant, and the dishes are special because they require more time to prepare and/or feature unusual ingredients. *Nhậu* is such an important part of Viet tradition that there is a entire cookbook, *Nghệ Thuật Làm Các Món Nhậu* by Le Hoa, devoted to it. Here in America, *nhậu* retains its male-centered connotation, although it is used generically by both sexes to mean a good time for all. People may *nhậu* to celebrate something or simply to hang out with friends and family.

Interestingly, the same foods are sometimes served to whet the appetite before a formal meal, but in this context they are called *món ăn chơi*, literally "foods for play," and refer to the light, rather than the substantive, part of the meal. In Western terms, such dishes would be considered starters (or appetizers) instead of merely snacks, and despite their secondary role, the cook is expected to prepare them from the best ingredients and offer them in a beautiful presentation. For example, skewers of lemongrass beef are usually served right off the grill at a casual meal, but they are artfully arranged on a plate, garnished, and accompanied by a dipping sauce in an attractive bowl when they are prepared as *món ăn chơi*.

When our family came to the United States, where there were no food hawkers on the corner, we had to satisfy our snacking needs at home. Sometimes we got takeout from Little Saigon delis (a Vietnamese American stand-in for the traditional vendors), which was both convenient and inexpensive, but the food was seldom as fresh and tasty as we were used to. Street hawkers typically specialize in only one or two items, and it's hard for a deli to do everything well. The lack of consistent quality inspired us to master our favorite snacks. As a result, small bites like beef and jicama hand rolls became a light lunch, rather than a quick snack on the run.

Indeed, food traditions are ever changing, and the recipes in this chapter highlight that evolution. For example, you'll get a sense of how Viet cooks co-opted French culinary ideas with the ubiquitous *bánh mì* (baguette sandwich), just as they adapted many southern Chinese classics, such as shrimp toasts and fried wontons, and made them integral to the Viet repertoire. Other foods, like the special-event salads, are distinctively Vietnamese. No matter their origin, these dishes draw on a broad range of ingredients and techniques to create the interplay of tastes and textures that is the hallmark of the Vietnamese kitchen.

BAKED SHRIMP TOASTS

Bánh Mì Tôm Quết Nướng

TRADITIONALLY DEEP-FRIED, shrimp toasts can be greasy affairs. During frying, the toasts soak up lots of oil and the shrimp topping often slides off the bread. A few years ago, chef Susana Foo, in her eponymous cookbook, offered an excellent solution for making this popular Chinese snack: baking the toasts. Her idea caught my eye, and I was fast to adapt the method for a Vietnamese version. The end product is a crispy, pinkish orange hors d'oeuvre that is delightfully grease free.

1 Position a rack in the middle of the oven and preheat to 250°F. Trim the crust from the bread slices and cut each slice into 4 triangles. Place the triangles on a baking sheet and bake for 25 to 30 minutes, or until dry but not browned. Set aside to cool completely. Increase the oven temperature to 350°F.

2 Refresh the shrimp by putting them in a colander and tossing them with a liberal amount of salt. Rinse immediately under lots of cold water and press gently to drain well. In a bowl, combine the shrimp, the ½ teaspoon salt, the cornstarch, sugar, pepper, garlic, egg white, and oil and mix well. Transfer to a food processor and process until a coarse paste forms. Return the paste to the bowl and stir in the scallion.

3 Coat a nonstick baking sheet with the butter. To make each toast, use a dinner knife or an icing spatula to spread a ¼-inch-thick layer of the shrimp paste on the top of a toast triangle. The paste should be as thick as the toast and cover all the corners. (If the toast browned on one side, spread the paste on that side, freeing up the other side to brown during baking.) As the toast triangles are topped, place them on the prepared baking sheet. Discard any leftover toasts or save for another use.

4 In a small bowl, stir together the egg yolk and water to make an egg wash. Brush the tops of the toasts with the egg wash. Bake the toasts for 10 to 12 minutes, or until the shrimp paste has turned pink-orange and the toast bottoms are golden brown. Let cool for 5 minutes before serving.

Makes about 48 small toasts, to serve 8 to 10

12 thin slices white bread
1 pound medium shrimp, peeled and deveined
Salt for refreshing shrimp, plus ½ teaspoon
1 teaspoon cornstarch
½ teaspoon sugar
⅛ teaspoon black pepper
2 cloves garlic, minced
1 egg, separated
1 tablespoon canola or other neutral oil
3 tablespoons minced scallion, green and white parts (2 or 3 small scallions)
3 tablespoons butter, melted
½ teaspoon water

NOTE

To freeze the unbaked assembled toasts, arrange them on an ungreased baking sheet (don't let them touch one another) and freeze until solid. Transfer the toasts to an airtight container, separating the layers with parchment paper, and freeze for up to 1 month. To serve, thaw at room temperature on a buttered baking sheet for 1 hour. Brush with the egg wash and then bake as directed.

GRILLED LEMONGRASS BEEF SKEWERS

Thịt Bò Nướng Xả

YEARS AGO, I tasted these grilled beef skewers at a restaurant in Orange County's Little Saigon, where they were served with a hoisin-based peanut sauce. When I got home, I researched the recipe in cookbooks published in Vietnam decades ago and developed this recipe, which includes shrimp sauce (*mắm tôm*) to give the beef a distinctive savory depth. Typical of food from Vietnam's central region, these skewers are rich and a bit salty. Dipped in the earthy sauce, they are addictively good—the perfect match for a cold beer, margarita, or gimlet.

Tri-tip steak (from the bottom loin), a flavorful cut that California cooks like to grill, is ideal for these skewers. A thick piece of flap steak (from the short loin), which is often used for carne asada, also works well. For the true flavors of the Southeast Asian table, grill the beef over charcoal or a gas grill. In the absence of a grill, use the broiler.

1 To make the marinade, combine the shallot, brown sugar, salt, and pepper in a mortar and pound into a rough paste. (Or, use an electric mini-chopper.) Transfer to a bowl, add the shrimp sauce, fish sauce, oil, lemongrass, and sesame seeds, and stir to mix. Set aside.

2 If you have time, place the beef in the freezer for about 15 minutes. It will firm up, making it easier to cut. Slice the beef across the grain into thin strips a scant ¼ inch thick, about 1 inch wide, and 2 to 3 inches long. (You may need to angle the knife to yield strips that are wide enough.)

3 Add the beef to the marinade and use your fingers to combine, making sure that each strip is coated on both sides. Cover with plastic wrap and marinate at room temperature for 1 hour. (For more tender meat, marinate in the refrigerator for up to 24 hours. Remove from the refrigerator 30 minutes prior to skewering.) Meanwhile, soak 24 to 30 bamboo skewers, each 8 to 10 inches long, in water to cover for at least 45 minutes.

continued

Makes 24 to 30 skewers, to serve 6 to 8

MARINADE

1 shallot, chopped (about ¼ cup)

1 teaspoon brown sugar

⅛ teaspoon salt

¼ teaspoon black pepper

1¼ teaspoons fine shrimp sauce

2 teaspoons fish sauce

2 tablespoons canola or other neutral oil

1 stalk lemongrass, trimmed and minced (about 3 tablespoons)

1½ tablespoons sesame seeds, toasted (page 332)

1¼ pounds tri-tip or flap steak, well trimmed (about 1 pound after trimming)

1½ cups Spicy Hoisin-Garlic Sauce (page 310)

Grilled Lemongrass Beef Skewers, pictured with Banana Blossom Salad (page 52)

4 To grill the beef, prepare a medium-low charcoal fire (you can hold your hand over the rack for no more than 5 or 6 seconds) or preheat a gas grill to medium-low. To broil the beef, position a rack about 4 inches from the heat source and preheat the oven for 20 minutes so it is nice and hot.

5 While the grill or broiler heats, drain the skewers and thread the beef onto them, putting 1 or 2 strips on each skewer. If you are broiling, put the skewers on an aluminum foil–lined baking sheet. Place the skewers on the grill rack or slip the baking sheet under the broiler. Grill or broil, turning the skewers once, for 3 to 4 minutes on each side, or until the beef is browned and a little charred at the edge.

6 Arrange the skewers on a platter and serve at once with the sauce on the side. Diners can dip the skewers in the sauce or spoon the sauce onto the skewers.

NOTE

These grilled beef strips are wonderful stuffed into a sandwich (page 34) or featured in a salad roll (page 32). They may also be used in place of the stir-fried beef in a rice noodle bowl (page 224). Or, roll them up with lettuce, mint, and cilantro in fresh rice noodle sheets (page 200); cut each roll into 2- to 3-inch lengths and serve with the hoisin-garlic sauce. You don't need to skewer the beef if using it in these ways, though it makes grilling the strips easier.

BEEF AND JICAMA HAND ROLLS

Bò Bía

LOADED WITH BEEF, crunchy texture, and heady sweet flavors, this specialty of southern Vietnam echoes Chinese *mu shu* pork and Malaysian and Singaporean *poh piah*. But instead of rolling the filling in a wheat flour–based wrapper, rice paper is used.

Bò bía are traditionally made by street vendors in a to-go format that recalls a Mexican burrito. When we lived in Saigon, my sister Ha and her best friend, Loan, were addicted to the rolls. On the way home from school, my parents or our driver would take them by one of the hawkers strategically positioned on a street corner, hot wok at the ready. Hand rolls and money were exchanged through the car window, with the girls giggling as they dove into their favorite snack.

Because we don't have those wonderful street vendors here, our family makes *bò bía* at home as a prelude to a big meal or the focus of a light lunch. We set things up at the table for everyone to assemble his or her own rolls. This do-it-yourself approach is ideal because these rolls, unlike salad rolls (page 32), can be messy and should be eaten as soon as they are made.

Serves 6 to 8 as a starter, or 4 as a light lunch

3 Chinese sweet sausages

3 tablespoons canola or other neutral oil

5 cloves garlic, finely minced

1/3 cup dried shrimp, rinsed under hot water and coarsely chopped

1 pound ground beef, preferably chuck, coarsely chopped to loosen

1 jicama, about 1/2 pound, peeled and cut into matchsticks

1/2 teaspoon salt

1 thick Egg Sheet (page 320) made with 2 eggs, quartered and cut into 1/2-inch-wide strips

1 head soft leaf lettuce such as butter, red leaf, or green leaf, leaves separated

20 rice paper rounds, 8 1/2 inches in diameter

1 1/2 cups Spicy Hoisin-Garlic Sauce (page 310)

1   In a small skillet, combine the sausages with water to reach halfway up their sides. Bring to a vigorous simmer over medium heat and cook until all the liquid has evaporated. The sausages will soften and plump up. Transfer them to a cutting board to cool.

2   Thinly slice each sausage on the diagonal, creating long slices. Put on a plate and set aside.

3   In a wok or large skillet, combine the oil and garlic over medium-low heat. When the garlic turns a pale blond, raise the heat to medium, add the shrimp, and sauté for about 30 seconds, or until fragrant. Raise the heat to medium-high, add the beef, and stir-fry for about 2 minutes, or until the beef is browned but not cooked through. Add the jicama and continue cooking for about 4 minutes, or until the jicama is soft but still slightly crunchy. Mix in the salt, then taste and adjust the seasoning with more salt if needed. Transfer to a serving bowl and keep warm.

4   To serve the rolls, set out all the components on the table, including separate small plates of Chinese sausage and egg strips, the sautéed beef and jicama, the lettuce leaves, the rice paper rounds and water bowls for dipping them, and the sauce. Explain to guests how to make their own hand rolls. First soften a rice paper round in the water and place on a dinner plate. (See page 331 for tips on working with rice paper.) When the rice paper is pliable and tacky, layer the ingredients on top in the following order, a lettuce leaf, some beef and jicama, a few slices of Chinese sausage, 1 or 2 egg strips, and a drizzle of sauce. Wrap up and enjoy.

NOTE

You can plump and slice the sausages several hours in advance, then cover and leave at room temperature. If the fat in the sausages congeals before you are ready to eat (which can be unappetizing), reheat the slices briefly in a dry skillet or microwave oven.

SOUTHERN SALAD ROLLS

Gỏi Cuốn

SOMETIMES LISTED ON RESTAURANT MENUS as fresh spring rolls or summer rolls, salad rolls, along with *phở*, have come to embody Vietnamese food to many non-Vietnamese. They typically combine the elements of a classic Vietnamese *gỏi* (salad) but wrapped in rice paper. Southern Vietnamese cooks usually slip a few aromatic Chinese chives into the mix. The chives, dark green, flat blades with a mild garlic flavor, are sold in Asian markets and are also easily grown from seeds. If they are unavailable, omit them and the rolls will still be tasty. Part of the genius of Vietnamese cooking is in how simple ingredients can be crafted into something that is both flavorful and attractive. These rolls reflect that talent.

1   To poach the shrimp, fill a small saucepan half full with water, add the salt, and bring to a rolling boil over high heat. Add the shrimp, remove from the heat, and let stand for 3 to 5 minutes, or until the shrimp have curled nicely and are pinkish orange. Lift them out with a slotted spoon and set aside to cool. Leave the water in the pan.

2   While the shrimp are poaching, trim any excess fat from the pork chop. Return the water in the pan to a rolling boil and drop in the pork. When the water starts bubbling at the edges of the pan, remove the pan from the heat and cover tightly. Let stand for 20 minutes. The pork should be firm yet still yield a bit to the touch. Remove the pork from the pan and let cool. Save the light stock for another use or discard.

3   Working with 1 shrimp at a time, lay it flat on a cutting board and cut in half horizontally. (Use the index and middle fingers of your noncutting hand to keep the shrimp in place as you wield the knife.) Devein the shrimp as necessary. Set aside on a plate.

Makes 16 rolls, to serve 6 to 8

1 teaspoon salt
24 small shrimp, peeled
1 boneless, thick pork
loin chop or 1/3 pound
boneless pork shoulder
1/3 pound small dried round
rice noodles, cooked in
boiling water for 3 to 5
minutes, drained, and
flushed with cold water
1 head butter lettuce, leaves
separated

12 to 16 sprigs cilantro
12 to 16 sprigs mint
32 to 48 Chinese chives
(about 1/2 small bunch),
optional

16 rice paper rounds,
8 1/2 inches in diameter
1 1/2 cups Spicy Hoisin-Garlic
Sauce (page 310)

4 Thinly slice the pork across the grain into strips about ⅛ inch thick, ½ inch wide, and 4 inches long. Add to the plate of shrimp.

5 Set up a wrapping station composed of a flat work surface (a cutting board, inverted baking sheet, or dish towel) and a bowl of water for dipping the rice papers. Place the shrimp, pork, noodles, lettuce, and herbs nearby.

6 Dip a rice paper round in water and then place it on your work surface. (See page 331 for tips on working with rice paper.) When the rice paper is pliable and tacky, fold a lettuce leaf in half along its central spine and then tear off the spine. Place the folded leaf on the lower third of the rice paper round. Put about ¼ cup of the noodles on top of the lettuce, spreading them in a rectangle. Lay a couple of pork strips on top (slightly overlapping, if necessary), and then arrange a few mint and cilantro leaves on top of the pork, spreading them out to distribute their flavors evenly.

Bring up the lower edge of the rice paper to just cover the herbs. Then roll the rice paper a half turn so that the lettuce is on top and visible through the rice paper. Add 3 shrimp halves, cut side up, to the unrolled portion of rice paper, lining them up snugly along the partially finished roll. Fold the sides of the round inward to cover the filling. Roll one more full turn, so that the orange sides of the shrimp are now facing up and visible through the rice paper. Tuck 2 or 3 Chinese chives into the roll, letting them extend out one end. Continue to roll until you have a snug cylindrical package. The rice paper is self-sealing.

Use a knife or scissors to trim the chives, leaving a ¾-inch "tail" extending from the end.

7 Repeat this process to make 16 rolls in all, placing the finished rolls on a serving platter. If the rolls seem too long to manage and eat comfortably, cut them in half on the diagonal. Serve the rolls with the sauce. Diners can dip the rolls into the sauce or spoon some sauce onto the rolls.

NOTE

While the pork and shrimp may be poached a day ahead, slice them on the day you wrap. The noodles may be cooked early in the day, covered with plastic wrap, and kept at room temperature. You may wrap the rolls 2 hours in advance of serving. Keep them covered with plastic wrap to prevent the rice paper from drying out and becoming unpleasantly tough. If you are cutting the rolls, do so just before serving, or they may lose their nice shape.

You can wrap other items in these rolls, too, but they must be thinly sliced so that they are flexible enough to roll. Seeded cucumber strips, julienned carrot, seared tofu strips, and slices of leftover grilled meats are among the possibilities. Different fresh herbs, such as Vietnamese coriander (*rau răm*) or Thai basil, may be incorporated to introduce different flavors. The elements that you need to preserve are the lettuce leaves and noodles, which give the rolls body, and the hoisin-garlic sauce, which marries all the flavors.

BAGUETTE SANDWICH

Bánh Mì

THERE IS ONE SANDWICH in the Vietnamese repertoire and it is a tour de force. Garlicky meats, marinated daikon and carrot, chiles, cucumber, and cilantro tucked into a baguette moistened with mayonnaise and Maggi Seasoning sauce, *bánh mì* merges European and Asian food traditions. Each mouthful reflects how Vietnamese cooks co-opted French ideas to create new foods.

All *bánh mì* use the same basic framework of ingredients, though a minority of makers use margarine or butter instead of mayonnaise. At Vietnamese delis, you make the call on the main protein element. The *đặc biệt* (special) is basically "the works," a smear of liver pâté and slices of various cold cuts that show off the art of Vietnamese charcuterie (pages 156 to 171). Follow the custom of Viet deli owners and use your imagination to fill the sandwich. Just make sure it is boldly flavored. Pieces of grilled lemongrass beef (page 28), oven-roasted chicken (page 80), five-spice pork steaks (page 143), or *char siu* pork (page 142; pictured here) are excellent. Seared or grilled firm tofu or leftover roasted lamb or beef will work, too.

The bread doesn't have to be one of the airy Vietnamese baguettes made with wheat and rice flours. (In the past, the best baguettes in Vietnam were made from wheat flour only and displayed an amazing crumb and crust.) You can use a regular baguette (though neither sourdough nor too crusty) or a Mexican *bolillo* (torpedo-shaped roll).

1 Slit the bread lengthwise, leaving it attached on the back side. Using your fingers or a bread knife, hollow out the insides, making a trough in each half. Discard the insides or save for another use, such as bread crumbs. If the bread is soft, crisp it briefly in a toaster oven preheated to 325°F, and then let it cool for a minute before proceeding.

2 Generously spread the cut sides of the bread with mayonnaise and then drizzle with Maggi Seasoning sauce. Layer the meat, cucumber, cilantro, chile, and pickle on the bottom half. Close the sandwich, cut in half crosswise for easy eating, and enjoy.

Makes 1 sandwich

1 petite baguette roll or 7-inch section from a regular baguette

Mayonnaise, preferably homemade

Maggi Seasoning sauce or light (regular) soy sauce

Liver pâté, boldly flavored cooked meat, and/or tofu, sliced and at room temperature

3 or 4 thin, seeded cucumber strips, preferably pickling (Kirby) or English

2 or 3 sprigs cilantro, coarsely chopped

3 or 4 thin slices jalapeño chile

1/4 cup Everyday Daikon and Carrot Pickle (page 192)

CORN AND COCONUT FRITTERS

Chả Bắp Rán

TENDER, FLAVORFUL, AND LIGHTLY CRISPY, these fritters release a heady coconut fragrance as they fry and are complemented by a spicy-sweet dipping sauce at the table. Traditionally, the corn was crushed in a mortar, but an electric mini-chopper or a food processor eases the workload with a fine result. For coconut cream with the best texture and flavor, make your own or use the thick, creamy plug that rises to the top of a can of Mae Ploy brand coconut milk.

1 To make the batter, place the corn in the bowl of an electric mini-chopper or food processor and pulse 12 to 15 times, pausing to scrape down the sides of the bowl. You want a semicohesive mass that holds together when you pinch a little between your fingers. Transfer to a small bowl and add the coconut cream, egg, flour, cornstarch, salt, and sugar. Stir to create a batter with the consistency of thick oatmeal. If it is too thin, add additional flour 1 teaspoon at a time. Set aside for 30 minutes.

2 To make the dipping sauce, in a small bowl, stir together the chile sauce, water, and sugar until the sugar dissolves. Taste and add more water and sugar if you want to decrease the heat level. Transfer to a shallow bowl for serving.

3 Line a large plate with paper towels and place next to the stove. Pour oil to a depth of 1 inch into a wok or 5-quart Dutch oven and heat over medium-high heat to 350°F on a deep-frying thermometer. (If you don't have a thermometer, stand a dry bamboo chopstick in the oil; if small bubbles immediately gather on the surface around the chopstick, the oil is ready.)

4 To make each fritter, scoop up about 2 teaspoons batter and gently scoot it into the hot oil. The fritters should be about 1½ inches in diameter. Cook only as many at one time as will fit without crowding. Fry the fritters, turning them once, for about

Makes about 20 fritters, to serve 4 to 6

1 cup fresh corn kernels, cut from about 2 ears corn, or thawed frozen corn kernels

¼ cup coconut cream, scooped from the top of an unshaken can of coconut milk or from freshly made coconut milk (page 318)

1 egg, lightly beaten

⅓ cup all-purpose flour

1½ teaspoons cornstarch

½ teaspoon salt

½ teaspoon sugar

DIPPING SAUCE

2 tablespoons Huy Fong brand Sriracha chile sauce or chile garlic sauce

2 teaspoons water

1 teaspoon sugar

Corn or canola oil for deep-frying

3 minutes total, or until puffed, golden brown, and crisp. Using a skimmer, transfer the fritters to the towel-lined plate to drain. If the fritters deflate, you need to fry them longer and perhaps lower the heat slightly. They should hold their shape and remain lightly crispy after frying.

5 Arrange the fritters on a plate and serve hot as finger food along with the dipping sauce.

FRIED SHRIMP CHIPS

Bánh Phồng Tôm

SHRIMP CHIPS, usually labeled shrimp crackers, are the Southeast Asian equivalent of the American potato chip. They are made by mixing a dough of primarily ground shrimp and tapioca starch, steaming it, slicing it, and setting the slices out in the hot sun to dry. The hard chips are then deep-fried in oil, puffing and expanding to about twice their original size. Made well, the essence of shrimp is captured in each chip.

Most cooks buy the dry chips, rather than make them. The frying is fast and neither messy nor oily. Plus, the chips may be fried hours in advance, making a bowl of *bánh phồng tôm* an easy accompaniment to cocktails. They are also used to scoop up salads, such as Cucumber and Shrimp Salad (page 46).

As with all snack foods, not all shrimp chips are equal. The inexpensive colorful ones sold in boxes are pretty but not much else. Indonesian shrimp chips, called *krupuk*, are consistently good and packed with real shrimp flavor. Imports from Vietnam are getting steadily better. Most of them are from Sa Dec, a city known for its tasty shrimp.

Dried shrimp chips

Corn or canola oil for
deep-frying

1 Line a large plate with paper towels and place next to the stove. Pour oil to a depth of ¾ to 1 inch into a wok or 5-quart Dutch oven and heat over medium-high heat to 350°F on a deep-frying thermometer. (If you don't have a thermometer, stand a dry bamboo chopstick in the oil; if small bubbles immediately gather on the surface around the chopstick, the oil is ready.)

2 Drop in 3 to 5 chips for each batch, keeping in mind that they will double in size. If you fry too many at a time, they will cook unevenly. Each will sink to the bottom, start to bubble, maybe curl, and then expand before rising to the top, where it will finish cooking. All of this happens in 4 to 5 seconds, so don't turn away. Once the chips float to the top, let them fry for only a few seconds longer. Don't let them brown or their delicate flavor will vanish. Using a skimmer, transfer the chips to the towel-lined plate to drain. This is fast-paced frying, so regulate the heat and adjust the size of your batches so that you are working at a comfortable speed.

FRIED WONTONS

Hoành Thánh Chiên

WHEN I WAS A CHILD, my mom often kept me busy making wontons, putting three or four packages of the skins and a big bowl of pork-and-shrimp filling in front of me. (That's 150 to 200 wontons!) She served the fried wontons to family and guests alike, who delighted in dipping the crispy morsels into our homemade sweet-and-sour sauce, a lighter version of the Chinese classic flavored with fish sauce instead of soy sauce.

1 To make the filling, in a bowl, combine the pork, shrimp, scallion, garlic, cornstarch, sugar, salt, and pepper and use chopsticks or a fork to mix well.

2 To fill the wontons, work in batches of 6 to 8 wonton skins. Place them on a work surface, such as large cutting board, inverted baking sheet, or tray. Using 2 teaspoons or demitasse spoons, place a scant teaspoon of filling (about the size of a ½-inch marble) in the center of a wonton skin. Dip a pastry brush in water and lightly brush the entire edge of the skin. Pick up a corner of the wonton skin and fold it over, enclosing the filling and forming a triangle. Press the edges of the triangle firmly with your finger to seal. Make sure that there are no air bubbles, or the wontons will bob around in the hot oil, and that the edges are well sealed, or the wontons will split open when they hit the hot oil. Place the finished wonton on a large plate or tray. Repeat until all the filling is used up.

3 Put a wire rack on a baking sheet and place the sheet next to the stove. Pour oil to a depth of 1½ inches into a wok or 5-quart Dutch oven and heat over medium-high heat to 350°F on a deep-frying thermometer. (If you don't have a thermometer, stand a dry bamboo chopstick in the oil; if small bubbles immediately gather on the surface around the chopstick, the oil is ready.)

Makes about 48 wontons, to serve 6 to 8

FILLING
1/3 pound ground pork
1/4 pound medium shrimp, peeled, deveined, and cut into pea-sized pieces
1 small scallion, white part only, finely chopped
1 small clove garlic, finely minced
1/2 teaspoon cornstarch
1/8 teaspoon sugar
Scant 1/2 teaspoon salt
1/8 teaspoon black pepper

48 square wonton skins (1-pound package)
Corn or canola oil for deep-frying
1 1/2 cups Sweet-and-Sour Sauce (page 312)

4 Working in batches of 4 to 6, slide the wontons into the hot oil and fry, turning once, for about 2 minutes on each side, or until golden brown. Using a skimmer, transfer to the rack to drain.

5 Arrange the wontons on a platter. Serve hot as finger food along with the sauce for dipping.

SAVORY MEAT PASTRIES

Pa-Tê Sô (Pâtés Chaud)

THE EASY AVAILABILITY of butter in America was a boon for my mother, who saw endless possibilities for perfecting French *pâtés chaud*, large puff pastry rounds filled with an aromatic meat mixture. She regularly made the rich pastries from scratch, and they were standard breakfast fare for my siblings and me growing up. As adults, we have scaled back our consumption, making the pastries smaller and serving them as finger food on special occasions. Shaping tiny round pastries is laborious, so we form logs and cut them into diamonds.

Unlike my mom, I don't have the patience or time to make my own puff pastry. Instead, I rely on a local bakery for frozen sheets of all-butter puff pastry or use the frozen puff pastry sold at supermarkets. The latter are usually sold two sheets to a box, with each sheet weighing about ½ pound and measuring about ten inches square.

1   To make the filling, in a bowl, combine the pork, beef, onion, garlic, Cognac, salt, and pepper and mix well. Set aside.

2   Line a baking sheet with parchment paper. Place the cold puff pastry on a lightly floured work surface. Using a sharp knife, cut into 3 equal strips. Put one-third of the filling on 1 strip, placing it lengthwise in a continuous line down the middle that reaches from end to end. Using your index finger or a pastry brush, lightly moisten 1 long edge of the strip with water. Without stretching the dough, lift the dry long edge of the strip to cover the filling. To create a smooth seam, flatten the moistened edge with your thumb, then roll the log to close. Repeat with the remaining strips and filling. Place the logs, seam side down, on the prepared baking sheet. Refrigerate for 30 minutes, or until firm. Meanwhile, position a rack in the middle of the oven and preheat to 400°F.

3   Using a sharp knife, cut each log on the diagonal at 1-inch intervals to create diamond shapes. Put the diamonds, seam side down and 1 inch apart, on the same prepared baking sheet. Brush the top of each pastry with the egg. Bake for 18 to 22 minutes, or until golden brown and crispy. Let cool for 5 minutes before serving.

Makes about 30 small pastries, to serve 8 to 10

FILLING

¼ pound ground pork

¼ pound ground beef, preferably chuck

1 tablespoon minced yellow onion

½ clove garlic, finely minced

2 teaspoons Cognac

¼ plus ⅛ teaspoon salt

¼ teaspoon black pepper

1 sheet puff pastry, about 10 inches square, thawed if frozen and kept refrigerated

1 egg, beaten

NOTE

At Vietnamese American bakeries, *pâtés chaud* are often labeled pork or chicken pies. These popular pastries can also be made in advance and then baked when needed. Fill the logs as directed in step 2 and then freeze them on the baking sheet for 1 hour, or until hard. Wrap each log airtight in plastic wrap and freeze for up to 2 months. Let thaw about halfway before cutting and baking as directed.

STUFFED SQUID WITH GINGER-LIME DIPPING SAUCE

Mực Nhồi

AS YOU FRY THESE STUFFED SQUID, the fragrant aromas that rise from the pan will have you dreaming of enjoying them along with a cold beer. Many Vietnamese cooks add minced garlic to the stuffing, but our family prefers ginger, a nod to ginger-centric northern Vietnam. The tart, spicy, salty dipping sauce heightens the flavors in the stuffing.

Select young, fresh squid with bodies about five inches long, not including the tentacles. For the best flavor, clean the squid yourself, rather than buying them already cleaned. Because both squid sizes and a cook's stuffing technique can vary, this recipe makes more stuffing than you will need. If only a little is left over, discard it. If there is a fair amount, mix in an egg or two and fry up into an omelet (see Pork and Mushroom Omelet, page 97, for cooking instructions).

1 Clean the squid as directed on page 323, reserving the tentacles. Finely chop the tentacles, and then put them in a bowl.

2 To make the filling, add the pork, mushrooms, noodles, onion, ginger, fish sauce, pepper, and sugar to the tentacles and use your fingers or a spatula to mix well.

3 Stuffing the squid bodies is difficult at first, but you will quickly get the hang of it. First, use a sharp knife to remove a scant ⅛ inch of the pointy tip of the squid bodies. This hole acts as a vent, so that air bubbles don't form that would prevent you from filling the entire cavity. Next, hold a body with one hand and use your other hand to stuff. Start out with a small amount of filling and push it in with your index or middle finger, gently squeezing the squid tube to force the filling to the tail end. (Or, fill a pastry bag outfitted with a ½-inch round tip and pipe in the filling.) Continue stuffing until only ½ to ¾ inch of the body remains unstuffed. *Do not overstuff* the squid, or it may burst during cooking. "Stitch" the opening closed by inserting a toothpick down through the wide end (head hole) and then back

continued

Serves 6

12 young squid, about
    1½ pounds total

FILLING
½ pound ground pork
4 dried shiitake mushrooms,
    reconstituted (page 332),
    stemmed, and finely
    chopped
1 bundle (1.3 ounces)
    cellophane noodles,
    soaked in hot water until
    pliable, drained, and cut
    into ¼-inch lengths

½ small yellow onion, finely
    chopped
½ teaspoon peeled and
    minced fresh ginger
2 teaspoons fish sauce
⅛ teaspoon black pepper
¼ teaspoon sugar

¼ cup canola or other
    neutral oil
⅔ cup Ginger-Lime Dipping
    Sauce (page 309)

up again. As the squid are stuffed, place them on a paper towel to blot up excess moisture. Discard any leftover filling or save for another use.

3   The initial searing of the squid can be fairly dramatic, so you may want to have a splatter guard handy. In a large skillet, heat the oil over medium-high heat. When it is hot, add the squid and sear, turning as needed, for about 2 minutes, or until lightly golden on all sides. Reduce the heat to medium and continue frying, moving the squid around to ensure even cooking. After

10 minutes, the squid should be tight and firm, like a well-filled balloon, and be nicely browned. Remove from the pan and let cool for 5 to 10 minutes.

4   To serve, remove the toothpick from each squid. Cut each squid on the diagonal into slices about ¼ inch thick. Arrange the slices on a platter, with the dipping sauce in a bowl in the center for people to help themselves. Serve the squid hot or at room temperature.

STUFFED SNAILS STEAMED WITH LEMONGRASS

Ốc Nhồi Hấp Lá Xả

A NORTHERN SPECIALTY, this dish traditionally features *ốc bươu* (apple snail), a freshwater mollusk with a shell that resembles the escargot shells sold in plastic tubes at gourmet markets. The chewy mollusk meat is made into a stuffing with mushroom and scallion and then steamed in the original shells with strips of ginger or lemongrass leaves. To eat the snails, you pull up the leaves, which lifts out the stuffing, and then you dip the stuffing into a ginger-lime sauce. Finally, you pour the aromatic cooking juice left over in the shell into a spoon and sip it like a fine consommé.

Because fresh Vietnamese snails aren't available in the States, I replicate this delicious dish with frozen apple snail or periwinkle meat. The yellowish chunks are sold in one-pound packages at Chinese and Vietnamese markets; sometimes periwinkle is available thawed and packed in Styrofoam trays. (Or, substitute conch or other sea snails normally used for chowder.) Without shells to stuff, I use ceramic egg cups or tall sake cups. The presentation isn't as provocative, but it is still lovely. Ribbons cut from lemongrass stalks, more aromatic and more readily available than ginger leaves, harness the stuffing in the cups and give the cooking juices a heady citrus flavor.

Serves 6

½ pound frozen apple snail or periwinkle meat, thawed overnight in the refrigerator

Salt for refreshing snail meat, plus ½ teaspoon

5 dried shiitake mushrooms, reconstituted (page 332), stemmed, and chopped

¼ cup minced scallion, white and green parts (about 2 medium scallions)

⅛ teaspoon sugar

¼ teaspoon black pepper

½ teaspoon peeled and minced fresh ginger

½ pound (scant 1 cup) Multipurpose Meat Paste (page 158)

1 hefty lemongrass stalk

⅔ cup Ginger-Lime Dipping Sauce (page 309)

1   To make the stuffing, first you must refresh the snail meat. Put it in a colander and toss with a liberal amount of salt. Rinse immediately under lots of cold water and press gently to drain well. Chop the snail meat into pea-sized pieces. Place in a bowl and add the mushrooms, scallion, sugar, ½ teaspoon salt, pepper, and ginger. Using a rubber spatula, mix in the meat paste, binding all the ingredients together.

2   Fill a steamer pan halfway with water and bring to a rolling boil over high heat. Lower the heat to keep the water hot. Cut off the base and peel off individual layers of the lemongrass stalk. Using scissors, cut each layer into ribbons ¼ inch wide and 7 inches long. You will need 24 ribbons, 2 for each cup. If the ribbons don't bend easily, return the water in the steamer to a boil and blanch them for 30 seconds; lower the heat once you're done.

3   Have ready 12 ceramic egg cups or sake cups. Cross 2 ribbons at a right angle to each other and push the midpoint of the cross into the bottom of a cup. (If 1 ribbon is stiffer than the other, put it on top to keep both ribbons in place.) There will be 4 equal lengths of lemongrass ribbon extending beyond the rim of the cup. To prevent the ribbons from shifting, hold the neck of the cup between your index and middle fingers, while using your thumb to hold down one end of the ribbon on top.

Use a spoon to stuff about 2½ tablespoons of the snail mixture into the cup. Don't stuff the mixture tightly. You need to provide passageways for the steam to get to the bottom of the cup where the cooking juices will collect. Nicely mound the top, and if desired, smooth it out with a finger dipped in water. Repeat with the remaining ribbons and stuffing. Place the filled cups in the steamer tray.

4   Return the steamer to a boil. Place the steamer tray over the boiling water, cover, and steam for 5 to 7 minutes, or until the stuffing has risen slightly, a sign of doneness. Using tongs, remove the cups from the steamer and let cool for 1 minute before serving.

5   Serve each person 2 cups. Accompany with individual shallow bowls of the sauce.

NOTE

The stuffing may be prepared 3 to 4 hours in advance, covered, and refrigerated.

If you grow lemongrass, use its leaves instead of ribbons cut from the stalk to harness the stuffing. Simply cut 7-inch lengths of the softer blades that grow out of the stalk portion of the plant. You will need 24 lengths of leaves.

DEVILED CRAB

Cua Farci

A HYBRID DISH (*cua* means "crab" in Vietnamese, and *farci* means "stuffed" in French), this deviled crab is enriched by butter and employs fish sauce to amplify the brininess of the crustacean. Many cooks stuff the crab shells with the raw filling and then fry them. Because it is hard to tell when the filling is cooked, I was taught to sauté it first, which also yields a more flavorful result. I also forgo frying and instead bake the filling in ramekins, topping them with bread crumbs for a crispy finish.

What makes this deviled crab special is fresh crabmeat and tomalley (liver) and fat, which you can only get if you start with a whole crab. (If you don't like the tomalley and fat, omit them for a less rich dish.) Find the freshest, feistiest crab you can, even if it is not a Dungeness, my local species. Live crabs are available at Asian and other markets, but already cooked crabs will work, too—as long as you have a trustworthy fishmonger. Ask when the crab was cooked. And if it has an ammonia-like smell, it is over the hill, so pass it up. You will need about ½ pound of crabmeat.

1 If you are using a live crab, cook, clean, and remove the crabmeat as directed on page 322. Set the meat and the tomalley and fat aside. If you are using a precooked crab, follow only the directions for cleaning the crab and removing the crabmeat and tomalley and fat. Position a rack in middle of the oven and preheat to 400°F.

2 In a large skillet, melt 3 tablespoons of the butter over medium heat. Add the garlic and sauté for about 30 seconds, or until fragrant. Add the onion and sauté for about 2 minutes, or until soft. Add the pork and cook, stirring to breaking it up into smaller pieces, for about 2 minutes, or until it is no longer pink. Add the mushrooms and cellophane noodles, stir to combine, and let cook for about 1 minute. Add the tomalley and fat, fish sauce, salt, and pepper and cook, stirring, for 1 minute to blend the flavors. Remove from the heat and add the crabmeat, incorporating it gently to maintain nice chunks. Taste and add up to ½ teaspoon fish sauce if the flavor lacks depth.

Serves 6 as a starter or as a light lunch with a green salad

1 Dungeness crab, about 2 pounds, preferably live

4 tablespoons unsalted butter

3 cloves garlic, finely minced

1 small yellow onion, finely chopped

1/3 pound ground pork, coarsely chopped to loosen

4 dried shiitake mushrooms, reconstituted (page 332), stemmed, and chopped

2 dried wood ear mushrooms, reconstituted (page 334), trimmed, and chopped (about 3 tablespoons)

1 bundle (1.3 ounces) cellophane noodles, soaked in hot water until pliable, drained, and cut into 1/2- to 3/4-inch lengths

1/2 teaspoon fish sauce

3/4 teaspoon salt

1/2 teaspoon black pepper

2 egg yolks, lightly beaten with 1/2 teaspoon water

2 tablespoons dried bread crumbs

3 Put six ½-cup flameproof ramekins on a baking sheet. Distribute the crab mixture evenly among the dishes. The filling compacts as it bakes, so press down lightly as you fill the molds. Brush the tops with the egg yolk, then sprinkle each one with 1 teaspoon of the bread crumbs. Cut the remaining 1 tablespoon butter into bits and dot the tops evenly.

4 Bake for 20 to 25 minutes, or until hot and lightly sizzling. Turn the oven to broil and slip the baking sheet under the broiler about 4 inches from the heat source. Broil for 3 to 5 minutes, or until the tops are nicely browned. Don't leave them in the oven any longer, or they will dry out. Transfer each dish to a plate and serve.

NOTE

You can prepare this dish a day in advance. Make the crab mixture, fill the baking dishes, cover, and refrigerate. Let the dishes sit at room temperature for about 30 minutes before brushing the tops with egg yolk, sprinkling with bread crumbs, and baking.

GROUND PORK OPTIONS

Most Vietnamese and Chinese markets, and some supermarkets, offer two kinds of ground pork, a fattier one and a leaner one. You won't see fat percentages posted, but the costlier one is leaner. There may even be coarsely ground pork (think of a chili grind), which has a texture similar to hand-chopped pork. Or, you can buy a shoulder roast and have it ground on the spot. It will have a fat content of 15 to 20 percent, making it excellent for these recipes, and it freezes beautifully. For smaller quantities, use pork shoulder (blade) steaks and do the chopping yourself (page 69). Try these various options and decide which one you prefer.

CUCUMBER AND SHRIMP SALAD

Gỏi Dưa Chuột

THIS IS PROBABLY THE MOST COMMONLY SERVED SALAD in the Vietnamese repertoire. Festive looking and tasty, *gỏi dưa chuột* often makes an appearance at our family celebrations. In fact, my mother made it for the one hundred guests at my wedding reception.

Vietnamese delis pack this popular salad for their customers with the dressing on the side. But those versions are often prepared with cucumbers that have thick, waxed skins. I recommend pickling or English cucumbers, as their skins are thin and not waxed and their flavors are superior. Small, briny bay shrimp are easily distributed throughout the salad, to accent every bite, while the chicken and pork lend richness. For an extra note of authenticity, serve the salad with Fried Shrimp Chips (page 37) or Toasted Sesame Rice Crackers (page 320) for scooping up bitefuls.

1 To make the dressing, in a small bowl, combine the lime juice, sugar, fish sauce, water, and chiles and stir to dissolve the sugar. Set aside to develop the flavors.

2 Trim off the ends of each cucumber, and then halve lengthwise. Use a teaspoon to remove the seeds from each half (the English cucumbers will have few seeds). Cut the halves crosswise into slices a scant ⅛ inch thick. A razor-sharp knife or a Japanese Benriner slicer (page 22) produces the most attractive, uniformly thin slices. A food processor can be used but will yield less satisfactory results. Put the cucumbers and carrot in a large bowl, add 1½ teaspoons of the salt and the sugar, and toss to mix. Set aside for 30 minutes to weep. A pool of juice will accumulate at the bottom of the bowl.

3 Drain the cucumbers and carrot in a colander and place under cold running water to rinse off as much salt and sugar as possible. Working in batches, wring out excess moisture in a nonterry dish towel: position a mound of the vegetables in the center, roll it up in the towel, and then twist the ends in opposite directions to force out the liquid. Do this 3 or 4 times. You want

Serves 4 to 6

DRESSING

¼ cup fresh lime juice (about 2 limes)

3½ tablespoons sugar

3 tablespoons fish sauce

2 tablespoons water

1 or 2 Thai or serrano chiles, finely chopped (optional)

2 to 2¼ pounds pickling (Kirby) or English cucumbers

1 carrot, peeled and finely shredded (page 51)

2½ teaspoons salt

1 teaspoon sugar

1 boneless, skinless chicken breast, about ¼ pound

1 boneless pork loin chop, about ¼ pound

¼ pound precooked bay or small salad shrimp

⅓ cup unsalted roasted peanuts, chopped

1 tablespoon sesame seeds, toasted (page 332) and crushed in a mortar

to extract enough water from the cucumber yet not completely crush it. (The cucumber will become a beautiful translucent green, in marked contrast to the color of the carrot.) Return the vegetables to the bowl and fluff them up to release them from their cramped state. Set aside.

4 Trim any excess fat from the pork chop. Fill a small saucepan half full with water, add the remaining 1 teaspoon salt, and bring to a rolling boil over high heat. Drop in the chicken breast and pork chop. When the water starts bubbling at the edges of the pan, remove the pan from the heat and cover tightly. Let stand for 20 minutes. The pork and chicken should be firm yet still yield a bit to the touch. Remove them from the pan. Reserve the light stock for another use or discard. When the pork and chicken are cool enough to handle, cut the pork into matchsticks, and shred the chicken with your fingers into thin pieces, pulling the meat along its natural grain. Let the pork and chicken continue to cool to room temperature and then add them to the vegetables.

5 Place the shrimp in a colander and rinse with cold running water, then press gently to drain well. Add the shrimp to the bowl of vegetables and meat.

6 Just before serving, add the peanuts and sesame seeds to the salad and toss to distribute evenly. Pour on the dressing and toss again. (If you don't want to bite into a piece of chile unexpectedly, strain the dressing over the salad.) Taste and adjust the flavors to your liking, balancing the sour, sweet, salty, and spicy. Transfer to a serving plate, leaving any unabsorbed dressing behind, and serve.

NOTE

You may ready the vegetables, pork and chicken, and shrimp a day in advance. Keep them in separate covered containers in the refrigerator, and return them to room temperature before tossing the salad. The dressing may be prepared several hours in advance.

SPECIAL-OCCASION SALADS

If you ask the cook, "What's on today's menu?" and the response includes a *gỏi* or *nộm*, you know it is a special occasion. *Gỏi* and *nộm* typically refer to colorful salads of meat, seafood, vegetables, herbs, peanuts, and sesame seeds usually served as a separate first course, instead of a side dish. Both words refer to the same type of dish, with *gỏi* the everyday term in southern and central Vietnam and *nộm* in the north.

These salads represent a careful balancing act among different flavors, colors, and textures, and a skilled Vietnamese cook runs through a mental checklist to make sure all three bases have been covered. One ingredient—vegetable, fruit, meat, fish, shellfish—usually makes up the bulk in the salad. If it naturally carries a lot of moisture, the first task is to expel the excess water, so that the ingredient will be relatively dry and crunchy. For example, cucumber and green papaya are tossed with salt and sugar to release their water and are then wrung out in a kitchen towel. Tiny raw silverfish are cooked and then drained. (Green cabbage is an exception, since it already has plenty of crunchiness and is not naturally moist.) Then the magic happens. When everything is combined, the main ingredient absorbs all of the other flavors like a sponge.

Vietnamese food aficionados may tell you that *gỏi* comes in more complex guises, built from exotic ingredients such as raw fish and sauces made from fish innards and astringent bananas, than you will find in this chapter. They are right, but it is these simpler salads that regularly appear on most Vietnamese tables.

For a lighter salad, omit the pork and/or chicken and double the amount of shrimp. Or, you may eliminate the shrimp and add more pork or chicken. Whatever you decide, include at least one of these elements, as they lend richness to the salad.

GREEN PAPAYA SALAD

Gỏi Đu Đủ

IN THE VIETNAMESE KITCHEN, papaya is more than just a sweet fruit. The mild, firm flesh of an unripened green papaya is treated like a vegetable. Green papaya may be pickled, added to soup, or featured in salads like this one. Here, crunchy, light jade papaya shreds are flecked with chopped herbs and bits of shrimp and pork and tossed with a dressing of lime juice, fish sauce, and garlic.

Look for green papayas at Vietnamese or Thai markets, Chinese markets with a Southeast Asian clientele, or Latin grocery stores. A bit of yellowing on the skin is fine, but make sure the flesh is neither soft nor mushy. Whole fruits will keep in the refrigerator for about a week.

1   To make the dressing, in a small bowl, stir together the lime juice, fish sauce, sugar, garlic, and chiles until the sugar dissolves. Set aside to develop the flavors.

2   Peel the papaya with a vegetable peeler and then cut off the stem. Halve the papaya lengthwise and use a spoon to scoop out and discard the seeds. Cut each half lengthwise into quarters, and then use a knife to remove the thin white layer lining the cavity. Using a Japanese Benriner slicer (page 22) or a food processor fitted with the largest shredder blade, shred the papaya pieces. Aim for thin strands about 1/16 inch thick, no more than 3/16 inch wide, and 2½ to 3 inches long (about the size of the shredded mozzarella you put on a pizza.)

3   Put the shredded papaya in a colander, add the sugar and 1½ teaspoons of the salt, and use both hands to massage the sugar and salt vigorously into the papaya. After a few minutes, the papaya will be a little slimy and limp yet still firm. At that point, rinse it under lots of cold running water to remove the salt and sugar.

Serves 4 to 6

DRESSING
1/4 cup fresh lime juice (about 2 limes)
2½ tablespoons fish sauce
2½ tablespoons sugar
1 small clove garlic, finely minced
1 or 2 Thai or serrano chiles, finely chopped (optional)

1 green papaya, about 2 pounds
1 teaspoon sugar
2½ teaspoons salt
½ pound medium shrimp, peeled and deveined
1 boneless pork loin chop, about 1/4 pound
3 tablespoons finely chopped fresh Vietnamese coriander or cilantro leaves

4 Working in batches, wring out excess moisture from the papaya in a nonterry dish towel: position a mound of the papaya in the center, roll it up in the towel, and then twist the ends in opposite directions to force out the liquid. Do this 3 or 4 times. You want to extract enough water from the papaya yet not completely crush it. Transfer the papaya to a large bowl and fluff it up to release it from its cramped state.

5 Fill a small saucepan half full with water, add the remaining 1 teaspoon salt, and bring to a rolling boil over high heat. Add the shrimp, remove from the heat, and let stand for 3 to 5 minutes, or until the shrimp have curled nicely and are pinkish orange. Lift them out with a slotted spoon and set aside to cool, leaving the water in the pan. When the shrimp are cool enough to handle, shred them with your fingers into ¼-inch pieces. Let the shrimp pieces continue to cool to room temperature and then add them to the bowl containing the papaya.

6 While the shrimp are cooling, trim any excess fat from the pork chop. Return the water in the pan to a rolling boil and drop in the pork. When the water starts bubbling at the edges of the pan, remove the pan from the heat and cover tightly. Let stand for 20 minutes. The pork should be firm yet still yield a bit to the touch. Remove the pork from the pan. Reserve the light stock for another use or discard. When the pork is cool enough to handle, cut it into matchsticks. Let the pork continue to cool to room temperature and then add it to the shrimp and papaya.

7 Just before serving, add the Vietnamese coriander to the salad and toss to distribute evenly. Pour on the dressing and toss again. (If you don't want to bite into a piece of chile unexpectedly, strain the dressing over the salad.) Taste and adjust the flavors to your liking, balancing the sour, sweet, salty, and spicy. Transfer to a serving plate, leaving any unabsorbed dressing behind, and serve.

NOTE

You may ready the papaya, shrimp, and pork a day in advance. Keep them in separate covered containers in the refrigerator, and return them to room temperature before tossing the salad. The dressing may be prepared several hours in advance.

When I am including this salad in a meal that contains a pork-based dish, I leave out the shredded pork and add more shrimp (use about ¾ pound total). If papaya isn't available or if you would like a slightly more assertive flavor, use daikon instead. Select young daikons (which have a milder taste) no more than 1½ inches in diameter.

To make another Vietnamese favorite, substitute sweet-and-spicy Asian beef jerky for the shrimp and pork. Purchase the thin, dark red sheets of jerky, packed in plastic wrap or in boxes, at a Chinese or Vietnamese market. Using scissors, cut about 3 ounces of the jerky into short strips that match the papaya strips; you will have about ¾ cup. Combine the papaya, jerky, and ¼ cup shredded fresh Thai basil leaves. Toss the mixture with the same dressing as for the pork and shrimp version, but use a little less, as you will have a slightly smaller amount of salad.

SPICY CABBAGE AND CHICKEN SALAD

Gỏi Bắp Cải Gà

UNLIKE THE OTHER SALADS in this chapter, this one uses vinegar in the dressing, rather than lime juice, for its tart edge. Raw cabbage and vinegar are great partners here, just as they are in any coleslaw.

Using a mortar to make the dressing is important, as it allows the garlic and chile to bloom. First, pound the garlic and chile. When they have broken up, switch to a circular motion, using the pestle to mash the mixture against the curved walls of the mortar, an action Vietnamese cooks refer to as smearing (*quẹt*) food. A richly hued orange-red paste emerges that has a perfume and flavor that cannot be achieved with a machine or hand chopping.

1 Fill a small saucepan half full with water, add the salt, and bring to a rolling boil over high heat. Drop in the chicken breasts. When the water starts bubbling at the edges of the pan, remove the pan from the heat and cover tightly. Let stand for 20 minutes. The chicken should be firm yet still yield a bit to the touch. Remove the chicken from the pan and reserve the light stock for another use (see Note) or discard. When cool enough to handle, shred with your fingers into thin pieces, pulling the meat along its natural grain. Put the chicken in a large bowl and let it cool to room temperature.

2 Meanwhile, put the onion in a small bowl and add the white vinegar just to cover. Set aside for 15 minutes; the vinegar will reduce the harshness of the onion. Drain well and add to the bowl with the chicken, along with the cabbage, carrot, and Vietnamese coriander.

Serves 4 to 6

1 teaspoon salt
2 boneless, skinless chicken
   breasts, 1/2 pound total
1 small red onion, thinly sliced
About 3/4 cup distilled white
   vinegar
1 small head green cabbage,
   about 1 pound, quartered
   through the stem end,
   cored, and cut crosswise
   into 1/4-inch-wide ribbons
1 carrot, peeled and finely
   shredded (page 51)
2 tablespoons finely chopped
   fresh Vietnamese
   coriander or cilantro
   leaves

DRESSING

1 or 2 Thai or serrano chiles,
   chopped
1 clove garlic, chopped
1/2 teaspoon sugar
Pinch of salt
3 tablespoons fish sauce
6 tablespoons unseasoned
   Japanese rice vinegar

3 To make the dressing, using a mortar and pestle, mash the chiles, garlic, sugar, and salt together into a fragrant orange-red paste. This releases and combines the oils from the chile and garlic. Scrape the paste into a bowl and add the fish sauce and rice vinegar, stirring to dissolve the sugar and salt and to combine well.

4 Just before serving, pour the dressing over the salad and toss to mix well. The salad will wilt slightly. Taste and adjust the flavors to your liking, balancing the sour, sweet, salty, and spicy. Transfer to a serving plate, leaving any unabsorbed dressing behind, and serve.

NOTE

The salad may be readied through step 3 up to 4 hours in advance. Cover the vegetables and chicken and refrigerate, and cover the dressing and leave at room temperature. Return the vegetables and chicken to room temperature before tossing.

Serve this salad with a bowl of Basic Rice Soup (page 67). Use the light stock left over from poaching the chicken as part of the liquid for making the soup. At the table, invite guests to put some of the salad into their soup. It not only cools the soup a bit (helpful in a tropical climate such as Vietnam), but also adds interesting texture and flavor.

Omit the chicken to create a zesty Vietnamese slaw that tastes good with all kinds of barbecue.

FINELY SHREDDING

When a recipe calls for finely shredding an ingredient, usually carrot or ginger, you don't need a four-sided box grater-shredder, nor do you need to cut perfect julienned strips. Instead, cut the item crosswise into coins or on the diagonal into slices a scant ⅛ inch thick. (Note that when you are cutting diagonal slices, the angle of your knife determines the overall length of the final shreds.) Assemble the slices into several short stacks—flat side against the cutting board for stability—and, using a sharp knife and keeping your knuckles well curled to avoid nicking your fingers, cut vertically at 1/16- to ⅛-inch intervals to create fine shreds. Don't expect the shreds to be uniform in length. In fact, some variation is fine—even attractive.

BANANA BLOSSOM SALAD

Nộm Hoa Chuối

MY MOTHER DISLIKES the slight astringency of this salad, but my father loves it. One day he secretly taught me how to make the salad. I was tickled then as now by its wild and tangly appearance, juicy texture, and earthy flavors. The element that brings the ingredients together is Vietnamese balm (*kinh giới*), a splendid herb with hints of lemongrass and mint.

You will find giant, burgundy teardrop-shaped fresh banana blossoms (illustrated on page 174), which are technically buds, in the produce section of Chinese and Vietnamese markets. Select one that feels firm and solid (not spongy) and has a tightly closed tip. The smaller the better because there is less astringency in the bracts (petal-like leaves) and flowers, which are both used here. The blossoms and balm are at their peak in the summer.

Illustrated on page 29

1   Fill a large bowl with cold water to a depth of 3 inches and add the vinegar (this acidulated solution will retard discoloration in the cut banana blossom). Place the bowl near the cutting board. Remove and discard any worn or soft outer bracts from the banana blossom and any exposed flowers underneath. Using a sharp knife, cut off and discard the protruding stem at the bottom. Halve the blossom lengthwise. Make a V-shaped cut in the middle of each half to remove the solid off-white center core.

Place each half, cut side down, and cut it crosswise into half circles 1/16 to 1/8 inch thick. As you cut, pause occasionally to deposit the pieces into the vinegar water. (There should be enough water to cover the cut pieces. Add more water if necessary.) After cutting the entire blossom, let the pieces soak for 10 minutes.

2   Pour off the water from the bowl and replace it with warm water. Use your hands to massage the blossom gently for a minute. When the water turns cloudy, drain the blossom in

Serves 4 to 6

- 2 tablespoons distilled white vinegar
- 1 banana blossom, 3/4 to 1 pound
- 1/2 pound bean sprouts, blanched in boiling water for 30 seconds and drained well
- 2 teaspoons salt
- 1 boneless pork loin chop or boneless, skinless chicken breast, about 1/4 pound
- 1 tablespoon sesame seeds, toasted (page 332)
- 1 1/2 teaspoons sugar
- 3 tablespoons dried shrimp, soaked in hot water to cover for 5 minutes to soften, drained, and finely chopped
- 1/3 cup unsalted roasted peanuts, finely chopped
- 1/3 cup lightly packed Vietnamese balm leaves, cut into thin strips
- 4 to 5 tablespoons fresh lime juice (2 or 3 limes)

a colander, and then rinse well under warm running water. Pick up handfuls of the blossom pieces, squeeze them to expel excess water, and put them in a large bowl. (Taste a piece of the blossom. If it is particularly astringent, discard about a quarter of the cut rounds of flowers, some of which will separate out to the bottom.) Add the bean sprouts and set aside.

3 Fill a small saucepan half full with water, add 1 teaspoon of the salt, and bring to a rolling boil over high heat. Drop in the pork (or chicken). When the water starts bubbling at the edges of the pan, remove the pan from the heat and cover tightly. Let stand for 20 minutes. The pork (or chicken) should be firm yet still yield a bit to the touch. Remove the pork (or chicken) from the pan and reserve the light stock for another use or discard. When cool enough to handle, cut the pork into matchsticks (or shred the chicken with your fingers into thin pieces, pulling the meat along its natural grain) and add to the banana blossom and bean sprouts.

4 In a mortar, crush the sesame seeds with the remaining 1 teaspoon salt and the sugar. Add to the salad along with the dried shrimp, peanuts, and Vietnamese balm, reserving a bit of the herb for garnish. Toss well to distribute the ingredients evenly. Add the lime juice, starting with 4 tablespoons. Toss well, taste, and adjust if needed with more lime juice, salt, and sugar. Transfer to individual plates or a platter, garnish with the reserved Vietnamese balm, and serve.

NOTE

The salad may be readied through step 3 up to a day in advance, covered, and refrigerated. Return it to room temperature before finishing.

SILVERFISH SALAD WITH SESAME RICE CRACKERS

Gỏi Cá

IF YOU HAVE EVER BEEN a guest at a Vietnamese eight-course fish feast (a variant of Saigon's famed seven-course beef dinner), you will have tasted a fish *gỏi* made with marinated raw fish, which you scooped up with a shrimp chip or the like. In our family, we have long enjoyed this lightly cooked version, created by my aunt Bac Hang.

She makes the salad with the teeny, tiny silverfish (not to be confused with the insect) sold at Chinese and Vietnamese markets. Piled high on a plate, the mound of white fish accented by orange carrot slivers, red onion, and chopped fresh herbs is beautiful. The silverfish are sold thawed in the seafood case, or in bricklike blocks in the frozen section (the latter look like freeze frames of a school of swimming fish). You will pay a little more for thawed silverfish because the excess water—and its weight—has been drained away. I usually buy the frozen package for long-term keeping. Silverfish have little flavor on their own, but they readily absorb the flavors of other ingredients, resulting in a delicious salad.

1 Place the silverfish in a colander and rinse under cold running water, then press gently to drain well.

2 Cook the fish in 2 batches to ensure even cooking. In a 10-inch nonstick skillet, heat 1½ tablespoons of the oil and half of the garlic over medium heat. When the garlic is sizzling and golden, add half of the fish and increase the heat to high. Sauté for 3 to 4 minutes, or until the fish turn from silver to white and take on a firm texture and a definite shape. Pour the cooked fish into a sieve placed over a bowl (or a colander in the sink) and let drain and cool. Repeat with remaining oil, garlic, and fish. Transfer the drained fish to a large bowl.

3 While the fish are cooling, in a bowl, combine the onion and carrot with the vinegar to cover and set aside for 15 minutes; the vinegar will reduce the harshness of the onion and soften the carrot. Drain, rinse under cold running water, and drain again.

Serves 4 to 6

- 1½ pounds thawed silverfish (from a 2-pound frozen block)
- 3 tablespoons canola or other neutral oil
- 6 cloves garlic, finely minced
- 1 small red onion, thinly sliced
- 1 carrot, peeled and finely shredded (page 51)
- About 1½ cups distilled white vinegar
- 3 tablespoons finely chopped fresh Vietnamese coriander or cilantro leaves
- ¼ cup unsalted roasted peanuts, chopped
- 1 tablespoon sesame seeds, toasted (page 332)
- ½ teaspoon Mellow Chile-Garlic Mix (page 315), optional
- 3 tablespoons fresh lime juice (1 or 2 limes)
- 1 teaspoon sugar
- 2½ tablespoons fish sauce
- 4 Toasted Sesame Rice Crackers (page 320), broken into shards

4 Add the onion, carrot, Vietnamese coriander, peanuts, sesame seeds, and chili-garlic mix to the fish. Toss well to distribute all the ingredients evenly. Combine the lime juice, sugar, and fish sauce in a small bowl, stir to dissolve the sugar, and then add to the fish. Toss well again. Taste and adjust the flavors to your liking, balancing the sour, sweet, salty, and spicy. Mound on individual plates or a platter and surround with some of the rice cracker shards. Serve the remaining shards on the side. At the table, invite guests to scoop up the salad with the cracker shards.

NOTE

The recipe may be readied through step 3 up to 8 hours in advance. Keep the fish and vegetables in separate covered containers in the refrigerator, and return them to room temperature before finishing the salad.

2. ESSENTIAL SOUPS

As refugees, our family was eager to absorb all the Americana we could to gain a sense of belonging. But despite our desire to learn and taste all things American, we rarely deviated from the Vietnamese custom of having casual weeknight soups called *canh*.

"A traditional Viet meal has *canh*, a meat dish, a vegetable, and rice," my parents repeated over and over. For that reason, Mom prepared her soups five days a week. In the late afternoon, she would take a break from her tailoring business to make dinner, cooking the soup first to allow the flavors to develop. When it came time to eat, the *canh*, no matter how simple it was, had to be majestically served in matching bowls to meet my mother's demand for dining formality. We would say "*nước sôi, nước sôi*" (boiling water, boiling water) as we carried the two hot bowls to the table, placing one at each end.

Hot they were. We couldn't escape *canh* even when the Santa Ana winds blew through Southern California and the steaming broth made us sweat. At one point my siblings and I complained about eating the soups all the time, and Mom fired back that *canh* helped our bodies adjust to outside temperatures by warming them up in cold weather and vice versa in hot weather. *Canh* was a sacred subject, so we didn't challenge her.

Canh is the generic term for everyday soups that are mostly made with water, not stock. The simplest version is made by seasoning the liquid leftover from boiling green vegetables for a meal. Associated with rustic living and hard times, this ascetic *canh* can be quite nice, especially with some dried shrimp added for flavor. Most *canh*, however, marry meat or seafood with vegetables and perhaps a last-minute herb garnish to make a homey and delicious soup. Indeed, a wide range of *canh* exist, and some cooks prefer complicated ones with stuffed vegetables, noodles, and other embellishments. I prefer straightforward soups that showcase the pure flavors of their ingredients. They

require less fuss and leave more time for cooking other dishes.

Cháo, a rice porridge eaten throughout Asia, was another kind of soup that regularly graced our family table. Known in English by its south Indian name, *congee*, or by its Cantonese name, *jook*, this soup is made with an astonishingly small amount of rice and lots of water and/or stock. Long simmering releases all the starch in the rice, yielding a creamy consistency. Whole chickens, ducks, or fish are sometimes used to flavor the soup and provide a meat accompaniment.

There are countless recipes for *cháo* to fit nearly any occasion and budget. Like many older Vietnamese, my dad believes that plain *cháo*—made with rice, water, and salt—is a curative, and he prescribed it for my siblings and me whenever we got sick, much like Western chicken soup. Because it was so bland, we hoped and prayed that Western medicine would hasten our recoveries and free us from his *cháo* diet. But as an adult, I can testify to its restorative powers. A larger budget or a special celebration may warrant my mom's *cháo bôi* (page 72), a northern Vietnamese classic containing chicken, shrimp, wood ear mushrooms, and tapioca pearls.

When Viet cooks want to impress or celebrate special occasions, they make *súp*, a name derived from the French *soupe*. Unlike *canh* or *cháo*, *súp* is served as a separate starter course at more formal meals. Delicately flavored, with varying textures and colors, some of these fancier soups are French inspired, while others are Chinese or Vietnamese in origin. All of them require more time because they are based on rich meat broths. They also demand the purchase of special ingredients, such as white fungus or asparagus, which is relatively costly in Vietnam.

The recipes in this chapter are organized by these three categories of soup, *canh*, *cháo*, and *súp*. The selections represent both my favorites and the remarkable range of Vietnamese soups.

RECIPES

NAPA CABBAGE AND SHRIMP SOUP

Canh Cải Kim Chi Nấu Tôm

ONE WAY TO IMBUE *canh* with flavor is to include lots of vegetables. This recipe, along with Opo Squash Soup (page 60) and Chicken Dumpling and Chrysanthemum Leaf Soup (page 61), amply illustrates this technique. Here, the broth is further enriched with the addition of dried shrimp, which contribute both brininess and color.

When I want a more special presentation, I cut the shrimp in half horizontally to yield two symmetrical halves. Once in the hot soup, the halves curl into beautiful spirals. This light soup is a great addition to nearly any Viet meal.

1   In a 4-quart saucepan, heat the oil over medium heat. Add the onion and cook gently, stirring occasionally, for about 4 minutes, or until fragrant and soft. Add the dried shrimp, salt, and fish sauce and cook for about 30 seconds to develop the flavors. Add the water, raise the heat to high, and bring to a boil. Skim and discard any scum that floats to the top. Add the cabbage and return to a boil. Lower the heat to a simmer and cook for 5 minutes, or until the cabbage has softened and the soup is golden. If you are not serving the soup right away, turn off the heat and cover.

2   Just before serving, return the soup to a simmer. Drop in the shrimp. When the shrimp have turned pink and curled, add the pepper. Taste and add extra salt or fish sauce, if necessary. Ladle into a serving bowl and garnish with the scallion. Serve immediately.

Serves 4 to 6 with 2 or 3 other dishes

1 tablespoon canola or other neutral oil

1 small yellow onion, thinly sliced

1 heaping tablespoon dried shrimp, rinsed under hot water and chopped

3/4 teaspoon salt

1 tablespoon fish sauce

6 cups water

3 cups firmly packed sliced napa cabbage (1/4-inch-wide ribbons)

1/2 pound small or medium shrimp, peeled and deveined

1/8 teaspoon white pepper

1 scallion, green part only, thinly sliced

MAXIMIZING SOUP ENJOYMENT

Vietnamese soups are enjoyed throughout the meal, not just at the start, which means you may always go back for more as long as some is left. You use the same bowl for soup that you use for rice, so don't set aside the soup bowl when it is empty. In fact, it is a Viet tradition to ladle *canh* into a bowl containing a little rice. This practice of eating *canh với cơm* (soup with rice) arose in times of hardship when meager diets consisted mostly of rice. Flavoring it with soup got people to consume more rice, which made them feel fuller. Nowadays, with food scarcity less of a concern for many people, *canh* still tastes good with a little rice in the bowl.

TOMATO EGG DROP SOUP

Canh Cà Chua Trứng

HERE IS THE VIETNAMESE VERSION of the familiar Chinese egg drop soup. At its heart is a base of onion and tomato, which is cooked down to concentrate flavors and impart a lovely color. The pork adds richness, and so do the eggs, which also contribute a creamy finish to round out the tangy notes. This soup was a weekly standard at our family dinner table, and my mom would sometimes substitute tofu cubes for the pork to vary the flavor. When I have extra time, I mince the pork by hand for an authentic touch. For instructions on how to do it, see page 69.

1 In a 4-quart saucepan, heat the oil over medium heat. Add the onion and cook gently, stirring occasionally, for about 4 minutes, or until fragrant and soft. Add the tomatoes and salt, cover, and cook for 4 to 6 minutes, or until the tomatoes have collapsed into a thick mixture. Stir occasionally and, if necessary, lower the heat to prevent the tomatoes from sticking or scorching.

2 Uncover and add the fish sauce and pork. Wield chopsticks or use a spoon to move the pork around the pan so that it breaks up into small pieces. This will make it possible to distribute the pork evenly among the bowls when serving. Add the water, raise the heat to high, and bring to a boil, using a ladle to skim and discard any scum that rises to the surface. Lower the heat to a simmer and cook, uncovered, for 15 to 20 minutes, or until the flavors have developed and concentrated sufficiently to produce a rich broth. If you are not serving the soup right away, turn off the heat and cover.

3 Just before serving, return the soup to a simmer. Taste and add extra salt or fish sauce, if necessary. Turn off the heat. Pour the beaten egg onto the soup in a wide circle, and then stir gently to break it up into chiffonlike pieces. Ladle the soup into a serving bowl. Garnish with the cilantro and a generous sprinkle of pepper and serve immediately.

Serves 4 to 6 with 2 or 3 other dishes

1½ tablespoons canola or other neutral oil

1 small yellow onion, thinly sliced

¾ pound ripe tomatoes, cored and coarsely chopped

¾ teaspoon salt

1½ tablespoons fish sauce

⅓ pound ground pork, coarsely chopped to loosen

5½ cups water

2 eggs, beaten

5 or 6 sprigs cilantro, coarsely chopped

Black pepper

OPO SQUASH SOUP

Canh Bầu

OPO SQUASH, a popular light green–skinned Asian gourd, shows off its delicate sweetness in this quick soup, which blends the opo with chicken or pork to yield a rich flavor that tastes like the broth simmered for hours. Look for opo squash at Asian or farmers' markets, selecting specimens that are blemish free and feel heavy for their size. When you gently squeeze the squash, it shouldn't yield to its spongy core, a sign of overmaturity. If an opo squash is unavailable, zucchini may be substituted. The flavor will be milder but still tasty.

1 Trim off both ends of the squash and cut it in half. Quarter each half lengthwise and remove the spongy seeded center. Cut each quarter into 1/2-inch cubes. Set aside.

2 In a 3- or 4-quart saucepan, heat the oil over medium heat. Add the onion and cook gently, stirring occasionally, for about 4 minutes, or until fragrant and soft. Add the chicken or pork and continue cooking for about 2 minutes, or until the meat begins to color. Add the salt and fish sauce and cook for 1 minute to develop the flavors. Add the water, raise the heat to high, and bring to a boil. Skim and discard any scum that floats to the top. Add the squash cubes and return to a boil. Lower the heat to a simmer and cook for about 15 minutes, or until the squash is tender and no longer floats on the surface. (The simmering time depends on the maturity of the squash; old squash with thick skin will take longer.) If you are not serving the soup right away, turn off the heat and cover.

3 Just before serving, return the soup to a simmer and add the white pepper. Taste and add extra salt or fish sauce, if necessary. Ladle into a serving bowl and garnish with the cilantro. Serve immediately.

Serves 4 to 6 with 2 or 3 other dishes

1 opo squash (about 1¼ pounds)

1 tablespoon canola or other neutral oil

1 small yellow onion, thinly sliced

½ pound boneless, skinless chicken thigh or boneless pork shoulder, well trimmed and cut into ¼-inch cubes

¾ teaspoon salt

1 tablespoon fish sauce

6 cups water

⅛ teaspoon white pepper

5 or 6 sprigs cilantro, coarsely chopped

CHICKEN DUMPLING AND CHRYSANTHEMUM LEAF SOUP

Canh Giò Nấu Cải Cúc

TO PUT A TASTY *CANH* on the table nightly requires that you make the most of staple ingredients like *giò*, a raw meat paste used extensively in the Viet kitchen. In fact, I freeze small amounts of this meat paste for whipping up classics like this fragrant soup laden with dumplings made from it. As the dumplings poach, they flavor the broth.

Edible chrysanthemum leaves (*cải cúc*) add their deep green color and musty floral perfume. Called *tong ho* in Cantonese and *shungiku* in Japanese, the greens are sold at Asian markets and are easy to grow, too. Watercress may be substituted.

1 Using your fingers, strip off the leaves and snap off the tender tops of each chrysanthemum stem. Discard the stems along with any discolored leaves and small buds. There should be about 3 cups packed leaves. Rinse the leaves well to remove any grit and drain in a colander. Cut the leaves into 1-inch pieces and set aside.

2 In a 3- or 4-quart saucepan, heat the oil over medium heat. Add the onion and cook gently, stirring occasionally, for about 4 minutes, or until fragrant and soft. Add the water and salt, raise the heat to high, and bring to a boil. Lower the heat to a simmer. Use 2 teaspoons or demitasse spoons to shape the dumplings. Scoop up a smallish mound of the paste with 1 spoon. (The dumplings nearly double in size, so you don't want to start with a huge spoonful of paste.) Pass the mound back and forth from 1 spoon to the other, forming it into a relatively smooth round or football shape. When you're satisfied, use the second spoon to push the dumpling gently off the spoon into the simmering broth.

3 After the dumplings float to the surface of the broth, let them simmer, uncovered, for 10 to 12 minutes, or until cooked through. Taste and season with up to 1 tablespoon fish sauce; how much you use depends on the saltiness of the meat paste. If you are not serving the soup right away, turn off the heat and cover.

Serves 4 to 6 with 2 or 3 other dishes

1/3 pound edible chrysanthemum leaves (about 1/2 bunch)	6 1/2 cups water
	3/4 teaspoon salt
1 tablespoon canola or other neutral oil	1/2 pound (scant 1 cup) Multipurpose Meat Paste (page 158)
1 small yellow onion, thinly sliced	Fish sauce
	Black pepper

4 Just before serving, return the soup to a simmer and add the chrysanthemum leaves. When they wilt and turn deep green, after about 1 minute, turn off the heat. Taste and add extra salt or fish sauce, if necessary. Ladle into a serving bowl and sprinkle with lots of black pepper. Serve immediately.

NOTE

This soup can also be prepared with meat paste made from pork.

GINGERY MUSTARD GREENS AND TILAPIA SOUP

Canh Cải Cá Rô

MY DAD AND I used to catch small perch at the local harbor for this soup. Amid the sailboats and cabin cruisers, we would lower our poles, the lines baited with thawed frozen peas, to catch the three- to four-inch-long fish, the American equivalent of Vietnamese *cá rô*. We would bring home about a dozen fish, and my mom would gut them for this classic Viet combination of sweet fish, sharp mustard greens, and ginger.

One day, Mom protested that cleaning the fish took too much time, so we stopped catching them, and the soup didn't grace our table for years. On a trip to Vietnam, I saw a fishmonger at Ben Thanh market in Saigon cleaning *cá rô*, which reminded me of how good this soup is. Back home, I decided to use whole tilapia, which is sometimes identified as *cá rô* in Viet markets. It worked just like traditional *cá rô* in this soup, but its larger size made it much easier to prep and cook. Now, this brightly flavored soup is back on my table as an ideal balance for bold, rich foods like Grilled Lemongrass Pork Riblets (page 145). Whole tilapia is sold at Asian and Latin markets.

1 In a 3- or 4-quart saucepan, combine the water, fish, half of the sliced onion, and 1/2 teaspoon of the salt and bring almost to a boil over medium-high heat. Lower the heat to a simmer and use a ladle to skim and discard any scum that rises to the top. Let simmer for 10 minutes, or until the flesh of the fish is opaque. Transfer the body sections to a plate, but leave the head in the broth. Let the broth simmer for another 10 minutes.

2 Meanwhile, let the body sections cool for a few minutes, then remove the meat and discard the skin and bones. A fork and a soupspoon are handy for this task. It is okay if the flesh does not come off in large pieces.

3 When the broth has finished simmering, remove from the heat and pour through a fine-mesh sieve into a clean saucepan. Discard the solids. Add 1 tablespoon of the fish sauce and cover and set aside if not serving right away.

Serves 4 to 6 with 2 or 3 other dishes

7 1/2 cups water

1 tilapia, 1 to 1 1/4 pounds, cleaned and cut into 3 sections (head and 2 body sections)

1 yellow onion, thinly sliced

3/4 teaspoon salt

1 1/2 tablespoons fish sauce

1 tablespoon canola or other neutral oil

1/8 teaspoon black pepper, plus extra for garnish

1/2 pound mustard greens, stems removed and leaves cut into bite-sized pieces (4 packed cups)

1 1/2 tablespoons peeled and minced fresh ginger

4 In a skillet, heat the oil over medium heat. Add the remaining onion and cook gently, stirring occasionally, for about 4 minutes, or until fragrant and soft. Add the fish and heat for about 1 minute, or until heated through, gently breaking it up into 1-inch pieces as it heats. Add the remaining 1/4 teaspoon salt and 1 1/2 teaspoons fish sauce and the 1/8 teaspoon pepper and cook for 1 to 2 minutes to allow the fish to absorb the flavors. If you are not serving the soup right away, turn off the heat and cover.

5 Just before serving, return the broth to a simmer. Add the mustard greens and cook for about 1 minute, or until they have wilted and turned deep green. Add the ginger and the fish and stir gently to distribute the fish evenly. Taste and add extra salt or fish sauce, if necessary. When the soup is at a simmer, turn off the heat and ladle into a serving bowl. Sprinkle with black pepper and serve immediately.

FRAGRANT AND SOFT ONIONS

The soups in this chapter, as well as many other recipes in this book, include gently cooking onions until they are fragrant and soft. This unhurried step is called *phi hành* and takes about four minutes to complete over medium heat. The purpose is to coax the sugars from the onions without browning them. You know the onions are ready when you stick your nose over the pan and the harshness of onion has been transformed into a sweet aroma. The onions will have lost their opacity and turned translucent, and they will have lost all their crispness and become limp. Note that *phi hành* shouldn't be confused with the crispy fried shallots called *hành phi*.

DUELING SOUP PHILOSOPHIES

There are two schools of *canh* making: the drop-into-boiling-water school and the sauté-first-then-simmer school. Cooks who follow the former practice argue that their method produces a pristine, clear broth. I prefer to extract extra flavor from some of the ingredients, such as onion, by sautéing them first and then adding the seasonings and water. A brief simmer follows and the soup is done. The broth is not quite as clear as with the drop-into-boiling water method, but the flavors are stronger.

BEEF AND VIETNAMESE CORIANDER SOUP

Canh Thịt Bò Nấu Rau Răm

THIS SIMPLE SOUP embodies the Vietnamese *canh* tradition. The peppery qualities of Vietnamese coriander (*rau răm*), one of the cuisine's most popular herbs, are fully displayed, with its headiness standing up well to the beef. Traditionally, hand-minced beef was used, but ground beef is both convenient and fully acceptable. For the best beef flavor, use the tastiest ground beef available, such as what you would select for a good hamburger. Natural, organic, or grass-fed beef is great. Also, remember that ground beef with a little fat, typically chuck, will add richness to the broth.

1 In a 3- or 4-quart saucepan, heat the oil over medium heat. Add the onion and cook gently, stirring occasionally, for about 4 minutes, or until fragrant and soft. Add the beef and wield chopsticks or use a spoon to move it around the pan so that it breaks up into small pieces. This will make it possible to distribute the beef evenly among the bowls when serving. When the beef turns color, after about 2 minutes, add the fish sauce and salt and cook for 1 minute to develop the flavors.

2 Add the water, raise the heat to high, and bring to a boil, using a ladle to skim and discard any scum that rises to the surface. Lower the heat to simmer and cook for about 15 minutes, or until the broth has reduced by about one-fifth. Taste to make sure the flavors have concentrated sufficiently to produce a rich broth. If they haven't, continue to simmer for a few more minutes. If you are not serving the soup right away, turn off the heat and cover.

3 Just before serving, return the soup to a simmer. Taste and add extra salt or fish sauce, if necessary. Turn off the heat, add the Vietnamese coriander, and give the soup a stir to wilt the herb. Ladle into a serving bowl and sprinkle with the pepper. Serve immediately.

Serves 4 to 6 with 2 or 3 other dishes

1 tablespoon canola or other neutral oil

1 small yellow onion, thinly sliced

2/3 pound hand-minced beef steak (page 69) or ground beef, preferably chuck, coarsely chopped to loosen

1 1/2 tablespoons fish sauce

3/4 teaspoon salt

7 cups water

1/3 cup chopped fresh Vietnamese coriander leaves

Black pepper

NOTE

For beef and bean sprout soup (*canh thịt bò nấu giá*), omit the Vietnamese coriander and add 1 1/2 cups bean sprouts in the last step once the soup is again at a simmer. As soon as the sprouts wilt, after about 30 seconds, turn off the heat. You want to leave a little crunch. Garnish with chopped cilantro.

SALMON WITH TOMATO, DILL, AND GARLIC SOUP

Canh Riêu Cá

WHEN *RIÊU* IS BROUGHT TO THE TABLE, expect a full-bodied soup laced with rich-tasting seafood and tangy tomato. Viet cooks prepare a fish *riêu* like this one as an everyday *canh*, or the more extravagant crab and shrimp *riêu* noodle soup (page 215) for a special occasion.

Carp is the fish typically used in this soup, but since it is not commonly available at regular markets, my family switched to salmon, which has the fattiness to pair perfectly with the tomato, dill, and garlic of a classic *riêu*. We used salmon steaks for years because the bones and skin enriched the broth. But steaks can be difficult to handle during cooking and later on in the bowl, so I now use salmon fillet. In the classic northern Vietnamese tradition, the fish is seared first to firm its flesh. The searing not only helps the fish hold its shape, but also provides a nice textural contrast in the finished soup.

1 Briefly blot the salmon dry with a paper towel before cutting it into 1-inch chunks. In a nonstick skillet, heat the 1/2 teaspoon oil over medium-high heat. Add the salmon and sear, turning once, for 1 to 2 minutes on each side, or until lightly browned. The fish will cook further in the soup. Transfer to a plate and set aside.

2 In a 3- or 4-quart saucepan, heat the remaining 1 tablespoon oil over medium heat. Add the onion and cook gently, stirring occasionally, for about 4 minutes, or until fragrant and soft. Add the tomatoes and salt, cover, and simmer for about 4 minutes, or until the tomatoes have collapsed. Uncover and add the salmon, fish sauce, and water. Raise the heat to high and bring to a boil, using a ladle to skim and discard any scum that rises to the surface. Lower the heat to a gentle simmer, so that the ingredients dance in the broth. Cook for 15 minutes to develop and concentrate the flavors. If you are not serving the soup right away, turn off the heat and cover.

Serves 4 to 6 with 2 or 3 other dishes

1 pound salmon fillet, skin removed	3/4 teaspoon salt
1 tablespoon plus 1/2 teaspoon canola or other neutral oil	1 tablespoon fish sauce
	6 cups water
1 small yellow onion, thinly sliced	3 tablespoons chopped fresh dill, feathery tops only
2/3 pound ripe tomatoes, cored and coarsely chopped	2 cloves garlic, finely minced
	Black pepper

3 Just before serving, return the soup to a simmer. Taste and add extra salt or fish sauce, if necessary. Add the dill and garlic and turn off the heat. Ladle into a serving bowl and sprinkle with the pepper. Serve immediately.

SOUR FISH SOUP WITH TAMARIND, PINEAPPLE, AND OKRA

Canh Chua Cá

RICH WITH CONTRASTS, this soup is easy to like. The tamarind and pineapple provide a sweet-and-sour edge, while the okra, tomato, and bean sprouts offer spongy, soft, and crunchy textures. The catfish and cumin ground the dish with their pungent, earthy qualities. If rice paddy herb (*rau om*) is available, use it for a citrusy accent.

Sour fish soups are eaten throughout Southeast Asia. The Viet version often includes sliced taro stems (*bạc hà*), a flavorless ingredient known for its ability to absorb other flavors. I generally omit the stems because they don't contribute much to the soup, and instead increase the amount of okra, which is added at the end. If you can't find fresh okra, use frozen whole okra, thawing it and slicing it before you add it to the pan. When fresh or frozen pineapple isn't around, don't resort to canned. It is not the same. The soup will be a bit tangier but equally sensational without the pineapple.

1 In a 4-quart saucepan, heat the oil over medium heat. Add the onion and cook gently, stirring occasionally, for about 4 minutes, or until fragrant and soft. Add the salt, sugar, fish sauce, tamarind liquid, and water, raise the heat to high, and bring to a boil. Lower the heat to a simmer, add the catfish and pineapple, and simmer for 5 minutes, or until the catfish and pineapple are tender but still firm. If you are not serving the soup right away, turn off the heat and cover.

2 Just before serving, return the soup to a simmer. Drop in the okra and cook for 2 minutes, or until tender but still firm. Add the tomatoes, bean sprouts, and cumin. When the bean sprouts have just wilted, after about 30 seconds, turn off the heat. Taste and add extra salt or fish sauce, if necessary. Ladle into a serving bowl, garnish with the cilantro, and serve immediately.

NOTE

For sour shrimp soup (*canh chua tôm*), use ¾ pound medium shrimp, peeled and deveined, instead of the catfish. Also, the pineapple is not optional. You need it for the extra flavor boost it delivers.

Serves 4 to 6 with 2 or 3 other dishes

1 tablespoon canola or other neutral oil

1 small yellow onion, thinly sliced

¾ teaspoon salt

1½ teaspoons sugar

1½ tablespoons fish sauce

¼ cup Tamarind Liquid (page 319)

5½ cups water

¾ pound catfish fillet, cut into 1-inch pieces

1 cup bite-sized chunks fresh or frozen pineapple (optional)

10 to 12 okra (⅓ pound total), stemmed and cut into 1-inch pieces

½ pound ripe tomatoes, cored, halved horizontally, seeded, and cut into wedges

2 cups bean sprouts (about ⅓ pound)

1 teaspoon ground cumin, or 3 tablespoons chopped rice paddy herb

5 or 6 sprigs cilantro, coarsely chopped

BASIC RICE SOUP

Cháo

WARM, CREAMY, AND COMFORTING, *cháo* is a staple of the Viet diet. It is eaten at all times of day, and is the magical antidote for whatever ails you—a stomachache, a cold, a hangover. With less than a cup of rice, you can create a pot of soup that will feed people in biblical proportions because it keeps thickening as it cooks and sits, requiring ever more liquid to thin it down.

At its most basic, *cháo* is rice simmered in liquid—water, homemade stock, or canned broth (the latter two are best)—until all its starch has been released. The thick finished soup is a versatile canvas. For a flavorful savory addition, eat it with Salted Preserved Eggs (page 101) or a sprinkle of Cotton Pork shreds (page 134). For richness, put a raw egg into the bowl before ladling in the hot soup. For a simple seafood soup, drop in raw peeled shrimp just before serving. Or, make one of the four *cháo* recipes that follow.

1 Put the rice in a heavy-bottomed 4-quart saucepan and add enough water to cover by 1 inch. Stir the rice with your hand 8 to 10 times around and then let the rice settle. Carefully pour out the milky water. Repeat this rinsing but without stirring the rice. These two rinsings remove some of the starch from the rice.

2 Add the stock, ginger, and scallions and bring to a boil over high heat. Lower the heat to a vigorous simmer, and then cover partially. To loosen but not lose its starch, the rice should bounce in the bubbling water without the water boiling over the pan sides. Let the soup cook for 5 minutes. Stir the rice to make sure none has stuck to the bottom and lower the heat to a gentle simmer.

3 Re-cover partially and continue cooking for 1 hour, or until the rice grains have bloomed and curled, releasing their starches to thicken the soup and turn it creamy white. There should be only a little separation between the rice and liquid. If you stir the soup, the rice should be suspended in the liquid.

Makes about 8 cups, to serve 4 as a light lunch, or 6 with 2 or 3 other dishes

3/4 cup long-grain rice	4 quarter-sized slices
2 1/2 quarts (10 cups) chicken	unpeeled fresh ginger
stock, homemade or quick	2 scallions, white part only
version (page 317)	Salt

4 Discard the ginger and scallion. Taste and add salt as necessary; the amount will depend on what liquid you used to make the soup. You now have a versatile soup base to which other flavorings may be added. This soup may be prepared a day in advance and reheated over medium heat with a bit of extra water to prevent scorching. It may thicken considerably after cooling, but you can always add water to thin it out. Avoid boiling the finished soup to prevent scorching.

RICE SOUP WITH BEEF AND GINGER

Cháo Bò

THIS RICE SOUP is the closing dish for the popular Vietnamese seven-course beef feast, where its primary role is to settle the stomach after six indulgent courses. At that point, I find it hard to enjoy the soup because I'm usually stuffed. But I regularly make this soup for lunch. It is a good way to get sustenance without feeling weighed down.

1 Divide the ginger among the soup bowls or put it in a large serving bowl. Similarly, add the beef, scattering it in small pieces. Don't mound it or it will cook unevenly. Sprinkle a pinch of salt on top and set the bowl(s) aside.

2 In a saucepan, bring the rice soup almost to a boil over medium heat, stirring frequently to prevent scorching. Ladle it over the beef. Garnish with the Vietnamese coriander, scallion, and pepper and serve immediately. Before eating, stir the beef from the bottom to ensure that it cooks in the hot soup and the flavors are well mixed.

NOTE

For extra richness, crack an egg into each bowl as you are dividing up the ginger and beef. Break the membrane of the yolk with the tip of a knife to facilitate cooking once the soup is added.

Serves 4 as a light lunch, or 6 with 2 or 3 other dishes

1 1/2 tablespoons peeled and finely shredded fresh ginger (page 51)

1/4 pound hand-minced beef steak (page 69) or ground beef, preferably chuck

Salt

8 cups Basic Rice Soup (page 67)

2 tablespoons chopped fresh Vietnamese coriander or cilantro leaves

1 scallion, green tops only, thinly sliced

Black pepper

MINCING AND
CHOPPING MEAT BY HAND

When a recipe calls for a small quantity of ground meat, try mincing it by hand for better flavor and texture. It doesn't take much time and you get to select the cut of meat. First, trim away any gristly bits, such as tendon. Then, using a sharp, heavy cleaver or a chef's knife, cut the meat into pea-sized pieces and mound them in a pile. Using a rocking motion, move the blade from one side of the pile to the other. Pause occasionally and lift the meat with the blade and fold it over on itself to keep it in a moderately compact mass. For a minced texture, chop until you have a rough pastelike consistency that is not as fine as typical ground meat. For a hand-chopped texture, the goal is a coarser finish, like a chili grind.

If you're ambitious and want to hand chop a large quantity of meat, use two knives of the same size and weight, working them as if you are drumming. Or, pulse the cut pieces of meat in a food processor or electric mini-chopper. The resulting texture isn't as uniform as doing it by hand but the convenience is greater.

RICE SOUP WITH CHICKEN

Cháo Gà

VIET COOKS PREPARE this *cháo* in several ways, and I prefer the easy northern approach of sautéing seasoned chicken and adding it to the hot soup. Traditionally, a chicken would be boned, its carcass cooked with the rice to make the soup, and the boneless meat sautéed and added later on. This old-fashioned approach saves fuel costs and time, but the residue from the bones ends up suspended in the soup. I prefer to use stock, either homemade or a blend of purchased broth and water. The final sprinkle of chopped Vietnamese coriander (*rau răm*) and sliced scallion adds contrasting color and flavor.

1 In a bowl, toss the chicken with the fish sauce and set aside to marinate for 15 minutes.

2 In a skillet, heat the oil over medium-high heat. Add the onion and cook gently, stirring occasionally, for about 3 minutes, or until fragrant and soft. Or, you may cook it longer until it is even a little caramelized, if you like. Add the chicken and sauté for about 4 minutes, or until cooked through.

3 Add the chicken mixture and any juices that have accumulated in the pan to the saucepan holding the rice soup. Place over medium heat and bring almost to a boil, stirring frequently to prevent scorching. Taste and add extra salt, as necessary. Ladle into individual soup bowls or a large serving bowl. Top with the Vietnamese coriander and scallion and serve immediately.

Serves 4 as a light lunch, or 6 with 2 or 3 other dishes

3/4 pound boneless, skinless chicken thighs or breasts, cut into small bite-sized pieces

1 1/2 tablespoons fish sauce

1 tablespoon canola or other neutral oil

1 small yellow onion, thinly sliced

8 cups Basic Rice Soup (page 67)

Salt

2 tablespoons chopped fresh Vietnamese coriander or cilantro leaves

1 scallion, green part only, cut into thin rings

RICE SOUP WITH FISH, GINGER, AND ONION

Cháo Cá

HERE IS A SOUP that my father taught me. In a ceviche-like approach, raw fish is marinated with onion, ginger, and cilantro. The semicooked mixture is then placed in the bottom of soup bowls, and the final cooking is done by the hot rice soup. When brought to the table, the seemingly plain white soup conceals a pleasant surprise of fish. Pair it with one of the salads in Chapter 1 for a Vietnamese soup-and-salad meal.

1 Run your thumb along the top of the fish fillet to check for errant bones. If you find some, cut along each side of the line of bones, cutting as close to the bones as possible to avoid waste, and discard the thin strip containing them. Slice the fish into pieces about 2 inches long, 1 inch wide, and 1/8 inch thick, angling your knife if necessary to get the needed width.

2 To remove some of the harshness of the onion, put it in a bowl and add hot tap water to cover. Let sit for 5 minutes, then drain and rinse under cold water.

3 To make the marinade, in a bowl, combine the salt, sugar, oil, fish sauce, vinegar, ginger, and cilantro. Add the fish and onion and use your hand to mix gently. Set aside for 30 minutes at room temperature to allow the fish to absorb the other flavors and turn slightly opaque. The fish may be refrigerated for several hours, but it should sit at room temperature for 20 minutes before serving to take the chill off.

4 In a saucepan, bring the rice soup almost to a boil over medium heat, stirring occasionally to prevent scorching. Meanwhile, divide the fish among the soup bowls, leaving any liquid behind. Ladle the hot soup over the fish. Garnish with scallion and pepper before serving. Before eating, tell diners to stir the fish from the bottom to ensure that it cooks in the hot soup and the flavors are well mixed.

Serves 4 as a light lunch, or 6 to 8 with 2 or 3 other dishes

3/4 pound mild white fish fillet such as red snapper, sea bass, cod, or halibut, skin removed

1 small red onion, thinly sliced

MARINADE

1/4 teaspoon salt

1/2 teaspoon sugar

1 tablespoon canola or other neutral oil

2 tablespoons fish sauce

2 1/2 tablespoons cider vinegar

2 tablespoons peeled and finely shredded fresh ginger (page 51)

2 tablespoons chopped fresh cilantro

8 cups Basic Rice Soup (page 67)

1 scallion, green part only, thinly sliced

Black pepper

RICE SOUP WITH CHICKEN, SEAFOOD, AND MUSHROOM

Cháo Bồi

AN ELEGANT PREPARATION of northern Vietnam, this soup is special-occasion fare. Rather than simmering the rice until it disintegrates into a silky creaminess, the grains are cooked until their ends "bloom" into flowerlike petals, an effect achieved by parboiling the rice and then simmering it for a shorter time than for standard *cháo*. Tapioca pearls thicken the soup and lend an interesting shimmer, and the halved shrimp turn into pink corkscrews as they cook, adding a final flourish to the presentation.

1 Fill a 5-quart saucepan half full with water. Bring to a rolling boil over high heat and add the chicken breast. Remove from the heat and cover tightly. Let stand for 20 minutes. The chicken should be firm to the touch yet still yield a bit. Remove the chicken from the pan. Leave the water in the pan. When the chicken is cool enough to handle, shred it by hand and set aside.

2 Return the water to a boil and add the rice. Parboil for 8 minutes, or until tender but still firm. Drain in a colander and rinse with cold water. Set aside.

3 In the same pan, bring the stock to a boil over high heat. Add the rice, chicken, and mushrooms, lower the heat to a gentle simmer, and cook for 10 minutes, or until the rice expands.

4 Meanwhile, in a skillet, heat the oil over medium heat. Add the onion and cook gently, stirring occasionally, for about 4 minutes, or until fragrant and soft. Add the shrimp and sauté for about 2 minutes, until they curl into corkscrews. Add the crabmeat and stir to distribute. Remove from the heat and set aside.

5 To prevent the tapioca pearls from clumping on contact with the hot soup, put them into a sieve and rinse briefly under cold water. When the rice has expanded in the soup, add the tapioca

Serves 8 to 10 as a starter, or 4 to 6 as a one-bowl meal

1 boneless, skinless chicken breast (about 1/4 pound)
1 cup long-grain white rice
3 quarts (12 cups) chicken stock, homemade or quick version (page 317)
4 or 5 dried wood ear mushrooms, reconstituted (page 334), trimmed, and cut into 1/4-inch-wide strips
2 tablespoons canola or other neutral oil
1 small yellow onion, thinly sliced
1/2 pound medium shrimp, peeled, deveined, and halved horizontally
1/3 cup freshly picked or thawed crabmeat
1/4 cup small tapioca pearls (about 1/8 inch in diameter)
Salt
1/3 cup chopped scallion, white and green parts
1/3 cup coarsely chopped fresh cilantro

pearls and cook for another 10 minutes. The opaque pearls will expand and become translucent. At that point, add the shrimp mixture, heat through, and adjust with salt, if necessary.

6 Ladle into individual bowls or a large serving bowl and sprinkle with the scallion and cilantro. Serve immediately.

CREAMY CORN AND SHIITAKE MUSHROOM SOUP

Súp Bắp Nấm Hương

WHEN PREPARING THIS CHINESE CLASSIC, Vietnamese cooks, like their northern neighbors, often rely on canned creamed corn, once considered an exotic foreign import in Asia. The velvety sweet-savory result fuses East and West. Here in the States, fresh corn is plentiful, and making this soup with kernels cut from the cob yields bright flavors that aren't cloying. Neither cornstarch nor egg is needed to create a creamy texture. The natural starch in the corn provides it. Some cooks add a variety of embellishments to the soup, but I prefer to keep it simple, using only sliced shiitake mushrooms for their flavor, texture, and visual appeal. Make sure you use the sweetest corn possible, whether from your local market or farm stand, fresh or frozen.

1   In a 4-quart saucepan, heat the oil over medium heat. Add the onion and cook gently, stirring occasionally, for about 4 minutes, or until fragrant and soft. Add the corn, salt, and water, cover, and cook for about 20 minutes, or until the corn is very tender. Remove from the heat and let cool for at least 10 minutes before proceeding.

2   Position a coarse-mesh sieve on top of another saucepan. In batches, purée the soup in a blender or food processor until velvety smooth. Pour each puréed batch through the sieve, pressing on the solids to extract as much liquid as possible. Discard the solids. Add the mushrooms and set the soup aside until ready to serve. (The soup may be made up to 2 days in advance, cooled, and refrigerated.)

3   Reheat the soup over medium-low heat, stirring occasionally to prevent scorching. If the soup is too thick, thin it with water. Taste and add extra salt, if necessary. Ladle the soup into a large serving bowl or individual bowls. Sprinkle with the chives and serve immediately.

Serves 6 to 8 with 2 or 3 other dishes

2 tablespoons canola or other neutral oil

1 yellow onion, chopped

6 cups corn kernels, cut from 6 to 8 ears, or 2 pounds frozen corn kernels, thawed

1 1/2 teaspoons salt

5 1/2 cups water

6 to 8 dried shiitake mushrooms, reconstituted (page 332), stemmed, and thinly sliced

2 tablespoons chopped fresh chives or thinly sliced green scallion tops

NOTE

Give the soup an earthy Thai edge by adding 4 or 5 Thai lime leaves (sometimes labeled *makrut* or kaffir leaves) when simmering the corn kernels. Remove and discard the leaves before puréeing.

FRESH ASPARAGUS AND CRAB SOUP

Súp Măng Tây Cua

LOADED WITH ASPARAGUS AND CRAB, this soup is elegant looking and delicately flavored. Vietnamese consider it special-occasion fare because it features asparagus, a pricey ingredient introduced by the French as an imported canned good. In Vietnamese, asparagus is *măng tây*, literally "French bamboo," an apt name as both asparagus and bamboo shoots grow quickly.

Resourceful Viet cooks often maximize the asparagus flavor by adding the spears and their canning liquid to the soup. But the taste is nonetheless rather flat, and canned asparagus is mushy. To achieve a strong asparagus flavor, I use fresh asparagus to prepare the soup. Asparagus declines in sweetness as soon as it is harvested, so choose only the freshest. Spring is asparagus season, and at farmers' markets the spears are sold within twenty-four hours of being cut. To keep them fresh, stand them in a tall container filled with about an inch of water. (If the ends look dry, trim them first.) Refrigerate the container; there is no need to cover it with plastic.

1 In a 4-quart saucepan, bring the stock to a boil over high heat. Add the asparagus, lower the heat to a simmer, and cook, uncovered, for 10 to 12 minutes, or until very tender and olive green. For this soup, you want to overcook the asparagus to extract more of its flavor. Remove from the heat, cover, and set aside for at least 30 minutes to allow the asparagus flavor to develop further.

2 Meanwhile, in a small skillet or saucepan, heat the oil over medium heat. Add the shallot and cook gently, stirring occasionally, for 3 to 4 minutes, or until fragrant and soft. Add the crabmeat and continue cooking for 1 to 2 minutes to develop the flavors. Add the fish sauce, pepper, and salt. Remove from the heat and set aside until serving.

3 Just before serving, bring the soup to a simmer. Add the crab mixture, stirring gently to distribute evenly. Taste and add extra salt, if necessary. Give the cornstarch mixture a stir and slowly pour it into the soup with one hand as you stir the soup with the other. Continue stirring for about 1 minute, or until the soup

Serves 4 to 6 with 2 or 3 other dishes

6 cups chicken stock, homemade or quick version (page 317)

3/4 pound asparagus, woody ends trimmed and cut on the diagonal into 1¼-inch pieces

1 tablespoon canola or other neutral oil

1 large shallot, thinly sliced (about 1/3 cup)

1/3 pound freshly picked or thawed crabmeat

1/2 teaspoon fish sauce

1/4 teaspoon black pepper

Pinch of salt

2 tablespoons cornstarch dissolved in 2 tablespoons stock or water

1 whole egg plus 1 egg yolk, beaten

is thickened. Turn off the heat. Pour the beaten egg onto the soup in a wide circle, and then stir gently to break it up into chiffonlike pieces. Ladle the soup into a large serving bowl or individual bowls and serve immediately.

WHITE TREE FUNGUS IN CLEAR BROTH

Súp Bạch Mộc Nhĩ

VIETNAMESE COOKING, like Chinese cooking, takes texture seriously. In fact, ingredients such as dried white tree fungus, a highly prized relative of the wood ear, lack flavor but offer interesting texture. Crunchy, resilient, and gelatinous, white tree fungus is expensive when compared with regular mushrooms and most other fungi and is thus saved for special occasions. It looks like crinkly, golden sponges and is sold in boxes or plastic bags at Chinese and Viet markets.

It is important to use a good chicken stock in this recipe. Both the mild-flavored fungus and the vegetables need the contrast of a rich backdrop. The resulting soup will remind you of an underwater scene, the florets of white tree fungus suspended like silvery blades of seaweed among the orange carrot slices and bright green snow peas. For extra flair, add hand-shredded poached chicken breast along with the carrot.

1 Put the white tree fungus in a bowl and add warm water to cover. Let sit for 15 minutes. The fungus will lighten, double in size, and become pliable. Drain and gently squeeze out the excess water. Break into 1-inch florets with your fingers, removing bits of dirt along the way. If the stem hasn't been well trimmed or seems too hard to chew easily, cut it off. You should have about 2 1/2 cups total.

2 In a 4-quart saucepan, bring the stock to a boil over high heat, and then lower the heat to a simmer. Salt the stock to taste and add the fungus and sugar. Let the soup simmer for 5 minutes. Add the carrot and continue cooking for 3 minutes longer, or until the carrot is tender but still firm. Add the snow peas and cook for 1 minute, or until tender and bright green.

3 Taste and add extra salt for greater depth, if necessary. If there are overly sour notes from the fungus, add a little more sugar. Ladle the soup into a serving bowl or individual soup bowls. Garnish with a sprinkle of pepper and the cilantro leaves and serve immediately.

Serves 4 to 6 with 2 or 3 other dishes

1 1/2 ounces dried white tree
   fungus (2 or 3 whole ones)
7 cups chicken stock,
   homemade or quick
   version (page 317)
Salt
1/2 teaspoon sugar
1 small carrot, peeled and
   thinly sliced into rounds
   or scored and thinly sliced
   into decorative pieces

12 snow peas, trimmed,
   strings removed, and
   cut on the diagonal into
   1/2-inch-wide pieces
Black pepper
Leaves from 5 or 6 sprigs
   cilantro

3. PRECIOUS POULTRY AND EVERYDAY EGGS

In Vietnam, pork and seafood are plentiful and inexpensive but poultry is not. Many people raise their own chickens and ducks to ensure a steady supply of eggs for frying, scrambling, steaming, and salting for everyday meals. But the birds themselves make their way to the table only on special occasions. When asked about poultry's exalted status, my mom responds, "Chickens were precious and valuable. That's why when guests were expected for a meal, someone would say, 'Go catch a chicken!'"

Indeed, now as then, if you don't raise your own poultry, you go to a market and buy a freshly killed bird or take home a live one to kill yourself. A resourceful head-to-tail rigor is applied to cooking every part of the bird, and in that necessary act of economy is an underlying appreciation for life.

It is hard to imagine graceful women like my mother, their wrists decorated by jade bracelets, cutting the throats of chickens and ducks or wringing the necks of smaller fowl. But that is what they do. In fact, any serious cookbook written in Vietnam offers details on how to pick, kill, and dress poultry. In *Làm Bếp Giỏi* (Cooking Well), a classic cookbook published in the early twentieth century, Mrs. Van Dai advised against buying scrawny old chickens or young ones that had not fully formed their plumage, which made them too hard to pluck. The ideal, she wrote, is a hen that is in between in age, with a full, round breast, an anus that is not large (a sign of having been overworked), and brilliantly colored fat. The feet should not be too big, the skin should be yellow, and when the hen is picked up, it should have some heft to it. Male ducks, she said, should be selected over females. In 1999, cooking teacher and writer Nguyen Dzoan Cam Van echoed the same notions in *Những Món Ăn Đãi Tiệc Và Gia Đình* (Dishes for Entertaining Guests and Family), signaling that times had not changed much. The enduring and crucial message in these works is this: good cooks carefully inspect and select their poultry.

America must have seemed like chicken heaven to my parents when our family arrived here. What was once a luxury was suddenly a readily available and economical option for feeding the family. Every week they scanned the supermarket mailers for sales on whole chickens. At the store, Dad would load up our cart with as many as Mom wanted (typically six), and if that was more than the advertised limit, we would make separate purchases to fill her order. Even though the cashiers never asked why we were buying so many chickens, I found the experiences embarrassing. Those were the days before membership-warehouse shopping became popular, and our bulk chicken purchases seemed to underscore our outsider lifestyle.

The awkwardness I felt always faded once we got home and Mom started transforming the chickens into marvelous dishes. She would debone them to make meat paste (*giò*, page 158), and set aside some legs, thighs, and drumettes for roasting in the oven and preparing curries. The chicken knees that she whacked off from the bottom of each drumstick were saved in the freezer for simmering with ginger in a traditional caramel sauce (page 316). The livers found their way into a pâté (page 168) or into a hoisin-garlic sauce (*tương*, page 310). She threw the bones into a big pot, and a few hours later she had a fragrant, golden stock. What was not used right away was wrapped in plastic and frozen for another day.

RECIPES

GARLICKY OVEN-ROASTED CHICKEN

Gà Rô-Ti

VIETNAMESE COOKS roast chickens in three ways: on the stove top in a pan with a little liquid for succulence, over charcoal for charred smokiness, or in the oven for crispy skin. The method mostly depends on the kind of heat source available. For example, ovens were traditionally luxurious home appliances in Vietnam. In 1966, my mom's oven was a metal box indirectly heated by hot charcoal set underneath and/or on top. When the Americans came, she was able to salvage a modern oven for her Saigon home kitchen.

After we arrived in America, Mom delighted in roasting this easy garlicky chicken for our family. With a reliable oven and affordable chicken, we ate *gà rô-ti* regularly with rice for dinner, sliced up and stuffed into a baguette sandwich (page 34) for lunch or a snack, and arranged atop sticky rice (page 246) for breakfast or lunch. When preparing *gà rô-ti* (which takes its name from the French term for roasting), use the more succulent parts—drumsticks, thighs, wings—for the best flavor.

1 To make the marinade, in a bowl large enough to accommodate the chicken, combine the garlic, sugar, salt, pepper, Maggi sauce, and oil and mix well. Add the chicken pieces and use your fingers to massage the marinade into the flesh, distributing the seasonings as evenly as possible. When possible, peel back the skin to get some marinade between the flesh and skin. Cover and marinate in the refrigerator for at least 2 hours or up to 24 hours for the best flavor.

2 Thirty minutes before roasting, remove the chicken from the refrigerator. Line a baking sheet with aluminum foil and put the chicken pieces, skin side down, on the sheet. Position a rack in the middle of the oven and preheat to 400°F.

3 Put the chicken in the oven. After about 15 minutes, you will hear gentle sizzling. At that point, using tongs, turn the pieces over and continue to roast until the skin is nicely browned and crispy and the juices run clear when a piece is poked in the meatiest part with a toothpick, bamboo skewer, or knife tip. The roasting time depends on the size of the pieces, but in general it will take 40 to 60 minutes total (including the initial 15 minutes). If a lot of fat and juices accumulate in the pan during roasting, remove the chicken from the pan, pour off the fat, and then quickly return the chicken and continue roasting. Serve the chicken hot, warm, or at room temperature.

Serves 4 to 6 with 2 or 3 other dishes

MARINADE
4 large cloves garlic, finely minced
1½ teaspoons sugar
¼ teaspoon salt
¾ teaspoon black pepper
3½ tablespoons Maggi Seasoning sauce or light (regular) soy sauce
2½ tablespoons canola or other neutral oil

4 pounds chicken drumsticks, thighs, and/or wings

GRILLED CHICKEN

Gà Nướng

MY PARENTS HAD TOLD ME so many times about how good chicken was in Vietnam that I couldn't wait to taste it for myself when I returned with my husband in January 2003. Our first day was in Hanoi, and after checking into the hotel, we set out into the streets looking for lunch. At a small, arty café, we ordered *gà nướng*, expecting something akin to *gà rô-ti* (opposite). Instead, the hipster waitress returned with plates of sliced grilled chicken thigh, rice, and the ingredients—salt, white pepper, lime, chile—for mixing up a dipping sauce. We took a few bites and then practically inhaled the rest, not because we were famished but because the dish was so unbelievably good. The toothsome meat and crispy skin were wonderful dipped in the tart-and-hot sauce. Nowadays, whenever I make this dish for an easy dinner, I am reminded of that memorable lunch.

1   To make the marinade, in a bowl large enough to accommodate the chicken, combine the sugar, salt, pepper, fish sauce, lime juice, and oil and mix well. Add the chicken pieces and use your fingers to massage the marinade into the flesh, distributing the seasonings as evenly as possible. When possible, peel back the skin to get some marinade between the flesh and skin. Marinate at room temperature for 30 minutes, or cover with plastic wrap and refrigerate for 2 hours.

2   If necessary, remove the chicken from the refrigerator 30 minutes before grilling. Prepare a medium-hot charcoal fire (you can hold your hand over the rack for only 3 to 4 seconds) or preheat a gas grill to medium (higher heat on a gas grill tends to burn the skin).

3   Place the chicken, skin side down, on the grill rack and grill, turning regularly to ensure even cooking, for about 12 minutes total, or until browned, a little singed by fire, and opaque throughout. Transfer to a plate and let rest for about 5 minutes.

4   Slice the chicken into strips a scant 1/2 inch thick. Arrange on a plate and serve with the dipping sauce.

Serves 4 to 6 with 2 or 3 other dishes

MARINADE
1/4 teaspoon sugar
1/2 teaspoon salt
1 1/2 teaspoons black pepper
1 tablespoon fish sauce
1 tablespoon fresh lime juice
2 tablespoons canola or other
   neutral oil

2 3/4 pounds chicken thighs,
   deboned and well trimmed
Salt, Pepper, and Lime
   Dipping Sauce (page 311)

NOTE

For a vegetarian version, substitute 2 pounds summer squashes for the chicken. Select zucchini or crookneck squashes between 5 and 6 inches long; trim the ends and halve each squash lengthwise. Or, use pattypan squashes about 3 inches in diameter, trim them, then halve crosswise. Toss in the marinade, grill, and serve with or without the dipping sauce.

CHICKEN AND GINGER
SIMMERED IN CARAMEL SAUCE

Gà Kho Gừng

THIS IS A CLASSIC northern interpretation of *kho*, homey simmered dishes that are part of everyday Viet meals. It reflects the simple art of Vietnamese cooking, requiring just a few ingredients yet yielding a savory result. The chicken releases its juices during cooking, which add to the overall flavor of the bittersweet caramel sauce, a Vietnamese staple. The ginger softens, mellows, and blends with the other ingredients as it cooks, but it still delivers a mild sharpness to the finished dish.

Traditionally, this *kho* calls for cutting bone-in, skin-on chicken into chunks. However, for the sake of ease and health, I, like many other Vietnamese Americans, now use boneless, skinless chicken thighs. Serve with lots of rice to sop up the sauce.

1 In a small saucepan, combine the chicken, ginger, caramel sauce, fish sauce, salt, and water and stir to distribute everything evenly. Cover and bring to a strong simmer over medium heat. Stir again to break up the chicken pieces and replace the lid. Cook for 10 minutes, stirring every now and again so that all the chicken is evenly exposed to the sauce. Fragrant plumes of steam will shoot from under the lid and the contents will boil vigorously. The sauce will increase in volume as the chicken releases its juices. If the contents threatens to boil over or the lid rattles, lower the heat.

2 After the 10 minutes, uncover and continue cooking for about 5 minutes, or until the sauce reduces and the color deepens to a rich reddish brown. Remove from the heat, cover, and let rest for 5 minutes.

3 Taste the sauce and adjust the flavor with extra fish sauce, if necessary. Transfer to a serving bowl, garnish with the scallion, and serve immediately.

Serves 4 with 2 or 3 other dishes

1²/₃ pounds boneless, skinless chicken thighs, well trimmed and cut into 1-inch chunks

Chubby 2-inch piece fresh ginger, peeled, thinly sliced, and smashed with the broad side of a cleaver or chef's knife

3 tablespoons Caramel Sauce (page 316)

2 tablespoons fish sauce

¹/₄ teaspoon salt

2 tablespoons water

1 scallion, green part only, chopped

NOTE

This dish may also be prepared in a small (1¹/₂-quart) clay pot. For details on clay pot cooking, see page 108.

CHICKEN, LEMONGRASS, AND POTATO CURRY

Cà-Ri Gà

> HERE IS A CURRY with big flavors, thanks to lots of lemongrass, curry powder, ginger, and chile flakes. The coconut milk unifies all the elements and enriches the dish. For the best Viet flavor, buy Vietnamese-style curry powder (page 327) at an Asian market. Serve the curry in a shallow bowl with a baguette for dipping or spoon it over rice or noodles.

1 In a food processor, process the lemongrass for about 3 minutes, or until it is a fine, fluffy mass. (You will see a whirling blizzard in the bowl.) Pause occasionally to scrape down the bowl. Add the ginger and pulse to chop finely. Add the onion and process until the mixture forms a paste.

2 In a large saucepan, heat the oil over medium heat. Add the lemongrass paste and sauté for about 2 minutes, or until fragrant. Add the curry powder and red chile flakes and continue sautéing for about 1 minute, or until the spices are fragrant. Add the chicken, salt, pepper, and coconut milk. The liquid should cover the chicken. If it doesn't, add water as needed. Bring to a simmer over medium heat and cook, uncovered, for 20 minutes.

3 Add the potatoes and return to a simmer. Cook for 10 to 15 minutes, or until the potatoes are tender. Turn off the heat, cover, and let stand for 30 minutes to develop the flavors.

4 Reheat the curry over low heat until hot, stirring occasionally to avoid scorching. Taste and adjust the flavors if needed. Add a bit of water to lighten or simmer to deepen. Serve with the lime wedges.

NOTE

For a lighter curry, use only 1 cup coconut milk and add water as needed to cover the chicken. If the resulting sauce is too watery,

Serves 4 to 6 with 2 or 3 other dishes

3 medium or 2 hefty stalks lemongrass, trimmed, quartered lengthwise, and coarsely chopped (about 2/3 cup)

Chubby 1-inch piece fresh ginger, peeled and coarsely chopped

1 yellow onion, coarsely chopped

2 tablespoons canola or other neutral oil

2 tablespoons Madras curry powder

1/2 teaspoon dried red chile flakes (optional)

2 1/2 pounds bone-in chicken thighs or drumsticks, skin removed (see Note)

1 1/2 teaspoons salt

1/2 teaspoon black pepper

1 can (13 1/2 ounces) coconut milk or 1 2/3 cups freshly made coconut milk (page 318)

4 white or red boiling potatoes, 1 1/4 to 1 1/2 pounds total, peeled and cut into 1-inch chunks

1 lime, cut into wedges

remove a few pieces of cooked potato, mash them, and stir back into the pan. To skin chicken drumsticks, use a cleaver or a heavy chef's knife suitable for chopping bones to whack through the bone about 3/4 inch from the knee-joint end. This releases the skin and enables you to pull it easily away from the flesh. Discard the knees and skin.

POACHED CHICKEN WITH LIME LEAVES

Gà Luộc Lá Chanh

FROM FRENCH *POULE AU POT* to Chinese Hainan chicken to this classic Vietnamese preparation, poached chicken offers clear, pure flavors. In my family, we enjoy the hot poaching broth as the soup course (*canh*) and slice up the cool chicken for the main dish. The chicken is strewn with fine strips of fresh, tender young lime or lemon leaves, to provide an unusual bright, citrusy contrast. Thai lime leaves, known also as *makrut* or kaffir leaves, are particularly wonderful if you can find them. At the table, we ladle the broth into our bowls and add a squirt of lime juice and a spoonful of rice. In between eating bowls of broth, we eat the chicken and citrus leaves with more rice, dunking them first in a sauce of lime juice, salt, and pepper. Add a simple stir-fried vegetable and you have a satisfying meal.

Purchase the best-quality chicken available for this recipe. Immersing it in an ice bath once it is cooked produces tight skin that Asian diners appreciate: a bit chewy and somewhat crunchy but not greasy. Also, as the chicken cools, a delicious layer of gelatinous juices forms between the skin and meat. Since cooling takes a while, you need to poach the chicken about four hours in advance of serving, or even the day before. Traditionally, the chicken is cut through the bone into small pieces for serving, but I prefer to slice the meat, except for the wings, off the bone.

1 Rinse the chicken and pat dry with paper towels. Cut off the wing tips and freeze, along with the neck (if it is included), for making stock, or discard them.

2 Select a pot that accommodates the chicken snugly with about 1 inch clearance between the top of the breast and the rim of the pot. Fill it half full with water and add the ginger, onion, and salt. Bring to a rolling boil over high heat and add the chicken.

3 When the pot returns to a boil, lower the heat to a gentle simmer. Bubbles should dance softly on the surface. Base the cooking time on the chicken's weight, poaching for 10 minutes per pound (a 3½-pound bird takes 35 minutes). Use tongs to rotate the chicken halfway through to ensure even cooking.

4 Near the end of the cooking time, select a bowl large enough to hold the chicken, fill it three-fourths full with ice water, and set it near the stove. When the chicken is done, use

Serves 4 to 6 with 2 or 3 other dishes

1 whole chicken, about
    3½ pounds, excess fat
    and tail removed
5 quarter-sized slices ginger,
    peeled or unpeeled, crushed
    with the broad side of a
    cleaver or chef's knife
½ yellow onion, thinly sliced
2 teaspoons salt
1 tablespoon fish sauce
12 fresh, tender young lime or
    lemon leaves, cut lengthwise
    into the narrowest strips
    possible and center rib
    discarded
Black pepper
Salt, Pepper, and Lime Dipping
    Sauce (page 311)

tongs to remove it from the pot and then plunge it into the ice water. Reserve the broth in the pot. Turn the chicken several times to expose it evenly to the ice water, then remove it from the bowl, draining the cavity well, and place it on a plate. Let it cool completely before slicing. The chicken may be prepared a day in advance; once it has cooled, cover it with plastic wrap and refrigerate, then bring to room temperature before slicing.

5 Add the fish sauce to the broth, bring to a boil over high heat, and boil until reduced by one-fourth, or until the flavor is concentrated enough for your taste. Turn off the heat, cover, and set aside while the chicken cools.

6 To serve, have ready 1 large serving plate or 2 smaller ones. Use a sharp knife to detach each wing at the shoulder joint. Separate the 2 sections of each wing, then chop them into smaller pieces with a heavy cleaver (or leave them whole). Arrange on the serving plate(s). Remove the breasts and the leg and thigh quarters from the chicken. Discard the back or save it for making stock. Cut the meat with skin attached off the bone and slice it into bite-sized pieces. Add the pieces, skin side up, to the serving plate(s), arranging them in an attractive pattern. (Diners may remove the skin while eating.) Scatter the lime leaves over the top.

7 If you like, skim the fat from the broth. Bring the broth almost to boil. Taste and add extra salt, if necessary. Strain the broth into a large soup bowl and sprinkle with pepper. Serve immediately with the chicken and dipping sauce.

NOTE

If citrus leaves are unavailable, garnish the chicken generously with chopped Vietnamese coriander (*rau răm*). Or, don't top the chicken with anything and serve it with Ginger-Lime Dipping Sauce (page 309); include sliced Thai or serrano chiles on the side so diners can add some heat to the sauce.

For a more substantial soup accompaniment, add small cubes of carrot or summer squash to the broth when reheating it for serving.

SOURCING HIGH-QUALITY CHICKEN

When shopping for high-quality chickens, you are typically faced with a wide range of confusing claims, including free-range, organic, naturally raised, kosher, and hormone and antibiotic free. And even birds with the most promising labeling are sometimes disappointing when you eat them. Some producers breed chickens to meet consumer desires for large breasts and low fat, while others raise birds with a high ratio of meat to bone. Even processing methods may affect the flavor. In other words, it is difficult to know how good a chicken is until you taste it.

The best way to sort out what birds are best where you live is to try all the types available and let your taste buds guide you. Perhaps you will prefer the chewy, flavorful meat of a slightly older chicken, or you will like a bird with a little more fat. Also, don't settle for what is in the meats section of your supermarket. Mine health-food stores, gourmet markets, and ethnic grocers, too. Talk to butchers, farmers, and chefs. If locally raised eggs are sold in your area, ask the vendor to help you find good chickens.

CHICKEN MEATBALLS
WITH SPICY HOISIN-GARLIC SAUCE

Nem Nướng

> FRAGRANT AND DELECTABLE, these meatballs are made from a fine chicken paste seasoned with toasted ground rice and enriched by tiny bits of pork fat. Although they are traditionally grilled, I cook them in the oven, where they are less likely to overbrown or even burn. They are served with rice paper, lettuce, fresh herbs, and a sweet-and-spicy sauce, and diners assemble their own hand rolls.
>
> You will need to soak 16 to 18 (8- or 10-inch) bamboo skewers in water for at least 45 minutes before you thread the meatballs onto them. At the table, set out kitchen scissors or knives for diners to cut their meatballs in half before wrapping them. (Like cherry tomatoes, these meatballs are hard to eat if left whole.) This is a hands-on dish that requires only a dinner plate at each place setting.

1   In a bowl, combine the chicken paste, fatback, and ground rice and use a rubber spatula to mix thoroughly. Lightly oil a baking sheet. Use 2 teaspoons to shape 1-inch meatballs: scoop up some of the paste with 1 spoon and pass it back and forth between the 2 spoons, molding it into a compact, nearly round ball and depositing the finished meatball onto the baking sheet. Repeat until all the paste has been shaped. To smooth out the meatballs, lightly oil your palms and roll each ball between them. Return the shiny orbs to the baking sheet.

2   You need to sear the meatballs before you skewer them, to help them keep their shape. In a large nonstick skillet, heat 1 teaspoon of the oil over medium-high heat. Add enough meatballs to cover about one-third of the skillet bottom. (If any meatball has flattened as it sat, give it a final roll between your hands before adding it to the skillet.) Sear the meatballs, shaking the skillet frequently so that they roll around. This helps them to color evenly and to keep their shape. When the meatballs have lost most of their pinkness and have turned off-white, slide them

continued

Serves 4 as a one-dish meal, or 6 to 8 with 2 or 3 other dishes

2 pounds Multipurpose Meat Paste (page 158), at room temperature

3 ounces pork fatback, blanched in boiling water for 1 minute until firm, drained, cooled, and finely diced (rounded 1/3 cup)

1/4 cup Ground Toasted Rice (page 321)

1 to 2 tablespoons canola or other neutral oil

About 32 rice paper rounds, 8 1/2 inches in diameter

Vegetable Garnish Plate (page 313)

2 1/4 cups Spicy Hoisin-Garlic Sauce (page 310)

onto a plate. This should take about 2 minutes. Repeat with the remaining meatballs.

3 Position a rack in the upper third of the oven and preheat to 475°F. Line a baking sheet with aluminum foil. Thread 4 meatballs on each skewer, spacing them about a thumb's width apart, and place the skewers on the prepared baking sheet. (Or, set the skewers on a plate, cover with plastic wrap, and refrigerate for up to 24 hours. Bring to room temperature before baking.)

4 Arrange the following at the table: rice papers, rice paper dipping bowl(s) filled with warm or hot water, vegetable garnish plate, and hoisin-garlic sauce. Set out a pair of kitchen scissors or a couple of knives for guests to cut the meatballs as they make their hand rolls.

5 Place the skewers in the oven and cook, turning them every 3 to 4 minutes, for 12 to 16 minutes, or until the meatballs have puffed up to the size of Ping-Pong balls and are lightly sizzling and golden. A few brown spots are fine. Remove from the oven and let cool briefly. When the meatballs have deflated and become wrinkly, transfer them to a platter and bring to the table.

6 Explain to any diners new to this dish how to make their hand rolls. First soften a rice paper round in the water bowl and place it on a dinner plate. (See page 331 for tips on working with rice paper.) When the rice paper is pliable and tacky, layer it with the ingredients in the following order: a piece of lettuce, a few cucumber slices, some torn herb leaves, 2 meatballs (each halved), and a drizzle of sauce. Wrap up and enjoy.

NOTE

These meatballs may also be prepared with meat paste made from pork.

FEAR OF FRYING

People love fried foods but too many home cooks are intimidated by deep-frying. If you are one of them, you will miss out on a number of my favorite recipes in this book. Here are some tips to smooth the way to success whenever you are deep-frying:

- Buy a deep-frying thermometer (same as a candy thermometer) and use a straight-sided pan (such as a Dutch oven) so you can clip it on. Position the tip of the thermometer just above the bottom of the pan so you are measuring the heat of the oil and not the metal.

- Get organized before you begin frying. Put the food on one side of the stove and the setup for draining the crispy results on the other side. Keep utensils such as a wire skimmer or tongs nearby.

- Put a few sheets of newspaper on the floor if you are worried about dirtying the kitchen. During or after frying, quickly wipe the stove and counter clean to prevent grease buildup.

- Never let the oil get so hot that it smokes. If it does, carefully move the pan to another burner. After the smoke dissipates, reheat the oil and continue frying.

- Fry in batches to avoid lowering the oil temperature. Always let the oil return to the appropriate temperature (regulate the heat as necessary) before adding the next batch.

- Recycle the oil used for deep-frying. After frying, let the oil cool completely, then strain it through a fine-mesh sieve. If the oil is cloudy or contains lots of unsavory bits, line the strainer with a paper towel or cheesecloth. Transfer the oil to a clean, dry jar or plastic bottle, cap tightly, and store in a cool, dry place. In general, I don't reuse oil once it has turned brown (as opposed to its golden color when new) or if it has picked up funky odors from frying foods like fish.

GARLICKY FRIED CHICKEN WITH SWEET-AND-SOUR SAUCE

Gà Chiên Xốt Chua Ngọt

IN THIS DISH FROM MY YOUTH, the chicken is marinated and poached before it is battered and fried until crunchy. Poaching the chicken first enables you to deep-fry in less time, yields more tender meat, and mellows the pungency of the garlic. Small pieces of bone-in chicken are traditionally used, but I prefer to fry boneless, skinless thighs for convenience. Rolling the chicken in *panko* (Japanese bread crumbs) yields a crispy shell that keeps for hours.

1 In a bowl, combine the chicken, garlic, sugar, and pepper and use your fingers or chopsticks to mix well. Set aside for 30 minutes to marinate. (Or, cover with plastic wrap and refrigerate overnight; bring to room temperature before poaching.)

2 Fill a large saucepan halfway with water and bring to a boil over high heat. Add the chicken. When the water returns to a boil, lower the heat to a simmer and poach for 1 minute, then drain the chicken into a colander. When cool enough to handle, lightly salt the chicken and set aside.

3 To make the batter, in a shallow bowl, stir together the flour and cornstarch. Make a well in the center, add the egg and water to the well, and then whisk the wet ingredients into the dry ingredients to yield a smooth, thick batter.

4 Put a wire rack on a baking sheet and set next to the stove. Set the chicken, the batter, and a bowl with the *panko* on the other side of the stove. Pour oil to a depth of 1½ inches into a wok or 5-quart Dutch oven and heat over medium-high heat to 350°F on a deep-frying thermometer. (If you don't have a thermometer, stand a dry bamboo chopstick in the oil; if small bubbles immediately gather on the surface around the chopstick, the oil is ready.)

5 Fry the chicken in 3 or 4 batches, to maintain the oil temperature and avoid crowding. Dip each piece into the batter, letting the excess drip back into the bowl, and then roll it in the *panko* and lower it into the hot oil. Fry for 6 to 8 minutes, or until golden brown. Using a skimmer, transfer the chicken to the rack. During frying, use the skimmer to remove any bits of *panko* from the oil and adjust the heat as needed to maintain the temperature.

6 Just before serving, slice the chicken into ½-inch-thick pieces, or keep the pieces whole. Arrange on a platter and serve hot, warm, or at room temperature with the sauce for dipping.

Serves 4 to 6 with 2 or 3 other dishes

2¼ pounds boneless, skinless chicken thighs, well trimmed and each cut into 2 or 3 pieces
3 cloves garlic, finely minced
¾ teaspoon sugar
½ teaspoon black pepper
Salt

BATTER
1 cup all-purpose flour
¼ cup cornstarch
1 egg
¾ cup plus 1 tablespoon ice water

2 cups panko
Corn or canola oil for deep-frying
1½ cups Sweet-and-Sour Sauce (page 312)

CHICKEN STIR-FRIED WITH LEMONGRASS AND CHILE

Gà Xào Xả Ớt

> T H E   I N G R E D I E N T S of this intensely flavored chicken dish resemble those of a curry, but here they are stir-fried, rather than simmered together in a sauce, to retain their individuality. You'll taste the sweetness of coconut milk and shallots, the heat of chiles (fresh and dried in the curry powder), and the citrus of lemongrass, plus the bell pepper adds color and softness.
>
> My mom makes a similar dish using whole skinless drumsticks. She cooks them first on the stove top with very little water so the meat absorbs all the flavors. Then she finishes the drumsticks in the oven, so the outside is dry while the inside stays moist. Her dish, which she regularly prepared for our family when I was growing up, inspired this quicker approach.

1 In a bowl, combine the chicken, salt, sugar, curry powder, and fish sauce and turn several times to coat the chicken evenly. Set aside to marinate at room temperature for at least 15 minutes or for up to 1 hour.

2 In a wok or large skillet, heat the oil over high heat until hot but not smoking. Add the shallot, chiles, and lemongrass and stir-fry for about 1 minute, or until fragrant. Add the chicken mixture and the bell pepper, quickly move them around to coat them with the aromatics, and then let the chicken cook, undisturbed, for about 1 minute, or until nicely seared. Using a spatula, flip the chicken pieces over and cook, undisturbed, for about 1 minute, or until nicely seared on the second side.

3 Add the coconut milk, lower the heat to a simmer, and cook for 6 to 8 minutes, stirring occasionally to ensure even cooking. As the coconut milk reduces, it will simmer vigorously. The chicken is done when the coconut milk is barely visible; it may have even begun to render some of its oil.

4 Transfer to a serving plate, sprinkle with the cilantro, and serve immediately.

Serves 4 to 6 with 2 or 3 other dishes

1 1/3 pounds boneless, skinless chicken thighs, well trimmed and cut into 1-inch chunks

1/2 teaspoon salt

1 1/2 teaspoons sugar

2 1/2 teaspoons Madras curry powder

2 1/2 teaspoons fish sauce

2 tablespoons canola or other neutral oil

1 large shallot, finely chopped (about 1/3 cup)

1 or 2 Thai or serrano chiles, finely chopped

1 stalk lemongrass, trimmed and finely chopped (about 3 tablespoons)

1 small red bell pepper, seeded and cut into 3/4-inch squares

1/2 cup coconut milk, canned or freshly made (page 318)

3 or 4 sprigs cilantro, coarsely chopped

CHICKEN STIR-FRIED WITH OYSTER MUSHROOMS AND SNOW PEAS

Gà Xào Nấm

THIS IS MY RIFF ON THE CLASSIC Vietnamese pairing of chicken and fresh straw mushrooms. Because only canned straw mushrooms are available here, I have used fresh oyster mushrooms, a good stand-in with a subtlety that complements the snow peas. If oyster mushrooms aren't available, use fresh shiitakes, removing their stems and slicing the caps into 1/4-inch-thick pieces. For a light meal, serve this quick stir-fry with Napa Cabbage and Shrimp Soup (page 58), a simple stir-fried vegetable like thinly sliced summer squash, and, of course, rice.

1 To make the marinade, in a large bowl, combine the salt, sugar, cornstarch, wine, and soy sauce and stir to dissolve the sugar and cornstarch. Add the chicken and mix to coat evenly.

2 To make the flavoring sauce, in a small bowl, combine the sugar, white pepper, cornstarch, water, soy sauce, oyster sauce, and sesame oil and stir well.

3 In a wok or large skillet, heat 1 tablespoon of the oil over high heat until hot but not smoking. Add the ginger and stir-fry for about 30 seconds, or until fragrant. Add the chicken in a single layer and cook, undisturbed, for about 1 minute, or until it begins to brown. Using a spatula, flip the chicken and stir-fry for 1 to 2 minutes, or until it has taken on color but is still slightly undercooked. Transfer to a plate.

4 Add the remaining 1 tablespoon oil to the pan and heat until hot. Add the onion and stir-fry for about 1 minute, or until fragrant. Add the mushrooms, snow peas, carrot, and 2 tablespoons of the water. Stir-fry for 1 minute, or until the water has evaporated. Repeat with the remaining 2 tablespoons water.

5 Return the chicken and its juices to the pan and stir-fry briefly to finish cooking. Add the flavoring sauce and stir-fry for 1 minute. Transfer to a serving plate and serve.

Serves 4 to 6 with 2 or 3 other dishes

MARINADE
1/4 teaspoon salt
1/2 teaspoon sugar
1 teaspoon cornstarch
1 teaspoon Shaoxing rice wine or dry sherry
1 tablespoon light (regular) soy sauce

3/4 pound boneless, skinless chicken breast, cut crosswise into slices 1/4 inch thick

FLAVORING SAUCE
1/2 teaspoon sugar
1/8 teaspoon white pepper
1 1/2 teaspoons cornstarch
1 tablespoon water
1 tablespoon light (regular) soy sauce
1 1/2 teaspoons oyster sauce
2 teaspoons sesame oil

2 tablespoons canola or other neutral oil
3 quarter-sized slices ginger, peeled and lightly bruised
1/2 small yellow onion, sliced lengthwise 1/4 inch thick
1/2 pound fresh oyster mushrooms, torn in half if large
1/4 pound snow peas, trimmed, strings removed, and cut in half on the diagonal if large
3-inch section carrot, peeled and thinly sliced on the diagonal
4 tablespoons water

FRAGRANT CRISPY QUAIL

Chim Cút Rán

SEVERAL YEARS AGO, my mom told me about one of the most memorable foods of her childhood: deep-fried birds the size of sparrows. They were prepared by itinerant Chinese cooks who would stop by her parents' home and offer various specialties, the best of which was this crunchy delicacy, eaten bones and all. The cooks never revealed their trade secrets, but several times Mom spied them dunking the birds in boiling water before frying them. The recipe sounded so simple and delicious that I decided to try to re-create the dish using quail.

This recipe is the result of my experiments. Rather than boiling the birds, I steam them, which better preserves the flavors of the marinade while gently cooking the meat. Then I coat the quail with seasonings that help to color and crisp their skin. After the coating dries, I quickly deep-fry them. The moment you bite into one of these freshly fried birds, the tangled aromas of rice wine and ginger come wafting out.

Look for quail at Asian and Mexican markets, where they are often sold frozen in six-pack trays. Check carefully before you buy, avoiding packages with freezer burn.

1 Rinse the quail and pat dry with paper towels. Check for pin feathers and pluck any you find.

2 To make the marinade, select a large, shallow bowl or deep plate that fits in your steamer tray. Add the salt, ginger juice, and wine and stir to dissolve the salt. Add the quail and use your fingers to coat each bird well with the marinade. Then, spoon the marinade into their cavities and rub it in with your fingers. Fold back each wing so that the wing tip is behind the neck, as if the quail is relaxing. Arrange the quail so that there is minimal overlap, to ensure even cooking. Put the bowl in the steamer tray and set aside to marinate for 15 minutes.

3 Fill the steamer pan halfway with water and bring to a rolling boil over high heat. Add the steamer tray, cover, and steam the quail for 9 to 11 minutes, or until there is no visible sign of pink rawness at the breast end. (Because the final frying is brief, the

Serves 4 as a main dish with 2 or 3 other dishes,
or 6 to 8 as a starter

6 quail, about 1/4 pound each,
thawed if frozen

MARINADE
3/4 teaspoon salt
2 teaspoons peeled and
grated fresh ginger,
pressed through a fine-
mesh sieve to extract
1 teaspoon juice
2 tablespoons Shaoxing rice
wine or dry sherry

2 tablespoons honey
2 tablespoons dark (black)
soy sauce
1/2 cup cornstarch
Corn or canola oil for
deep-frying

quail should be cooked through at this point. However, be careful not to steam away their juiciness.) While the quail steam, place a wire rack on a baking sheet.

4 When the quail are ready, transfer them to the rack, angling them as if they are reclining or standing, so the liquid in the cavities drains out. When cool enough to handle, blot dry with paper towels, removing any bits of residue from the skin.

5 In a small bowl, whisk together the honey and soy sauce. Using your fingers, coat each quail evenly with the mixture. Place the quail on a plate. Wash and dry the rack and return it to the baking sheet.

6 Put 1/4 cup of the cornstarch in a zip-top plastic bag. Standing near the sink, put a quail into the bag and shake a few times to dust lightly. Remove the quail and pat it between your hands over the sink to remove excess cornstarch. Put the quail, breast side up, on the rack. Repeat with the remaining quail, adding the remaining 1/4 cup cornstarch to the bag as needed. Set the quail aside for about 3 hours. As the quail sit, they will dry and absorb the cornstarch. They are ready to fry when most of the powdery white coating has turned light brown. Just before frying, give each quail a quick pat to remove any excess cornstarch.

7 Pour oil to a depth of 1 1/2 inches into a wok or 5-quart Dutch oven and heat over medium-high heat to 350°F on a deep-frying thermometer. (If you don't have a thermometer, stand a dry bamboo chopstick in the oil; if small bubbles immediately gather on the surface around the chopstick, the oil is ready.)

8 Because the quail brown quickly, you need to use a two-hands, two-utensils frying technique. With a skimmer in one hand and a large spoon in the other, lower a quail into the hot oil. Then immediately spoon the hot oil over the quail so that it fries to a nice, even brown. This only takes 30 to 45 seconds. To make sure the quail is browning evenly, occasionally use both utensils to lift and dip or rotate it in the oil. Because the color deepens slightly once the quail is out of the pan, pull it from the oil when it is just shy of a rich brown. Balance it between the skimmer and spoon as you lift it out, letting any excess oil drip back into the pan, and then return the quail to the rack. Repeat with the remaining quail. Once all the quail are fried, use a paper towel to blot away any clinging oil.

9 To serve, cut each quail in half along the breastbone and place on a large platter. Take to the table and start nibbling.

NOTE

These quail may be reheated in a preheated 350°F oven or toaster oven. Halve them first and put them cut side down to reheat. They are ready when you can hear them gently sizzling, usually about 10 minutes.

You may also serve these quail with Salt, Pepper, and Lime Dipping Sauce (page 311); omit the chiles if desired.

HONEY-ROASTED DUCK LEGS

Đùi Vịt Quay Mật Ong

FEW DISHES CAN BEAT THE MAGNIFICENCE of a whole roast duck, a treat that most Vietnamese purchase at Chinese barbecue shops. For an easier at-home version that is just as rich and succulent, I use whole duck legs (thigh and drumstick). They are relatively inexpensive at Asian markets, and they freeze well, which means you can stock up for when you don't have time to shop.

The legs are steamed first, during which most of the fat melts away, and then they are roasted to crisp the skin. Finally, the honey glaze is applied, which puts a lacquerlike finish on the skin while the meat stays moist. A simple hoisin dipping sauce adds a little extra sweetness to each bite. Present the duck with Everyday Daikon and Carrot Pickle (page 192) or Tangy Mixed Vegetable Pickle (pages 194) and accompany with a green vegetable stir-fried with just salt and a touch of sesame oil, a light soup such as Creamy Corn and Shiitake Mushroom Soup (page 74), and rice.

1 To make the glaze, in a small saucepan, combine the garlic, ginger, five-spice powder, salt, honey, light and dark soy sauces, and wine. Place over medium heat and bring to a boil. Remove from the heat. When the bubble action ceases, pour the glaze through a fine-mesh sieve place over a medium-sized bowl, pressing on the solids with the back of a spoon to extract as much liquid as possible. Let the glaze cool completely.

2 Select a large, shallow bowl or deep plate that fits in your steamer tray. Add the salt, wine, and ginger juice and stir to dissolve the salt. Add the duck legs and use your fingers to coat the duck legs well with the marinade. Arrange the duck legs so that there is minimal overlap, to ensure even cooking. Put the bowl in the steamer tray and set aside to marinate for 15 minutes.

continued

Serves 4 to 6 with 2 or 3 other dishes

GLAZE

4 cloves garlic, smashed with the broad side of a cleaver or chef's knife

Chubby 1-inch piece fresh ginger, thinly sliced and smashed with the broad side of a cleaver or chef's knife

3/4 teaspoon Chinese five-spice powder

1/4 teaspoon salt

6 tablespoons honey

2 tablespoons light (regular) soy sauce

1 tablespoon dark (black) soy sauce

1 tablespoon Shaoxing rice wine or dry sherry

3/4 teaspoon salt

2 tablespoons Shaoxing rice wine or dry sherry

2 teaspoons peeled and grated fresh ginger, pressed through a fine-mesh sieve to extract 1 teaspoon juice

6 whole duck legs, trimmed of excess fat and skin and backbone removed, if necessary

2 tablespoons hoisin sauce

3 Fill the steamer pan halfway with water and bring to a rolling boil over high heat. Add the steamer tray, cover, and steam the duck for 25 minutes. The skin will pull back from the flesh, and cooking juices will collect in the bowl. Transfer the duck legs to a plate and discard the cooking juices. (The legs may be cooled, wrapped in plastic wrap, and refrigerated overnight. Bring to room temperature before roasting.)

4 Position a rack in the lower third of the oven and preheat to 425°F. To promote heat circulation and allow the fat to drip away from the duck, place a flat roasting rack on a foil-lined baking sheet. Put the duck, skin side up, on the rack, spacing the legs as far apart from one another as possible. Roast for 35 to 40 minutes, or until the skin is crisp and lightly golden. Turn on the exhaust fan as the duck roasts, as the dripping fat can cause smoke. If more than 2 tablespoons of fat accumulates in the pan during roasting, remove the duck from the rack, make a spout in one corner of the foil, and pour off the fat. Then quickly return the duck to the rack and continue roasting.

5 When the duck is ready, using tongs, lift each leg from the rack, roll it in the glaze to coat evenly, and hold it above the bowl to allow excess glaze to drip off. Return the duck to the rack,

skin side up. Roast the legs for 5 minutes and then again coat them with the glaze. Roast for 3 to 5 minutes longer, or until the glaze richly colors the duck. Remove from the oven and let cool for 10 minutes.

6 After glazing the duck legs the second time, return the remaining glaze to the small saucepan and add the hoisin sauce to make a dipping sauce. Warm over medium heat, adding a spoonful or two of water if needed to balance out the flavor. Pour into a small serving bowl.

7 Using a heavy cleaver, chop the legs through the bone into bite-sized pieces. Or, slice the meat off the bone. Arrange the duck on 2 plates or a platter and serve with the sauce.

NOTE

To serve this duck as an appetizer, slice the meat off the bone and serve it with small Shortcut Plain Steamed Buns (page 267). Diners split the buns open, stuff them with duck, and drizzle on a bit of sauce. For directions on how to remove the backbone from a duck leg so that you can slice the meat easily, see the Note that accompanies Duck and Chinese Egg Noodle Soup (page 221).

PORK AND MUSHROOM OMELET

Chả Trứng Chiên

ALTHOUGH THEY ARE NOTHING MORE than egg and the classic Vietnamese combination of pork, onion, and mushrooms, these omelets are rich, savory, chewy, and a bit crispy at the edge, and they taste remarkably good. Enjoy them hot from the pan, at room temperature, or even cold. The wedges are usually served with rice, though I have also stuffed them into baguette sandwiches (page 34).

1 In a bowl, combine the pork, wood ear mushrooms, shiitake mushrooms, scallions, salt, and pepper. Using a fork, break the pork into small pieces and mix it well with the other ingredients. Add the eggs and mix until thick.

2 In an 8-inch nonstick skillet, heat 2 teaspoons of the oil over medium-low heat. Give the egg mixture a stir and pour half of it into the skillet, spreading it out into an even layer. When it starts bubbling at the edge, cover and cook gently for 4 minutes, or until the top is opaque yellow and slightly cooked. Uncover and fry for 3 to 4 minutes, or until the underside is golden brown. Using a spatula, quickly and confidently flip the omelet. Dribble in 1 teaspoon of the oil at the side of the pan and continue to cook for 2 to 3 minutes, or until browned on the second side. Slide the finished omelet onto a serving plate and keep warm in a low oven. Repeat with the remaining egg mixture and oil.

3 To serve, cut each omelet into 6 to 8 wedges and arrange on 2 plates or a platter. Put the chiles, fish sauce, and soy sauce in separate small bowls on the table. Let diners craft their own dipping sauce by muddling some chiles in either the fish sauce or soy sauce.

Makes 2 small flat omelets, to serve 4 to 6 with 2 or 3 other dishes

2/3 pound ground pork, coarsely chopped to loosen

2 dried wood ear mushrooms, reconstituted (page 334), trimmed, and chopped (about 3 tablespoons)

3 dried shiitake mushrooms, reconstituted (page 332), stemmed, and chopped

3 scallions, white and green parts, chopped

3/4 teaspoon salt

1/4 plus 1/8 teaspoon black pepper

5 eggs, beaten

2 tablespoons canola or other neutral oil

1 or 2 Thai or serrano chiles, thinly sliced (optional)

Fish sauce and light (regular) soy sauce for serving

EGG, SHRIMP, AND SCALLION PANCAKES

Trứng Chiên Tôm

LONG BEFORE I KNEW ABOUT Chinese American egg foo yong, I was dipping these tasty pancakes in fish sauce and soy sauce and enjoying them with hot rice. When my mother was short of time, she would prepare a couple of plates full of these yellow, pink, and green pancakes for dinner. They are incredibly easy to whip up and yet taste fancy. The edges get fluffy and crispy from frying in a liberal amount of oil, and each rich bite contains a bit of tasty shrimp.

I don't devein the shrimp for these pancakes because I have found that it leaves unattractive lumps. But if you prefer to devein them, do so.

1   Refresh the shrimp by putting them in a colander and tossing them with a liberal amount of salt. Rinse immediately under cold water and press gently to drain well. Put the shrimp in a bowl, add the eggs and scallions, and mix well.

2   Put enough oil into a large nonstick skillet to coat the bottom thinly. Place over medium heat and heat until a drop of egg immediately sizzles and bubbles upon contact with the oil. To make each pancake, ladle about 2 tablespoons of the egg mixture into the skillet, making sure that a few shrimp are included in each portion, and then quickly nudge the shrimp in each pool of egg so they don't overlap. Fry only as many pancakes at once as will fit without crowding, about 3 pancakes at a time in a 12-inch skillet. Don't worry about the shape each one takes, as they are meant to be free-form. When the edges of a pancake are set and lightly browned, after about 2 minutes, use a spatula to turn it carefully. (If the pancakes have stuck together, use the spatula to separate them before flipping.) Fry for another 30 seconds to 1 minute, until browned on the second side. Transfer the finished pancakes to a plate and keep warm while you fry the rest.

3   Arrange the pancakes on 2 plates or a platter and serve with the fish sauce for dipping.

Serves 4 to 6 with 2 or 3 other dishes

1 pound medium shrimp, peeled

Salt

5 eggs, beaten

2 scallions, white and green parts, chopped

Canola or other neutral oil for frying

Fish sauce or light (regular) soy sauce for serving

FRAGRANT STEAMED EGG, PORK, AND CELLOPHANE NOODLES

Trứng Mắm Hấp

THE FEATURED INGREDIENT in this homey egg dish is *mắm nêm*, a thick, taupe sauce made of salted and fermented fish that is pungent and earthy like a delicious stinky cheese but mellows when combined with other ingredients. This southern Vietnamese seasoning is usually labeled fish sauce, but is different than light, clear regular fish sauce, or *nước mắm*. Before using it, shake the small, long-necked bottle vigorously to blend the solids and liquid. In this recipe, the cellophane noodles absorb the savory depth of the sauce and plump up during steaming to give the egg mixture its firm texture.

At Vietnamese restaurants in the United States, a small piece of this steamed egg is often included as a side item on rice plates. At my house, I prefer to serve it as a main dish, accompanied by rice, a quick soup (*canh*), and stir-fried water spinach (page 178).

1 In a skillet, heat the oil over medium heat. Add the onion and sauté for 1 minute, or until sweetly fragrant. Add the pork, using a spatula to break it into small pieces, then cook, stirring, for 3 minutes, or until it is still a little pink. Add as much of the fermented fish sauce as needed to create a robust-smelling mixture and then add the salt, pepper, and sugar. Continue cooking, stirring often, for about 2 minutes, or until the pork is completely done. Transfer to a bowl and let cool for 10 minutes.

2 Meanwhile, fill the steamer pan halfway with water and bring to a rolling boil over high heat.

3 Add the eggs, cellophane noodles, and scallions to the pork and combine well with a spatula. Oil an 8-inch round or square cake pan and line the bottom with parchment paper. Pour in the egg mixture. Use the spatula to distribute the ingredients evenly and smooth the top. Place the pan in the steamer tray.

4 Place the steamer tray over the boiling water, cover, and steam the egg mixture for 40 minutes, or until a toothpick inserted in the center comes out clean. Turn off the heat and uncover. Let cool for 10 minutes before removing the pan.

Serves 4 to 6 with 2 or 3 other dishes

1 tablespoon canola or other neutral oil

1/2 small yellow onion, finely chopped

3/4 pound ground pork, coarsely chopped to loosen

1 1/2 to 2 tablespoons fermented fish sauce

1/2 teaspoon salt

1/2 teaspoon black pepper

3/4 teaspoon sugar

6 eggs, lightly beaten with 2 tablespoons water

1 bundle (1.3 ounces) cellophane noodles, soaked in hot water until pliable, drained, and cut into 2-inch lengths

2 scallions, white and green parts, chopped

5 Run a knife around the inside edge of the pan to loosen the egg, then invert a plate on top of the pan. Invert the pan and plate together and lift off the pan. Peel off the parchment paper and then invert the steamed egg onto a serving plate. Cut into wedges or squares. Serve hot or warm.

SALTED PRESERVED EGGS

Trứng Muối

> SALTING EGGS is a simple preservation method used throughout Asia. Egg shells are porous, and after weeks of curing eggs in brine, the yolks turn bright yellow and richly flavored, while the whites become creamy and salty. The salted eggs are usually boiled and eaten as a snack or light meal with plain rice or Basic Rice Soup (page 67). The yolks are also used alone in special preparations, such as Moon Cakes (page 300).
>
> Traditionally, duck eggs are salted, but chicken eggs are easier to find and more affordable in the United States. Any kind of salt works, but fine sea salt doesn't crystallize after boiling like both regular table salt and pickling salt sometimes do.

1   In a small saucepan, combine the salt and water and bring to a boil. Remove from the heat and let cool completely.

2   Carefully place the eggs into a large earthenware crock, glass jar, or plastic container. Pour the cooled brine over the top. To keep the eggs submerged, place a quart-sized zip-top plastic bag half filled with water or a small dish on top. Set the eggs in a cool, dark place for 3 to 4 weeks.

The curing time depends on how salty you like the eggs. During the last week of curing, test the readiness of the eggs by taking one from the brine, rinsing it, and then placing it in a saucepan with water to cover by 1 inch. Bring to a boil over medium heat, lower to a gentle simmer, and cook for 8 to 10 minutes. Remove from the heat, flush with cold water, and remove the egg. When it is cool enough to handle, peel it and taste. If it is salty enough, remove the remaining eggs from the brine. Otherwise, leave the eggs in the brine for a few more days.

3   Store the salted eggs in the refrigerator for up to 1 month. The eggs continue to get saltier the longer they sit. If the whites become too salty, you can still enjoy the yolks. Alternatively, before refrigerating the eggs, boil them to stop the curing process and then refrigerate them, and they are ready to eat at any time. Boiled salted eggs also keep for 1 month.

Makes 1 dozen

1 cup fine sea salt
4 cups water

1 dozen extra-large or jumbo chicken eggs

4   To serve the boiled eggs, cut them lengthwise into quarters. If they don't peel cleanly, cut them with their shells on. (Tap with a knife blade to crack the shell and make cutting easier, then use a spoon to scoop out the egg.) Arrange on a plate and serve.

NOTE

When I use the salted yolks in moon cakes, I salt the eggs for the full 4 weeks because the extra saltiness is a nice contrast to the sweet elements of the cakes. Schedule yourself to make moon cakes within the first week after the eggs are ready, to ensure that the yolks retain their beautiful round shape. You don't boil the salted eggs used for moon cakes. Instead, you separate the whites and yolks, discard the whites, and bake the yolks.

4. BOUNTIFUL FISH AND SHELLFISH

The foods of Vietnam feature a glorious variety of marine life. The country's twenty-one-hundred-mile-long coastline (roughly equal to the Atlantic coast of the United States) delivers an abundance of tuna, mackerel, grouper, and other fish. The ocean also provides spiny lobsters, sweet crab, tasty squid, and flavorful shrimp, plus the silvery anchovies used for fish sauce and the tiny *ruốc* shrimp that go into fermented shrimp sauce (*mắm ruốc/mắm tôm*), both staple condiments of the Vietnamese kitchen. Indeed, seafood is so bountiful in Vietnam that cooks often combined it with meat in dishes.

But the ocean isn't the only source of fish. Vietnam is bisected by a dense network of rivers and streams fed by heavy cyclical rains. Much of the country's population lives in areas where rice is easily grown—the Red River Delta in the north near Hanoi and the Mekong River Delta in the south near Saigon—and wherever rice is cultivated, water and freshwater fish are bountiful. In fact, the Mekong River is one of the world's most productive inland fisheries. Starting at the Tibetan plateau and flowing some twenty-six hundred miles through six countries—China, Myanmar, Thailand, Cambodia, Laos, and Vietnam—to the South China Sea, the river offers a myriad of habitats for freshwater marine life. Numerous variations in climate, geology, terrain, and water flow make it easy to believe that perhaps as many as seventeen hundred species of fish live in the Mekong River basin—and that is not counting other edible aquatic animals, such as turtle, eel, shrimp, crab, and worm.

Not surprisingly, fish is the primary source of protein for the hardworking farmers and fishers of Vietnam's river deltas. Their lives are shaped by their river, whose seasonal rise floods the low-level plains and rice paddies. "When the water rises," my father recalls, "there are lots of fish that end up in the rice field. If there's no farm work, you go fishing in the paddy. Some people dig ponds to capture extra fish that may be eaten later or taken to market." In recent years, this kind of industriousness has fueled the development of aquaculture in Vietnam, and now the country is a major world exporter of catfish and shrimp.

What do people typically do with all the fish? Depending on the type, it may be dried or salted and fermented for long keeping. For everyday meals, fresh fish is simply prepared, most often simmered in a caramel-based sauce to create a dark, bittersweet savory *kho*. A meal of rice, a simple soup (*canh*), a boiled green vegetable, and fish *kho* is Viet soul food.

The rivers and paddies also provide unusual ingredients such as *rươi*, rich-tasting worms that are mixed with eggs and fried into an omelet. Northerners have a soft spot for their regional bounty of small freshwater crabs that go into *bún riêu cua*, a tomatoey rice noodle soup (page 215). People from Hue boast of their *cơm hến*, an intricate brothy rice dish featuring a tiny mollusk from the Perfume River, which passes through the city, while southerners enjoy their *cá lóc* (snakehead fish) in many guises, cooked in soup, grilled, simmered into a *kho*, fried, steamed, dried, and salted and fermented.

The recipes that follow reflect how Vietnamese immigrants like my family have kept these fish and shellfish traditions alive in their kitchens. Some recipes highlight how traditional Vietnamese cooking techniques, such as simmering in caramel sauce and creating fish pastes, are applied to locally available fresh seafood. Other recipes use standard cooking methods—grilling, steaming, frying, stir-frying—and familiar ingredients to create foods with a distinctive Viet imprint.

RECIPES

SEAFOOD SAFETY TIPS

- Purchase wisely. Patronize a reputable vendor or market that does a brisk business.

- Make friends. Fishmongers, like butchers, greengrocers, and farmers, will educate and help you make the best food choices. Ask them questions.

- Inspect carefully. Look, touch, and smell. Seafood should look vibrant, feel firm, and smell clean. When selecting a whole fish, look for clear, bulging eyes and moist, red gills. If seafood comes prepackaged on Styrofoam trays, check the "packed on" and "sell by" dates.

- Be flexible. If the seafood you want doesn't look good, select an alternative or go elsewhere.

- Temperature matters. Refrigerate fresh seafood or freeze frozen seafood when you get home. Cook and clean live crab the day you buy it.

- Use it quickly. The shelf life of fish and shellfish varies according to type, but in general they are highly perishable.

- Heed but explore. Find out how public health warnings apply to your specific life situation.

- Shop responsibly. Investigate restrictions on specific catches brought about by sustainability issues and keep your purchases to well-managed fisheries.

SHRIMP SIMMERED IN CARAMEL SAUCE

Tôm Kho

FOR EVERYDAY MEALS, Viet cooks often prepare *kho*, simple dishes simmered in a bittersweet caramel-based sauce. Similar to the Chinese braising technique called red cooking, Vietnamese *kho* cooking transforms ingredients into richly colored and flavored foods. Economical to prepare but lavish tasting, these dishes also keep well for days, a plus in the old days of no refrigeration.

If you are new to seafood *kho* dishes, start with this one. You will experience shrimp in a totally new way. Nowadays it seems a mistake to overcook seafood, but here you purposely do it to allow the flavors to penetrate thoroughly. The shrimp cook vigorously, releasing juices that combine with the other seasonings to create a dark, tasty sauce. The onion nearly disintegrates, and the final addition of oil lends a rich note. Traditional cooks use extra lard or oil to give the shrimp, which are still in the shell, an appetizing sheen, but I use peeled shrimp because they are easier to chew.

1 Refresh the shrimp by putting them in a colander and tossing them with a liberal amount of salt. Rinse immediately under lots of cold water and press gently to drain well. In a shallow saucepan, combine the shrimp, 1/8 teaspoon salt, the fish sauce, and the caramel sauce and bring to a vigorous simmer over high heat. Add the onion and pepper and give the mixture a big stir to distribute the ingredients evenly. Continue cooking over high heat for another 10 to 14 minutes, or until the shrimp have turned an orange-brown and have a pleasant sweetness and chewiness. The total cooking time depends on the size of the shrimp.

As the shrimp cook, they curl and release their juices to combine with the other ingredients. Expect a strong boil throughout and turn the shrimp occasionally with a spoon. If the pan begins to appear dry, splash in some water to coax the shrimp to cook longer. The juices eventually concentrate into a mahogany-colored sauce. When the shrimp are done, there should only be a few tablespoons of sauce left.

2 Turn off the heat, add the oil, and stir to coat the shrimp. Taste and sprinkle in more pepper for added flavor. Transfer to a shallow bowl, scatter the scallion on top, and serve.

Serves 4 with 2 or 3 other dishes

1 1/2 pounds medium or
  large shrimp, peeled and
  deveined
Salt for refreshing shrimp, plus
  1/8 teaspoon
1 1/2 tablespoons fish sauce
2 tablespoons Caramel Sauce
  (page 316)

1 small yellow onion,
  thinly sliced
1/2 teaspoon black pepper,
  preferably freshly ground
1 1/2 tablespoons canola or
  other neutral oil
1 scallion, green part only,
  chopped

NOTE

This dish may also be prepared in a small (1 1/2-quart) clay pot. Cook the shrimp with the lid on for at least half of the time to maintain a high temperature. For details on clay pot cooking, see page 108.

CATFISH SIMMERED IN CARAMEL SAUCE

Cá Kho Tộ

IN THIS CLASSIC southern Vietnamese *kho*, catfish steaks are simmered for about an hour, which turns them a mahogany brown and gives them a deep savory flavor tinged with sweetness. You may enrich the dish with oil, though I prefer the old-world technique of my mom's friend Mrs. Ly, who renders pork fat and simmers the cracklings with the fish.

Buy a whole fresh catfish (about three pounds, gutted weight) at a Chinese, Southeast Asian, or Latin market and ask the fishmonger to cut it into one-inch-thick steaks. Use the center-cut steaks for this recipe and save the head, collar, and tail pieces to make Sour Fish Soup with Tamarind, Pineapple, and Okra (page 66), in place of the fillet. Serve the *kho* with the soup, a boiled green vegetable or Crunchy Pickled Bean Sprout Salad (page 193), and rice. For the best taste, combine a little piece of the fish, some rice, and a bit of sauce in each bite.

1   Thoroughly clean the catfish steaks, removing membranes and blood that the fishmonger may have overlooked. On a dinner plate or in a bowl, stir together the brown sugar, pepper, salt, caramel sauce, and fish sauce. Add the catfish and coat with the mixture, turning the steaks to make sure that all surfaces are evenly exposed to the seasonings. Set aside for 15 minutes to marinate.

2   Select a shallow saucepan in which the fish steaks will fit snugly in a single layer. If you are using the fatback, put it into the saucepan and cook over medium heat for about 12 minutes, or until it renders liquid fat and turns into golden cracklings; lower the heat slightly if the pan smokes too much. Pour out all but 1 tablespoon of the fat, keeping the cracklings in the pan, then return the pan to medium heat. (If you are using oil, heat it in the saucepan over medium heat.) Add the garlic and scallions and sauté for about 30 seconds, or until fragrant.

continued

Serves 4 with 2 or 3 other dishes

1½ pounds catfish steaks, each about 1 inch thick

2 teaspoons brown sugar

½ teaspoon black pepper

¼ teaspoon salt

2 tablespoons Caramel Sauce (page 316)

1½ tablespoons fish sauce

2 ounces pork fatback, cut into ½-inch dice, or

1 tablespoon canola or other neutral oil

2 large cloves garlic, sliced

5 scallions, white part only, cut into 1½-inch lengths

3 Add the catfish and all the seasonings from the plate to the pan. There may be some intense bubbling. Adjust the heat to a simmer, cover, and cook for 10 minutes to develop the flavors, checking midway to make sure there is enough liquid in the pan. If the pan seems dry, splash in a little water. During this initial period, the fish will more or less cook in the steam trapped in the pan. Expect the liquid to bubble vigorously. Soft plumes of steam may shoot from under the lid.

4 Uncover, add water almost to cover the fish, and bring to a gentle simmer. Cover and cook for 30 minutes. The fish will be at a hard simmer. Uncover and adjust the heat, if necessary, to continue at a gentle simmer. Cook for another 15 to 18 minutes, or until the liquid has reduced by half and has thickened slightly, forming a sauce.

5 Taste the sauce and adjust the flavor with a pinch of brown sugar to remove any harsh edges, or a sprinkling of fish sauce for more savory depth. Carefully transfer the fish to a shallow bowl. Don't worry if the steaks break up a bit. Pour the sauce over the fish and serve.

NOTE

To cook this dish in a clay pot (described at right), use a small (1½-quart) Japanese *donabe* about 8 inches wide. Marinate the fish in the pot. Use a small skillet to prepare the cracklings (or heat up the oil) and to sauté the garlic and scallions, then add them to the clay pot, bring to a simmer, and proceed as directed in step 3.

COOKING IN CLAY POTS

Vietnamese cooks of the past relied on clay pots for preparing everyday *kho* dishes and rice. They were inexpensive but also prone to cracking and breaking, instantly ruining the meal. When affordable aluminum pots became available in Vietnam in the mid-1940s, people embraced their modern convenience. Nowadays, clay pots are seldom used by Vietnamese cooks, but the term *clay pot* is sometimes used to describe *kho* dishes. In fact, the *tộ* in the catfish *kho* recipe name refers to a type of clay pot typically used for making the dish.

Despite these changes in the Viet kitchen, you may simmer *kho* in a clay pot. There is no flavor advantage, but the vessels are charming and can go from stove to table. Most Asian markets and housewares shops stock two styles: the off-white, high-sided Chinese sand pot and the squat Japanese *donabe*, which are often richly glazed and usually have a wide bottom. A sand pot is inexpensive, but the higher-priced *donabe*, made in Japan and China and constructed of dense clay, heats up faster and is sturdier. The wide-bottomed *donabe* is ideal for *kho* dishes that call for the ingredients to be arranged in a single layer. Common clay pot sizes include extra small (1 quart), small (1½ quart), medium (2½ to 3 quart), and large (4 to 5 quart).

Clay pots are designed for cooking food in liquid. Any sautéing or searing steps must be done in a regular pan. Some cooks season their clay pots before using them, but I don't. They can be set directly on the burner of a gas stove, but require a heat diffuser on an electric stove. Always have a clay pot at room temperature, never chilled, before you put it on the burner; heat it gradually to prevent cracking; and never raise the heat above medium. Once the contents are at a simmer, make sure any liquid you add is *at least* warm. To maintain the life of a clay pot, avoid using sharp utensils and clean it with mild detergent, hot water, and gentle wiping.

SALMON AND GALANGAL
SIMMERED IN CARAMEL SAUCE

Cá Kho Riềng

> MOST PEOPLE are introduced to galangal, a relative of ginger, by way of Thai curries and seafood soups. The rhizome is seldom used in Vietnamese cooking, but when it is, it is paired with other bold-flavored ingredients. Here, its pungent heat brightens a northern fish *kho*, with the bittersweet caramel sauce tempering its fire. Use the smaller amount of galangal if you want a dish with less intensity. Although salmon isn't native to Vietnam, it takes on the robust flavors of the *kho* remarkably well.
>
> Fresh side pork (pork belly), which you can find at Asian markets, is the stealth ingredient here, enrobing everything with its richness to create a unique surf-and-turf combination. The result is spicy, savory, and a touch sweet.

1 In a bowl, stir together the brown sugar, pepper, salt, caramel sauce, and fish sauce. Add the salmon and turn to coat evenly. Set aside for 15 minutes to marinate.

2 Select a shallow saucepan in which the fish steaks will fit snugly in a single layer. Arrange the galangal slices on the bottom. Place the fish steaks on top, and drizzle with the marinade. Put the pork in the open spaces between the steaks.

3 Bring to a vigorous simmer over medium-high heat. Adjust to a simmer, cover, and cook for 10 minutes, checking midway to make sure there is enough liquid in the pan. If the pan seems dry, splash in a little water. During this stage, the fish will more or less cook in the steam trapped in the pan. The liquid will bubble vigorously, and plumes of steam may shoot from under the lid.

4 Uncover, add water almost to cover the fish, and bring to a gentle simmer. Cover and cook for 1 hour. Uncover and adjust the heat, if necessary, to continue at a gentle simmer. Cook for another 15 to 18 minutes, or until the liquid has reduced by half and has thickened slightly, forming a sauce.

5 Taste the sauce and adjust the flavor with a pinch of brown sugar to remove any harsh edges, or a sprinkling of fish sauce for more

savory depth. Carefully transfer the fish to a shallow bowl. Don't worry if the steaks break up a bit. Surround the fish with the pork pieces, pour the sauce over the fish and pork, and serve. To eat, put fish and pork on your rice and spoon on a bit of sauce.

Serves 4 to 6 with 2 or 3 other dishes

2 teaspoons brown sugar

1/4 teaspoon black pepper

1/4 teaspoon salt

2 1/2 tablespoons Caramel Sauce (page 316)

1 1/2 tablespoons fish sauce

2 salmon steaks, each 10 to 12 ounces and about 1 inch thick

6 to 8 slices fresh galangal, each about 1/8 inch thick, or 3 to 5 slices dried galangal

1/3 pound lean side pork (pork belly), cut into 1/4-inch-thick strips and then into 1-inch squares

NOTE

To simmer the fish in a clay pot, use a small (1 1/2-quart) Japanese *donabe* about 8 inches wide. For details on clay pot cooking, see opposite.

GRILLED TROUT HAND ROLLS

Cá Nướng Trui

THESE HAND ROLLS are a simple and healthful do-it-yourself meal: you assemble the ingredients and invite guests to do the rest. It is a relaxing experience, with everyone making their own hand rolls, eating, sipping cold beverages, and chatting. In Vietnam, freshwater *cá lóc* (snakehead fish) is often used for this dish, encased in clay and roasted in rice straw, wrapped in banana leaf and grilled over charcoal, or just placed directly on the grill. I prefer the simplicity of the last approach. Trout is the perfect substitute for *cá lóc*, as its sweet flesh stands up well to grilling. The skin crisps wonderfully, too.

1   Rinse the trout well, removing any membranes and blood that the fishmonger may have overlooked. Pat dry with paper towels. Lay the trout flat on your work surface and, with a sharp knife, score each fish crosswise at 3 or 4 places, about 1¼ inches apart. (For scoring tips, see the Note on page 124.) To enrich the fish and to help it more easily release from the grill rack, rub it with a little oil, inside and out. Season the cavity and then the skin with salt and pepper. Set aside.

2   Arrange the noodles on 2 plates in 2-inch mounds for easy serving. Set the noodles out on the table with the rice paper rounds and water bowls for dipping them, the vegetable garnish plate, and the dipping sauce. Set each place with a dinner plate. Have the scallion oil garnish ready.

3   To cook the trout, prepare a medium charcoal fire (you can hold your hand over the rack for only 4 to 5 seconds) or preheat a gas grill to medium. Grill the trout, turning once, for 5 to 6 minutes on each side, or until the skin is crisp and lightly browned. The trout is ready when the meat is opaque. Peek inside the cavity; there should be no sign of blood. Use 2 spatulas to transfer the fish to a platter. Scatter 2 tablespoons of the scallion oil garnish on top of each fish and bring the rest of the garnish to the table.

Serves 4 as a light lunch or dinner

2 whole trout, 1 pound each, cleaned with head and tail intact
Canola or other neutral oil
Salt and black pepper

ACCOMPANIMENTS
²/₃ pound dried small round rice noodles, cooked in boiling water for 3 to 5 minutes, drained, and flushed with cold water

About 24 rice paper rounds, 8½ inches in diameter
Vegetable Garnish Plate (page 313)
1½ cups Tamarind-Ginger Dipping Sauce (page 312) or Basic Dipping Sauce (page 308)
½ cup Scallion Oil Garnish (page 314)

4   Explain to any diners new to this dish how to make their rolls. First soften a rice paper round in the water bowl and place it on a plate. (See page 331 for tips on working with rice paper.) When the rice paper is pliable and tacky, layer the ingredients on top in the following order: a lettuce leaf, some torn herb leaves, a few cucumber slices, some noodles, a little scallion oil garnish, a piece of fish, and a drizzle of sauce. Wrap up and enjoy.

GRILLED SHRIMP AND SQUID

Tôm với Mực Nướng

A GREAT WAY TO COOK SHRIMP is to grill them whole, with heads and shells intact. The unpeeled shrimp cook in their own juices, staying moist, and the shells pick up a little char, releasing a sweet, toasty aroma. Since I also like grilled squid, I often serve a mixed grill of squid and shrimp. Squid with tubes only about five inches long are especially tender.

The best shrimp to grill are big white ones that have edible thin shells. To find them, head to an Asian market, where you will also find the squid. Before cooking the shrimp, follow Vietnamese tradition and neatly trim them. Then, cut the squid to create fringe that will curl back during grilling, to resemble trumpet flowers. I recommend cleaning the squid yourself because the flavor is superior to that of precleaned squid. To create a full menu, add one of the *canh* soups (pages 58 to 66) and some grilled summer squash (see the Note that accompanies Grilled Chicken on page 81).

1   Using scissors, snip off the antennae, pointy tip, jagged rostrum, legs, and feet of each shrimp (see page 115). Set aside.

2   To prepare the squid tubes, lay a tube flat on a cutting board. Holding it down on the pointed end, use a sharp knife to make 3 cuts about 3/4 inch long at the open end, creating fringe. Make sure to cut through both layers. With your hand, roll the tube to check for wide sections where another fringe or two may need to be cut. Repeat with the remaining the squid tubes and set aside.

3   To make the marinade, in a bowl, whisk together the sugar, fish sauce, lime juice, and oil. Add the shrimp and squid and toss to coat well. Marinate for 15 minutes, or until the grill is ready.

4   Prepare a medium-hot charcoal fire (you can hold your hand over the rack for only 3 to 4 seconds) or preheat a gas grill to medium-high. Grill the shrimp for about 3 minutes on each side and the squid for about 2 minutes on each side. The shrimp are cooked when they are a brilliant color, a bit charred, and toasty smelling. The squid are ready when they are opaque and the fringe has curled.

Serves 4 to 6 with 2 or 3 other dishes

32 large head-on white
   shrimp in their shells,
   about 2 pounds total
20 young squid, about
   2 pounds total, cleaned
   (page 323) and tentacles
   discarded or saved for
   another use

MARINADE

1/2 teaspoon sugar

1 1/2 tablespoons fish sauce

1 tablespoon fresh lime juice

2 tablespoons canola or other
   neutral oil

Salt, Pepper, and Lime
   Dipping Sauce (page 311)

5   Transfer the shrimp and squid to a plate and serve with the dipping sauce. If you are new to eating shrimp with their heads on, here is how it is done: First twist off the head and suck the opened end, where the heady reddish orange brains are. Whether or not you eat the rest of the head is up to you. Eat the remainder as usual.

SHRIMP IN SPICY TAMARIND SAUCE

Tôm Rang Me

SHRIMP CAN BE PAIRED with strong flavors—in this case, a tangy and sweet tamarind sauce with a touch of heat—and still retain their briny character. The tartness of the tropical pod comes through in the sauce, but it is balanced by the other seasonings, just as it is in a well-prepared Indian tamarind chutney.

These shrimp are at home with a bowl of rice for soaking up the sauce, but they also make an interesting cross-cultural hand roll tucked into a warm corn tortilla and eaten like a taco. As long as you have frozen cubes of tamarind liquid on hand, this recipe is quick to prepare.

1 To make the flavoring sauce, in a small bowl, combine the sugar, tamarind liquid, fish sauce, and chile sauce and stir to dissolve the sugar. Because tamarind liquid varies, taste the sauce and adjust the flavors, if necessary. Add extra sugar to reduce tartness, fish sauce for more savory depth, chile sauce for extra heat, or water to dilute.

2 Refresh the shrimp by putting them in a colander and tossing them with a liberal amount of salt. Rinse immediately under lots of cold water and press gently to drain well.

3 In a wok or large skillet, heat the oil over high heat until hot but not smoking. Add the shallot and garlic and stir-fry for about 30 seconds, or until fragrant. Add the shrimp and stir-fry for about 1 minute, or until they have turned pinkish orange and are half cooked. They will release juice and look shiny.

4 Give the flavoring sauce a stir, pour it over the shrimp, and stir to coat the shrimp. Let the sauce come to a vigorous boil, stirring occasionally to keep the elements moving. The sauce will reduce to a thickish consistency in 2 to 3 minutes.

5 Transfer the shrimp and sauce to a deep plate or shallow bowl. Garnish with the cilantro and serve immediately.

Serves 4 with 2 or 3 other dishes

FLAVORING SAUCE
1 1/2 tablespoons sugar
1/4 cup Tamarind Liquid (page 319)
2 tablespoons fish sauce
2 teaspoons Huy Fong brand Sriracha chile sauce

1 1/2 pounds large shrimp, peeled and deveined
Salt
2 tablespoons canola or other neutral oil
1 shallot, finely chopped (about 1/4 cup)
2 cloves garlic, minced
3 or 4 sprigs cilantro

REFRESHING PEELED SHRIMP

Most shrimp sold in the United States are frozen, so whenever I use peeled raw shrimp in a recipe, I like to return a bit of the sea to them. I do this by tossing the shrimp with a liberal amount of salt, and then immediately rinsing them under cold running water. This simple step gives the shrimp a fresher flavor.

PAN-SEARED TUNA STEAKS WITH GINGERY DIPPING SAUCE

Cá Thu Chiên

THIS RECIPE WAS INSPIRED by a grilled tuna steak that I ordered at a sleepy roadside restaurant in Vietnam. Working tableside on a small charcoal brazier, the young waiter cooked a half-inch-thick tuna steak with care and patience. Back in my home kitchen, I decided to adapt the recipe to the stove top. I find that pan searing allows greater control than grilling over the doneness of the lean, meaty steaks, yielding juicier results.

There are no tricks here. The tuna steaks are coated with the same seasonings used for Grilled Shrimp and Squid (page 111), and the gingery dipping sauce offers a good contrast to the richness of the fish. Serve with Chicken Dumpling and Chrysanthemum Leaf Soup (page 61), boiled *gailan* (Chinese broccoli) or regular broccoli (which are both good with the dipping sauce), and rice.

1 Pat the tuna steaks dry with paper towels. To make the marinade, in a bowl large enough to accommodate the tuna steaks, whisk together the sugar, fish sauce, lime juice, and oil. Add the steaks and turn them to coat well. There's no need to let the steaks marinate.

2 Heat a 12-inch nonstick skillet over medium-high heat until hot. To test if it is ready, flick a drop of water into it. It should immediately dance and then evaporate. Add the tuna steaks and let them cook, undisturbed, for 2 minutes. The tuna should brown nicely on the underside, perhaps even with some dark caramelized spots. Using tongs, carefully turn the steaks over. Without disturbing them, let them cook for about another 1½ minutes for rare or 3 minutes for medium-rare.

To check for doneness, nick the steaks with the tip of a paring knife. A rare steak should be opaque at the edges and translucent red and cool in the middle. A medium-rare steak should be opaque at the edges and reddish pink in the middle. For a medium steak, cook for medium-rare but let the steak rest for 5 minutes under a foil tent before cutting. The steak will continue to cook as it rests.

Serves 4 with 2 or 3 other dishes

3 tuna steaks, each ½ pound and about 1 inch thick

⅔ cup Ginger-Lime Dipping Sauce (page 309)

MARINADE
½ teaspoon sugar
1½ tablespoons fish sauce
1 tablespoon fresh lime juice
2 tablespoons canola or other neutral oil

3 Transfer the steaks to a cutting board. Cut each steak into ¼-inch-thick slices. Arrange the slices on a platter and serve immediately with the dipping sauce.

WOK-SEARED SHRIMP WITH GARLIC AND CHILE

Tôm Rang Tỏi Ớt

> THIS VIETNAMESE VERSION of Chinese salt-and-pepper shrimp is bursting with bold flavors, and the high-heat searing seals in the juices. Use shrimp in their shells for the extra crunch and smokiness they develop during searing. Ideally their heads will be intact, too, as the juices trapped in the heads add to the richness of the finished dish. Purchase white shrimp with edible thin shells for this recipe; they are usually available at Asian and Latin markets.

1 Using scissors, snip off the antennae, pointy tip, jagged rostrum, legs, and feet of each shrimp (see below). Pat dry with paper towels and set aside.

2 In a bowl large enough to accommodate the shrimp, stir together the white pepper, sugar, salt, and tapioca starch. Add the shrimp and toss with your fingers to coat well. Set aside.

3 In a wok or skillet, heat 2 tablespoons of the oil over high heat until hot but not smoking. Add half of the shrimp and spread them into a single layer. Let the shrimp sear and brown for 1 minute. Flip the shrimp over and sear the second side for 1 minute. They should curl and turn pinkish orange. Transfer the shrimp to a plate and repeat with the remaining shrimp, using an additional 2 tablespoons oil.

4 Lower the heat to medium and add the remaining 2 tablespoons oil. Add the garlic and chiles and stir-fry for about 30 seconds, or until fragrant. Don't let the garlic burn. Return the shrimp to the pan and stir-fry for about 1 minute, or until some of the garlic and chile adhere to the shrimp. Transfer to a plate and serve hot.

Serves 4 to 6 with 2 or 3 other dishes

1 1/2 pounds medium white shrimp in their shells, preferably with heads intact	2 1/2 teaspoons tapioca starch or cornstarch
1 1/4 teaspoons white pepper	6 tablespoons canola or other neutral oil
1 1/4 teaspoons sugar	5 or 6 cloves garlic, chopped
1 teaspoon salt	2 to 4 Thai or serrano chiles, thinly sliced

HOW TO TRIM SHRIMP

When shrimp are served with their shells intact, Vietnamese cooks like to trim them before they cook them to rid the shrimp of any parts that may be unpleasant or harmful to eat. If they are head-on shrimp, the antennae, pointy tip of the head, jagged rostrum atop the head, the legs, and the feet should go. The tails are optional. If they are headless shrimp, the feet are trimmed and sometimes the tails.

To trim shrimp, use kitchen scissors and work over a plastic bag to catch the unwanted bits. Hold the shrimp near its tail with the feet facing up. Snip away at the unwanted parts. If the head is attached, turn the shrimp over and remove the remaining jagged part between the eyes.

WOK-SEARED CRAB
WITH SCALLION, GARLIC, AND PEPPER

Cua Rang Hành Tỏi Tiêu

EATING THIS CRAB is somewhat akin to eating a pile of barbecued ribs. Coated with a garlicky-sweet-spicy sauce, the crab requires a little work to get at all the delicious bits (and perhaps a cold beer to wash things down), but your effort pays off.

Vietnamese cooks traditionally cut up live crabs before stir-frying them. That is a run-of-the-mill task for fearless types like my mom. Most cooks, however, wince at the thought of chopping up a live crustacean, especially one with large claws. To avoid getting pinched, I briefly boil the crab, which also sets the meat and tomalley, making the crab easy to take apart.

Since freshness is crucial, use whatever kind of live crab is available in your area, the feistier the better for optimal flavor. Asian markets are typically reliable sources. In Northern California, I'm blessed with the large Dungeness crab. Outfit the table with metal nutcrackers, communal bowls for holding shells, and a finger bowl for each person.

1 Fill a 5- or 6-quart pot two-thirds full with water and bring to a rolling boil over high heat. Use tongs to grasp the crab at the rear. Holding it top side down, slide it head first into the pot. If it thrashes about, press down on it with the tongs until it is still. After its legs have completely folded inward, let it gently cook for 5 minutes longer. Transfer the crab to a baking sheet or platter. Set it aside for about 10 minutes, or until it is cool enough to handle.

2 To clean the crab, use the directions on page 322 for guidance. Scrape the tomalley and fat from the shell and body section into a liquid measuring cup. If you don't like the tomalley and fat, substitute the beaten egg. Do not remove the meat from the legs and body section. Use a knife to quarter the body section, setting the pieces aside on a plate. To make the claws and legs easier to eat, gently crack each one just to break the shell, adding it to the plate with the body sections. (A metal nutcracker is handy for cracking.)

3 To make the flavoring sauce, add the oyster sauce, sugar, fish sauce, and pepper to the tomalley and fat (or egg) and stir to

Serves 2 or 3 as a main course, or 4 to 6 with 3 or 4 other dishes

1 live Dungeness crab, 2 to 2¼ pounds

1 egg, beaten (optional)

FLAVORING SAUCE

2 tablespoons oyster sauce

1½ teaspoons sugar

1 teaspoon fish sauce

¾ teaspoon black pepper, preferably freshly ground

5 large cloves garlic, coarsely chopped

2 scallions, cut into 1½-inch lengths, white and green parts separated

3 quarter-sized slices fresh ginger, peeled and smashed with the broad side of a cleaver or chef's knife

2 tablespoons canola or other neutral oil

mix well. Add enough water to make 2/3 cup. Set near the stove, along with the crab, garlic, white and green scallion sections, and ginger.

4   In a wok or large skillet, heat the oil over medium-high heat until hot but not smoking. Add the garlic, white scallion sections, and ginger and stir-fry for about 30 seconds, or until fragrant. Add the crab and stir-fry for 2 to 3 minutes to heat the crab through, taking care not to burn the garlic.

5   Give the flavoring sauce a stir and pour it over the crab. Raise the heat to high and keep stir-frying for another 2 to 3 minutes. As you stir-fry, the sauce will bubble vigorously and then reduce to coat the crab. (If the pan ever seems dry, splash in some water.) The crab is done when all the visible meat is opaque. Add the green scallion sections and cook for 30 seconds longer, or until the scallions have wilted slightly.

6   Transfer the crab to a platter and serve. Remind diners to eat with both hands and to suck the sauce from the outside of each piece before breaking in to get the meat. A crab's pointy leg tip is perfect for digging out the meat. If you are serving the crab with rice, advise diners to mix some of the scallions and other tasty bits on the platter into their rice.

NOTE

For a crab-loving crowd, double or triple this recipe. Unless you have a gigantic wok or skillet and a powerful stove, it's easier to stir-fry the crab in batches. In between batches, quickly wash and dry the pan to avoid burning bits of sauce on the bottom when you cook the next crab. Keep the finished crab in a warm oven while you are cooking the rest.

CRISPY CATFISH WITH ONIONS AND GINGER

Cá Trê Chiên Hành Gừng

WHENEVER OUR FAMILY gets together for dinner at my parents' house, this dish is usually on the menu. To make it, catfish fillets are cut into pieces and panfried to a golden crisp. When the fish is removed from the pan, the oil that remains is used to sauté onion and ginger into a heady mixture that is finished with fish sauce and water and then served like a relish.

Most catfish sold today are farm-raised and thus lean, so don't skimp on the oil. Also, the fish splatters during frying, so you might want to use a splatter guard and/or put newspaper on the floor around the stove to speed cleanup.

1 To cut each fillet into equal-sized pieces that will cook evenly, first cut off a 2½-inch piece from the thin, flat end of the fillet. Then halve the fillet lengthwise and cut the halves into 2- to 2½-inch-long pieces. Set aside near the stove.

2 Turn the oven on to warm (175° to 200°F). Pour in enough oil to film the bottom (6 to 7 tablespoons) of a 12-inch nonstick skillet and heat over medium heat. When the oil is hot, add half of the fish, laying the pieces flat in the skillet. The fish shrinks during frying, so you can crowd it a bit. Fry the fish, undisturbed, for 12 minutes, or until the bottom edges are deeply golden.

3 Using chopsticks or a spatula, turn each piece over; expect some sputtering and splattering. The cooked side should be orange-yellow and very crispy; tap it to check. Fry the second side for about 7 minutes, or until deeply golden and crispy. If the pan gets too hot and the fish starts to burn rather than brown, lower the heat slightly. Transfer the fish to a paper towel–lined plate and slip it into the oven to keep warm. Repeat with the remaining pieces, adding more oil if needed.

4 When all the fish is fried, lower the heat to medium-low. There should be a generous 2 tablespoons oil remaining in the pan; add or discard oil as necessary. Add the onion and ginger

Serves 4 to 6 with 2 or 3 other dishes

2 pounds catfish fillets, preferably large
Canola or other neutral oil
1 large yellow onion, halved and sliced lengthwise ¼ inch thick
Chubby 5-inch piece fresh ginger, peeled and finely shredded (see page 51)
2½ tablespoons fish sauce mixed with 6 tablespoons water
3 or 4 sprigs cilantro

and sauté gently for 15 to 20 minutes, or until they have collapsed to about one-third of their original volume. If the pan ever seems dry, splash in some water or add extra oil.

5 Add the fish sauce mixture, stir to incorporate, and raise the heat to medium-high. When the mixture begins to bubble, turn off the heat. Let sit for a few minutes. The liquid will thicken into a light sauce.

6 Make a bed of the onion and ginger on a platter, reserving a bit of the sauce. Arrange the catfish on top and drizzle on the reserved sauce. Garnish with the cilantro and serve.

FRIED SMELTS

Cá Tẩm Bột Chiên Dòn

IN VIETNAM, THE DELICATE ANCHOVIES (*cá cơm*) used for making fish sauce are also fried and enjoyed as a snack like a Spanish tapa or as part of a meal along with a simple soup, boiled or stir-fried vegetable, and rice. Even though these small fish are sold frozen at Viet markets, I like to use smelts, which are the perfect North American substitute. Delicate and sweet, they have soft, edible bones that allow you to "eat them like French fries," as a fishmonger once told me. And the batter remains crispy long after the last fish is fried. Use the freshest smelts you can find or substitute other small fish available in your area, such as fresh anchovies.

1 To prepare the smelts for frying, work near the sink with a plastic bag nearby to hold unwanted bits. First, cut off their heads. If the smelts are less than 3/4 inch wide, simply cut off the belly (the guts will go with it) by making an angled cut from the neck down to the small anal opening. For larger smelts, slit the fish open along the belly and remove the guts. Rinse each fish under running water and use your finger to scoop out any remaining viscera. Pat the fish dry with paper towels. Transfer to a bowl and toss with the salt, pepper, and sugar.

2 To make the batter, in a bowl, stir together the all-purpose flour, rice flour, and cornstarch. Make a well in the center, pour in the ice water, and then stir together the wet and dry ingredients to make a smooth, thick batter. If it seems heavy like pancake batter, add water by the teaspoon until it thins slightly.

3 Put a wire rack on a baking sheet and place next to the stove. Set the fish and the batter on the other side of the stove. Pour oil to a depth of 1 1/2 inches into a wok or 5-quart Dutch oven and heat over medium-high heat to 350°F on a deep-frying thermometer. (If you don't have a thermometer, stand a dry bamboo chopstick in the oil; if small bubbles immediately gather on the surface around the chopstick, the oil is ready.)

Serves 8 to 10 as a snack, or 4 to 6 with 2 or 3 other dishes

2 pounds smelts or other
    small white-fleshed fish,
    preferably 1/2 to 1 inch
    wide
3/4 teaspoon salt
1/2 teaspoon black pepper
1/2 teaspoon sugar

BATTER
1 cup all-purpose flour
1/2 cup rice flour
1/4 cup cornstarch
1 1/3 cups ice water

Corn or canola oil for
    deep-frying
Salt, Pepper, and Lime
    Dipping Sauce (page 311)

4 When the oil is ready, take a fish by the tail and drag it through the batter, letting the excess drip back into the bowl. Lower the fish into the hot oil. Repeat with a few more fish, being careful not to crowd the pan. Fry, stirring the fish occasionally so they don't stick together, for 5 to 7 minutes, or until the batter-coated bodies are golden and the tails are golden brown. Using a skimmer, transfer the fried fish to the rack.

5 When all the smelts are fried, pile them on a plate and serve with the dipping sauce.

SHRIMP AND CRAB ROLLS

Chả Giò

CHẢ GIÒ, WHICH ORIGINATED IN SAIGON, are among Vietnam's national dishes. They are often misleadingly translated as spring rolls, because they seem like a riff on the Chinese spring roll, or as imperial rolls, a translation of *pâté imperial*, their French moniker. But these rolls are not reserved for royalty, nor are they exclusively eaten during the Spring Festival (Chinese New Year). And their filling, wrapper, and accompaniments are uniquely Vietnamese. Out of culinary pride, I encourage people to call these rolls *chả giò*, their southern Viet name.

The rolls are made in varying sizes. Cooks with great manual dexterity create thumb-sized rolls. Lacking such skill and patience, I make stubby cigar-sized ones and cut them up before serving. Larger ones also involve less labor when frying up enough for a special lunch or dinner. Some Vietnamese American cooks use Filipino lumpia or Chinese spring roll wrappers, which are made of wheat flour and fry up crisp, but an authentic flavor is lost. For the best results, use rice paper made of all rice flour or of rice and tapioca flours.

Makes 20 to 24 rolls, to serve 4 to 6 as a one-dish meal

FILLING

Generous 1/4 teaspoon salt

3/4 teaspoon black pepper

2 tablespoons fish sauce

1 egg

2 dried wood ear mushrooms, reconstituted (page 334), trimmed, and finely chopped (about 3 tablespoons)

3 dried shiitake mushrooms, reconstituted (page 332), stemmed, and finely chopped

1 bundle (1.3 ounces) cellophane noodles, soaked in hot water until pliable, drained, and cut into 1/2-inch lengths

1 small yellow onion, minced

3 scallions, white and green parts, finely chopped

1 cup firmly packed coarsely grated jicama, squeezed gently to remove excess water

3/4 pound small or medium shrimp, peeled, deveined, and cut into pea-sized pieces

1/4 pound crabmeat, preferably picked from a freshly cooked crab (see page 322)

1/2 pound ground pork, coarsely chopped to loosen

5 tablespoons sugar

5 cups warm water

20 to 24 rice paper rounds, 8 1/2 inches in diameter

Corn or canola oil for deep-frying

Vegetable Garnish Plate (page 313)

1 1/2 cups Basic Dipping Sauce made with garlic (page 308)

1 To make the filling, in a large bowl, whisk together the salt, pepper, fish sauce, and egg until blended. Add the wood ears, shiitakes, noodles, yellow onion, scallions, jicama, shrimp, crabmeat, and pork and stir to combine, breaking up the pork into small pieces as you mix. Set aside. (The filling may be made up to 1 day in advance, covered with plastic wrap, and refrigerated.)

2 In a wide, shallow bowl or baking dish, combine the sugar and water and stir to dissolve the sugar. This sugar water helps the rolls to color and crisp. If there isn't enough liquid to allow the rice paper to be fully immersed, mix more. Place the bowl or dish at your work station, which should also include the rice paper rounds, filling, a platter for holding the finished rolls, and a spread-out dish towel on which to shape the rolls. (The dish towel absorbs excess water and typically makes the rice paper tackier and easier to roll smoothly. If you find that the rice paper sticks too much to the dish towel, switch to a cutting board.)

3 To make each roll, slide a rice paper round into the sugar water. Let it sit for 5 seconds to moisten both sides well, then place it on the dish towel and let sit for another minute to soften. Repeat with another rice paper and set it next to the first one. (Once the first rice paper has softened, you can begin rolling it while the other one rests.) Center 2 heaping tablespoons of the filling on the lower third of the softened rice paper. Use your fingers to shape the filling into a solid 4-inch-long log about 1 inch in diameter. Lift the bottom edge over the filling, making sure it is smooth. To reinforce to the ends, which brown quickly, use the side of each little finger to crease the ends before folding in the sides. Roll from the bottom up to finish. The rice paper is self-sealing. Try to make sure the cylinder is free of air pockets, so the roll doesn't burst during frying. (Rolls that burst still taste good but they aren't pretty.) Place the roll seam side down on the platter. Dip a new rice paper round and get to work on the one that is now ready. Work in this rhythm until all the filling is used. As the platter fills, don't stack the rolls or they may stick and tear.

4 Another key to preventing the rolls from bursting during frying is to maintain a moderately low oil temperature. Given

that, a 5-quart Dutch oven and a deep-frying thermometer are the best equipment ensemble for frying the rolls, as they make monitoring the oil easy. Put a wire rack on a baking sheet and place the baking sheet and a paper towel–lined plate (for blotting away excess oil) next to the stove. Put the platter of rolls on the other side of the stove.

Pour oil to a depth of 1½ inches into the Dutch oven and heat over medium-high heat to 325°F on a deep-frying thermometer. Start adding the rolls, placing them seam side down. Set the rolls as far apart from one another as possible to prevent them from sticking, and add as many as the pan can hold comfortably without crowding. When the oil reaches 350°F, steady the temperature by lowering the heat to medium. Let the rolls fry for 5 to 10 minutes, or until crispy and golden. The frying time and color depth depend on the rice paper; some papers stay light while others darken. Bubbles will form in the rolls. Ignore small ones, but if a huge one prevents a roll from frying evenly, let the bubble set to a crisp, remove the roll from the oil, tap it against the cooling rack to burst and remove the bubble, and then return the roll to finish frying.

5 When a roll is ready, use tongs to remove it from the oil. Put it on the towel-lined plate briefly to remove excess oil and then set it on the rack to cool. Add a new roll to the hot oil and continue frying until all are cooked. As needed, regulate the heat to maintain the temperature. When you are through, briefly refry any rolls that have softened during cooling.

6 Use scissors to cut each roll into 3 or 4 pieces, and put them on 2 plates or platters. Serve with the vegetable garnish and sauce. To eat, wrap pieces in the garnishes and dip.

NOTE

The best way to refresh leftover uncut rolls is to refry them. Return them to room temperature, then arrange them in a saucepan or deep skillet in a single layer. Add oil to cover and heat over medium heat. When the oil gently bubbles, monitor the rolls. They'll soon be crisp and renewed.

CLASSIC STEAMED FISH WITH PORK, MUSHROOM, AND NOODLES

Cá Hấp

PRESENTED ON A PLATTER just moments out of the steamer, a whole steamed fish reflects the cook's care and attention to obtaining the freshest ingredients possible. Ideally, the fish was plucked live from a tank at the market. Barring that, it met its end shortly before the cook selected it from a bed of ice.

This recipe, with its mixture of pork, ginger, onion, mushrooms, and cellophane noodles, is one of the classic Viet ways to steam fish, with the various flavors and textures melding beautifully during cooking. The flavorings are light, so select a mild-tasting white-fleshed fish to complement them. I like striped bass, which is readily available and has delicate flesh, as well as bones that aren't troublesome; a whole trout weighing about 1 1/2 pounds is another good option. The dish is perfect for entertaining because most of the work may be done hours in advance. Add White Tree Fungus in Clear Broth (page 76), a simply seasoned stir-fried vegetable, and rice for an elegant meal.

1 To make the filling, heat the oil in a 10-inch skillet over medium heat. Add the onion and ginger and sauté for about 1 minute, or until fragrant. Add the pork and mushrooms and use chopsticks or a spatula to break the meat into small pieces so that it will be well distributed later. Cook, stirring, for about 2 minutes, or just until the pork is no longer pink, then remove from the heat. Add the fish sauce, noodles, and scallions and stir for about 1 minute, or until the noodles are soft and transparent. Season to taste with pepper and set aside. (The filling may be prepared up to 4 hours in advance. Let cool, cover, and refrigerate; bring to room temperature before using.)

2 Rinse the fish well, removing any membranes and blood that the fishmonger may have overlooked. Generously rub the fish inside and out with salt, then rinse thoroughly under cold running water. Pat the fish dry with paper towels. Lay the fish flat on your work surface and, with a sharp knife, score it crosswise at 3 or 4 places, spacing the slits about 1 inch apart. (See Note for scoring tips.)

continued

Serves 4 to 6 with 2 or 3 other dishes

FILLING
2 tablespoons canola or other neutral oil

2 tablespoons finely chopped yellow onion

Chubby 1 1/2-inch piece fresh ginger, peeled and minced

1/4 pound ground pork, coarsely chopped to loosen

4 dried shiitake mushrooms, reconstituted (page 332), stemmed, and thinly sliced

2 tablespoons fish sauce

1 bundle (1.3 ounces) cellophane noodles, soaked in hot water until pliable, drained, and cut into 4- to 6-inch lengths

2 scallions, green part only, cut into 2-inch lengths

Black pepper

1 whole striped bass, 1 3/4 to 2 pounds, cleaned with head and tail intact

Salt

2 scallions, white part only, cut lengthwise into thin strips

1 Roma tomato, cored, cut lengthwise into 3 wedges, and seeds removed

4 to 6 sprigs cilantro

3 Set aside a few white scallion strips for garnish and tuck the remainder into the score marks. Select a heatproof plate or nonreactive cake or pie pan 1 inch smaller in diameter than your steamer tray. (Ideally, you will be able to serve the fish from whatever you choose, thus avoiding the need to transfer it to a serving plate.) Lay the fish on the plate or pan, bending it as needed. Stuff half of the filling in the cavity and arrange the rest over the fish. Put the tomato wedges on top and place the plate in the steamer tray.

4 Fill the steamer pan half full with water and bring to a rolling boil over high heat. Place the tray in the steamer, cover, and steam the fish for 18 to 22 minutes, or until a knife inserted at the thickest part easily pierces the flesh all the way to the bone.

5 When the fish is done, turn off the heat. Use pot holders or a Chinese steamer retriever (see Note) to remove the plate or pan from the steamer (you may find it easier to put the steamer tray on the counter first). Since the dish is hot, I like to slide it onto a platter and carry it to the table. If you want to transfer the fish to a warmed serving platter, use 2 wide spatulas, and remember to pour the delicious juices onto the platter, too. Garnish with the reserved scallion strips and the cilantro. Serve immediately.

NOTE

For beautiful score marks, hold the knife at a 45-degree angle to the backbone, with the blade pointed toward the head. Make the first cut about 1 inch below the collar and continue from there. Stop 2 inches from the tail or it may break off during cooking. Each cut should be about three-fourths of the way to the bone.

A Chinese steamer retriever is an ingenious three-armed gadget that expands to grip onto the lip of a bowl or plate used for steaming, making removal from a hot steamer tray a snap. Constructed of thin aluminum and plastic, it looks wimpy but isn't. Put your thumb through the ring and move the plastic part like a syringe. The arms open and close to reach around an item and grasp it tight. This inexpensive gadget is sold at Chinese housewares and restaurant-supply shops. Remember, though, it only works on dishes with a lip.

SERVING AND ENJOYING WHOLE FISH

Once you have delivered the fish to the table, take the lead to serve your guests. Use a serving spoon to dig into and lift pieces of flesh gracefully from the bone. The score marks are good guides. Make sure garnishes and juices are included with each portion. Once the top side has been eaten, gently peel the central bone away from the flesh. This may be done by holding the neck with chopsticks and peeling it back from head to tail, or vice versa. Toward the end, use the serving spoon to support the removal of the bone in one piece. Set the bone to one side of the platter. Carefully push the short bones edging the fish away from the flesh and continue the feast.

It is customary to eat both the skin and the flesh of a whole fish. The fish cheeks are saved for special guests. And the eyes are for connoisseurs.

STEAMED SALMON WITH GARLIC AND GINGER

Cá Hấp Tỏi Gừng

THIS STEAMED FISH RECIPE, given to our family by our Chinese Vietnamese friend Uncle Su, is special. During cooking, the bold seasonings mix with the sweet fish juices to create a wonderful sauce for flavoring the flesh and a bowl of hot rice. Fresh salmon steaks or fillets are a fine substitute for the heads, which my parents prefer. You can also try the sauce atop other moderately flavored fish that have some richness to their flesh, such as sablefish. Avoid lean, dense fish, such as halibut or swordfish, which dry out and toughen when steamed.

1   To make the flavoring sauce, in a small bowl, combine the sugar, pepper, oyster sauce, and soy sauce and stir to dissolve the sugar. In a small skillet or saucepan, heat the oil over medium heat. Add the garlic and sauté for 15 to 20 seconds, or until fragrant. Add the ginger and cook for about 1 minute, or until aromatic and pliant. Pour in the oyster sauce mixture and bring to a boil. Add the chopped scallion, stir to combine, and remove from the heat. Set aside. (The sauce may be prepared up to 4 hours in advance. Let cool, then cover it to prevent it from drying out. Keep at room temperature until ready to use.)

2   Select a heatproof plate or nonreactive cake or pie pan 1 inch smaller in diameter than your steamer tray. (Ideally, you will be able to serve the fish from whatever you choose, thus avoiding the need to transfer it to a serving plate.) Set aside a few scallion strips for garnish and scatter the rest on the plate or pan. Arrange the fish on top and pour on the flavoring sauce. Place the plate or pan in the steamer tray.

3   Fill the steamer pan half full with water and bring to a rolling boil over high heat. Place the tray in the steamer, cover, and steam the fish for 8 to 10 minutes, or until a knife inserted at the thickest part easily pierces the flesh all the way to the bottom.

Serves 4 to 6 with 2 or 3 other dishes

FLAVORING SAUCE

1¼ teaspoons sugar

¼ teaspoon black pepper

2 tablespoons oyster sauce

2 tablespoons light (regular) soy sauce

2½ tablespoons canola or other neutral oil

3 cloves garlic, finely chopped

Chubby 2-inch piece fresh ginger, peeled and finely shredded (see page 51)

3 scallions, green part only, chopped

1 scallion, white part only, cut lengthwise into thin strips

1¼ pounds salmon fillet, halved crosswise into 2 equal pieces, or 2 salmon steaks, 10 to 12 ounces each

4 to 6 sprigs cilantro

4   When the fish is done, turn off the heat. Use pot holders or a Chinese steamer retriever (see Note, opposite) to remove the plate or pan from the steamer (you may find it easier to put the steamer tray on the counter first) and place it on a platter. Or, use 2 wide spatulas to transfer the fish to a warmed serving platter and pour the juices on top. Garnish with the reserved scallion strips and the cilantro and serve immediately.

SALMON CAKES WITH DILL AND GARLIC

Chả Cá Salmon

SMOOTH, WELL-SEASONED meat and seafood pastes have many uses in the Vietnamese kitchen. Here, a pinkish orange salmon paste is shaped into small cakes before undergoing a two-step cooking process: an initial steaming to cook the cakes, followed by broiling, grilling, or frying to crisp the outside. The cakes are sliced and served as an appetizer or dunked into Simple Dipping Sauce (page 309) and eaten with rice for dinner. If you have enjoyed Thai fried fish cakes (*tod mun*), these will remind you of them.

When my mother came to the States, she substituted salmon for the rich-tasting tuna she had used in Vietnam. I have since prepared the cakes with the ahi tuna available here, but the results were too firm and dry. The fattier salmon is superior. If you can't find skinless salmon fillet, buy $2^{1}/_3$ pounds of skin-on fillet and remove the skin before you cut the fish into chunks. The cakes can be frozen after they are steamed and then thawed and crisped for a good last-minute meal or snack. The recipe is also easily halved, but I advise you to make the whole batch and tuck away the extras for when you need a quick dish.

1 Cut the salmon into 1-inch chunks, discarding any errant bones you discover along the way. (Bevel-tipped tweezers, particularly the professional kind used for fish, will speed any bone removal.)

2 To make the marinade, in a bowl, whisk together the sugar, baking powder, cornstarch, fish sauce, oil, egg whites, and pepper until blended. Add the salmon and mix well with a rubber spatula to coat thoroughly. Cover with plastic wrap and refrigerate for at least 4 hours or up to overnight.

3 Grind the salmon in 2 batches (or in 3 or 4 batches if you have only a small food processor): In a large-capacity food processor, finely chop half of the onion and garlic, stopping the machine as needed to scrape down the bowl. Add half of the salmon and process until a smooth, stiff, sticky paste forms, again stopping the machine as needed to scrape down the bowl. Pass a spatula through the paste; it should have a resilient,

Makes 14 to 16 cakes, to serve 8 to 10

2 pounds skinless salmon fillet

MARINADE
2½ teaspoons sugar
1 tablespoon plus 1 teaspoon baking powder
2 teaspoons cornstarch
3 tablespoons fish sauce
2 tablespoons canola or other neutral oil
2 egg whites
½ teaspoon black pepper

1 large yellow onion, cut into 1-inch chunks
2 cloves garlic, chopped
¼ cup lightly packed finely chopped fresh dill, feathery tops only
Canola or other neutral oil

almost bouncy texture. Transfer the paste to a bowl. Repeat with the remaining onion, garlic, and salmon. Add the dill to the paste and mix well with the spatula.

4 Fill the steamer pan half full with water and bring it to a rolling boil over high heat. While the water heats, cut out sixteen 4-inch squares of parchment paper and place them on the counter. Set a small, shallow bowl filled with water alongside. Using a spring-action 3-ounce ice-cream scoop, scoop up a heaping mound of paste and release it onto a paper square. (If you don't have an ice-cream scoop, use a 1/4-cup measuring cup to scoop and a rubber spatula to push the paste onto each paper square.) Dip the heel of one hand in the bowl of water and rub the mound of paste in a circular motion to flatten the top. Aim for a cake the size of an average burger, about 1/2 inch thick and 31/2 inches in diameter. Smooth the sides with wet fingers. The cake doesn't have to be perfectly round or flat. Repeat to make more cakes. You may steam the cakes in batches as you shape them or wait until you shape them all.

5 When you are ready to steam, pick up the cakes by their paper squares and place them in the steamer tray, spacing them 1 inch apart. Place the tray in the steamer, cover, and steam each batch for 6 to 7 minutes, or until the cakes have puffed up and are lighter in color, the signs of doneness. Remove the steamer tray from the steamer pan and set aside to cool. (If you have 2 trays, have the other one ready for steaming.) Repeat the steaming until all the cakes are cooked and then let them cool completely. As the cakes cool, they deflate and their color brightens. (At this point, the cooled cakes can be double wrapped in plastic wrap or placed in an airtight container and refrigerated for up to 5 days or frozen for up to 3 months. Bring to room temperature before continuing.)

6 Discard the paper squares from the cooled cakes. Now you must choose the second cooking method, which will crisp the cakes and deliver a golden brown finish. Each method has its advantages and all produce delicious cakes. For sheer ease, lightly coat the cakes with oil and broil in a toaster oven, turning them once, for about 15 minutes total. For a tasty charred edge, lightly coat the cakes with oil and grill over a medium-hot fire on a charcoal grill or medium-high heat on a gas grill, turning them once, for 6 to 8 minutes total. For the most authentic taste and the most evenly crisp exterior, blot excess moisture from the cakes with a paper towel, heat oil to a depth of 1 inch in a wok or Dutch oven to 350°F, and deep-fry for 1 to 2 minutes. In each case, let the crisp cakes cool for 1 minute, then cut into 1/4-inch-thick slices and serve.

5. CLASSIC MEATS

The menus in Vietnamese restaurants are full of beef dishes— *phở* (beef noodle soup), shaking beef (wok-seared steak cubes), beef stir-fried with all manner of vegetables, even seven-course beef feasts—and customers regularly order them. Yet when it comes to cooking at home, Vietnamese nearly always favor pork. That preference is obvious at any Viet butcher counter, where the display space given over to pork far exceeds that for beef, and in the pages of most Vietnamese-language cookbooks, where pork recipes leave little room for beef dishes in the meats chapter.

The popularity of pork is largely due to the fact that pigs are relatively easy to raise and mature quickly. In agricultural societies like Vietnam, keeping a few pigs, along with flocks of chickens and ducks for eggs, has long been a sound strategy for feeding a family. When a hog is slaughtered, every part of the carcass is used: the leg and neck bones are simmered for fragrant broth, the ribs are grilled, chunks of leg meat are cooked in caramel sauce, and the loin is transformed into a preserved shredded meat. Lard, cracklings, headcheese, and blood sausage are more options for minimizing waste.

Today, fewer Vietnamese home cooks, particularly those in urban areas, face the challenge of using up a whole pig, but pork is still prized for its versatility. In the same meal, ground pork may be part of an egg drop soup (page 59) and star in a main dish, such as pork with lemongrass (page 132). Indeed, pork can turn up in any course, from an appetizer like deviled crab to a special-occasion sweet like moon cakes (page 300).

Of course, beef and water buffalo are both eaten in Vietnam as well. But the water buffalo has traditionally been regarded as the country's primary work animal, not a source of food, and the Vietnamese did not consume much beef until the arrival of the French in the late nineteenth century. The colonialists brought with them a love of beef, particularly *bifteck* (beefsteak), and to satisfy their appetite, they ordered the slaughtering of many cows. Unwanted portions of the carcasses were left to the Vietnamese, and although it remains a point of dispute, some people insist that *phở* was created by northern cooks in search of a way to use the supply of scraps.

But the seventy-five years of French colonial rule was just a blip on Vietnam's long history, and while the Vietnamese did acquire a taste for beef during that time, it was and continues to be considered a special meat. When beef is eaten, it is usually in small portions because it is costlier and harder to find than pork. For years after my family settled in America, we delighted in having pan-seared beef steaks on Friday nights, but the meat was always sliced and presented on a platter. It didn't seem natural for each of us to eat an entire steak. That also explains why you will rarely see roast-sized cuts of beef at an Asian butcher counter.

The Vietnamese also enjoy a variety of specialty meats, including rabbit, goat, venison, and dog. These are usually saved for celebratory occasions with friends and family, either at home or, particularly in the case of dog, at a restaurant that specializes in the meat. Rabbit is often featured in a French-style stew with white wine, tomato, and mushroom. Goat may be cooked in a curry or wrapped in caul fat and grilled. Venison preparations are similar to those for beef, while dog is usually seasoned with galangal and then grilled, stewed, or made into sausages.

continued

RECIPES

SAUTEED, STIR-FRIED, AND PAN-SEARED

ROASTED AND GRILLED

SIMMERED WITH CARAMEL SAUCE (KHO)

STEWS

I have never tasted dog meat, but my parents and others attest to its amazing richness. "When someone was grilling dog meat, you could smell the fragrance for blocks," Dad remembers. If this seems off-putting (or worse), consider that dogs, like pigs, were domesticated in China long ago, as archaeological discoveries in Neolithic sites have proved, and were undoubtedly a chief source of meat in the region that is now Vietnam at the same time. Also, the Vietnamese raise only a certain type of dog for eating, while others are raised solely as pets.

Although I have not included any of these specialty meats in this chapter, I have assembled a broad selection of classic pork and beef dishes that reflect the modern, everyday Vietnamese kitchen. You will find recipes for sautéing, grilling, and oven roasting pork and beef stir-fries that blend East and West. And to showcase the Vietnamese knack for slow-cooking meats, I have included a handful of my favorite stews and *kho*.

MEAT TIPS

Because the names for meat cuts vary by country, region, and store, you will be a better cook if you know where a cut comes from on the body of a cow or pig. For example, pork shoulder, which also goes by pork butt, Boston butt, Boston shoulder, and pork shoulder blade, is the meat from the upper portion of a pig's shoulder. Since that part of the animal gets little exercise, the rich, flavorful meat cut from it is perfect for grilling, roasting, and stewing. Such knowledge is the first step to shopping smarter and cooking better. To learn more, ask your butcher questions about the cuts in his or her counter and study professional meat charts (an Internet search for "meat charts" will yield plenty of results) to become better acquainted with what you are buying.

Some cuts used in this book are sold primarily at Chinese and Vietnamese butcher counters. If you have never been to one, here is some advice for your first visit:

- Before you go, decide what you need. For help on deciphering the offerings, review the meat chapter in Bruce Cost's *Asian Ingredients*.

- Go in the morning or on a weekday, when the butchers are more likely to have time to answer questions.

- If you know a little Chinese, Vietnamese, or Spanish, use it. Nowadays, many large Asian markets employ Spanish-speaking butchers. When there is a language barrier, don't hesitate to point at different parts of your body.

- Direct eye contact and a smile go a long way toward getting good service.

- When you find a butcher counter you like, patronize it regularly and you are more likely to get good service every time you shop there.

CARAMELIZED MINCED PORK

Thịt Heo Băm

SIMPLE TO PREPARE, this traditional dish is meant to be eaten in small quantities with lots of rice. The pork cooks slowly in a skillet with salty-sweet seasonings until it starts rendering a little fat and turns reddish brown. The caramelized, crispy results recall the delicious bits that stick to the bottom of the pan when you sear meat. The final addition of scallion lends a touch of color.

You can also eat this minced pork with *cơm nắm* (page 241), cooked rice shaped by hand into compact balls or logs. When I was a child, my father used a wet dish towel to knead hot rice into thick logs, which he then let cool before slicing. My siblings and I would pick up a piece with our fingers, firmly press it against some of the minced pork, and eat it out of hand.

1   In a 12-inch skillet, heat the oil over medium heat. Add the onion and cook gently, stirring, for about 4 minutes, or until fragrant and soft. Add the pork and use a large slotted spoon to stir, poke, and break it into small pieces. Cook, stirring occasionally, for about 4 minutes, or until the meat has lost most of its pink color.

2   Add the fish sauce, caramel sauce, and sugar, increase the heat to medium-high, and continue cooking for 10 to 12 minutes. Stir the mixture frequently and spread it out so it fills the bottom of the pan, giving it plenty of space to cook evenly. If there are large pieces left, take time to mash them into smaller ones. During cooking, the pork will release its juices, start browning, render a little fat, and finally gently fry. It will sizzle and maybe pop.

Halfway through, as the meat darkens, monitor it carefully, stirring rhythmically and constantly to prevent burning. During the last 2 to 4 minutes, the pan will get hotter and the pork will seem lighter and easier to stir around. As the cooking intensifies, the bottom of the skillet will darken with tiny dark brown bits. At this point, lower the heat to medium to steady the browning. Keep stirring to coax the meat into browning a bit more. When it is a beautiful reddish brown, it is done.

Serves 4 with 2 or 3 other dishes

1/4 cup canola or other
   neutral oil
1 small yellow onion,
   finely chopped
1 1/4 pounds ground pork,
   roughly chopped to loosen

2 1/2 tablespoons fish sauce
2 teaspoons Caramel Sauce
   (page 316)
1 teaspoon sugar
2 scallions, green part only,
   chopped

3   Remove from the heat and stir in the scallions. Transfer to a serving dish or shallow bowl, leaving behind the excess fat. Let the meat sit for 5 minutes to darken and crisp up—the flavors will intensify, too—before serving.

MINCED PORK WITH LEMONGRASS AND SHRIMP SAUCE

Thịt Heo Xào Mắm Ruốc

THIS RECIPE is my re-creation of a dish prepared by Le Thang, the chef and owner of the now-defunct Dong Ba restaurant in Little Saigon in Westminster, California. The modest eatery, named after the famous outdoor market in Hue, showcased the rustic dishes of central Vietnam, and although the *mì Quảng* noodle soup and *bánh bèo chén* (rice pancakes steamed in small bowls) were superb, the minced pork was my favorite.

Conceptually, this dish is similar to the recipe for Caramelized Minced Pork (page 131), but it takes on a distinctive central Vietnamese character from the bold use of lemongrass, chile, garlic, and shrimp sauce. Indeed, the generous amount of lemongrass acts as more of a main ingredient than a seasoning, while the chopped shrimp, roasted peanuts, and toasted sesame seeds add layers of flavor and texture. The result is salty, sweet, spicy, rich, and dangerously addictive. Enjoy this dish with plenty of rice, adding some cucumber to each bite for a cool and crunchy contrast.

1 In a 12-inch skillet, heat the oil and red chile flakes over medium heat. When the oil becomes fragrant and pale orange, add the garlic and sauté for about 30 seconds, or until aromatic. Add the pork and use a large slotted spoon to stir, poke, and break it into small pieces. Cook, stirring occasionally, for about 2 minutes, or until the meat has lost most of its pink color.

2 Add the shrimp and lemongrass and give the mixture a big stir to incorporate. Sprinkle in the sugar, pour in the shrimp sauce, and let the mixture cook for 10 to 12 minutes. Stir it frequently and splash in some water whenever the skillet seems dry or if caramelized bits are sticking to the bottom. You want an intensely spicy, salty flavor, so don't add too much water. The mixture should gently sizzle as it cooks. This dish is done when the pork has turned reddish brown.

3 Remove from the heat and stir in the peanuts. Transfer to a serving plate or shallow bowl and sprinkle on the sesame seeds. Garnish with the cucumber slices or place them alongside, and then serve.

Serves 4 to 6 with 2 or 3 other dishes

¼ cup canola or other neutral oil

1 teaspoon dried red chile flakes

4 large cloves garlic, minced

½ pound ground pork, coarsely chopped to loosen

12 medium shrimp, peeled, deveined, and cut into pea-sized pieces

3 hefty or 5 medium stalks lemongrass, trimmed and minced (about 1 cup)

4 teaspoons sugar

2 tablespoons fine shrimp sauce diluted with ¼ cup water

2 tablespoons unsalted roasted peanuts, coarsely chopped

1 teaspoon sesame seeds, toasted (page 332)

1 small English cucumber or 2 pickling (Kirby) cucumbers, halved lengthwise, seeded, and thinly sliced

PAN-SEARED TOMATOES STUFFED WITH PORK

Cà Tô-Mát Farci

SEVENTY-FIVE YEARS of French domination left many influences in the Viet kitchen. Because I grew up eating these stuffed tomatoes on a regular basis, it never crossed my mind that they were adapted from a traditional French idea. It should have: *farci* means "stuffed" in French and *tô-mát* is a Vietnamese transliteration of the French *tomate*.

My edition of *Larousse Gastronomique* offers nine recipes for stuffing tomatoes. Here's a tenth, flavored with a shot of fish sauce, of course. As a hybrid dish, these savory, slightly tangy tomatoes can be enjoyed with chopsticks as part of a traditional Viet dinner or with knife and fork as part of a Western-style meal. For the best results, select firm, slightly underripe tomatoes that will hold their shape nicely after cooking.

1   Trim off the crust from the bread, put the bread in a small bowl, and cover with water. While the bread softens, prepare the tomatoes for stuffing. Halve each tomato crosswise. Seed the tomato halves (see page 152), then use a teaspoon to remove the meaty insides to create a tomato cup; remember to be gentle near the stem. Reserve the insides for another use, such as Tomato Egg Drop Soup (page 59).

2   To make the stuffing, drain the bread and squeeze firmly to extract excess liquid. In a bowl, combine the bread, pork, onion, garlic, fish sauce, salt, and pepper. Mix thoroughly with a fork and then divide into 8 roughly equal portions. Blot the inside of each tomato cup with a paper towel to remove excess moisture. Stuff each tomato cup, pressing gently to ensure that the stuffing reaches all the crevices. Mound the stuffing a bit, if necessary.

3   In a 12-inch skillet, heat the oil over medium-high heat. Place each tomato cup, skin side down, in the skillet. Cover with a lid or piece of aluminum foil and cook for 5 minutes to brown the tomatoes and begin cooking the filling.

continued

Serves 4 to 6 with 2 or 3 other dishes

1 slice white bread, preferably from a rustic country loaf

4 slightly underripe tomatoes, each about 3 inches in diameter

1 pound ground pork

1/2 small yellow onion, minced

1 clove garlic, minced

2 teaspoons fish sauce

1/2 teaspoon salt

1/4 teaspoon black pepper

3 tablespoons canola or other neutral oil

4 Uncover the skillet and be ready for a little drama. Using 2 spatulas, carefully turn each cup over, stuffing side down. (Expect a dark brown circle in the center of the tomato where it was frying. It's okay if the skin breaks.) Lower the heat to medium and cook, uncovered, for 10 to 12 minutes; use a splatter guard, if needed. After 5 minutes, check the stuffing side to see if it is browning too quickly, lowering the flame if necessary. You want a gentle sizzle. When the tomatoes show signs of collapse and there is some wrinkling in the skin, they are done.

5 Use a spatula to transfer the cups to a platter, placing them stuffing side down for an attractive presentation, then serve. Advise diners to use a spoon or knife to break each cup into smaller manageable pieces for easy eating.

NOTE

For an extra treat, make "dirty" rice by sautéing some cooked rice in the oil that remains from cooking the tomatoes. This works best if the tomatoes were seared in a nonstick skillet.

COTTON PORK

Thịt Ruốc Bông

IN THE VIET KITCHEN, preserved dried meats include not only Chinese sausages and jerky, but also these fine, salty pork shreds, named for their resemblance to cotton fibers. Mixed into a bowl of hot rice (add a pat of butter for richness) or creamy rice soup (page 67), the chewy shreds add savory depth to otherwise plain foods. They also turn up tucked into baguette sandwiches (page 34) or sprinkled atop rice crepe rolls (page 270).

You may buy *thịt ruốc bông* in tubs at Viet delis and Chinese markets (called pork *sung* or pork *fu* in Chinese), but I prefer to make my own. That way, there is no MSG and I know that quality ingredients were used. Eaten a little at a time, a batch lasts months. Use boneless pork loin that has been trimmed of any pearlescent silver skin and fat; Chinese markets often sell such well-trimmed cuts. Or, you can purchase a boneless center-cut pork loin roast, cut and trim the center portion, and reserve the balance for another use.

Makes about 3 cups (about 7 ounces)

2 pieces center-cut boneless
    pork loin, each 2 inches
    thick and about 1¼ pounds
    total, well trimmed (about 1
    pound total after trimming)

3½ tablespoons fish sauce
2½ tablespoons water

1 Select a saucepan in which the pork will fit snugly in a single layer. Put the pork in the pan, add the fish sauce and water, place over medium heat, and bring to a simmer. Cover, lower the heat to a gentle simmer, and cook for 18 minutes. Periodically rotate the meat so that it cooks evenly. Although plumes of steam will eventually shoot from under the lid, the simmering should never be so vigorous that the lid rattles. (A vigorous simmer will toughen the meat and make it difficult to shred.) If it does, adjust the heat. When done, the pork should yield a little when pressed in the center. Transfer the meat to a plate and let cool for 20 minutes. Reserve the cooking liquid.

2 Put a heavy-bottomed 12-inch nonstick skillet near your work area. Use your fingers to pry and tear the pork along the grain into jagged pieces ¼ to ½ inch thick. To form the shreds, work with 1 piece of pork at a time and cover the rest of the pieces with plastic wrap or an inverted bowl to keep them moist and soft. Tear the piece apart, using your fingers and nails to separate it into the finest, longest shreds possible—they'll resemble fine wood shavings—dropping the shreds into the skillet as you work. If a piece feels particularly hard, squeeze it between your fingers to crush the fibers. The resulting pile of white shreds will feel damp. Strain the reserved cooking liquid onto the meat and stir to combine.

3 To dry the pork, heat the skillet over medium-low heat. When you hear a gentle sizzle, use a wooden spoon to stir and then spread out the meat to fill the skillet bottom. Let the meat dry for a few minutes and stir and spread again. Repeat this process to help the pork dry with minimal browning. The meat is done when it makes little noise in the skillet, looks fuzzy and stringy, and appears dry but remains slightly damp (like a well-wrung dish towel). A little steam may still rise from the skillet. This process will take 18 to 20 minutes total. Avoid overdrying the shreds, which will cause them to break later.

4 Remove from the heat and let cool completely. Transfer the shredded pork to an airtight container and place in the refrigerator, where it keep for up to about 3 months. Or, you may freeze it for up to 6 months. Bring to room temperature before eating.

PAN-SEARED BEEF STEAKS

Thịt Bò Bít-Tết

I OFTEN PAN-SEAR STEAKS Vietnamese style, with lots of garlic, black pepper, and Maggi Seasoning sauce, a favorite condiment of the Vietnamese. Thinly slice the steaks so guests may help themselves with chopsticks, plus the juices released are delicious mixed into a bowl of rice. Or, make the steaks part of a Western knife-and-fork meal (*bít-tết* is the Viet transliteration of the French *bifteck*) and serve with crispy fried potatoes instead of rice (see Stir-Fried Beef with Crispy Fried Potatoes, page 140, for guidance on cooking the potatoes).

1 Trim the steaks of any gristle. If you are using top sirloin, cut into 4 steaks of roughly equal size. To make the marinade, in a shallow bowl large enough to accommodate the steaks, combine the garlic, pepper, Maggi sauce, and oil and mix well. Add the steaks and use your fingers to coat all sides. Set aside for 30 minutes, turning the steaks over after 15 minutes.

2 Heat a 12-inch heavy-bottomed or cast-iron skillet over medium heat until hot. To test if it is ready, flick a drop of water into it. It should immediately dance and then evaporate. Add the steaks and let them cook, undisturbed, for 6 minutes. The steaks should be well browned on the underside. Use tongs to turn the steaks over. Cook them on the second side, undisturbed, for another 4 minutes for rare, 5 minutes for medium-rare, and 6 minutes for medium. If you are unsure about the doneness of the meat, nick a steak with the sharp point of a paring knife and check the color.

3 Transfer the steaks to a plate and tent loosely with aluminum foil. Let rest for 5 minutes before thinly slicing across the grain. Arrange the slices on a platter and include the juices, too. Serve immediately.

Serves 4 to 6 with 2 or 3 other dishes

4 New York strip (top loin) or tri-tip (bottom sirloin) steaks, each 8 to 10 ounces and about 1 inch thick, or 2 to 2 1/2 pounds top sirloin steak, about 1 inch thick

MARINADE

4 large cloves garlic, minced

3/4 teaspoon black pepper

3 tablespoons Maggi Seasoning sauce, preferably Chinese made, or light (regular) soy sauce

3 tablespoons canola or other neutral oil

BEEF STIR-FRIED WITH CAULIFLOWER

Thịt Bò Xào Bông Cải

IN CLASSIC STIR-FRIES such as this one, beef, a special-occasion meat in Vietnam, is paired with a vegetable that is equally prized and costly. Here, it is cauliflower, traditionally considered a luxury vegetable in Vietnam because it used to be grown only in the cool areas around Dalat. To allow these precious ingredients to shine, they are treated simply with little sauce and only a few other ingredients.

Taking a cue from Chinese cooks, I use flank steak for stir-frying. Cut across the grain into small pieces, it cooks up to an inimitable tenderness. To complement the beef, I select cauliflower that tastes sweet, looks dense, and feels heavy for its size.

Serves 2 to 3 as a main dish, or 4 to 6 with 2 or 3 other dishes

Beef Stir-Fry Marinade
(page 319)

3/4 pound flank steak, cut
across the grain into strips
about 3 inches long, 1/4
inch thick

3 cups small cauliflower florets,
about 2 inches long and
1 inch wide at the bud end

2 tablespoons canola or
other neutral oil

1/2 small yellow onion, sliced
lengthwise 1/2 inch thick

2 cloves garlic, finely chopped

Black pepper

3 or 4 cilantro sprigs

1   In a bowl, combine the marinade and beef and mix well. Set aside to marinate while you ready the other ingredients.

2   Bring a large saucepan of salted water to a boil. Add the cauliflower and parboil for 1 minute, or until crisp tender. Drain and flush with cold water to cool quickly.

3   In a wok or large skillet, heat 1 tablespoon of the oil over medium-high heat until hot but not smoking. Add the onion and stir-fry for about 30 seconds, or until fragrant. Add the garlic and stir-fry for about 15 seconds, or until aromatic. To prevent the onion and garlic from getting stuck under the beef and charring, bank them on one side of the pan. Raise the heat to high and add the beef, spreading it out into a single layer. Let it cook, undisturbed, for about 1 minute. When the beef begins to brown, use a spatula to flip and stir-fry it, incorporating the onion and garlic, for another 1 to 2 minutes, or until the beef is still slightly rare. Transfer to a plate.

4   Add the remaining 1 tablespoon oil to the pan. When it is hot, add the cauliflower and stir-fry for about 1 minute, or until heated through. Return the beef, onion, and garlic, along with any juices, to the pan and stir-fry quickly to combine. If the ingredients start to look dry, splash in a little water and cook until it evaporates. This hydrates and removes bits sticking to the bottom. Continue stir-frying to heat and finish cooking the beef, splashing in more water if needed. When the beef no longer shows signs of rareness, after about 1 minute, it is done.

5   Transfer the beef and cauliflower to a serving plate, top with a generous sprinkle of pepper, and garnish with the cilantro. Serve immediately.

BEEF STIR-FRIED WITH CHINESE CELERY

Thịt Bò Xào Cần Tàu

CHINESE CELERY has a wonderfully intense and rather wild flavor when eaten raw, which explains why it is always cooked before serving, as in this simple stir-fry. It looks like pencil-thin stems of Western celery with roots attached, and in a bunch, it could be mistaken for Italian parsley because the leaves are similar. At a Chinese or Viet market, choose Chinese celery that looks crisp and fresh (check the roots) and use it within a couple of days of purchase.

1   In a bowl, combine the marinade and beef and mix well with chopsticks or your fingers. Set aside to marinate while you ready the other ingredients.

2   Trim off the celery roots and then use your fingers to snap off some of the large leaves at the top. (I usually leave about half the leaves). Cut the stems into 2-inch lengths. Put the stems into a colander and rinse thoroughly. Bits of dirt are often stuck in the hollows. Drain well. The celery cooks easily in the stir-frying, so there is no need to parboil it first.

3   In a wok or large skillet, heat 1 tablespoon of the oil over medium-high heat until hot but not smoking. Add the onion and stir-fry for about 30 seconds, or until fragrant. Add the garlic and stir-fry for about 15 seconds, or until aromatic. To prevent the onion and garlic from getting stuck under the beef and charring, bank them on one side of the pan. Increase the heat to high and add the beef, spreading it out into a single layer. Let it cook, undisturbed, for about 1 minute. When the beef begins to brown, use a spatula to flip and stir-fry it, incorporating the onion and garlic, for another 1 to 2 minutes, or until the beef is still slightly rare. Transfer to a plate.

4   Add the remaining 1 tablespoon oil to the pan. When it is hot, add the celery and stir-fry for about 3 minutes, or until

Serves 2 to 3 as a main dish, or 4 to 6 with 2 or 3 other dishes

Beef Stir-Fry Marinade (page 319)	1 pound (about 2 bunches) Chinese celery
3/4 pound flank steak, cut across the grain into strips about 3 inches long, 3/4 inch wide, and a scant 1/4 inch thick	2 tablespoons canola or other neutral oil
	1/2 small yellow onion, sliced lengthwise 1/2 inch thick
	3 cloves garlic, finely chopped
	Black pepper

the celery has softened and collapsed to about one-third of its original volume. Return the beef, onion, and garlic, along with any juices, to the pan and stir-fry quickly to combine. (Unless the celery is bone-dry, you won't need to splash in any water; the celery tends to weep a bit.) Continue stir-frying to heat and finish cooking the beef. When the beef no longer shows signs of rareness, after about 1 minute, it is done.

5   Transfer the beef and celery to a serving plate and top with a generous sprinkle of pepper. Serve immediately.

STIR-FRIED BEEF WITH CRISPY FRIED POTATOES

Thịt Bò Xào Khoai Tây Chiên

THIS IS A FINE EXAMPLE of a Vietnamese hybrid dish. In many Viet cookbooks, the prescribed method for cooking potatoes is the double-fry approach (a Belgian technique introduced by the French), which yields nongreasy potatoes that are crispy on the outside and tender on the inside. Atop the perfectly fried potatoes is a mound of stir-fried beef, the juices of which penetrate the potatoes to give them great savoriness. Enjoy this East-meets-West dish as is, with a boiled green vegetable or green salad to round out the meal. Or, treat it like a stir-fry and eat it with rice (as I like to) as part of a traditional Viet meal.

1 To remove excess starch from the potatoes, put the slices in a large bowl and fill with cold water. Stir the potatoes with your hand and pour out the cloudy water, as if you are rinsing rice. Repeat until the water is clear. Add enough water to cover the potatoes by 1 inch. Add a tray of ice cubes and refrigerate for at least 30 minutes or for up to several hours. The colder the potatoes are, the better their interiors will fry.

2 Line a baking sheet with a triple layer of paper towels and place next to the stove. Pour oil to a depth of 1¹/₂ inches into a 5-quart Dutch oven and heat over medium heat to 325°F on a deep-frying thermometer. (If you don't have a thermometer, stand a dry bamboo chopstick in the oil; if small bubbles gather on the surface around the chopstick in a few seconds, the oil is ready.)

3 While the oil heats, drain the potatoes, discarding any unmelted ice cubes. Blot the potatoes thoroughly dry with paper towels or lint-free dish towels. Set the potatoes near the stove. In a bowl, combine the marinade and beef and mix well with chopsticks or your fingers. Set aside to marinate while you fry the potatoes.

Serves 2 or 3 as a main dish, or 4 to 6 with 2 or 3 other dishes

4 russet potatoes, about
  ¹/₂ pound each, peeled,
  halved lengthwise, and
  cut into ¹/₄-inch-thick half
  circles
Corn oil or canola oil for deep-
  frying, plus 1 tablespoon
  for stir-frying
Beef Stir-Fry Marinade
  (page 319)
³/₄ pound flank steak, cut
  across the grain into strips
  about 3 inches long,
  ³/₄ inch wide, and a scant
  ¹/₄ inch thick

Salt
¹/₂ small yellow onion, sliced
  lengthwise ¹/₂-inch thick
2 cloves garlic, finely chopped
Black pepper
3 or 4 sprigs cilantro

4   When the oil is ready, increase the heat to medium-high. (The cold potatoes will cause the oil temperature to drop dramatically.) Carefully add the potatoes to the oil, which will suddenly boil and sound like falling rain. As the potatoes fry, use a skimmer or spoon to stir them gently in the oil. When they start to turn gold, after about 8 minutes, use the skimmer to transfer them to the baking sheet, spreading them out to drain. Let them cool for at least 10 minutes before refrying. (You may let them sit for up to 3 hours, in which case you must cover and refrigerate the marinating beef and then return it to room temperature before stir-frying.)

5   For the second frying, reheat the oil over medium-high heat to 350°F. Pick up the potatoes by the triple layer of paper towels and use your hand to scoot them off into the oil. Fry, stirring frequently, for 4 to 6 minutes, or until crispy and golden brown. Meanwhile, line the baking sheet with new paper towels. Using the skimmer, transfer the finished potatoes to the paper-lined baking sheet, spreading them out to drain. Lightly salt the potatoes while they are hot and transfer to a platter.

6   In a wok or large skillet, heat the 1 tablespoon oil over medium-high heat until hot but not smoking. Add the onion and stir-fry for about 30 seconds, or until fragrant. Add the garlic and stir-fry for about 15 seconds, or until aromatic. To prevent the onion and garlic from getting stuck under the beef and charring, bank them on one side of the pan. Increase the heat to high and add the beef, spreading it out into a single layer. Let it cook, undisturbed, for about 1 minute. When the beef begins to brown, use a spatula to flip and stir-fry it, incorporating the onion and garlic, for another 2 to 3 minutes, or until the beef no longer looks rare and is done.

7   Transfer the beef, onion, and garlic to the platter holding the potatoes, centering it on top of the potatoes and leaving a golden rim for an attractive presentation. Sprinkle with pepper and garnish with the cilantro. Serve immediately.

CHAR SIU PORK

Thịt Xá Xíu

WHEN MY NIECES AND NEPHEWS were toddlers, they loved this oven-roasted pork, tinged with char. They requested it whenever they visited grandma's house, and she would cut it into tiny pieces and serve it atop sticky rice. I share their enthusiasm but savor the pork in many other ways, too: with regular rice, as a filling in steamed *bao* (page 265), stuffed into baguette sandwiches (page 34), added to wonton noodle soup (page 222), and as part of moon cake filling (page 300).

A mainstay of Chinese barbecue shops and a Viet favorite, *xá xíu* is the Vietnamese transliteration of the Cantonese *char siu* (*thịt* means meat.) To make the pork look appetizing, it is often prepared with food coloring, sold by the bottle at most Viet markets. But chemical coloring isn't needed here. The marinade imparts an appealing reddish brown.

1 Quarter the pork lengthwise into strips about 6 inches long and 1 1/2 inches thick. If there are odd-sized pieces, they should be of the same thickness.

2 To make the marinade, in a large bowl, whisk together the garlic, sugar, five-spice powder, hoisin sauce, honey, wine, light and dark soy sauces, and sesame oil. Add the pork and use a spatula or tongs to coat evenly. Cover with plastic wrap and refrigerate for 6 to 8 hours, turning the pork 2 or 3 times.

3 Remove the pork from the refrigerator 45 minutes before cooking. Position a rack in the upper third of the oven and preheat to 475°F. Line a baking sheet with aluminum foil and place a flat roasting rack on the pan. Put the pork on the rack, spacing the pieces 1 inch apart. Reserve the marinade.

4 Roast, basting with the marinade every 10 minutes, for 30 to 35 minutes. To baste, use tongs to pick up each piece and roll it in the marinade before returning it to the rack, turning the pork over each time. The pork is done when it looks glazed, is slightly charred, and most important, registers about 145°F on an instant-read thermometer. Remove from the oven.

Makes about 1 1/2 pounds, to serve 4 to 6 with
    2 or 3 other dishes

2 1/3 pounds boneless pork
    shoulder, well trimmed
    (about 2 pounds after
    trimming)

MARINADE
2 cloves garlic, minced
2 tablespoons sugar
1/2 teaspoon Chinese
    five-spice powder

3 tablespoons hoisin sauce
2 tablespoons honey
1 1/2 tablespoons Shaoxing rice
    wine or dry sherry
2 tablespoons light (regular)
    soy sauce
1 tablespoon dark (black)
    soy sauce
2 teaspoons sesame oil

5 Let the meat rest for 10 minutes to finish cooking and seal in the juices. Thinly slice the pork across the grain and serve warm or at room temperature. Or, let it cool completely, wrap tightly, and freeze for up to 3 months. This pork reheats well in a microwave oven.

GRILLED GARLICKY FIVE-SPICE PORK STEAKS

Thịt Heo Nướng Ngũ Vị Hương

THE MENU AT VIETNAMESE RESTAURANTS in the United States often includes an inexpensive, homey rice plate with grilled pork chops flavored with Chinese five-spice powder, garlic, and onion. Unfortunately, I have often found the dish disappointing, with the rib chops dry and thin. Even with a knife and fork, the meat—typically broiled, rather than the advertised grilled—is hard to cut.

After a number of dissatisfying rice plates, I decided to make the pork at home. To avoid dry meat, I opted for pork shoulder steaks. The slightly fatty, flavorful steaks turned out to be perfect for absorbing the bold marinade and remained moist after grilling. Sliced up before serving, the meat is easily managed with chopsticks, too, and I include a dipping sauce for extra flavor. Serve the pork with rice and a salad or a stir-fried or sautéed vegetable for a light meal. Add a soup such as Opo Squash Soup (page 60) and you have a traditional Vietnamese menu. Use any leftovers for baguette sandwiches (page 34) or Mixed Rice (page 245).

1 If the pork steaks are large, cut them into pieces about the size of your hand. To make the marinade, in a baking dish or shallow bowl large enough to accommodate the steaks, combine the garlic, shallot, five-spice powder, oil, fish sauce, salt, sugar, and pepper and mix well. Add the steaks and use your fingers to coat all the surfaces well. Cover with plastic wrap and refrigerate for at least 2 hours or up to 8 hours for the best flavor.

2 Remove the pork from the refrigerator 30 minutes before cooking. Prepare a medium charcoal fire (you can hold your hand over the rack for only 4 to 5 seconds) or preheat a gas grill to medium.

Grill the steaks, turning once, for 5 to 7 minutes on each side, or until browned and a little charred on the edges.

3 Transfer the steaks to a plate, cover with foil, and let rest for 10 minutes before slicing. Provide each diner with an individual dish for the dipping sauce.

Serves 4 to 6 with 2 or 3 other dishes

2 1/2 pounds bone-in or boneless pork shoulder (blade) steaks, each about 1/2 inch thick

MARINADE
5 cloves garlic, finely minced
1 large shallot, minced (about 1/3 cup)
1 1/4 teaspoons Chinese five-spice powder
2 tablespoons canola or other neutral oil
1 tablespoon fish sauce
1/2 teaspoon salt
3/4 teaspoon sugar
1/4 teaspoon black pepper

1/3 cup Simple Dipping Sauce (page 309)

GRILLED LEMONGRASS PORK RIBLETS

Sườn Nướng Xả

THESE ADDICTIVE BITE-SIZED RIBLETS are perfumed by lemongrass, and the addition of caramel sauce to the marinade—a trick of the trade often used by food vendors in Vietnam—imparts deep color and flavor. Honey is a fine substitute that results in a slightly sweeter finish. Removing the tough membrane from the underside of the rack (a technique borrowed from American barbecue masters) and a long marinade yield riblets that are chewy-tender.

The rack of spareribs must be cut through the bone into long strips. Don't attempt this yourself. Instead, ask your butcher to do it. Serve the riblets as an appetizer or with rice for a satisfying meal. For a Viet twist on the classic American barbecue, pair the ribs with Grilled Corn with Scallion Oil (page 183) and a green salad or Russian Beet, Potato, and Carrot Salad (page 186).

1   Starting from one end, remove the tough white membrane from the underside of each rib strip: Slide the tip of a knife underneath the membrane that lies between 2 rib bones, lift it up and cut it. Then, use a pair of pliers or a dish towel to grab the membrane and pull it away from the ribs. Several pulls may be required to remove it all. Trim any small membrane patches that remain with a knife. When done, remove as much fat from the rib strips as you like. Cut each strip between the bones or cartilage into individual riblets.

2   To make the marinade, combine the garlic, shallot, brown sugar, and pepper in a mortar and pound to a rough paste. (Or, use an electric mini-chopper.) Transfer to a large bowl and add the caramel sauce, soy sauce, fish sauce, oil, and lemongrass, mixing well. Add the riblets to the marinade and mix well to coat all surfaces. Your hand is the best tool for this. Cover with plastic wrap and refrigerate for 24 hours.

3   Thirty minutes before cooking, remove the bowl from the refrigerator. For the best flavor, grill the riblets. Prepare a medium charcoal fire (you can hold your hand over the rack for only 4 to 5 seconds) or preheat a gas grill to medium.

continued

Serves 8 to 10 as an appetizer, or 4 to 6 with 2 or 3 other dishes

3¹/2 to 4 pounds meaty pork spareribs, cut crosswise through the bone into long strips about 2 inches wide

MARINADE
3 cloves garlic, chopped
1 large shallot, chopped (about ¹/3 cup)
1 tablespoon light brown sugar
¹/2 teaspoon black pepper
2 tablespoons Caramel Sauce (page 316) or honey
2 tablespoons light (regular) soy sauce
1 tablespoon fish sauce

2 tablespoons canola or other neutral oil
2 medium or 1 hefty stalk lemongrass, trimmed and minced (about 6 tablespoons)

1 small English cucumber or 2 pickling (Kirby) cucumbers, halved lengthwise and sliced on the diagonal
1 or 2 Thai or serrano chiles, thinly sliced
Light (regular) soy sauce for serving

Alternatively, position a rack in the upper third of the oven and preheat to 475°F. Arrange the riblets on an aluminum foil–lined baking sheet for roasting. (The riblets taste nearly as good oven roasted as they do grilled.)

4 Arrange the riblets on the grill rack, or slip the baking sheet into the oven. Cook for 12 to 15 minutes, or until browned and a little charred on the edges. Extra-thick pieces will require a little more time. Monitor the ribs closely as they cook, turning them over or moving them around (if you are grilling) to ensure even cooking and prevent burning.

5 Transfer the riblets to a serving platter. Garnish with the cucumber or serve it alongside. At the table, let diners craft their own dipping sauce by muddling some chiles in a little soy sauce. Feel free to use fingers for eating.

PORK AND EGGS SIMMERED IN COCONUT JUICE AND CARAMEL SAUCE

Thịt Heo Kho Trứng

A CLASSIC SOUTHERN *KHO*, this combination of pork and eggs spotlights the importance of texture in Vietnamese cooking. The cut used here is pork leg (fresh ham), purchased and cooked with the skin (rind) attached. The meat is slowly simmered until tender, with a slight dryness offset by the unctuous skin and fat. The eggs develop an interesting contrast of chewy white and buttery yolk, while the sauce made from coconut juice is softly sweet.

You may need to abandon your fear of fat when preparing this dish. It is important to use a piece of pork leg with its fat and skin intact, or the meat will be dry and lack richness. The cut is widely available at Viet and Chinese markets and sometimes at regular supermarkets. The meatier upper butt of the leg (the portion typically used for smoked hams) is best, rather than the lower shank. At the table, you may eat just the meat, using chopsticks to detach and set aside the unwanted bits. Crunchy Pickled Bean Sprout Salad (page 193) is a traditional accompaniment, along with plenty of rice.

Viet cooks vary the size and type (duck or chicken) of eggs they use. I prefer medium chicken eggs. Canned coconut juice works in place of the liquid inside a fresh, young coconut. Choose a brand with the least amount of sugar for the best flavor.

Serves 4 to 6 with 2 or 3 other dishes

1¹/₂ pounds boneless pork
    leg with skin and fat
¹/₄ cup Caramel Sauce
    (page 316)
3 tablespoons fish sauce
1 tablespoon sugar

6 medium eggs, hard boiled
    and peeled
1¹/₂ cups canned coconut
    juice, strained of bits of
    coconut meat

1   Examine the pork skin for any stray hairs and use a sharp knife to scrape and remove any you find. Cut the meat into long chunks about 1 inch thick and 2 to 3 inches long. Each piece should have some fat and skin attached. Put the pork into a 3- or 4-quart saucepan and add the caramel sauce, fish sauce, and sugar. Give everything a stir with a rubber spatula or spoon to coat the meat with the seasonings. Set aside to marinate for 45 minutes, turning the meat every 15 minutes.

2   Cover the pan and bring to a simmer over medium heat. Uncover and stir to ensure that each piece of meat is well exposed to the bubbling seasonings. Re-cover and simmer for 5 minutes, or until the pork is a gorgeous golden brown.

3   Add the eggs, coconut juice, and water just to cover. Bring to a boil, uncovered, over medium-high heat. Use a spoon to skim and discard any scum that rises to the surface and then lower the heat to a simmer. Cover partially and cook for 1¹/₄ hours, rotating the pork and eggs occasionally to ensure that they cook evenly. Uncover and continue simmering for 15 minutes after uncovering, or until the meat is tender when pierced with the tip of a knife and the sauce is reduced by half.

4   Remove from the heat and let stand for a few minutes so that the fat collects on the surface, then use a ladle or spoon to skim it off. (Or, let cool, cover, and refrigerate overnight to congeal the fat, making the task much easier; reheat before continuing.) Return to a simmer and taste the sauce. Add extra fish sauce and/or sugar to create a deeper savory, sweet flavor, or water to lighten the flavor.

5   To serve, transfer the pork, whole eggs, and sauce to a shallow bowl. Let diners halve the eggs as they eat them, using their soup spoon (or provide a knife) to cut them. Or, halve the eggs in the kitchen and serve the pork in a large, deep dish with the halved eggs rimming the meat.

NOTE

You may use a medium-sized clay pot (2¹/₂ to 3 quart) for cooking this *kho*. For details on clay pot cooking, see page 108.

A *KHO* FOR EVERY OCCASION

This chapter, like the chapters on poultry and seafood, includes recipes for *kho*, savory-sweet dishes in which meat, poultry, seafood, or tofu is usually simmered in a caramel-based sauce. The reddish brown dishes that result are deeply flavored and perfect with rice. They are traditionally cooked in clay pots, which is why the *kho* recipes include tips on preparing them in the earthenware vessels.

Quick *kho* preparations, such as the ones that feature chicken (page 82) and shrimp (page 105), are ideal when you don't have much time to put a meal on the table. Others, like the three recipes in this chapter, require long simmering to yield tender, succulent meat, and while certainly fit for everyday eating, are also served on special occasions. For example, a meal during Tet, the Vietnamese Lunar New Year celebration and the most important holiday of the year, would be incomplete without at least one *kho*. Southerners like to simmer pork with eggs, as is done here. Raised by northerners, I always offer two *kho* for Tet: one with pork riblets and the other with beef flank and ginger (pages 148 and 149, respectively). All of them deliver a true taste of Vietnam.

PORK RIBLETS SIMMERED IN CARAMEL SAUCE

Sườn Kho

THIS *KHO* involves a little more work than the pork and eggs *kho* on page 146. You must first marinate the meat and then sear it before it settles into its long simmer. The extra steps produce a rich, roasty undercurrent of flavor that permeates the dish.

These riblets have special meaning for my mom because her family prepared them for their month-long Tet festivities. An entire pig was slaughtered for the celebration, and the ribs were used in this *kho*. Since it reheats well, it is the perfect make-ahead dish for the Lunar New Year, a time when everyone is supposed to relax, rather than slave in the kitchen. When purchasing the ribs, remember to ask the butcher to cut them into strips for. For the best flavor, sear the riblets on a grill.

1 Cut each rib strip between the bones or cartilage into individual riblets. In a large bowl, combine the onion, sugar, pepper, and 3 tablespoons of the fish sauce and mix well. Add the riblets and toss to coat evenly. Cover with plastic wrap and refrigerate for at least 2 hours or up to overnight.

2 Remove the bowl from the refrigerator about 45 minutes before searing. Prepare a hot charcoal fire (you can hold your hand over the rack for only 2 to 3 seconds) or preheat a gas grill to high. Remove the riblets from the marinade, reserving the marinade, and sear on the grill, turning as needed, for about 10 minutes total.

Alternatively, broil the riblets on a foil-lined baking sheet for about 8 minutes on each side, or until lightly charred.

3 Transfer the seared riblets, the reserved marinade, and any cooking juices to a 5-quart Dutch oven and add the remaining 3 tablespoons fish sauce, the caramel sauce, and water almost to cover. Bring to a boil over medium-high heat. Adjust the heat to a simmer, cover, and cook for 45 minutes. Uncover and adjust the heat so that the riblets simmer vigorously. Cook for about 20 minutes, or until the riblets are tender when pierced with a knife. The sauce will have reduced, but there will still be plenty.

Serves 4 to 6 with 2 or 3 other dishes

3 pounds meaty pork spareribs, cut crosswise through the bone into long strips 1½ to 2 inches wide	1 teaspoon black pepper
	6 tablespoons fish sauce
	6 tablespoons Caramel Sauce (page 316)
½ large yellow onion, minced	2 scallions, green part only, chopped
1 tablespoon sugar	

4 Remove from the heat and let stand for a few minutes so that the fat collects on the surface, then skim it off. Return to a simmer and taste the sauce. Add extra fish sauce to create a deeper savory flavor, or water to lighten it. Transfer the riblets and sauce to a bowl. Sprinkle the scallion on top and serve.

NOTE

You may use a medium-sized clay pot (2½ to 3 quart) for cooking this *kho*. For details on clay pot cooking, see page 108.

BEEF FLANK AND GINGER SIMMERED IN CARAMEL SAUCE

Thịt Bò Kho Gừng

HERE'S A WONDERFUL *KHO* that transforms an unusual-looking but exceptionally flavorful beef cut into elegant, tasty morsels. The cut, known as rough flank (a.k.a. beef *nạm* or beef plate), is a favorite for stewing and other types of long cooking. You have probably eaten slices of it in restaurant bowls of *phở*, where it is typically identified as flank (though it is not the same as the flank steak used for stir-fries). It is usually displayed as upright rolls in Chinese and Vietnamese markets; when unrolled, it is long and narrow, with loosely textured meat separated by layers of tough membranes. If you are unfamiliar with the cut, it may appear strange at first, but I urge you to try it. Look for meaty pieces with a minimal amount of membrane. If the cuts are small, buy two pieces, select the choicest parts for this recipe, and save the trimmings for another use, such as *phở* (page 209).

In this recipe, the beef is tied into small rolls that are simmered for hours. It absorbs the seasonings and softens, while still retaining a characteristic slight chewiness. Sliced into beautiful spirals, the meat is presented in a pool of dark, savory sauce. Each intense bite is beefy, bittersweet, salty, and gingery. Enjoy the dish with bowls of hot rice.

1 To form the rolls, first look at the beef closely to figure out how best to cut four 1/2-pound pieces. In general, it is easier to manage pieces 1/2 to 3/4 inch thick and about 5 inches long. If the meat is a single thick piece, use your knife to separate it into 2 pieces, cutting along one of the layers of tough membranes, before dividing again to arrive at 4 pieces. If the meat is in more than 1 piece, the thickness is determined for you.

After cutting the meat, pat each piece dry again with paper towels to make it easier to handle. Roll 1 piece with the grain so that the tough membrane forms the outside of the roll. Use kitchen string to secure the roll at regular intervals along its length. Repeat with the remaining pieces.

2 Select a saucepan in which the rolls will fit snugly in a single layer. Arrange half the ginger coins flat on the bottom. Put the rolls on top. Scatter the remaining ginger coins over the rolls and pour in the fish sauce. Bring to a simmer over medium heat. Cover and cook for 5 minutes to develop the flavors.

continued

Serves 4 to 6 with 2 or 3 other dishes

2 pounds meaty beef rough flank, rinsed and blotted dry with paper towels

Chubby 3-inch piece fresh ginger, peeled and sliced into 1/8-inch-thick coins

3 tablespoons fish sauce

3 tablespoons Caramel Sauce (page 316)

3 Uncover, add the caramel sauce and water to cover, and bring to a boil over medium-high heat. Use a spoon to skim and discard any scum that rises to the surface, then cover, lower the heat to a simmer, and cook for 1 hour. Uncover and continue to cook, adjusting the heat as needed to maintain a simmer, for 1 hour longer, or until the beef is tender. To test for doneness, press your finger against the meat; it should give but feel firm, like the flesh at the base of your thumb. (If making the dish in advance, remove from the heat at this point, let cool, then cover and refrigerate overnight. Remove as much of the fat congealed on top as desired before reheating and continuing.)

4 Transfer the rolls to a plate and set aside to cool until warm and firm, which will make them much easier to slice. Return the sauce to a boil and reduce to about 3/4 cup reddish brown liquid. Skim off some of the fat from the surface (if you haven't refrigerated the dish overnight and skimmed it already) and then taste the sauce to make sure it has a good deep flavor. If it isn't flavorful enough, continue to reduce it. If it is too strong, lighten it with a splash of water.

5 To serve, snip and remove the string from each roll. Slice the rolls into 1/8- to 1/4-inch-thick spirals and arrange on 2 warmed plates. (Because the meat isn't hot when served, warming the plates is important.) Reheat the sauce, if necessary, and then spoon it over the meat. Put the ginger coins in a small separate dish for anyone who wants a sharp, spicy bite. Before serving, check the beef to make sure it is warm. If necessary, pop the plates into a microwave oven to reheat. Serve immediately.

NOTE

If when you cut the rolls, the outer membrane seems leathery and too tough to chew comfortably, remove it or try slicing thinner spirals.

To cook this dish in a clay pot, use a small (1 1/2-quart) Japanese *donabe* about 8 inches wide. For details on clay pot cooking, see page 108.

BEEF STEWED WITH TOMATO, STAR ANISE, AND LEMONGRASS

Bò Kho

THIS STEW IS SO POPULAR that practically every Viet cook has his or her own version. I have read recipes that call for curry powder, annatto seeds, tomato paste, and beer. But this is how my mother learned to make *bò kho* decades ago. Although in Vietnam it is traditionally eaten for breakfast, here in the States it has become lunch or dinner fare in the Vietnamese American community. It may be served in shallow bowls with warm French bread for sopping up the flavorful sauce, or it may be spooned over rice or wide rice noodles (*bánh phở*). The addition of chopped Vietnamese coriander or Thai basil leaves is something that my parents picked up when we lived in Saigon. Also, despite the name, this is not a *kho* dish. Here, *kho* means "to simmer" or "to stew." No caramel sauce is involved.

Traditionalists like to use the boneless beef shank sold at Chinese and Viet markets for this dish, which they cook for hours to yield a chewy-tender result. Once in the States, my family switched to beef chuck, which is flavorful, suited to long cooking, and more readily available.

1   In a bowl, combine the beef, lemongrass, fish sauce, five-spice powder, ginger, brown sugar, and bay leaf. Mix well with chopsticks to coat the beef evenly. Set aside to marinate for 30 minutes.

2   In a heavy-bottomed 5-quart Dutch oven, heat the oil over high heat until hot but not smoking. Working in batches, add the beef and sear on all sides, then transfer to a plate. Each batch should take about 3 minutes. Reserve the lemongrass and bay leaf from the marinade and discard the rest.

3   Lower the heat to medium-low, add the onion, and cook gently, stirring, for 4 to 5 minutes, or until fragrant and soft. Add the tomato and salt and stir to combine. Cover and cook for 12 to 14 minutes, or until the mixture is fragrant and has reduced to a rough paste. Check occasionally to make sure the tomato mixture is not sticking to the bottom of the pan. If it is, stir well and splash in some water.

continued

Serves 4 to 6 as a main course

2 1/3 pounds boneless beef chuck, well trimmed (about 2 pounds after trimming) and cut into 1 1/2-inch chunks

1 hefty stalk lemongrass, loose leaves discarded, cut into 3-inch lengths, and bruised with the broad side of a cleaver or chef's knife

3 tablespoons fish sauce

1 1/2 teaspoons Chinese five-spice powder

2 1/2 tablespoons peeled and minced fresh ginger

1 1/2 teaspoons brown sugar

1 bay leaf

3 tablespoons canola or other neutral oil

1 yellow onion, finely chopped

2 cups peeled, seeded, and chopped fresh tomato or 1 can (14 ounces) crushed tomato

Generous 1/2 teaspoon salt

2 star anise (16 robust points total)

3 cups water

1 pound carrots, peeled and cut into 1-inch chunks

1/4 cup chopped fresh Vietnamese coriander or Thai basil leaves

4   When the paste has formed, add the beef, lemongrass, bay leaf, and star anise, give the contents of the pot a bit stir, and cook, uncovered, for another 5 minutes to allow the flavors to meld and penetrate the beef. Add the water, bring to a boil, cover, lower the heat to a simmer, and cook for 1¼ hours, or until the beef is chewy-tender (a sign that it is close to being done). To test for doneness, press on a piece; it should yield but still feel firm.

5   Add the carrots and return the stew to a simmer, adjusting the heat if needed. Cook, uncovered, for about 30 minutes, or until the carrots and beef are tender. (This stew may be made up to 2 days in advance. Let cool, cover, and refrigerate, then bring to a simmer before continuing.)

6   Just before serving, do a final taste test. Add salt or a shot of fish sauce to intensify the overall flavor. Or, splash in a bit of water to lighten the sauce. Transfer the stew to a serving dish, removing and discarding the lemongrass, bay leaf, and star anise. Garnish with the Vietnamese coriander and serve.

HOW TO SEED TOMATOES

Holding each tomato half over a bowl or the sink, squeeze gently to release the seeds and gelatinous insides. For reluctant seeds, use a finger to loosen them. Then, with a swift shaking motion of the wrist, empty out the seeds.

MOCK TURTLE STEW OF PORK, PLAINTAIN, AND FRIED TOFU

Thịt Heo Nấu Giả Ba Ba

THE VIETNAMESE LOVE EXOTIC MEATS, and when such delicacies are unavailable, they enjoy dishes that mimic the real thing. This northern stew features a stand-in for *ba ba*, a freshwater snapping turtle that thrives in the south, where heavy rains offer it perfect muddy living conditions. Since the turtles are hard to find in the drier, colder north, cooks there add extra pork instead. The original southern stew also calls for pork belly.

Although I've never tasted the real stew, I grew up eating the mock version, which, with its brilliant yellow color, robust flavors, and varied textures, is excellent in its own right. The fried tofu has a meaty consistency, and thick rounds of unripe plaintain (peel included) add interesting starchiness, astringency, and texture. Both ingredients soak up the sauce and complement the savory, rich chunks of pork. While pork shoulder works well, the best way to imitate *ba ba* meat and the classic stew is to use skin-on boneless pork shank (available at Chinese and Viet markets). It provides a nice balance of chewy meat and gelatinous skin to imitate the turtle, while its fat recalls the original pork belly.

The sour cream is a substitute for a tangy fermented rice mash called *mẻ*, a favorite northern Vietnamese ingredient that is scarce in the States. Fresh red perilla and garlic add the final flourishes to a delicious combination of flavors. Serve the stew with plenty of rice.

1 If using pork shank, exam the pork skin for any stray hairs and use a sharp knife to scrape and remove any you find. Regardless of the cut used, cut the pork into 1½- to 2-inch chunks. Transfer to a bowl.

2 In a small bowl, stir together one-third of the onion, the turmeric, shrimp sauce, fish sauce, and sour cream. Pour over the pork and use a rubber spatula to coat the meat well. Set aside to marinate for 45 minutes.

3 Meanwhile, trim both ends of the plantain. Use a vegetable peeler to remove the outermost layer of the peel. A fibrous ⅛-inch-thick layer of peel should remain. Cut the plantain into ¾-inch-thick rounds. Drop the pieces into a saucepan of boiling water and boil for 2 minutes to remove some of the astringency. Drain and pat dry with paper towels.

continued

Serves 4 to 6 with 2 or 3 other dishes

- 1½ to 1¾ pounds boneless pork shoulder, or 1 skin-on boneless pork shank, 1½ to 1¾ pounds
- 1 yellow onion, minced
- 1 tablespoon ground turmeric
- 1½ tablespoons fine shrimp sauce
- 2½ tablespoons fish sauce
- ⅓ cup sour cream, preferably full fat
- 1 unripe plantain, 8 to 10 ounces (see Note)
- 12 to 14 ounces regular or medium-firm tofu (in cakes or 1 block), drained
- Corn or canola oil for deep-frying, plus 2 tablespoons for frying
- 3½ cups water
- 2 cloves garlic, minced
- ½ cup lightly packed fresh red perilla leaves, cut into ¼-inch-wide ribbons

4 Cut the tofu into 1-inch cubes. Put into a colander to drain briefly, then use paper towels to blot any excess moisture. Pour oil to a depth of 1 1/2 inches into a wok or 5-quart Dutch oven and heat over medium-high heat to 350°F on a deep-frying thermometer. (If you don't have a thermometer, stand a dry bamboo chopstick in the oil; if small bubbles immediately gather on the surface around the chopstick, the oil is ready.) Working in batches, gently drop the tofu into the hot oil, which will vigorously foam. The tofu will sink to the bottom and eventually float to the top. As it fries, use a skimmer to push the cubes around to ensure even frying and to separate any that stick together. After 4 to 6 minutes, the cubes should be golden and crispy. Use the skimmer to lift them out of the oil, shaking it over the pan briefly to drain off the excess, and then place on paper towels to drain. Set aside. (You may fry the tofu a few hours in advance; let cool, cover, and leave at room temperature.)

5 To cook the stew, heat the 2 tablespoons oil in a heavy-bottomed 5-quart Dutch oven over medium heat. Add the plantain rounds and sear gently on each side for about 3 minutes total, or until light yellow. Using a slotted spoon, transfer to a plate and set aside. Add the remaining onion and sauté for about 3 minutes, or until fragrant. Add the pork, scraping the marinade into the pan, too. Increase the heat to medium-high and cook, stirring constantly, for about 3 minutes, or until the meat has firmed up and each chunk displays definite shape. Add the water and bring to a boil. Cover, lower the heat to a simmer, and cook for 30 minutes.

6 Add the plantain and continue simmering, covered, for 15 minutes; expect the skin to break away from the plantain. Uncover and use a spoon or ladle to skim away some of the fat floating on the surface. Add the tofu, making sure all the cubes are exposed to the stewing liquid. Adjust the heat to a vigorous simmer and continue to cook, uncovered, for 15 minutes, or until the tofu soaks up the seasonings, the sauce thickens slightly, and the meat is chewy-tender when pierced with the tip of a knife. (The stew may be made up to 2 days in advance. Let cool, cover, and refrigerate, then bring to a simmer before continuing.)

7 Just before serving, taste and adjust the flavors, adding a sprinkle of fish sauce to intensify the taste or water to lighten it. Stir in the garlic and red perilla, saving a few herb ribbons for garnish. Transfer the stew to a shallow serving bowl, garnish with the reserved herb, and serve.

NOTE

Although the herb of choice here is red perilla (*tía tô*), you may substitute 1/4 cup coarsely chopped fresh cilantro. The flavor isn't the same but is still quite good. When shopping for the plantain, select a green fruit for greater authenticity or a greenish yellow–brown one for a less starchy, less astringent result.

6. THE ART OF CHARCUTERIE

Bite into a *bánh mì*, gaze at the refrigerated section of an Asian market, or step inside a Viet deli and you are in the world of Vietnamese charcuterie. An Eastern tradition threaded with Western influences, it includes smooth, thick sausages perfumed by banana leaf, marbled headcheese, pinkish red garlicky pork, dried Chinese sausages, and French-style liver pâtés. Some have the snap of an old-fashioned hot dog, others boast a velvety richness from the addition of diced fatback, and one is crispy from deep-frying. Central elements of Vietnamese culinary tradition, these charcuterie specialties may begin a meal, be featured in a dish, or be used as a garnish.

At the heart of the charcuterie repertoire is *giò*, a versatile meat paste that may be boiled, steamed, fried, roasted, or grilled. Somewhat like French forcemeat, the smooth paste is used to create a multitude of delicious foods, from meatballs to dumplings to sausages. Traditionally the paste is made by hand pounding a still-warm lean pork leg from a freshly killed pig. In the past, this task, which requires rapid movements without stopping, was left to professionals, skilled men of great upper body strength and endurance. (Home cooks lacked the outsized mortar, the physical capability, and the ready access to the meat.) Sitting on a low stool astride the huge stone mortar, the *giò* maker worked on large chunks of pork, initially crushing them with heavy blows from a hardwood dumbbell-shaped pestle. He then would switch to two pestles and rhythmically and quickly transform the meat to a paste. He paused only briefly to gather the meat in the mortar and to add ingredients such as fish sauce and diced pork fat, depending on the intended use of the paste. To ensure that the result was smooth, rather than mealy, and tasty, the pounding had to be steady and even and the seasonings had to be well balanced. Indeed, a professional *giò* maker was regarded as both an athlete and a craftsman.

When French Moulinex food processors arrived in Vietnam in the late 1960s, avid home cooks who could afford the expensive appliances snapped them up for making the paste. Using a machine allowed cooks to marinate the meat and then push a button to transform it into a perfectly smooth mass. But food processors don't incorporate as much air into the mixture as the mortar and pestle do, so a leavening agent, such as baking powder, was added to yield a lighter result. Also, while the pestle merely crushed the muscle fibers, retaining the desired firm texture, the food processor blade cut the fibers, producing an overly soft, mealy texture. This prompted the addition of tapioca or potato starch to stiffen the paste and help it cohere.

Nowadays, the machine method is the standard for Viet cooks abroad, who use it not only for *giò*, but for all their chicken, beef, and seafood pastes as well. When my family left Saigon in 1975, there were *giò* shops that sold machine-made paste and those that sold hand-pounded paste, and recipes recently published in Vietnam still call for a mortar and pestle. A hand-pounded paste takes a lot more work, but it also has a slightly deeper flavor and a heartier texture.

This chapter provides instructions on how to prepare *giò* by machine and by hand, and how to use the paste for a number of popular sausages. I have also included a liver pâté and two cold cuts. The recipes are not particularly difficult, nor do they require long curing times or special equipment. Many people purchase their charcuterie from markets or delis, but I have found that it is always more satisfying—and tastes better—when you make it at home.

RECIPES

MULTIPURPOSE MEAT PASTE

Giò

A CORNERSTONE OF VIETNAMESE COOKING, this smooth meat paste is the most important recipe in the charcuterie repertoire and forms the base of three sausages in this chapter. It is also used to make meatballs (page 86), acts as the binder for Stuffed Snails Steamed with Lemongrass (page 42), and may be shaped into dumplings similar to French quenelles and poached in a quick *canh*-style soup (page 61).

This recipe, which calls for chicken rather than the traditional pork, is my mother's modern American approach to *giò*. Chicken, a luxury meat in Vietnam that is affordable here, is easier to work with and yields a particularly delicately flavored and textured paste. Additionally, chicken breasts and thighs are readily available at supermarkets, while pork leg, the cut typically used, isn't. A recipe for the pork paste appears in the Note that follows.

1 Slice each breast and thigh across the grain into 1/4-inch-thick strips. When cutting the breast tenders, remove and discard the silvery strip of tendon. Keep any visible fat for richness, but trim away any cartilage or sinewy bits, as they won't grind well.

2 To make the marinade, in a bowl large enough to fit the chicken, whisk together the baking powder, tapioca starch, sugar, fish sauce, and oil. Add the chicken and use a rubber spatula to mix well. Cover tightly with plastic wrap and refrigerate for at least 8 hours or up to overnight. The chicken will stiffen as it sits.

3 Remove the chicken from the refrigerator and use a spoon to break it apart. Working in batches, grind the chicken in a food processor until a smooth, stiff, light pink paste forms. (This step takes several minutes and the machine will get a good workout.) Stop the machine occasionally to scrape down the sides. When you are finished, there should be no visible bits of chicken and the paste should have a slight sheen. Using the rubber spatula, transfer each batch to another bowl, taking care to clean well under the blade.

Makes about 2 1/2 pounds

1 pound boneless, skinless chicken breasts

1 1/4 pounds boneless, skinless chicken thighs

MARINADE

1 tablespoon baking powder

2 tablespoons tapioca starch

1 tablespoon sugar

5 tablespoons fish sauce

3 tablespoons canola or other neutral oil

4 The paste is ready to use, or it can be covered and refrigerated for up to 3 days. For long-term keeping, divide it into 1/2- and 1-pound portions (a scant 1 cup paste weighs 1/2 pound), wrap in a double layer of plastic wrap, and freeze for up to 2 months.

NOTE

To make a pork version of the paste, use 2 pounds well-trimmed boneless pork leg (fresh ham). Look for a boneless, skinless pork leg roast at a Chinese or Vietnamese market. The slightly domed, oval cut is usually near other lean cuts, such as pork loin. Buy about 2 1/3 pounds because there is always some waste. If that cut isn't available, buy a piece of pork leg (about 2 3/4 pounds) and remove the fat and skin yourself. Make sure that you remove any pearlescent silver skin or gristle from either cut and then slice it across the grain into 1/4-inch-thick strips (like you would for a stir-fry). Marinate the pork in a mixture of 1 tablespoon baking powder, 3 1/2 tablespoons tapioca starch, 1 tablespoon sugar, and 5 tablespoons each fish sauce, canola or other neutral oil, and water. Process and store as directed for the chicken version. Makes about 2 1/2 pounds.

Whether you have made the chicken or the pork paste, use a powerful spray from your kitchen faucet to rinse the paste off your equipment. The paste sticks and attacking it with a sponge can be messy.

POUNDING *GIÒ* BY HAND

To make *giò* the old-fashioned way, you must first hand pound the meat and then add the marinade ingredients. Use a large Thai stone mortar and pestle, which can be found reasonably priced at Asian restaurant-supply and housewares shops. My 9-inch-wide mortar has a 5-cup capacity bowl that is 6 1/2 inches wide and 4 inches deep. The 8-inch-long pestle is about 2 inches wide at the base. Select a pestle that fits your hand comfortably. (Stone pestles, heavier than the wooden one mentioned in the chapter introduction, make pounding easier.)

To minimize physical strain, I sit on a low kitchen stool and put the mortar on a solid table or box, with the rim of the mortar slightly below my knee. You may also sit on the floor with the mortar between your legs. Place a thick towel under the mortar to protect the work surface. Regardless of your setup, you want to sit astride the mortar and efficiently use your upper body strength to work the pestle. It takes about 35 minutes to produce a full batch of paste, so you may want to halve the recipe. To yield *giò* that is close to the traditional version, pound pork (see Note, above), which works better than chicken. The beef mixture used for making Beef, Dill, and Peppercorn Sausage (page 161) is also a good candidate for hand pounding.

1 Cut the meat into 1/4-inch-thick strips as instructed in the recipe. Blot the meat dry with paper towels to prevent it from sliding around the mortar.

2 In a small bowl, whisk together the marinade ingredients. Set aside near the pounding station. (Hand-pounded *giò* doesn't traditionally call for leavener and starch, but I find that they guarantee a silkier result that is neither too dense nor too firm.)

3 Put about 1/2 pound of the meat (or a quantity you find manageable) in the mortar and start pounding with a steady rhythm, pausing only to remove any gristly bits that come loose. After about 4 minutes, the meat should have gathered into a mass and, perhaps, even stuck to the pestle, allowing you to use the pestle to lift the meat from the mortar and pound it down again. Keep pounding for another 2 minutes to make the meat cohere into a smooth mass that resembles a ball of dough. Use a rubber spatula or plastic dough scraper to transfer the meat to a bowl. Repeat with the remaining meat.

4 Add all the marinade ingredients to the meat, stirring with a fork until the marinade is no longer visible. In batches, pound the meat for about 3 minutes longer to combine all the ingredients well. You should hear a suction noise as air is mixed in. The finished paste will feel firm and look ragged, and small nuggets of meat will be suspended in the paste. Transfer the paste to a clean bowl and repeat with the remaining meat.

CLASSIC SILKY SAUSAGE

Giò Lụa

GIÒ LỤA IS THE MOST WIDELY EATEN of all the Vietnamese charcuterie. A kind of Vietnamese mortadella, the smooth, light-colored sausage is sliced and tucked into baguette sandwiches (page 34), eaten with regular or sticky rice, or presented as part of a charcuterie assortment with pickled vegetables. Cut into matchsticks, it is used as a garnish for *bún thang*, a popular Hanoi noodle soup (page 217).

Although *giò lụa* is stocked in the refrigerated food aisle of nearly every Vietnamese deli and market, I make mine at home. It's easy. All you need is some meat paste, which may be freshly made or thawed, a piece of banana leaf, and some foil. You shape the paste into a log, wrap it in the foil and then in the leaf, and then boil it. The finished sausage will keep for up to a week in the refrigerator, but it is at its best soon after cooking, when the flavor of the banana leaf still lingers on the meat.

Illustrated on page 260

1   Fill a 4- or 5-quart pot two-thirds full with water and bring to a boil over high heat. Lower the heat and cover to keep warm.

2   Shaping and wrapping the paste is like rolling a very stubby cigar. Put a 12-by-18-inch piece of heavy-duty aluminum foil on your work surface with a short side closest to you. Center the piece of banana leaf on the foil. Use a rubber spatula to deposit the paste near the bottom edge of the leaf (the edge closest to you), roughly shaping it into a fat 5-inch-long log. Do not get any paste on the foil. Roll up the leaf to encase the paste, creating a cylinder 3 inches in diameter. Place the cylinder at one of the short ends of the foil and roll it up, letting the foil naturally overlap to form a silver tube. Finish by sealing the ends closed and then folding them toward the center. Because the paste expands during cooking, you need to tie the package with kitchen string to secure it. In general, a cross tie followed by another loop around the sausage—much like tying a very small roast—works well. There is no need to be fancy, but to ensure the shape and compactness of the paste, make sure the string is taut.

Makes one 1-pound sausage

1 pound (about 2 cups) Multipurpose Meat Paste (page 158)	5-by-12-inch piece fresh or thawed, frozen banana leaf, trimmed of brown edges, rinsed, and wiped dry

3   Return the pot of water to a boil. Drop in the sausage and boil for 40 minutes, replenishing with extra boiling water as needed. During cooking, the foil will darken and the sausage will puff up, push against the string, and eventually float. Don't be alarmed; it will deflate afterward.

4   Use tongs to remove the cooked sausage from the pot. Let cool completely before untying and removing the foil. Keep the banana leaf in place. Put the sausage in an airtight container or zip-top plastic bag and refrigerate until serving.

BEEF, DILL, AND PEPPERCORN SAUSAGE

Giò Bò

THE TERM *GIÒ* IS USED NOT ONLY for the ubiquitous meat paste, but also for describing any charcuterie that is log shaped. Most *giò*-style charcuterie is wrapped in banana leaf, including this wonderful sausage spiked with dill and crushed black peppercorns. Because beef is a luxury meat in Vietnam, *giò bò* is a special treat. It is not commonly sold at delis and markets, which is fine because it is simple to make at home. Lean top round steak (a.k.a. London broil) yields great flavor and a fine texture.

Illustrated on page 164

1   Cut the beef across the grain into ¼-inch-thick strips (like you would for a stir-fry).

2   To make the marinade, in a bowl, whisk together the baking powder, tapioca starch, sugar, fish sauce, oil, and water. Add the beef and use a rubber spatula to mix well. Cover tightly with plastic wrap and refrigerate for at least 8 hours or up to overnight. The beef will stiffen as it sits.

3   Remove the meat from the refrigerator and use a spoon to break it apart. Using a large-capacity food processor, grind all the meat at once, stopping the machine occasionally to scrape down the sides. When the meat has been transformed into a stiff and somewhat coarse paste (fine bits of meat are still visible), stop the machine. Add the dill and pepper and restart the machine to finish grinding the mixture to a smooth, stiff mauve paste. Using the rubber spatula, transfer the mixture to another bowl, taking care to clean well under the blade. (If you have only a small food processor, grind in 2 batches, dividing the dill and pepper in half.) Grinding the meat will take several minutes and will give your machine a workout.

continued

Makes one 1¼-pound sausage

1¼ pounds top round steak
     (London broil), trimmed of
     all gristle, rind, and fat
     (1 pound after trimming)

MARINADE
1½ teaspoons baking powder
2 tablespoons tapioca starch
1½ teaspoons sugar
2½ tablespoons fish sauce
2½ tablespoons canola or
     other neutral oil
2½ tablespoons water

3 tablespoons chopped fresh
     dill, feathery tops only
Generous ½ teaspoon black
     peppercorns, toasted
     in a dry skillet for about
     1 minute, until fragrant,
     then crushed with a
     mortar and pestle
5-by-12-inch piece fresh or
     thawed, frozen banana leaf,
     trimmed of brown edges,
     rinsed, and wiped dry

4 Fill a 4- or 5-quart pot two-thirds full with water and bring to a boil over high heat. Lower the heat and cover to keep warm.

5 To shape and wrap the sausage, put a 12-by-18-inch piece of heavy-duty aluminum foil on your work surface with a short side closest to you. Center the piece of banana leaf on the foil. Use a rubber spatula to deposit the paste near the bottom edge of the leaf (the edge closest to you), roughly shaping it into a fat 5-inch-long log. Do not get any paste on the foil. Roll up the leaf to encase the paste, creating a cylinder 3 inches in diameter. Place the cylinder at one of the short ends of the foil and roll it up, letting the foil naturally overlap to form a silver tube. Finish by sealing the ends closed and then folding them toward the center. Because the paste expands during cooking, you need to tie the package with kitchen string to secure it. In general, a cross tie followed by another loop around the sausage—much like tying a very small roast—works well. There is no need to be fancy, but you do want to ensure the shape and compactness of the paste, so make sure the string is taut.

6 Return the pot of water to a boil. Drop in the sausage and boil for 45 minutes, replenishing with extra boiling water as needed. During cooking, the foil will darken and the sausage will puff up, push against the string, and eventually float. Don't be alarmed; it will deflate afterward.

7 Use tongs to remove the cooked sausage from the pot. Let cool completely before untying and removing the foil. Keep the banana leaf in place. Put the sausage in an airtight container or zip-top plastic bag and refrigerate until serving. It will keep for up to 1 week, but as with the previous sausage, it is at its best soon after cooking, when the flavor of the banana leaf still lingers on the meat.

NOTE

To pound the meat paste with a mortar and pestle, see page 159. When adding the marinade ingredients to the pounded beef, add the dill and peppercorns, too. Wrap and boil as directed.

ROASTED CINNAMON SAUSAGE

Chả Quế

WHEN GROUND MEAT or meat paste is enhanced by other seasonings and cooked in an unusual manner, rather than just boiled, it is elevated to the realm of *chả*, a term used for fancier charcuterie. So if the name of a dish includes the word *chả*, expect to be seduced.

Here, the meat paste receives a dose of cinnamon, which adds a deep spicy-sweet flavor without being cloying (much as it does to many savory Middle Eastern dishes). To accentuate the perfume and color that cinnamon lends to the paste, the mixture is traditionally spread onto a large section of bamboo and cooked on a spit over a wood fire. As the bamboo spins, a chewy skin forms and a heady aroma wafts through the air. When cut from the bamboo, the ready-to-eat sausage is curved like pieces of cinnamon bark.

In the States, my mom tried substituting a large metal juice can for the bamboo and an electric rotisserie for the spit. If things weren't just right, the paste slipped off the can and was ruined. The method here, which uses an inverted baking sheet, is much easier, although it doesn't yield the characteristic curved shape. The taste, however, is splendid, especially when the sausage is made with strong, sweet Vietnamese cassia cinnamon.

Illustrated on page 251

Makes 1 scant pound

1 pound (about 2 cups) Multipurpose Meat Paste (page 158)	2¹/₂ teaspoons sugar 1 teaspoon ground cinnamon

1 Position a rack in the middle of the oven and preheat to 375°F. Invert a baking sheet and cover the bottom with heavy-duty aluminum foil.

2 Put the paste in a bowl and sprinkle on the sugar and cinnamon. Mix vigorously with a rubber spatula to distribute the dark specks of cinnamon evenly.

3 Transfer the paste to the prepared baking sheet. Use the rubber spatula to spread the paste into a 1-inch-thick rectangle (to mimic the bamboo) or disk. Wet the palm of your hand with water and rub it in a circular motion to smooth the top. Wet your fingers and smooth the sides. To prevent the paste from puffing up too much and cooking unevenly, use a skewer or toothpick to poke holes in it, spacing them about 1 inch apart and making sure to touch bottom.

4 Bake the paste for 25 to 30 minutes, or until the top is dry and light brown and a skewer or toothpick inserted in the middle comes out clean. During baking, a puffy, shiny skin forms. Remove from the oven and let cool completely. As the sausage cools, the skin deflates, crinkles, and darkens.

5 To serve, cut the sausage into 3 long sections and then crosswise into ¹/₄-inch-thick slices. Store leftover sausage in an airtight container or zip-top plastic bag in the refrigerator for up to 1 week.

RICH AND CRISP SAUSAGE

Chả Mỡ

> NOT ONLY IS THIS SAUSAGE in the fancy *chả* category, like Roasted Cinnamon Sausage (page 163), but it is also sinfully good. *Mỡ* means fat, in this case diced pork fatback, which is combined with the classic meat paste and specks of ground pepper. Shaped into a thick disk, the mixture is cooked twice, first steamed and then fried or baked. The two-step process allows you to keep the meat on hand for last-minute cooking, ensuring that it is perfect at serving time. Sliced while still warm, it is crispy on the outside and rich on the inside. For a traditional pairing, serve a few of the slices between steamed sticky rice cakes (page 254).

1 Fill the steamer pan halfway with water and bring to a rolling boil over high heat. Meanwhile, put the paste, fatback, and pepper in a bowl. Use a rubber spatula to mix well, making sure the pork fat is evenly distributed. Deposit all the paste in the center of the banana leaf and use the spatula to spread it into a disk 6 inches in diameter and 1 inch thick. Wet your palm with water and rub it in a circular motion to smooth the top. Wet your fingers and smooth the sides.

2 Lift up the leaf, place it in the steamer tray, and place the tray in the steamer. Cover and steam for 20 to 25 minutes, or until a toothpick inserted in the center comes out clean. Turn off the heat and uncover. When the steam has dissipated, transfer the sausage on the leaf to a rack and let cool completely. Fresh from the steamer, the sausage will be white and slightly inflated. As it cools, it returns to its original size and the outside turns pale yellow. (The steamed sausage may be well wrapped and refrigerated for up to 1 week. Return it to room temperature before proceeding.)

Clockwise from top left: Tangy Mixed Vegetable Pickle (page 194); Headcheese (page 170); Rich and Crisp Sausage ; and Beef, Dill, and Peppercorn Sausage (page 161)

Makes 1 pound

1 pound (about 2 cups) Multipurpose Meat Paste (page 158)

2 ounces pork fatback, blanched in boiling water for about 1 minute until firm, cooled, and finely diced (generous 1/4 cup)

1/2 teaspoon black pepper, preferably freshly ground

8-inch-square piece fresh or thawed, frozen banana leaf, trimmed of brown edges, rinsed, and wiped dry

Corn or canola oil for deep-frying (optional)

3 You may deep-fry or bake the sausage for the final cooking. Traditionally it is deep-fried, which yields great color, while baking, of course, is easier. Cut the sausage into 3 fairly long pieces that will yield nice slices when cut. To deep-fry, pour oil to a depth of 1 1/2 inches into a wok or Dutch oven and heat to 350°F on a deep-frying thermometer. (If you don't have a thermometer, stand a dry bamboo chopstick in the oil; if small bubbles immediately gather on the surface around the chopstick, the oil is ready.) Add the sausage pieces and fry, turning with tongs for even coloring, for about 4 minutes, or

continued

until golden and crisp. Using tongs, transfer to paper towels to drain, blot with more towels, and let cool for 1 to 2 minutes.

To bake, place the 3 sausage pieces in a toaster oven set to the highest heat (broil) and cook, for about 4 minutes on each side, or until golden and crisp. The pieces will hiss and pop, so monitor closely to prevent charring. The color isn't as even with baking as it is with deep-frying and the sausage takes longer to cook, but there is typically less hassle for the cook. Remove from the toaster oven, briefly blot with paper towels, and let cool for 1 to 2 minutes.

4   To serve, slice into ¼-inch-thick pieces and serve piping hot.

NOTE

For tips on finding fatback, see page 169.

GARLICKY SANDWICH MEAT

Thịt Bánh Mì Ổ

MRS. HIEU, a friend of my parents, is an avid cook, and one of her specialties is this garlicky pork. When my mother first tried the meat, stuffed in a baguette sandwich, she said it instantly reminded her of pork from her favorite Saigon street vendors. Indeed, it is so good that Mrs. Hieu used to sell her pork to Little Saigon delis in Orange County, California.

Mrs. Hieu's method calls for seasoning, rolling, and tying boneless pork shank, a funnel-shaped, rich cut sold at Chinese and Viet markets. Instead of boiling or steaming the meat in the traditional manner, she bakes it in the oven, a method that yields more concentrated flavor. That's her secret. My recipe utilizes Mrs. Hieu's approach, but since pork shank can be hard to roll and tie securely (the meat slides around), I forgo tying it and instead roll the meat in heavy-duty foil. Food coloring gives this cold cut its characteristically pinkish red rind, without which it is rather gray. You may decide against this superficial yet cheery touch, but it is authentic.

Makes 2 rolls, about 1 3/4 pounds total

1 skin-on, boneless pork shank, about 2 pounds	2 1/4 teaspoons salt
	2 teaspoons sugar
	1/4 teaspoon Chinese five-spice powder
SEASONING MIXTURE	
3 large cloves garlic, finely minced and mashed with the broad side of the knife	3 or 4 drops red food coloring mixed with 1 teaspoon water (optional)
1 teaspoon black peppercorns, toasted in a dry skillet for about 1 minute, until fragrant, then crushed with a mortar and pestle	Boiling water

1 Pork shank typically comes as a single circular cut with unbroken skin. Find the part of the skin where no meat is attached and cut at that spot so the shank will lay flat. If you have purchased a cut from a large shank, skip this step. Lay the pork skin side up. Exam it for stray hairs and use a sharp knife to scrape and remove any you find. Locate the white cord of tendon in the thick layer of fatty tissue. The tendon is hard to chew, so cut it out with a boning knife. Trim any other loose bits of tendon or fat to neaten the shank, and then halve it into 2 chunky pieces each about 6 inches long.

2 To make the seasoning mixture, in a small bowl, stir together the garlic, pepper, salt, sugar, and five-spice powder to form a paste. Rub the paste on the meaty side of each piece of pork, taking care to get it into the crevices. Flip the pork over so the skin side faces up. Dip your fingers into the diluted food coloring and paint the skin pinkish red.

3 Position a rack in the middle of the oven and preheat to 375°F. Shape each piece of pork into a chubby roll that will more or less hold its shape; if necessary, spiral the meat to manipulate it. Don't expect the skin to surround the meat completely. Put a 12-by-18-inch piece of heavy-duty aluminum foil on your work surface with a short side closest to you. Center 1 pork roll, skin side down, on the foil about 3 inches from the edge closest to you. Holding the roll together with one hand, lift up the bottom edge of foil and tightly roll up the pork, encasing it in a foil tube. Finish by sealing the ends closed and then folding them toward the center. Repeat with the other piece of pork and a second piece of foil.

4 Put the rolls, seam side up, in a baking dish and add boiling water to the dish, filling it a generous 1/4 inch deep. Bake for 1 1/2 hours, replenishing the water midway. If you wish to check the internal temperature of the rolls to see if they are done, it should be about 170°F on an instant-read thermometer. Use tongs to transfer the rolls to a plate and then let cool completely.

5 Refrigerate the rolls for 8 hours or up to overnight before unwrapping. To neaten the rolls, scrape off the gelatinous juices and/or fat. Because the meat and skin are a little chewy, slice the rolls as thinly as possible (1/8 to 1/16 inch thick) for stuffing sandwiches or nibbling alone. Also, always cut them when they are cold for the thinnest slices. The rolls will keep in an airtight container or zip-top plastic bag in the refrigerator for up to 1 week or in the freezer for up to 1 month.

NOTE

When purchasing the pork shank for these rolls, buy a little extra for a batch of Headcheese (page 170). Both cold cuts are excellent in Vietnamese baguette sandwiches (page 34).

CHICKEN LIVER PÂTÉ

Pa-Tê Gan Gà

IN MY MOM'S SAIGON KITCHEN, the food processor, a modern luxury appliance, was reserved for making *giò*, while the old-fashioned hand-crank meat grinder was used for delicious liver pâtés like this one. We regularly enjoyed it, tucked into *bánh mì* or simply smeared on a baguette slice.

In the traditional Viet interpretation of French pâté, pork or beef liver, pork meat, and fatback are seasoned with lots of garlic and sometimes Cognac and Chinese five-spice powder (a substitute for French *quatre épices*). Some cooks add tapioca starch or flour as a binder, and, when available, they line the mold with caul fat for encasing the meat mixture. The pâté is then steamed, steamed and baked, or baked in a water bath, the method usually depending on whether or not the cook has an oven.

When my mother came to the States and switched from pork to chicken for making *giò*, she began saving the leftover livers for this light, elegant pâté. She also started making the pâté in a food processor. If you want a more intense liver flavor, use half pork and half chicken liver, or make an all-pork version, cutting the liver into 1-inch cubes before processing. Don't skimp on fat, or the results will be dry and tough. Meat today tends to be lean, and this recipe needs the fat to achieve the right taste and texture. You will end up with a large pâté—the better to impress others with your efforts.

1 Put the onion and garlic in a food processor and pulse to mince. Transfer to a large bowl and add the pork fatback, chicken livers, ground pork and beef, eggs, Cognac, pepper, salt, and five-spice powder. Mix well with a rubber spatula.

2 Working in batches, grind the ingredients in the food processor to a fine, smooth, light tan mixture, transferring each batch to another bowl as it is ready. Each batch will take a few minutes, and you will have to pause occasionally to scrape down the sides. When all the ingredients have been ground, beat them with the spatula to blend well. If you want to check the seasoning, sauté a spoonful in a little skillet until it is well done, let cool, taste, and then correct if necessary.

3 Position a rack in the middle of the oven and preheat to 350°F. Bring a kettle of water to a boil and lower the heat to keep it hot.

Makes one 3-pound loaf

1 small yellow onion, cut into ½-inch chunks

5 large cloves garlic, roughly chopped

½ pound pork fatback, cut into ½-inch pieces (about 1 cup)

1 pound chicken livers, yellowish membranes trimmed

⅔ pound ground pork, coarsely chopped to loosen

⅓ pound ground beef, preferably chuck, coarsely chopped to loosen

2 eggs

3 tablespoons Cognac

¾ teaspoon black pepper, preferably freshly ground

1 tablespoon salt

¾ teaspoon Chinese five-spice powder

Butter for greasing pan and parchment paper

2 or 3 bay leaves

4 Butter a 6-cup loaf pan. Pour in the pâté mixture and smooth the top with the spatula. Bang the pan on the countertop or table to remove air bubbles. Center the bay leaves on top of the pâté. Butter a piece of parchment paper large enough to cover the top of the pâté and place it, buttered side down, over the pâté. Then cover the pâté with aluminum foil, allowing a 1-inch overhang. Place the loaf pan in a baking or roasting pan. Pour enough boiling water into the pan to come 1 inch up the sides of the loaf pan. Bake the pâté for 1½ to 1¾ hours, or until the internal temperature registers about 160°F on an instant-read thermometer.

5 Remove the baking pan from the oven and set the pâté aside to cool for 1 hour. Place a twin pan (or board) and a 5-pound weight, such as a brick or a few food cans, directly on top of the pâté; this compacts it and creates a smooth texture. When the pâté is completely cool, remove the weight. Refrigerate it and let it mature for 1 or 2 days.

6 To serve, unmold the cold pâté, removing and discarding the foil and parchment paper. Cut the pâté into thin slices or a thick slab. Blot away the juices with paper towels and then lay the slices or slab on a serving plate. Let the pâté come to room temperature before serving. You can include it in a Western-style charcuterie spread, or use it in your next Vietnamese baguette sandwich. The pâté keeps well in the refrigerator for 10 days. I advise against freezing it, however, as it turns soggy.

FINDING FATBACK

Pork fatback is an old-fashioned cooking fat that can be difficult to find. Your best bet is to go to a market that caters to a pork-loving clientele, such as an Asian or Mexican market. The fatback may not be in the meat case, but just ask the butcher for it. At my local Mexican market, the butcher is always tickled by my request for *grasa* (fat). He proudly emerges from the cooler with a thick piece with the *cuero* (skin) still attached.

To ensure that I have a supply if fatback on hand, I buy a pound or two. I set aside the portion I am using immediately and then I divide the remaining fat into pieces the size of a deck of playing cards (about two ounces), wrap each one tightly in plastic wrap, and freeze them all in a zip-top plastic bag. Fatback will keep in the freezer for up to nine months. Before using or freezing fatback, remove any skin, if necessary. A little meat attached is fine.

HEADCHEESE

Giò Thủ

YOU MAY ENCOUNTER Vietnamese headcheese in a *bánh mì*, but it isn't an everyday charcuterie. When made at home, it is considered special-occasion fare and is often presented as an hors d'oeuvre with other cold meats and tangy pickled vegetables. Dense, firm Vietnamese headcheese is not as gelatinous as its Western counterpart. The meats are boiled, cut up, and then slowly sautéed to release the gelatin, which helps all the elements stick together. Strips of fluffy egg sheets are added for color. The mixture is wrapped in banana leaf and tied, rolled up in plastic and aluminum foil, or packed into an empty food can and left to cool at room temperature and congeal. It is then ready for serving, but time in the refrigerator improves its flavor.

    This recipe is my mother's "refined" version and doesn't require buying a whole pig's head. She omits snouts and instead uses just ears, tongue, and pork shank (all readily available at a Chinese or Vietnamese market), a combination that offers a nice textural balance. To mold the mixture, I use an empty food can. The twenty-ounce cans that once held fruits like lychees and jackfruit produce well-proportioned, handsome results, and their ridge-free walls make unmolding easy. Lining the can with banana leaf imparts fragrance and flavor.

Illustrated on page 164

Makes 1¼ pounds

½ pound pig ears
    (2 medium-large ears)
½ pound pork tongue
    (1 small tongue)
Salt
½ pound skin-on, boneless
    pork shank
1 small yellow onion, halved
1 egg, lightly beaten
1 teaspoon canola or other
    neutral oil

3 or 4 dried wood ear
    mushrooms, reconstituted
    (page 334), trimmed, and
    cut into ¼-inch-wide
    strips (¼ to ⅓ cup)
2 pieces fresh or thawed,
    frozen banana leaf, one
    4 inches square and one
    5 by 12 inches, trimmed of
    brown edges, rinsed, and
    wiped dry
1 tablespoon fish sauce
¼ plus ⅛ teaspoon black
    pepper, preferably freshly
    ground

1   Examine the ears for stray hairs and use a sharp knife to scrape and remove any you find. If there are lots of hairs, remove just the long ones. Hairs on the rim can be get cut off later. A few short ones are okay.

2   To rid the ears and tongue of impurities, put them in a large saucepan with 1 teaspoon salt and water to cover. Bring to a boil over high heat and boil for 5 minutes. Drain in a colander and rinse well with cold water. Set the ears aside. Use a vegetable peeler or sharp knife to remove the white top layer of the tongue from the tip to the fuzzy back; there's no need to remove the bottom layer.

3   Return the tongue and ears to the saucepan. Add the pork shank, onion, 2 teaspoons salt, and water to cover by 1½ inches.

Bring to a boil over high heat and boil for 45 minutes. Remove from the heat and set aside for 45 minutes, or until cool enough to handle.

4 Meanwhile, use the egg and oil to prepare a thick egg sheet (page 320) in an 8-inch nonstick skillet. Quarter the egg sheet and then cut into 1/2-inch-wide strips. Set aside with the wood ear mushrooms.

5 For the mold, select an empty can (such as a 20-ounce fruit can) that has a capacity of 2 1/2 cups and is about 3 1/2 inches in diameter and 4 1/2 inches tall. To line the bottom of the can, stand the can on the 4-inch square of banana leaf and press to create an impression of the bottom. Use scissors to cut out the circle, making it slightly smaller than the impression. Drop it into the can and use a spatula or spoon to make sure it lays flat. Cut a 9-by-12-inch piece of heavy-duty aluminum foil. To stiffen the foil, so that it is easier to slide it into the can, fold one of the long edges over by 1 inch. Shape the foil by wrapping it around the outside of the can, letting the edges overlap. Hold the foil as a loose tube and slide it into the can, with the folded edge touching the bottom. Again, make sure it is snugly in place. Use the remaining larger piece of banana leaf to line the wall of the can by coiling it into a short tube and sliding it into the can. Make sure it is snug. Set the mold near the stove.

6 Remove the ears, tongue, and pork shank from the pan. Discard the broth. Halve each ear lengthwise and cut the pieces into scant 1/2-inch-wide strips. Halve the tongue lengthwise and scrape out any dark, soft bits lingering in the center. Cut each half crosswise into 1/4-inch-thick pieces. Slice the pork shank into domino-sized pieces about 1/4 inch thick.

7 Put all the meats into a 10-inch nonstick skillet and place over medium heat. When the sizzling begins, gently stir the meats, lowering the heat slightly when they brown. As the ears release their gelatin, the white cartilage becomes more visible. Keep stirring to coax more gelatin out. After 10 minutes, the mixture should hiss, pop, and be sticky. Touch a piece of meat

and it will feel tacky. Add the egg and mushroom pieces and continue cooking for about 5 minutes, or until they are tacky, too. (Some of the skin on the ear pieces will have receded enough for you to see a good 1/8 inch of cartilage.) Sprinkle in the fish sauce and pepper and keep stirring and cooking for another 2 to 3 minutes, or until the ingredients are tacky again. Remove from the heat. The total cooking time will be less than 20 minutes. Taste and add 1 or 2 big pinches of salt for extra depth; don't dilute the gelatin with more fish sauce.

8 Use a large spoon to transfer the mixture to the prepared can. As you add each spoonful, push down on it firmly to compact the mixture. It is okay for some of it to rise above the rim of the can. The foil tube will hold it in place and it will all fit. Fold the foil to close the top and press firmly to compact the contents further. Weight it down first with a smaller can and then with a larger can on top. You want weights totaling 2 1/2 to 3 pounds. When the contents are completely cool, remove the weights and refrigerate for 8 hours or overnight.

9 To unmold, use a can opener to remove the bottom of the can. Put the can holding the headcheese atop a smaller can and firmly push the headcheese out. Remove the foil but keep the banana leaf to maintain its aroma for serving time. Store the headcheese in an airtight container or zip-top plastic bag in the refrigerator for up to 1 week or in the freezer for 1 month.

CUT IT COLD, SERVE IT SOFT

All of the charcuterie in this chapter, with the exception of Rich and Crisp Sausage (page 165), which is served hot or warm, should be cut cold, straight from the refrigerator. The cold meats are firm and easy to handle, so you will get nice, thin slices. But before digging in, let the meats sit at room temperature to take the chill off. They will soften a little and be more flavorful.

7. VEGETABLES FOR ALL SEASONS

Vegetables are woven throughout the Vietnamese table. A plate of vegetables and herbs arrives with a bowl of noodle soup; cucumbers, jicama, and greens join meats and seafood in rice-paper rolls; and everyday soups (*canh*) usually include a vegetable for flavor, texture, and color.

But vegetables also play a feature role in the cuisine, most noticeably as one of the four components of the classic Vietnamese four-dish meal of a soup, a meat or seafood dish, a vegetable dish, and rice. The cooking techniques for these vegetable dishes are generally familiar, but the ingredients, such as water spinach, or the way they are combined, such as the popular Russian Beet, Potato, and Carrot Salad (page 186), may surprise those unfamiliar with the repertoire. Tofu recipes are included in this chapter, too, as Vietnamese cooks typically treat the soybean-based food as a vegetable, serving it both alongside meat and seafood preparations and as the main dish.

As with many Asian cuisines, pickled and preserved vegetables are an important part of Viet cooking, providing contrasting texture and flavor to other foods on the table. Classics such as central Vietnam's garlicky daikon and carrot (*dưa món*) complement a variety of menus, while a baguette sandwich needs sweet pickled vegetables to balance the richness of the meats. Pickled shallots serve the same tempering role at special-event meals, such as the feasts held during Tet. Pickles and preserved vegetables are eaten so often that Vietnamese cooks don't bother canning them, finding it more practical to make regular supplies and store them in the refrigerator, where they last for weeks and sometimes months.

Like all cooking, vegetable dishes demand high-quality ingredients. In the United States, we increasingly live with year-round supplies of vegetables and fruits imported from around the globe. But many Asian vegetables have yet to be mass-produced, so their availability and freshness still follow seasonal rhythms, as a trip to any Asian market or farmers' market where Asian vegetables are sold will illustrate. In California, Southeast Asian farmers, mostly Laotian and Hmong, truck their harvests from the Central Valley to farmers' markets all over the state.

As you become familiar with the selection, you'll discover that spring, fall, and sometimes winter, depending on where you live, deliver an exceptional bounty of cool-weather produce, including Chinese celery, chrysanthemum leaves, daikon, *gailan* (Chinese broccoli), napa cabbage, bok choy, and *gai choy* (Chinese mustard cabbage). When the temperature rises, especially during the long, hot days of summer, it is peak time for warm-season crops like long beans, Chinese chives, banana blossoms, green papaya, Chinese and Japanese eggplants, chiles, opo squash, water spinach, and amaranth. Vietnamese herbs also thrive in these warm conditions, and I make sure to savor them at their best.

If you like a particular Asian vegetable and can't find it, you can grow it (see Resources, page 335, for seed sources). If you can neither find it nor grow it, you will discover that you can still prepare many Vietnamese vegetable dishes with what is readily available at regular markets.

RECIPES

BASIC BOILED VEGETABLE

Rau Luộc

VIETNAMESE COOKS regularly prepare vegetables by simply boiling them in salted water. It is a fast and healthy method, and boiled vegetables are the perfect partner for a robust, saucy dish like a *kho* or a piquant stir-fry. If you have eaten Cantonese dim sum, you may recall how the ubiquitous plate of boiled *gailan* (Chinese broccoli) and oyster sauce harmonizes with and counters the richness of the other foods on parade. The same concept applies here. The boiled vegetables are served plain if they accompany saucy or boldly flavored dishes and with a dipping sauce if they don't. During lean times, the leftover cooking liquid is served as a light broth or transformed into a modest soup (*canh*) for the meal.

Leafy greens such as water spinach and amaranth, cabbage, cauliflower, green beans, and long beans are all good candidates for boiling. Many Vietnamese farmers grow sweet potatoes and squashes, and the leaves from those plants are boiled as well. I particularly like dark green brassicas (crucifers), such as broccoli, *gailan*, and *gai choy* (Chinese mustard cabbage), for their high nutrient value, tender yet firm texture, and sweet, slightly spicy bite.

In her classic *Làm Bếp Giỏi*, cookbook author Mrs. Van Dai wrote, "Rau héo gần như cá ươn," which roughly means, "Wilted vegetables are almost like spoiled fish." Check the cut stem ends of vegetables to see if they were recently trimmed, and avoid greens that have tired, sad leaves. At home, simply wash, trim, and cut the vegetable into bite-sized pieces.

The vegetables must be cooked quickly in plenty of water to capture their best qualities. For tender leafy greens such as water spinach, use enough water to cover. Make sure other vegetables are covered by at least 3 inches of water. Add

Clockwise from far left: green papaya, banana blossom (whole blossom and single bract with exposed flowers), water spinach, Thai chiles, fresh galangal, and lemongrass

a generous teaspoon of salt for each quart of water, bring the water to a rapid boil over high heat, and then add the vegetable. Give the pot a stir and then cook the vegetable just until tender (sample cooking times follow). Drain the vegetable in a colander and flush with cold water to cool quickly. Serve the vegetable warm or at room temperature. Accompany with Ginger-Lime Dipping Sauce (page 309) or Tamarind-Ginger Dipping Sauce (page 312), if desired.

VEGETABLE COOKING TIME *	
Cauliflower and broccoli (cut into 1-inch florets)	4 to 5 minutes
Gai choy and green cabbage (cut into 2-inch pieces)	2 to 3 minutes
Gailan (cut into 2-inch lengths; split thick stems lengthwise for even cooking)	Add the stems first; after the water returns to a boil, add the leafy parts and cook for 2 to 3 minutes
Green beans and long beans (cut into 2-inch lengths)	3 to 4 minutes
Water spinach, amaranth, and sweet potato or squash vines (use the leaves and tender tops; bite into a raw stem to see if it is tender enough to eat)	Less than 1 minute, or until leaves wilt
* Start timing when the vegetables are added to the boiling water.	

WINTER SQUASH SIMMERED IN COCONUT MILK

Bí Đỏ Hầm Dừa

> THIS ELEGANT and easy-to-prepare stew is one of my favorite vegetarian dishes. The Garnet sweet potato (usually mistakenly labeled a yam) has bright orange flesh, and the raw peanuts deliver protein and crunch. When peanuts are boiled, simmered, or steamed, they become beanlike, revealing their true identity as legumes. You may need to look for shelled raw peanuts at Chinese and Southeast Asian markets, as they are rarely carried in regular supermarkets.
>
> I often use pinkish tan–skinned banana squash for this recipe, which is typically sold in pieces wrapped in plastic. It is easy to peel and you can buy just as much as you need for the stew. Select a piece that has deep-colored flesh, more orange than yellow. Or, you may use your favorite winter squash, such as butternut, in place of the banana squash.

1 To give the peanuts a head start in cooking, put them in a small saucepan with water to cover by 1 inch. Place over medium heat, bring to a boil, and boil for about 15 minutes, or until the nuts are chewy but crunchy and about half cooked. Bite into a nut to see if they are ready. Meanwhile, put the squash cubes in a medium saucepan, add the salt and sugar, and toss the squash to coat. When the peanuts are ready, drain and add to the squash.

2 Add the coconut milk and water to the squash and peanuts and bring to a simmer over medium heat. Cook for 3 to 5 minutes, or until the squash has slightly softened. Add the sweet potato and stir gently to combine well. The liquid should just cover the vegetables; if it doesn't, add water as needed. Continue at what sounds like a loud simmer for 15 to 20 minutes, or until the squash and sweet potato are tender but not mushy. Test for doneness by poking a few pieces with a knife. You want the sweet potato and squash to retain some of their individuality, the peanuts to still have a bit of crunch, and the sauce to be a creamy yellow.

3 Remove from the heat and let stand for a few minutes to allow the flavors to settle. During that time, the sauce will

Serves 2 to 3 as a main dish, or 4 to 6 with 2 or 3 other dishes

1/2 cup raw peanuts

3/4 pound banana squash, peeled and cut into 1-inch cubes

Generous 1/2 teaspoon salt

1 teaspoon sugar

1 cup coconut milk, canned or freshly made (page 318)

1 cup water

1 small Garnet sweet potato, about 1/2 pound, peeled and cut into 1-inch cubes

1 tablespoon chopped fresh cilantro

thicken and deepen in color. If you are not serving the stew right away, cover the pan.

4 If the stew has cooled, bring it back to a near simmer over medium-low heat. Check the sauce and thin it with 1 to 2 tablespoons water if it is too thick. Taste it as well and adjust the flavor with extra pinches of salt and/or sugar, if necessary. Then transfer to a serving bowl, sprinkle with the cilantro, and serve immediately.

WATER SPINACH STIR-FRY

Rau Muống Xào

IT IS HARD TO IMAGINE the Viet table without water spinach (a.k.a. morning glory in English, *rau muống* in Vietnamese, and *ong choy* in Cantonese; illustrated on page 174), a long, tubular leafy green that is part of the lifeblood of the country and appears in many guises. The tender tops with their pointy leaves are often boiled or stir-fried. The hollow stems are sometimes laboriously split into slender pieces, dropped in water to curl, and then the crunchy raw spirals are used as a garnish for certain noodle dishes, such as Crab and Shrimp Rice Noodle Soup (page 215); as a bed for a beef stir-fry; or as a lightly dressed salad. Water spinach is also pickled.

Even today my parents become wistful at the mention of a rustic meal of boiled *rau muống*, soup prepared from the leftover cooking liquid, a heady fish *kho*, and rice. So, it was a sad moment when we arrived in the United States to discover that we could not afford water spinach, which cost nearly two dollars a pound and was not widely available. What had once been an everyday vegetable was suddenly a splurge. When my parents did buy it, my mother would stir-fry the greens with garlic and fermented shrimp sauce (*mắm tôm*) and finish the dish with lots of lime. Aromatic, earthy, and tangy, the traditional combination was a comforting reminder of our culinary roots.

Nowadays, *rau muống* is thankfully much less expensive and is easily found at Chinese and Southeast Asian markets. During the peak summer season, prices are downright cheap. Here are two options for stir-frying the bounty: first, the soulful dish of my youth, followed by a more modern preparation flavored with garlic and oyster sauce, which pairs well with Eastern and Western dishes (try it with a steak). If you can't find water spinach, Western spinach can be used for either of the two stir-fries that follow.

Serves 4 to 6 with 2 or 3 other dishes

1 bunch water spinach,
  13/4 to 2 pounds

1 Take each stem of water spinach and snap, twist, or cut off the bottom 4 inches, which tend to be too fibrous to eat. (As a test, try chewing on some of the hollow stem to see how much you should discard; in general, stems over 1/4 inch wide are too tough. Tough stem sections may be split for noodle soup; see page 216 for details.) Cut the trimmed water spinach into 3-inch sections and wash well in several changes of water, discarding any unsavory parts. Drain in a colander.

2 In a large pot, bring a generous amount of water (enough to cover the water spinach) to a rolling boil. Add the water spinach, moving it around with chopsticks or a spoon to ensure even cooking. Once it has wilted, after just under a 1 minute, drain it in the colander and flush with cold water. Press gently to expel excess water and then place near the stove and use for one of the following stir-fries. You may also ready the water spinach several hours in advance of stir-frying; cool, cover, and keep at room temperature.

WATER SPINACH STIR-FRIED WITH SHRIMP SAUCE AND LIME

Rau Muống Xào Mắm Tôm

FLAVORING SAUCE

2 teaspoons fine shrimp sauce

1 teaspoon fish sauce

1½ tablespoons water

2 tablespoons canola or other neutral oil

3 cloves garlic, finely chopped

Trimmed, cut, and blanched water spinach (opposite)

2 limes, cut into wedges

1 To make the flavoring sauce, in a small bowl, combine the shrimp sauce, fish sauce, and water and stir to mix well. Set aside.

2 In a wok or large skillet, heat the oil over medium-high heat until hot but not smoking. Add the garlic and stir-fry for 15 seconds, or until fragrant Add the water spinach and stir-fry for about 3 minutes, or until heated through. Add the flavoring sauce and toss with the greens to distribute evenly. Remove from the heat and squeeze half of the lime wedges over the water spinach. Stir gently and transfer to a serving plate. Serve with the remaining lime wedges for diners who enjoy a tangier dish.

SELECTING AND STORING WATER SPINACH

To minimize waste, select freshly cut bunches with stems no wider than ¼ inch. Once home, trim the ends (like a bunch of flowers), wrap the bottom 3 to 4 inches of stems in damp paper towels, and store in a plastic bag in the refrigerator to keep crisp. Cook the greens within a couple days.

WATER SPINACH STIR-FRIED WITH GARLIC

Rau Muống Xào Tỏi

FLAVORING SAUCE

¾ teaspoon sugar

1½ teaspoons fish sauce

1½ tablespoons oyster sauce

2 teaspoons canola or other neutral oil

3 cloves garlic, finely chopped

Trimmed, cut, and blanched water spinach (opposite)

1½ tablespoons canola or other neutral oil

1½ teaspoons cornstarch dissolved in 2 teaspoons water

1 To make the flavoring sauce, in a small bowl, combine the sugar, fish sauce, oyster sauce, and oil and stir to mix well. Stir in half of the garlic and set aside.

2 In a wok or large skillet, heat the oil over medium-high heat until hot but not smoking. Add the remaining garlic and stir-fry for about 15 seconds, or until fragrant. Add the water spinach and stir-fry for about 3 minutes, or until heated through. Give the flavoring sauce a stir to recombine and then add it to the pan and toss with the greens to distribute evenly. When the water spinach starts releasing its taupe-colored juices, add the cornstarch mixture. Cook for another minute, or until the sauce thickens slightly and the spinach takes on a silky finish. Transfer to a plate and serve.

CABBAGE AND EGG STIR-FRY

Bắp Cải Xào Trứng

BECAUSE COOL-SEASON CROPS such as cabbage and cauliflower are difficult to grow in Vietnam, they enjoy a special status. In fact, my dad remembers how his mother carefully tended the cabbage heads in the family garden, covering each one with a cooking pot to encourage the leaves to curl.

When we came to the States and found cabbage so readily available, my mother began fixing this easy stir-fry regularly for our weeknight suppers. I have since followed suit, and also sometimes serve it as a simple lunch with rice. The naturally sweet and spicy cabbage ribbons are enriched by a coating of egg, while a final splash of fish sauce adds a nutty, briny flavor.

1 In a wok or large skillet, heat the oil over medium-high heat until hot but not smoking. Add the garlic and stir-fry for about 15 seconds, or until fragrant. Add the cabbage and stir-fry for about 2 minutes, or until heated through and glistening. Splash in 1 tablespoon of the water to facilitate cooking and prevent browning. Continue stir-frying, adding the remaining 1 tablespoon water if the cabbage threatens to scorch.

2 After 2 to 3 minutes, when the cabbage has softened but is still crisp tender, splash in the fish sauce, pour in the egg, and stir-fry briefly to distribute the egg evenly. Before the egg firmly sets—you want a slightly custardy texture—remove from the heat. Transfer the cabbage to a plate and top with a generous amount of pepper for some spicy heat. Serve immediately.

Serves 4 with 2 or 3 other dishes

2 tablespoons canola or
    other neutral oil
2 cloves garlic, finely
    chopped
1/2 head green cabbage,
    cored and sliced into
    1/4-inch-wide ribbons
    (4 cups packed)

1 to 2 tablespoons water
2 teaspoons fish sauce
1 egg, beaten
Black pepper

ASPARAGUS AND SHIITAKE MUSHROOM STIR-FRY

Măng Tây Xào Nấm Hương

ASPARAGUS IS OFTEN THOUGHT OF as a vegetable that requires delicate seasoning, but this hearty stir-fry proves that notion wrong. The sweet, heady sauce is essentially the same sauce called for in Water Spinach Stir-Fried with Garlic (page 179), but the addition of meaty shiitake mushrooms produces a more robust dish. Prepare this easy stir-fry during springtime when asparagus is at the height of its season, or substitute 1¼ pounds green beans or long beans other times of the year. Be sure to use high-quality dried mushrooms, and don't skimp on the soaking time, or they won't develop their naturally full flavor or velvety texture.

1 Bring a large saucepan filled with salted water to a boil. Add the asparagus and parboil for about 1 minute, or until just tender but still firm. Drain and rinse under cold water to stop the cooking. Set aside. Have the mushrooms cut and ready to cook.

2 To make the flavoring sauce, in a small bowl, combine the sugar, fish sauce, oyster sauce, oil, and water and stir to dissolve the sugar. Set aside. (The asparagus and the sauce may be readied several hours in advance and kept at room temperature.)

3 In a wok or large skillet, heat the oil over medium heat until hot but not smoking. Add the asparagus and mushrooms and stir-fry for about 3 minutes, or until heated through. Raise the heat to medium-high. Give the flavoring sauce a stir to recombine, then add to the pan and stir to distribute evenly. When only a little sauce is visible, after about 1 minute, transfer the vegetables to a plate and serve.

Serves 4 to 6 with 2 or 3 other dishes

Salt

1½ pounds asparagus, woody ends trimmed and cut on the diagonal into 1½- to 2-inch pieces (generous 1 pound after trimming)

6 to 8 dried shiitake mushrooms, reconstituted (page 332), trimmed, and cut into ¼-inch-thick strips

FLAVORING SAUCE

½ teaspoon sugar

1½ teaspoons fish sauce

1 generous tablespoon oyster sauce

2 teaspoons canola or other neutral oil

1½ tablespoons water

1½ tablespoons canola or other neutral oil

CRISPY EGGPLANT SLICES

Cà Tím Rán

EGGPLANTS ARE PREPARED IN MANY WAYS by Viet cooks, but my two favorites are deep-fried, as in this recipe, and grilled or roasted until smoky and soft, as in Grilled Eggplant with Seared Scallion (page 184). Here, I coat thickish eggplant slices with a thin batter, which yields deep-fried pieces with a moist interior and a delicate crust that remains crisp well after frying. For the best results, use slender, firm, blemish-free Chinese, Italian, or Japanese eggplants. They have an appealing meatiness and fry better than large globe eggplants.

1   Trim off the stem and flower ends from each eggplant and then cut the eggplants into scant 1/4-inch-thick slices. You can cut rounds or you can angle the knife slightly for a diagonal cut. To lessen the bitterness of the eggplants, place the slices in a bowl, cover with water, and let stand for 10 minutes.

2   Meanwhile, make the batter. In a shallow bowl, stir together the all-purpose flour, rice flour, cornstarch, sugar, and salt. Make a well in the center, pour the ice water into the well, and then whisk the water into the flour mixture to create a silky batter. Set aside.

3   Drain the eggplant in a colander. Lay the slices flat in a single layer on a dish towel. Top with a second dish towel and press gently to blot excess moisture. (You may instead use paper towels for this step.)

4   Put a wire rack on a baking sheet and place the baking sheet next to the stove. Gather up the eggplant slices and set them and the batter on the other side of the stove. Pour oil to a depth of 1 inch into a wok or 5-quart Dutch oven and heat over medium-high heat to 350°F on a deep-frying thermometer. (If you don't have a thermometer, stand a dry bamboo chopstick in the oil; if small bubbles immediately gather on the surface around the chopstick, the oil is ready.)

Serves 4 to 6 with 2 or 3 other dishes

3/4 pound Chinese, Italian, or Japanese eggplants

BATTER
2/3 cup all-purpose flour
1/3 cup rice flour
3 tablespoons cornstarch
3/4 teaspoon sugar
Scant 1/2 teaspoon salt
1 cup ice water

Corn or canola oil for deep-frying
1/3 cup Simple Dipping Sauce (page 309) mixed with 1 clove garlic, minced

5   Fry the eggplant slices in 3 or 4 batches to avoid crowding the pan and lowering the oil temperature. Dip each slice into the batter, letting the excess drip back into the bowl, and then gently drop it into the hot oil. Fry, turning once and adjusting the heat as needed to maintain an even temperature, for about 2 minutes on each side, or until golden and crispy. Move the slices around as they fry and split up any that stick together. When the slices are ready, transfer them to the rack to drain.

6   When all the eggplant slices are fried, arrange them on a serving plate. Serve immediately with the dipping sauce.

GRILLED CORN WITH SCALLION OIL

Bắp Nướng Mỡ Hành

PEOPLE OFTEN ASK ME what I remember about my life in Vietnam. I always respond that my memory is filled with photographic images of people and places, but because I was only six years old when we fled, I had not yet experienced enough of life to have fuller pictures. However, one of my most vivid memories is of our cook, Older Sister Thien, squatting and fanning the small charcoal brazier on which she grilled corn on the cob. As the corn cooked to a charred chewy sweetness, she brushed on scallion oil made with home-rendered lard. The aroma and taste were heavenly.

Here is my updated version with regular cooking oil. With so many varieties of corn available in summertime, you should have no trouble finding the sweetest one for grilling. This is traditionally a snack food, but it is also a wonderful addition to an Eastern or Western barbecue. Parboiling the ears before grilling ensures that the corn is evenly cooked and the grill work is fast.

Illustrated on page 144

Serves 6 with 2 or 3 other dishes

6 ears corn, husks and silk removed   Kosher salt

½ cup Scallion Oil Garnish (page 314)

1 Bring a large pot filled with salted water to a rolling boil. Plunge the corn into the water and parboil for 4 minutes. Remove the corn and set aside. If the pot isn't big enough to accommodate all the ears at once, parboil them in batches. (The corn may be parboiled several hours in advance, cooled, covered, and kept at room temperature.)

2 Prepare a medium-hot charcoal fire (you can hold your hand over the rack for only 3 to 4 seconds) or preheat a gas grill to medium-high. Lay the ears on the grill rack and grill, rolling them often, for about 5 minutes total, or until they are marked by rich brown areas on all sides. There is no need to brown the entire ear.

3 Brush some scallion oil on top of each ear, and then roll that side down to face the flames. Let cook for 30 seconds to develop the flavors. You want some of the scallion bits to stick to the kernels, though a fair amount will fall off. Now brush the second side of each ear and again turn to cook for 30 seconds. Transfer the corn to a serving plate and garnish with any leftover scallion oil. Sprinkle lightly with the salt and serve.

GRILLED EGGPLANT WITH SEARED SCALLION

Cà Tím Nướng

IN VIETNAM, small clay charcoal-fired braziers are used to cook dishes like this smoky eggplant topped with scallion and served with a garlic-chile dipping sauce. Here in the States, I often make this dish in the summer when the farmers' market is brimming with an incredible array of eggplants. (The vegetable is at its sweetest in August and September.) You can cook the eggplant over a gas burner, or even bake it, but you'll have the best results on a grill. Small globe eggplants, meaty Italian eggplants, and slender Japanese eggplants all work well for this recipe.

1 To expose each eggplant fully to the heat, peel off the pointy flaps of the cap but leave the stem attached. Use a fork to poke 6 to 8 sets of holes into each eggplant to prevent it from exploding while cooking (skip this step if you are oven roasting).

2 To cook the eggplants on a grill, prepare a hot charcoal fire (you can hold your hand over the rack for only 2 to 3 seconds) or preheat a gas grill to high. Grill the eggplants, turning frequently, for 12 to 15 minutes, or until the skin is black and dry and the flesh is soft.

To cook the eggplants on a gas stove top, turn on the burner to high and place the eggplants, one at a time, directly on the burner grate. Cook the eggplant, rotating it often, for 10 to 15 minutes, or until it has sagged and is pleasantly smoky and charred. Run the exhaust fan during cooking to avoid filling your kitchen with smoke. If the eggplant isn't sufficiently soft in the middle, finish it off in a preheated 450°F oven.

To oven roast the eggplants, position a rack in the middle of the oven and preheat to 450°F. Split each eggplant in half lengthwise and place, cut side down, on an aluminum foil–lined baking sheet. Roast for 30 to 45 minutes, or until the eggplant halves are soft and oozing a bit of juice.

Serves 4 with 2 or 3 other dishes

2½ pounds small globe, Italian, or Japanese eggplants

2 scallions, green part only, thinly sliced

2 tablespoons canola or other neutral oil

⅓ cup Simple Dipping Sauce (page 309) mixed with 1 clove garlic, minced

3 When the eggplants are cool enough to handle, remove the skin. (The eggplants may be cooked and peeled several hours in advance of serving, covered, and kept at room temperature.) Cut the flesh crosswise into 2-inch sections. Use your fingers to separate the flesh into strips, placing them in a lovely pile on a serving plate. If the strips weep lots of liquid, pour it off the plate. Top with a mound of scallions.

4 In a butter warmer or small saucepan, heat the oil until it starts to smoke. Remove from the heat and immediately pour the oil over the scallions. The scallions will sizzle as they sear from the hot oil. Serve at once with the dipping sauce.

RUSSIAN BEET, POTATO, AND CARROT SALAD

Rau Củ Trộn (Salade Russe)

INTRODUCED TO VIETNAM BY THE FRENCH as *salade russe*, this salad is a fine example of how Viet cooking blurs culinary and cultural traditions. Home cooks incorporated it into their repertoire, and I grew up treating it as any other Viet vegetable dish. During the summer, my mother served it with roasted chicken that had been marinated in garlic and Maggi Seasoning sauce.

While there are many versions of this salad, I prefer combining the three root vegetables with chopped egg and a creamy herb vinaigrette. Use red beets for a beautiful magenta salad, pink or golden beets for a jewel-toned salad. For an interesting barbecue menu, serve the salad with Grilled Lemongrass Pork Riblets (page 145), Grilled Corn with Scallion Oil (page 183), and a lightly dressed green salad.

Illustrated on page 144

Serves 6 to 8 with 2 or 3 other dishes

1 Position a rack in the middle of the oven and preheat to 400°F. Place the beets in a baking dish and add water just to cover the bottom of the dish. Cover tightly with aluminum foil and bake for 45 minutes to 1 hour, or until easily pierced with a knife. (A covered ovenproof saucepan may be used instead; if the pan has a heavy bottom, heat the pan on the stove top until the water simmers before putting it in the oven.) Remove from the oven, uncover, and let cool.

2 When the beets are cool enough to handle, cut off the stem and root ends and use your fingers to slip off the skin. Cut each beet into 1/2-inch dice and put into a small bowl. Toss with the vinegar and season lightly with salt. Set aside for at least 15 minutes to let the flavors develop.

3 Meanwhile, make the dressing. In a bowl large enough to accommodate the finished salad, whisk together the vinegar, oil, mayonnaise, salt, and pepper. Add the shallot and herbs and stir to mix. Set aside near the stove.

3 beets, stems trimmed with about 1/2 inch intact (about 1 1/4 pounds after trimming)

2 tablespoons cider vinegar, red wine vinegar, or white wine vinegar

Salt

DRESSING

4 1/2 tablespoons cider vinegar, red wine vinegar, or white wine vinegar

1/4 cup canola or other neutral oil

1/4 cup mayonnaise, preferably whole egg

3/4 teaspoon salt

1/4 teaspoon black pepper

1 shallot, finely chopped, rinsed under water, and well drained (about 1/4 cup)

2 tablespoons finely chopped fresh herbs such as dill, mint, parsley, and/or tarragon

Salt

2 large carrots, 8 to 10 ounces total, peeled and cut into 1/2-inch dice

3 or 4 white or red boiling potatoes, about 1 1/4 pounds total, cut into 1/2-inch dice

3 eggs, hard boiled, peeled, and chopped

4 Bring a saucepan filled with salted water to a rolling boil and add the carrots. When the water returns to a boil, cook the carrots for 5 to 7 minutes, or until tender but still moderately firm. Using a slotted spoon or skimmer, lift out the carrots, shake briefly over the pan to drain off excess water, and then add to the bowl holding the dressing.

5 Return the water to a rolling boil. While the water is heating up, put the potatoes in a large bowl and fill with cold water. Stir the potatoes with your hand and pour out the cloudy water. Repeat until the water is clear. Drain the potatoes well and add to the boiling water. When the water returns to a boil, cook the potatoes for 4 to 6 minutes, or until tender but still moderately firm. Drain well in a colander and, while still hot, add to the bowl holding the carrots and dressing and toss well.

6 Add the beets and egg and toss again. Taste and add extra salt and pepper, if necessary. Cover with plastic wrap and refrigerate to chill thoroughly before serving.

MORE SALAD OPTIONS

When a meal includes hybrid dishes that combine Viet and Western flavors, such as Pan-Seared Beef Steaks (page 136) and Beef Stewed with Tomato, Star Anise, and Lemongrass (page 151), a green salad is always a good accompaniment. My mother used to offer an iceberg lettuce salad seasoned with onions that had been marinated in distilled white vinegar, vegetable oil, salt, pepper, and sugar. Her old-fashioned approach, a bracing nod to the French colonial period, has thankfully given way to salads made with more tender lettuces and more nuanced dressings. Nowadays, because of the variety of oils and vinegars available, you can fashion all manner of light vinaigrettes, flavoring them perhaps with freshly grated ginger, unseasoned rice vinegar, soy sauce, and/or a touch of sesame oil, and use them to dress an equally varied selection of salad greens.

To stay within the purely Vietnamese repertoire, make a *gỏi* or *nộm* (special-event salads, pages 46 to 55). Although these salads are mostly served as first courses preceding an array of elaborate dishes, they make great side salads, too. For casual meals, I often omit the pork, chicken, and/or shrimp to save time, with results that are less luxurious but still tasty and refreshing.

PANFRIED STUFFED TOFU WITH FRESH TOMATO SAUCE

Đậu Hũ Nhồi Thịt Xốt Cà

OF ALL THE VIETNAMESE TOFU DISHES, this recipe and the deep-fried tofu on page 191 are the ones I ate most often as a child. To this day, my mom still panfries double batches of stuffed tofu so that she and my dad can reheat individual servings in the toaster oven over the course of several days.

For this recipe, use tofu sold in large, bricklike blocks, rather than smaller cakes, as it is easier to cut the big blocks to size. Regular tofu is a little difficult to stuff but produces a delicate, silky interior. The exterior doesn't hold its crispiness but is delicious nonetheless. Medium-firm tofu is easier to stuff and holds its crispiness for a long time, but the interior is chewy and less delicate. Firm tofu is too hard and silken tofu is much too soft. When tomatoes are out of season, substitute a 14 ½-ounce can of whole tomatoes, drained and chopped, and use ¼ cup of the canning liquid in place of the water. Or, skip the tomato sauce altogether and instead dip the tofu in Simple Dipping Sauce (page 309) or a combination of soy sauce and fresh chiles.

1 To make the filling, in a small bowl, combine the pork, scallion, mushrooms, egg, fish sauce, pepper, and cornstarch mixture and beat vigorously with a fork until well blended. Set aside.

2 Drain the tofu and cut into ½-inch-thick pieces each about 2¼ inches square. You may have to cut the tofu in half crosswise. There will be 8, 10, or 12 pieces, depending on the size and shape of the block. Lay a piece flat on your work surface and cut a horizontal slit in it, stopping ½ to ¼ inch shy of the opposite side to avoid splitting the piece in half. Make sure the cut is equally deep on both sides. Repeat with the remaining pieces.

3 To fill each tofu piece, hold it in one hand and use the other hand to open it up carefully like a tiny book. If the top flap naturally lays open, let it rest on the soft part of the thumb. Otherwise, use the thumb to keep the flap peeled back. Use a fork or small spatula to spread a layer of filling about ¼ inch

continued

Serves 3 to 4 with 2 or 3 other dishes

FILLING

⅓ pound ground pork, coarsely chopped to loosen

1 scallion, white and green parts, finely chopped

2 dried shiitake mushrooms, reconstituted (page 332), stemmed, and finely chopped

1 egg, lightly beaten

1 tablespoon fish sauce

¼ teaspoon black pepper

1 teaspoon cornstarch dissolved in 2 teaspoons water

1 large block regular or medium-firm tofu, 16 to 19 ounces

Canola or other neutral oil for panfrying

SAUCE

2 cloves garlic, minced

1½ cups peeled, seeded, and finely chopped ripe tomato

¼ cup water

1 tablespoon fish sauce

Salt

Sugar

thick on one side. Lower the top flap and press the filling gently into place. Don't worry if the tofu tears a little. As you work, place the stuffed tofu squares on a double layer of paper towels to absorb excess water.

4   Preheat the oven to 175° to 200°F for keeping the tofu squares hot once they are fried. Pour enough oil into a 12-inch nonstick skillet to film the bottom (about 4 tablespoons) and heat over medium heat. Panfry the tofu in 2 batches to avoid crowding, and give each stuffed square a final blotting on a paper towel before you lay it gently in the skillet. Fry for 4 to 6 minutes, or until the bottom is golden brown; the timing will depend on the density of the tofu. Using 2 spatulas, carefully flip the tofu over and fry the second side for 4 to 6 minutes, or until golden brown and the filling is cooked. Transfer the cooked tofu to a plate and place in the oven. Repeat with the remaining tofu.

5   Lower the heat slightly and pour off all but 2 tablespoons of the oil from the pan. To make the sauce, add the garlic to the pan and sauté for about 15 seconds, or until fragrant. Add the tomato, water, and fish sauce, bring to a simmer, and cook for about 5 minutes, or until the tomato breaks down and the flavors have blended. (Extra water may be needed, depending on the juiciness of the tomato.) When the sauce has thickened slightly, taste and season it with a little salt to deepen the flavor and with a little sugar to balance the tartness.

6   Remove from the heat and spoon the sauce onto the center of a platter or 2 serving plates. Arrange the stuffed tofu on top and serve.

VIET TOFU

In the markets in Little Saigon in Southern California, trays of still-warm fresh tofu are delivered daily. Wrapped in plastic and glistening with condensation, the fat, spongy, brick-sized cakes are too beautiful to resist. Poke at one and it will jiggle. You can't get fresher tofu unless you patronize a *lò đậu hủ* (literally, "tofu oven"), a Viet tofu shop.

If you come across this medium-firm tofu, buy some and enjoy it the same day to appreciate its freshness. To keep for about two weeks, remove the plastic, put the tofu in a tub of water, cover, and refrigerate, changing the water every third day.

DEEP-FRIED TOFU SIMMERED WITH SCALLION

Đậu Hũ Chiên Tẩm Hành Lá

VIET COOKS OFTEN deep-fry cubes of tofu until crisp and golden and then add them to a stir-fry or a simmering liquid (in this case, a mixture of fish sauce, water, and scallion). Fried tofu absorbs other flavors especially well, yet holds its shape and retains its faintly nutty overtones. The end result is a chewy, almost meaty quality.

Look for regular or medium-firm tofu for deep-frying, never the silken type or the firm type that is best for grilling. Freshly made tofu (see opposite) will puff up during frying and then deflate as it cools; packaged tofu won't do that and will be denser after it is out of the oil. Both will have excellent flavor. When building your menu, treat this recipe as the main savory dish and accompany it with a vegetable dish and/or meat-and-vegetable stir-fry, a simple soup, and rice.

1 In a wide, shallow saucepan or 10-inch skillet, combine the water and enough fish sauce to create a lightly savory liquid. The tofu will completely absorb this liquid, so make it a little less strong than you would like. Place the pan next to the stove.

2 Pour oil to a depth of 1½ inches into a wok or 5-quart Dutch oven and heat over medium-high heat to 350°F on a deep-frying thermometer. (If you don't have a thermometer, stand a dry bamboo chopstick in the oil; if small bubbles immediately gather on the surface around the chopstick, the oil is ready.)

3 Fry the tofu cubes in 2 or 3 batches to avoid crowding the pan and lowering the oil temperature. Gently drop the tofu into the hot oil, which will foam vigorously. The tofu will immediately sink to the bottom and then eventually float up. As the tofu cubes fry, use a skimmer to push them around to ensure even frying and to separate any that stick together. After 4 to 6 minutes, the cubes should be golden and crispy. Use the skimmer to lift them out of the oil and then shake it over the pan briefly to drain away excess oil. Put the tofu directly into the saucepan holding the fish sauce and water. Repeat until all the tofu is fried. (You can fry

Serves 4 with 2 or 3 other dishes

½ cup water
2 to 3 tablespoons fish sauce
1½ pounds regular or medium-firm tofu (in cakes or large blocks), cut into 1-inch cubes, drained well in a colander, and patted dry

Corn or canola oil for deep-frying
3 scallions, green part only, chopped

the tofu several hours in advance, cover, and keep at room temperature. Just before serving, add the tofu to the fish sauce and water and continue with the recipe.)

4 Place the pan over medium heat, bring the tofu and sauce to a simmer, cover, and cook, stirring occasionally to expose all the surfaces to the seasonings, for 3 minutes, or until the tofu absorbs the liquid. Uncover, scatter in the scallion, and give everything a big stir. Transfer to a shallow bowl and serve immediately.

EVERYDAY DAIKON AND CARROT PICKLE

Đồ Chua

THE VIETNAMESE NAME for this fast pickle literally translates as "sour stuff." Although it doesn't sound enticing, it is exactly what you want to serve whenever you need a simple garnish (or side) that is tart, sweet, and crunchy. I keep a jar of it in the refrigerator for stuffing baguette sandwiches (page 34), for serving alongside grilled meats such as Grilled Garlicky Five-Spice Pork Steaks (page 143), and for adding to Duck and Chinese Egg Noodle Soup (page 220).

Some people like the vegetables on the sweet side, but I prefer a tangy flavor and therefore use less sugar. When selecting daikons, look for evenly shaped, firm, smooth, unblemished roots.

1 Place the carrot and daikons in a bowl and sprinkle with the salt and 2 teaspoons of the sugar. Use your hands to knead the vegetables for about 3 minutes, expelling the water from them. They will soften and liquid will pool at the bottom of the bowl. Stop kneading when you can bend a piece of daikon so that the ends touch but the daikon does not break. The vegetables should have lost about one-fourth of their volume. Drain in a colander and rinse under cold running water, then press gently to expel extra water. Return the vegetables to the bowl if you plan to eat them soon, or transfer them to a 1-quart jar for longer storage.

2 To make the brine, in a bowl, combine the 1/2 cup sugar, the vinegar, and the water and stir to dissolve the sugar. Pour over the vegetables. The brine should cover the vegetables. Let the vegetables marinate in the brine for at least 1 hour before eating. They will keep in the refrigerator for up to 4 weeks.

Makes about 3 cups

1 large carrot, peeled and cut into thick matchsticks

1 pound daikons, each no larger than 2 inches in diameter, peeled and cut into thick matchsticks

1 teaspoon salt

2 teaspoons plus 1/2 cup sugar

1 1/4 cups distilled white vinegar

1 cup lukewarm water

NOTE

Sometimes the daikon develops a strong odor as it sits in the jar. This doesn't mean that the pickle has gone bad. Before serving it, open the jar and let it sit for about 15 minutes to allow the odor to dissipate.

CRUNCHY PICKLED BEAN SPROUT SALAD

Dưa Giá

THIS SOUTHERN VIETNAMESE SPECIALTY is technically a pickle because the vegetables steep in brine, but it is eaten in large amounts, more like a salad, with intensely flavored pork and fish *kho* (dishes simmered in caramel sauce). The texture and flavors of the vegetables provide the perfect bright contrast to the inky, deep flavors of *kho*.

Flat, delicately flavored Chinese chives are traditionally combined with the bean sprouts and carrot. Because these chives can be hard to find, I often substitute leafy green scallion tops. Select small scallions the width of a chopstick or medium scallions. Larger ones can be too harsh. If you can find Chinese chives, substitute a nickel-sized bunch for the scallions.

1 To make the brine, in a small saucepan, combine the sugar, salt, vinegar, and water and heat over medium heat, stirring occasionally until the sugar and salt have dissolved. Remove from the heat and set aside to cool completely.

2 Up to 2 hours in advance of serving, combine the bean sprouts, carrot, and scallions in a bowl. Pour the cooled brine over the vegetables and then use your fingers to toss the vegetables in the brine. Set aside to marinate for 30 minutes, turning the vegetables 2 or 3 times to expose them evenly to the brine. At first, there won't be enough brine to cover the vegetables, but they will eventually shrink in volume. When the vegetables are ready for eating, the brine will almost cover them and they will have a pleasantly tangy flavor and lots of crunch. Taste to make sure they have sat long enough.

3 Once you are satisfied with the flavor, drain the vegetables and pile them high on a plate. Serve them within 2 hours to enjoy them at their peak.

Makes 4 to 5 cups, to serve 4 to 6 with 2 or 3 other dishes

2/3 cup sugar

1 1/2 teaspoons salt

1 cup distilled white vinegar

1 cup water

1 pound bean sprouts

1 carrot, peeled and cut into matchsticks

5 small or 4 medium scallions, green part only, cut into 1 1/2-inch lengths

TANGY MIXED VEGETABLE PICKLE

Dưa Góp

MY MOM, WHO WAS BORN IN NORTHERN VIETNAM, grew up with this regional pickle. Quan, my brother-in-law, is addicted to it, and when he visits her, he never fails to find the jar that she always keeps in her fridge. While *dưa góp* sometimes contains different ingredients, such as green papaya, this combination of cauliflower, bell pepper, and carrot offers a nice balance of flavor, color, and texture.

Traditionally the pickle is served with rich meats and fried fish, but the vegetables are great alone as a quick nibble or as part of a charcuterie platter (Vietnamese or otherwise), antipasto spread, or sandwich plate.

1 In a large bowl, combine the salt and lukewarm water and stir with your hand or a spoon to dissolve the salt. Add all the vegetables. The water should just cover them. If it doesn't, add more lukewarm water as needed. Set aside for 4 to 6 hours. The vegetables will soften and become slightly chewy.

2 Meanwhile, prepare the brine. In a saucepan, combine the vinegar, sugar, and cold water and heat over medium heat, stirring occasionally until the sugar has dissolved. Remove from the heat and set aside to cool completely.

3 Drain the salted vegetables but do not rinse them. Put them in a 2- or 3-quart glass or plastic container. Pour in just enough of the brine to cover and discard the balance. Cover the container and refrigerate overnight. The pickle is ready to eat the next day. It will keep well in the refrigerator for about 3 weeks. Beyond that, it loses its edge.

NOTE

If you decide to prepare a double batch, you will only need 1 1/2 recipes of the brine.

Makes about 8 cups

1/4 cup salt

3 cups lukewarm water

1 large or 2 medium red bell peppers, 8 to 10 ounces total, seeded and cut into strips 1/2 inch wide and 1 1/2 inches long

2 large or 3 medium carrots, 8 to 10 ounces total, peeled and cut on the diagonal into pieces a scant 1/4 inch thick and 2 inches long

1 small head cauliflower, about 1 1/4 pounds, trimmed and cut into 1-inch florets

2 cups distilled white vinegar

1 1/4 cups sugar

2 cups cold water

PICKLED SHALLOTS

Dưa Hành

LOVELY TO LOOK AT, these rosy shallots are also wonderful to eat. Their delightful tanginess and mild bite cut the richness of foods like beef or pork *kho* and Viet sausages, headcheese, or pâté. They are also good in a Western salad or sandwich. Tipplers might even try a few in a gin on the rocks.

These shallots are a must for Tet celebrations. In fact, there is a traditional Tet couplet that includes *dưa hành* as one of the required foods for the holiday. My family doesn't wait for the Lunar New Year to eat them, however. My mom and I make them year-round, using this recipe from my late aunt, Bac Dao. A widow most of her life, she often prepared large batches of various foods and divided them up among her family and friends. These shallots were usually among her gifts.

Use small shallots (sold at Asian markets in red plastic net bags, each weighing about a pound) that are firm and without sprouts or mold. If shallots aren't available, substitute red pearl onions (sold at most supermarkets).

Makes about 2 cups

10 ounces (about 2 cups) small shallots, unpeeled and each no larger than 1 inch in diameter	2 tablespoons salt dissolved in 1 cup water
	1/2 cup sugar
Boiling water	1 cup distilled white vinegar

1 Put the shallots in a small heatproof bowl and pour boiling water over them to cover. Let stand for 2 to 3 minutes, during which the skins will loosen and wrinkle. Pour off the hot water and add cold water to cool the shallots quickly. Drain in a colander.

2 To peel each shallot, use a small, sharp knife to cut off a bit of the stem end. Working from the stem end, peel away the outer skin and any dry-looking layers underneath to reveal a glossy, smooth shallot. Separate any Siamese-twin bulbs to remove the skin fully. Finally, cut away the root end, taking care to leave enough so the shallot won't fall apart. Repeat with the remaining shallots.

3 Return the peeled shallots to the bowl and pour in the salt solution. There should be enough for the shallots to float a bit. Let them stand at least overnight or up to 24 hours to remove some of their harshness.

4 Drain and rinse the shallots well under cold running water. In a small saucepan, combine the sugar and vinegar and bring to a rolling boil, stirring occasionally until the sugar has dissolved. Add the shallots and when the liquid returns to a simmer, immediately remove the pan from the heat. Use a slotted spoon to transfer the shallots to a 1-pint jar. Pour in the hot vinegar solution to fill to the rim. Set aside to cool, uncovered, then cover and refrigerate.

5 Allow the shallots to mature for 5 days before serving. They will keep refrigerated for several weeks, though they are likely to be long gone by then.

SWEET AND SALTY PRESERVED RADISH

Củ Cải Dầm

WHEN YOU WANT A SALTY-SWEET ADDITION to your food, look to these bits of golden radish. The pickle is made using the packaged salted radish, commonly labeled salted or preserved turnip, sold at Chinese and Vietnamese markets (check the dried vegetable aisle). The plastic packages come in different sizes, and the radishes are packed in a variety of forms, from minced to whole. I prefer to start out with chunky thick strips the size of a finger and cut them myself. Don't be put off by any musty smells emanating from the package. After the contents are rinsed, soaked in water, and seasoned, the off odor disappears and the crisp strips become a wonderful and rather delicate treat. In less than an hour, the radish is ready for eating or long-term storage. I snack on the strips straight from the jar, or serve them with rice or chopped up in bowls of Hanoi Special Rice Noodle Soup (page 217).

1 Put the radish in a colander and rinse with cold running water. Transfer to a heatproof bowl and add boiling water to cover by 1 inch. Set aside for 20 minutes to allow the radish to soften and expand a little. Drain and, if necessary, cut the radish into strips about 1/4 inch wide and 2 inches long.

2 Return the strips to the bowl, add the sugar, fish sauce, and ginger, and toss to coat the strips evenly. After 10 to 15 minutes, they are ready to eat. Don't expect much liquid because the radish soaks up most of the fish sauce.

3 To store the radish, tightly pack the strips and the seasonings into a small glass jar and refrigerate for up to 6 months. When using them, remove strips from the bottom of the jar, which will be more flavorful. After you pull out what you need, stir the remainder around in the jar to expose them evenly to the seasonings. If the radish strips get too salty, rinse briefly with water before eating.

Makes about 1¼ cups

1 package (7 ounces) Chinese salted radish (turnip) strips
Boiling water
2 tablespoons sugar
3 tablespoons fish sauce

3 quarter-sized slices fresh ginger, peeled and smashed with the broad side of a cleaver or chef's knife

GARLICKY PRESERVED DAIKON AND CARROT

Dưa Món

A SPECIALTY OF CENTRAL VIETNAM, these preserved vegetables pack plenty of punch in each garlicky, savory, sweet, and crunchy morsel. Served as a small side dish, they are a flavorful addition to any meal and even make a bowl of plain rice satisfying. Traditionally, the vegetables are cut into thick, stubby sticks, salted, and then partially dried outdoors on bamboo trays before they are left to sit in a mixture of fish sauce, sugar, and garlic. Here in the States, the oven speeds up the process considerably. I use small young daikons and large carrots and cut them into rounds instead of sticks.

Makes about 1¹/₂ cups

1¹/₂ pounds daikons, each about 1¹/₂ inches in diameter, peeled and cut into ¹/₄-inch-thick rounds	1¹/₂ tablespoons salt
	¹/₄ cup sugar
	¹/₂ cup water
¹/₂ pound carrots, each about 1 inch in diameter, peeled and cut into ¹/₄-inch-thick rounds	3 to 4 tablespoons fish sauce
	2 large cloves garlic, sliced

1   Put the daikons and carrots in a bowl and toss well with the salt. Set aside for 3 hours to allow the vegetables to weep. Drain in a colander and rinse with cold running water. Pat dry.

2   Set the oven to the lowest possible heat setting, which is usually "warm" or 175°F. You want a temperature of between 140° and 160°F, so hang an oven thermometer where it can be easily read and keep the oven door open the entire time. For drying racks, use 2 wire racks, covering each with a layer of cheesecloth to prevent the vegetables from falling through.

3   Lay the vegetables flat on the racks. To maximize air circulation, place the drying racks directly on the oven racks and run the exhaust fan. Let the vegetables dry for about 2 hours, checking the oven temperature every 30 minutes. The vegetables are ready when they are about one-third their original size and barely damp to the touch. Each chewy piece should be ¹/₁₆ to ¹/₈ inch thick. Together they should weigh about 4¹/₂ ounces and fill 1¹/₄ cups.

4   Meanwhile, in a small saucepan, combine the sugar and water and bring to a boil, stirring occasionally until the sugar has dissolved. Remove from the heat and let cool completely. Add enough of the fish sauce to create a pleasant sweet-and-savory flavor. Cover and set aside.

5   When the vegetables are dried, put them in a bowl and cover with warm water. Squeeze gently a few times and then drain in a colander, squeezing again to remove excess saltiness. Return the vegetables to the bowl and toss with the garlic. Pack them into a 1-pint jar and pour in the fish sauce solution. Push the vegetables down so they are covered with liquid. Set aside, uncovered, until cool.

6   Cover the jar and refrigerate the vegetables for 4 days before eating. They will keep in the refrigerator for up to 6 months. If they get too salty, rinse briefly with water before eating.

8. NOODLES FROM MORNING UNTIL NIGHT

My love of noodles began when I was five years old, on a visit with my parents to a small *phở* shop in Saigon. Perched on a wooden bench, I wielded chopsticks and spoon with remarkable aplomb, considering my age. As I worked my way to the bottom of the bowl, my parents held their heads high, while the owner marveled at their daughter's advanced eating skills. My memory of that proud moment, and the heady broth, savory beef, and chewy-tender noodles, is one of the most vivid from my childhood.

Once we arrived in the United States, casually slipping into a noodle joint or pausing at a street-side vendor for a noodle snack wasn't possible anymore, and so we enjoyed homemade noodle dishes instead. Preparing good noodles—whether soupy, dry, or saucy—requires time and care, which made it a weekend activity. After the requisite eight o'clock Sunday morning mass, our family would often skip the donuts-and-coffee social and head straight home to assemble bowls of noodle soup for a traditional Viet breakfast. Chicken *phở*, beef *phở*, and orange-hued Hue beef noodle soup were standard menu items. We also enjoyed delicate *bún thang*, my mother's favorite northern Vietnamese soup, which she worked diligently to perfect.

No matter what type of soup was on the menu, Mom made the broth and readied the other ingredients on Saturday. When we returned home from church, she would quickly change out of her traditional *áo dài* and head to the kitchen, marshaling us into action on the way. While she heated the fragrant broth, some of us set the table and others formed the noodle-soup assembly line. Things often got manic for two reasons: for proper enjoyment, noodle soup must be piping hot when it is served,

and our family of seven hadn't consumed anything all morning except communion wafers, so we were ravenous.

As we assembled the bowls, we took care to meet various personal preferences, such as Dad's fondness for noodles and Ha's dislike of raw onion. The order of assembly in each bowl was exactingly prescribed: first a mound of noodles, next the meat neatly arranged in a flat pattern on top so the hot broth would efficiently warm everything, and finally, after tasting and adjusting the seasoning one last time, my mother ladled the broth on top.

In Viet culinary terms, noodle soups are called *món nước*, or "watery dishes." If Vietnamese don't eat them at breakfast, they have them for lunch or a snack. They are considered *món phụ*, or "secondary dishes," and are never eaten as the main meal of the day, which is usually a multiple-dish dinner. In fact, when my father lived in Saigon, he sometimes went out for a late-evening bowl of *phở* even though he had eaten supper, explaining that the noodles settled his stomach before bedtime.

Theoretically, you can enjoy Vietnamese noodle dishes all day long, especially if you eat like folks do in Vietnam, in smallish portions that allow for sampling a wide variety of foods throughout the day. From a morning bowl of soup noodles, you might move on to a dry noodle dish (*món khô*) that features small round rice noodles (*bún*) and stir-fried beef or grilled pork or fish. In Vietnam, street-side vendors and restaurants often specialize in just one of these dry noodle dishes. At Vietnamese restaurants

continued

RECIPES

in America, these one-dish meals are often grouped under the heading *bún*, for the vermicelli-sized rice noodles they use.

Stir-fried, panfried, or sautéed noodles are either grouped with the dry noodle dishes or are included in the broad category of stir-fried foods (*món xào*). In both cases, they differ from their soup and *bún* counterparts because they are normally included in multiple-dish meals, rather than eaten on their own. When you make them, you will also notice that they carry certain Chinese influences, such as the use of Chinese chives and egg noodles.

In this chapter, you will find some of the best-known recipes from these classic noodle categories. They are drawn from the country's three major regional kitchens—southern, central, and northern—and they call for five of the most popular types of noodle, three made from rice flour, one from wheat flour, and one from bean starch. Yet together these dishes reflect only a small part of Vietnam's big and varied noodle table.

TYPES OF NOODLES

In Vietnam, noodles are such an important part of daily life that they are typically purchased fresh from a neighborhood vendor. My mother says, "We never knew about dried noodles until we came to the United States." Indeed, go to Vietnam today and you will find freshly made noodles sold at markets and used by both home and professional cooks. In the United States, fresh Vietnamese noodles are not nearly as commonplace, but plenty of good-quality dried noodles are available. There are countless types in the national repertoire, so here are only the major ones.

Flat rice noodles - *Bánh phở* (Baan fuh)

These noodles are available fresh or dried in small, medium, and large widths. The dried noodles cook up to a terrific chewy texture that is nearly as good as fresh. Keep several packages (14 or 16 ounces are most common) of each width in the pantry to make noodle dishes on demand. If the sizes are not printed on the packages, think of the noodles as Italian pasta: small is the width of linguine (1/8 inch) or narrower; medium is roughly the width of fettuccine (1/4 inch); and large is about the width of *pappardelle* (1/2 inch). Depending on how they will be used, the

dried noodles may be soaked first and then stir-fried or plunged into boiling water, or they may be simply boiled.

If available, try fresh *bánh phở*, stocked in the refrigerated sections of Chinese and Viet markets. The extrathin variety (about 1/16 inch wide) is for *phở* and requires only a brief dunk in boiling water before serving. The uncooked noodles will keep well for a week in the refrigerator. Nearby you will usually find wide fresh rice noodles that are the same as wide Chinese *fun* noodles. Often labeled *bánh hủ tiếu* (the Viet term for Chinese rice noodles), they are just another type of *bánh phở*. Although I seldom use them, uncut sheets of fresh rice noodles, or *bánh ướt*, are also sold, and may be used to roll up foods such as Grilled Lemongrass Beef Skewers (page 28). Purchase these latter two noodles only if they are soft and at room temperature, which means buying them not long after they are delivered to the market, and then eat them same day. Unfortunately, *bánh hủ tiếu* and *bánh ướt* are usually hard and cold by the time I find them, which is why the widest dried rice noodles are a better option. (Alternate names for dried noodles: rice sticks and *chantaboon*.)

Round rice noodles - *Bún* (Boon)

A Viet kitchen would be incomplete without *bún*. Most Vietnamese abroad keep these round rice noodles in dried form in their cupboard, though pricey fresh ones are sometimes sold at Viet markets. The dried noodles, imported from China, are available in small, medium, large, and extralarge widths. Resembling vermicelli noodles, the smallest *bún* is the handiest and most widely used for Viet cooking. Look for packages of wiry, flat skeins or straight sticks. For decades, Pagoda brand (Bun Thap Chua) has served cooks well. Newer Sailing Boat brand also cooks up to a satisfying toothsome texture. I only use large or extralarge *bún* for making Hue beef rice noodle soup (page 212). In general, I don't use the medium width, but some people like that size. Medium, large, and extralarge *bún* are sold as straight

Clockwise from top left: dried round rice noodles (small); dried fine rice noodles; cellophane noodles; dried round rice noodles (extra-large); fresh flat rice noodles (small); dried flat rice noodles (large, medium, and small); and (in the center) fresh Chinese egg noodles

sticks in colorful plastic packaging. (Alternate names: rice sticks, Jiangxi rice sticks, Jiangxi rice vermicelli, and rice vermicelli.)

Fine rice noodles - *Bánh hỏi* (Baan hoy)

These fine, delicate strands are a special-event food eaten with grilled meats and crispy pieces of Chinese roast pork. If the noodles are purchased fresh (packaged on a Styrofoam tray and resembling a mound of wide-mesh cheesecloth), you don't need to cook them. If they are dried, you will need to soak and steam them. *Bánh hỏi* is usually served as small, flat sheets arranged in layers on a plate, with scallion oil (page 314) between the layers. (It is customary to cut the noodles into manageable sections.) The noodles and meat are encased in soft lettuce and dipped into *nước chấm* (page 308). When the noodles are served with Chinese roast pork, the dipping sauce is basically sweet but with a slight edge from the addition of rice vinegar.

Cellophane noodles - *Miến* (Mee-en)

Made from mung bean starch, *miến* are featured in many Viet classics, from soup noodles to stir-fries, steamed fish to *chả giò* (page 120). They are only available dried, and as they cook and expand, they absorb flavors and adhere to other ingredients. Often labeled bean thread, these white or semiclear noodles are just 1/32 inch thick and are sold in coils of various weights. I find that the most useful packages are made of pink plastic netting and hold eight individually wrapped coils. In some packages, the coils weigh 1.3 ounces and in others 2 ounces. Don't be afraid to break up a bundle to get the quantity you need for a recipe. Also, beware of package weight misprints, and if you are unsure, use a scale to double check. You need to soak the noodles in hot water until they are soft and pliable before using, usually about fifteen minutes. Snip them into shorter lengths for soups and stir-fries, or chop with a knife for stuffing. (Alternate names: vermicelli, bean thread noodles, glass noodles, silver noodles, long rice, transparent noodles, and *bún tàu*.)

Chinese egg noodles - *Mì* (Mee)

Fresh Chinese egg noodles are superior to dried. Made from wheat flour and eggs, they are usually dusted with cornstarch to keep them from sticking and to provide a light, silky texture. When searching the refrigerated section of Asian markets for *mì*, look for noodles that appear dry, rather than moist, and supple. They should be pale yellow rather than bright yellow, which indicates the use of food coloring; check the ingredients list to make sure. There are many widths available; the recipes in this book call for thin noodles (1/16 inch thick) for soup and medium noodles (1/8 inch thick) for panfrying. Uncooked *mì* will keep for a couple weeks in the refrigerator and may be frozen for up to six months. Fresh noodles or thawed frozen noodles may be used in the recipes in this chapter. Fluff them up before cooking.

NOODLE BOILING BASICS

Many recipes in this chapter call for boiling noodles, which must be done correctly for a successful dish. The first step is to pick the right pot. You need one large enough to hold lots of water and with sufficient space in case the noodles foam up. For example, you need a five-quart pot to cook one pound of noodles.

Fill the pot with water and bring to a rolling boil. Unlike cooking Italian pasta, you don't need to salt the water. While the water is heating, put a large colander—it needs to be large, so the noodles drain quickly—in the sink for draining the noodles. Put a small inverted bowl or cup at the bottom to prevent the cooked noodles from gathering and clumping as they cool.

When the water is at a hard boil, add the noodles. As soon they go in, stir them with chopsticks to separate and submerge all the strands, and then occasionally swirl them around again as they cook. Most Asian noodles cook fast, so as soon as the water returns to a boil, begin watching the pot. Like most Asians, I like noodles that are tender yet still firm and chewy to the bite. Trust your own taste, as you may find that you like them more tender.

As soon as the noodles are done, drain them in the colander. Flush with cold water to stop the cooking and rinse off the excess starch. Pick up the colander and give it a few sideways shakes to expel the excess water. Once the noodles are cool, fluff them with your fingers.

NOODLE SOUP TIPS

Making Asian noodle soups is an art form that merits a cook's time and attention. There are no convenience products or shortcuts, so be prepared to give over a few hours to putting a soup together. Here are some tips to help you make and appreciate good noodle soups.

- To create a great soup, you must first create a great broth. Avoid a hard boil when making the broth or it will turn cloudy. Leave a bit of fat in it for richness; otherwise, you will have a fat-free, healthful broth that lacks the necessary mouthfeel. When adjusting the seasonings in the broth, shoot for an intense savoriness. Remember, the other ingredients are not heavily seasoned, so the broth should be saltier than what you are normally accustomed to. If you find that you have gone too far, just dilute it with a little water.

- Delicious soup also requires noodles that are warm. They should be cooked or reheated as you assemble the bowls. The two *phở* recipes require blanching raw noodles in boiling water. For other soups, the noodles are cooked ahead of time, and you can reheat them in boiling water or in the microwave oven. When blanching or reheating noodles in boiling water, use a large pot and big vertical-handle strainer (sold at Asian markets and housewares stores) to dunk and drain the noodles efficiently, and don't rinse the noodles after they are done. (If the strainer is unavailable, a regular mesh sieve is the next best choice.)

- Serving noodle soups requires a number of last-minute steps, so ready as many elements as you can in advance. For example, make the broth a day ahead. Before serving, set the table and put out any garnishes and condiments, enlisting a family member or friend to help you.

- The noodle soups in this chapter yield moderate-sized servings. At home, I use $3^1/_2$- to 4-cup porcelain bowls about seven inches in diameter, roughly the size of the "small" bowls used in Vietnamese American noodle shops. If you are accustomed to the snack-sized bowls of noodle soup in Vietnam, these servings will seem large.

- At the table, eat the noodle soup with gusto. Approach the bowl with a two-handed technique. First, wielding chopsticks in one hand and a Chinese soup spoon in the other, stir up the soup to distribute the flavors. Then, taste and adjust the flavors with condiments and/or garnishes. Dip and wiggle thin slices of hot chile in the broth to release their oil, and then leave them in if you dare. Strip fresh herb leaves from their stems, tear up the leaves, and drop them into your bowl. A squeeze of lime gives the broth a tart edge, which is especially nice if the broth is too sweet or too bland; if greater savory depth is needed, a shot of fish sauce will remedy the situation. Many people squirt hoisin sauce and Sriracha chile sauce directly into their bowls of *phở*, but a well-prepared broth suffers from such additions. Finally, eat the soup with both utensils, using the chopsticks to pick up the noodles and the spoon to deliver broth and other goodies to your mouth. Add more garnishes as you eat, and slurp to show the cook your appreciation.

- Bank your efforts by freezing leftover broth and cooked meats for another day. When you have a craving for noodle soup, you will be able to assemble it with a lot less work. Both the broth and meats may be kept frozen for several months.

CHICKEN AND CELLOPHANE NOODLE SOUP

Miến Gà

FOR VIETNAMESE LIVING ABROAD, a trip to Saigon would be incomplete without a visit to Ben Thanh Market, a huge maze of fresh food and sundries. Near the center is a food court where vendors hawk popular Viet treats. As you sample their wares, you are apt to strike up conversations with other gluttonous Viet *kiều* (Vietnamese expats). On one occasion, a man from Texas visiting his family for Tet told me part of his daily routine while in Vietnam included eating *miến gà*, which was so deliciously light that it allowed him to order more dishes from other vendors.

This noodle soup is easy to prepare. Most versions contain shallot, garlic, and chicken giblets, but our family enjoys a simpler preparation that focuses on just a few ingredients, most of which go into the hot stock moments before serving and are then ladled directly into the waiting bowls, with no fancy assembly required. For a nice lunch, present large servings of this soup with a special-event salad (pages 46 to 55). Or, offer it in smaller portions for an elegant beginning to a celebratory meal. This recipe is easily halved.

1 In a large pot, bring the stock to a boil over high heat. Drop in the chicken breast. When the water starts bubbling at the edges of the pan, remove the pan from the heat and cover tightly. Let stand for 20 minutes. The chicken breast should be firm yet still yield a bit to the touch. Remove it and let cool, then shred with your fingers into small bite-sized pieces, pulling the meat along its natural grain. Set aside.

2 Add the fish sauce and rock sugar to the stock and then bring it to a boil over medium-high heat. Taste and add salt, if necessary. Add the chicken, mushrooms, and noodles. As soon the soup returns to a boil, remove from the heat. The noodles will have become clear and plump. Taste once more to check the seasoning and adjust with fish sauce or salt.

3 Ladle into soup bowls. Because the noodles are slippery, hold a ladle in one hand to scoop up some soup and chopsticks in the other hand to move noodles into the ladle. Garnish with a sprinkle of the Vietnamese coriander and lots of pepper. Serve immediately. Pass the chiles at the table.

Serves 6 as a light lunch, or 10 to 12 as a starter

3 quarts (12 cups) chicken stock, homemade or quick version (page 317)

3/4 pound boneless, skinless chicken breast

2 tablespoons fish sauce

3/4-inch chunk yellow rock sugar (about 3/4 ounce)

Salt

4 dried wood ear mushrooms, reconstituted (page 334), trimmed, and cut into 1/4-inch wide strips (about 1/3 cup)

1/2 pound cellophane noodles, soaked in hot water until pliable, drained, and cut into 6-inch lengths

1/2 cup lightly packed fresh Vietnamese coriander or cilantro leaves, finely chopped or whole

Black pepper

2 or 3 Thai or serrano chiles, thinly sliced (optional)

CHICKEN PHO

Phở Gà

WHILE BEEF *PHỞ* may be the version that most people know and like, chicken *phở* is also excellent. In recent years, there has been a renewed interest in *phở gà* within the Vietnamese American community, and a handful of restaurants are specializing in the delicate noodle soup. Some of them use free-range *gà chạy* or *gà đi bộ* (literally "jogging chicken" or "walking chicken"), yielding bowls full of meat that has a flavor and texture reminiscent of traditionally raised chickens in Vietnam. If you want to create great chicken *phở* yourself, take a cue from the pros and start with quality birds.

    If you have never made *phở*, this recipe is ideal for learning the basics. It calls for fewer ingredients than other *phở* recipes, so you can focus on charring the onion and ginger to accentuate their sweetness, making a clear broth, and assembling steamy hot, delicious bowls. While some cooks flavor chicken *phở* broth with the same spices they use for beef *phở*, my family prefers using coriander seeds and cilantro to distinguish the two.

Serves 8

BROTH

2 yellow onions, about 1 pound total, unpeeled

Chubby 4-inch section fresh ginger, unpeeled

1 chicken, about 4 pounds, excess fat and tail removed

3 pounds chicken backs, necks, or other bony chicken parts

5 quarts water

1$\frac{1}{2}$ tablespoons salt

3 tablespoons fish sauce

1-inch chunk yellow rock sugar (about 1 ounce)

2 tablespoons coriander seeds, toasted in a dry skillet for about 1 minute until fragrant

4 whole cloves

1 small or $\frac{1}{2}$ large bunch cilantro (bound stems about 1 inch in diameter)

BOWLS

1$\frac{1}{2}$ to 2 pounds small flat rice noodles, dried or fresh

Cooked chicken from the broth, at room temperature

1 yellow onion, sliced paper-thin, soaked in cold water to cover for 30 minutes and drained

3 or 4 scallions, green part only, thinly sliced

$\frac{1}{3}$ cup chopped fresh cilantro, leafy tops only

Black pepper

OPTIONAL GARNISHES

3 cups bean sprouts (about $\frac{1}{2}$ pound)

10 to 12 sprigs mint

10 to 12 sprigs Thai basil

12 to 15 fresh culantro leaves

2 or 3 Thai or serrano chiles, thinly sliced

2 or 3 limes, cut into wedges

MAKE THE BROTH

1 Place the onions and ginger directly on the cooking grate of a medium-hot charcoal or gas grill or a gas stove with a medium flame, or on a medium-hot burner of an electric stove. Let the skin burn (if you're working indoors, turn on the exhaust fan and open a window), using tongs to rotate the onions and ginger occasionally and to grab and discard any flyaway onion skin. After 15 minutes, the onions and ginger will have softened slightly and become sweetly fragrant. There may even be some bubbling. You do not have to blacken the entire surface. When amply charred, remove from the heat and let cool.

2 Rinse the cooled onions under warm running water, rubbing off the charred skin. Trim off and discard the blackened root and stem ends. Use a vegetable peeler, paring knife, or the edge of a teaspoon to remove the ginger skin. Hold it under warm water to wash off any blackened bits. Halve the ginger lengthwise and bruise lightly with the broad side of a cleaver or chef's knife. Set the onions and ginger aside.

3 Rinse the chicken under cool water. Detach each wing by bending it back and cutting it off at the shoulder joint. Add the wings and neck, if included, to the chicken parts. If the heart, gizzard, and liver have been included, discard them or save for another use. (Some cooks like to simmer the heart and gizzard in water and slice them for adding to the noodle bowls.) Set the wingless chicken aside.

4 Remove and discard any loose pieces of fat from the chicken parts. Wielding a heavy cleaver designed for chopping bones, whack the bones to break them partway or all the way through, making the cuts at 1- to 2-inch intervals, depending on the size of the part. This exposes the marrow, which enriches the broth.

5 To achieve a clear broth, you must first parboil and rinse the chicken parts. Put them in a stockpot (about 12-quart capacity) and add cold water just to cover. Bring to a boil over high heat and boil vigorously for 2 to 3 minutes to release the impurities. Dump the chicken parts and water into the sink (make sure it is clean), and then rinse the parts with water to wash off any

clinging residue. Quickly scrub the stockpot clean and return the chicken parts to it. Add the chicken, breast side up.

6 Pour in the 5 quarts water and snuggle the chicken in between the parts so that it is covered with water. Bring to a boil over high heat and then lower the heat to a gentle simmer. Use a ladle or large, shallow spoon to skim off any scum that rises to the top. Add the onions, ginger, salt, fish sauce, rock sugar, coriander seeds, cloves, and cilantro and cook, uncovered, for 25 minutes, adjusting the heat if needed to maintain a gentle simmer. At this point, the chicken is cooked; its flesh should feel firm yet still yield a bit to the touch. Use a pair of tongs to grab the chicken and transfer it to a large bowl. Flush the chicken with cold water and drain well, then set it aside for 15 to 20 minutes until it is cool enough to handle. Meanwhile, keep the broth at a steady simmer.

7 When the chicken can be handled, use a knife to remove each breast half and the whole legs (thigh and drumstick). Don't cut these pieces further, or they will lose their succulence. Set them aside on a plate to cool completely, then cover with plastic wrap and refrigerate; bring them to room temperature before assembling the bowls.

8 Return the leftover carcass to the stockpot and adjust the heat to simmer the broth gently for another 1 1/2 hours.

9 Strain the broth through a fine-mesh sieve (or a coarse-mesh sieve lined with cheesecloth) positioned over a pot. Discard the solids. Use a ladle to skim as much fat from the top of the broth as you like. (To make this task easier, you can cool the broth, refrigerate overnight, lift off the solidified fat, and then reheat before continuing.) Taste and adjust the flavor with additional salt, fish sauce, and rock sugar. There should be about 4 quarts (16 cups) broth.

continued

ASSEMBLE THE BOWLS

10 If using dried noodles, cover them with hot tap water and let soak for 15 to 20 minutes, or until they are pliable and opaque. Drain in a colander. If using fresh rice noodles, untangle them, place in a colander, and rinse briefly under cold running water.

11 Cut the cooked chicken into slices about 1/4 inch thick, cutting the meat off the bone as necessary. If you don't want to eat the skin, discard it first. Set the chicken aside. Ready the yellow onion, scallions, cilantro, and pepper for adding to the bowls. Arrange the garnishes on a plate and put on the table.

12 To ensure good timing, bring the broth to a simmer over medium heat as you are assembling the bowls. (For an extra treat, drop in any unused white scallion sections and let them poach in the broth. Add the poached scallion sections—called *hành chần*—to a few lucky bowls when ladling out the broth.)

At the same time, fill a large pot with water and bring to a rolling boil. For each bowl, place a portion of the noodles on a vertical-handle strainer (or mesh sieve) and dunk the noodles in the boiling water. As soon as they have collapsed and lost their stiffness (10 to 20 seconds), pull the strainer from the water, letting the water drain back into the pot. Empty the noodles into a bowl. If you like, once you have finished blanching the noodles, you can blanch the bean sprouts for 30 seconds. They should wilt slightly but retain some crunch. Drain and add to the garnishes.

13 Top each bowl of noodles with chicken, arranging the slices flat. Place a mound of yellow onion in the center and then shower some scallion and cilantro on top. Finish each bowl with a sprinkle of pepper.

14 Raise the heat and bring the broth to a rolling boil. Do a final tasting and make any last-minute flavor adjustments. Ladle about 2 cups broth into each bowl, distributing the hot liquid evenly to warm all the ingredients. Serve immediately with the plate of garnishes.

BEEF PHO

Phở Bò

DESPITE THE FUN and convenience of eating *phở* at a local noodle soup spot, nothing beats a homemade bowl. What inevitably makes the homemade version *đặc biệt* (special) is the care that goes into making the broth, the cornerstone of *phở*.

One of the keys to a great broth is good leg bones, which are often sold at supermarkets as beef soup bones. Avoid neck bones; instead, look for soup bones made up of knuckle and leg bones that contain marrow. At Asian markets, beef leg bones are precut and bagged in the meat department. Vietnamese markets will sometimes have whole leg bones at the butcher counter, and you can specify how you want them cut. A butcher who divides large sections of beef carcasses into small retail cuts is likely to have good bones. For the most fragrant and flavorful broth, I recommend the bones of grass-fed or natural beef.

Serves 8

BROTH

2 yellow onions, about 1 pound total, unpeeled

Chubby 4-inch piece fresh ginger, unpeeled

5 to 6 pounds beef leg bones, in 2- or 3-inch pieces

6 quarts water

5 star anise (40 robust points total)

6 whole cloves

3-inch cinnamon stick

1⅓ pounds boneless beef chuck, rump, brisket, or cross-rib roast, well trimmed (about 1 pound after trimming) and cut into pieces about 2 inches wide, 4 inches long, and 1½ inches thick

1½ tablespoons salt

Scant ¼ cup fish sauce

1-inch chunk yellow rock sugar (about 1 ounce)

BOWLS

1½ to 2 pounds small flat rice noodles, dried or fresh

Cooked beef from the broth

½ pound eye of round, sirloin, London broil, or tri-tip steak

1 yellow onion, sliced paper-thin, soaked in cold water to cover for 30 minutes and drained

3 or 4 scallions, green part only, thinly sliced

⅓ cup chopped fresh cilantro, leafy tops only

Black pepper

OPTIONAL GARNISHES

3 cups bean sprouts (about ½ pound)

10 to 12 sprigs mint

10 to 12 sprigs Thai basil

12 to 15 fresh culantro leaves

2 or 3 Thai or serrano chiles, thinly sliced

2 or 3 limes, cut into wedges

MAKE THE BROTH

1 Place the onions and ginger directly on the cooking grate of a medium-hot charcoal or gas grill or a gas stove with a medium flame, or on a medium-hot burner of an electric stove. Let the skin burn (if you're working indoors, turn on the exhaust fan and open a window), using tongs to rotate the onions and ginger occasionally and to grab and discard any flyaway onion skin. After 15 minutes, the onions and ginger will have softened slightly and become sweetly fragrant. There may even be some bubbling. You do not have to blacken the entire surface. When amply charred, remove from the heat and let cool.

2 Rinse the cooled onions under warm running water, rubbing off the charred skin. Trim off and discard the blackened root and stem ends. Use a vegetable peeler, paring knife, or the edge of a teaspoon to remove the ginger skin. Hold it under warm water to wash off any blackened bits. Halve the ginger lengthwise and bruise lightly with the broad side of a cleaver or chef's knife. Set the onions and ginger aside.

3 To achieve a clear broth, you must first parboil and rinse the beef bones. Put them in a stockpot (about 12-quart capacity) and add cold water just to cover. Bring to a boil over high heat and boil vigorously for 2 to 3 minutes to release the impurities. Dump the bones and water into the sink (make sure it is clean), and then rinse the bones with water to wash off any clinging residue. Quickly scrub the stockpot clean and return the bones to the pot.

4 Pour in the 6 quarts water, bring to a boil over high heat, and lower the heat to a gentle simmer. Use a ladle or large, shallow spoon to skim off any scum that rises to the top. Add the onions, ginger, star anise, cloves, cinnamon stick, beef, salt, fish sauce, and rock sugar and cook, uncovered, for 1 1/2 hours, adjusting the heat if needed to maintain a simmer.

5 At this point, the boneless meat should be slightly chewy but not tough. Press it and it should feel like the flesh at the base of your thumb. When it is cooked to your liking, use tongs to transfer it to a bowl of cold water to cover. Let the meat soak

for 10 minutes to prevent it from drying out and turning dark. Drain the meat, set aside on a plate to cool completely, then cover with plastic wrap and refrigerate. Meanwhile, maintain the broth at a steady simmer for 1 1/2 hours longer.

6 Strain the broth through a fine-mesh sieve (or a coarse-mesh sieve lined with cheesecloth) positioned over a pot. If desired, remove any bits of gelatinous tendon from the bones to add to the cooked beef in the refrigerator. Discard the remaining solids. Use a ladle to skim as much fat from the top of the broth as you like. (To make this task easier, you can cool the broth, refrigerate overnight, lift off the solidified fat, and then reheat before continuing.) Taste and adjust the flavor with salt, fish sauce, and rock sugar. There should be about 4 quarts (16 cups) broth.

ASSEMBLE THE BOWLS

7 If using dried noodles, cover them with hot tap water and let soak for 15 to 20 minutes, or until they are pliable and opaque. Drain in a colander. If using fresh rice noodles, untangle them, place in a colander, and rinse briefly under cold running water.

8 Cut the cooked beef across the grain into slices about 1/16 inch thick. For the best results, make sure it is cold. Freeze the raw beef for 15 minutes, then slice it across the grain into pieces 1/16 inch thick. Set all the beef slices aside. Ready the yellow onion, scallions, cilantro, and pepper for adding to the bowls. Arrange the garnishes on a plate and put on the table.

9 To ensure good timing, bring the broth to a simmer over medium heat as you are assembling the bowls. (For an extra treat, drop in any unused white scallion sections and let them poach in the broth. Add the poached scallion sections—called *hành chần*—to a few lucky bowls when ladling out the broth.)

At the same time, fill a large pot with water and bring to a rolling boil. For each bowl, place a portion of the noodles on a vertical-handle strainer (or mesh sieve) and dunk the noodles in the boiling water. As soon as they have collapsed and lost their stiffness (10 to 20 seconds), pull the strainer from the water, letting the water drain back into the pot. Empty the noodles into a bowl. If you like, once you have finished blanching the noodles, you can blanch the bean sprouts for 30 seconds. They should wilt slightly but retain some crunch. Drain and add to the garnishes.

10 Top each bowl of noodles with cooked and raw beef, arranging the slices flat. Place a mound of yellow onion in the center and shower some scallion and cilantro on top. Finish with a sprinkle of pepper.

11 Raise the heat and bring the broth to a rolling boil. Do a final tasting and make any last- minute flavor adjustments. Ladle about 2 cups broth into each bowl, distributing the hot liquid evenly to warm all the ingredients. Serve immediately with the plate of garnishes.

NOTE

To add more types of beef to the soup, head to a Vietnamese or Chinese market. At the butcher counter, buy a small piece of book tripe (*sách*), which is precooked. Before using, rinse and gently squeeze dry. Thinly slice it into fringelike pieces and add them to the bowl during assembly. The hot broth will warm them up like the other meats.

In the refrigerated food case or frozen-food aisle, you will find small packages of precooked crunchy beef meatballs (*bò viên*). Slice each one in half and drop into the finished broth to heat through. When you are ready to serve, ladle them out with the broth to top each bowl. Serve with hoisin and Sriracha chile sauces on the side for dipping.

To use the beef *nạm* trimmings left over when you make Beef Flank and Ginger Simmered in Caramel Sauce (page 149), simmer the meat in the broth for about 2 hours, or until chewy yet tender. Thinly slice the meat with the grain at assembly time and add to the bowl during assembly. At *phở* shops, this meat is identified as flank.

SPICY HUE BEEF AND RICE NOODLE SOUP

Bún Bò Huế

AMONG VIETNAMESE NOODLE SOUPS, *bún bò Huế* is second only to *phở* in popularity. But while *phở* is delicate and nuanced, *bún bò* is earthy and spicy, characteristic of central Viet cooking and of the elegant yet rustic table of Hue, the former imperial capital. And although its name suggests an all-beef affair, the soup actually combines beef and pork.

To make great *bún bò Huế*, I heed the advice of our family friend Mrs. Nha, a Hue native who insists that the broth be made with beef bones, not the pork bones widely used today. From my mom, I learned to sauté the onion and boneless meat for a deeply flavored broth. On my own, I discovered that simmering the annatto in the broth yields a nice rich color. (Most cooks fry the seeds in oil to release their color and then add the oil to the finished broth.)

Shop for the various meats you need at a Viet or Chinese market, where you will find beef shank (shin) in long pieces, boneless pork leg with a layer of fat and skin, and slices of pork hock, often prepackaged in Styrofoam trays.

Serves 8

BROTH

4 pounds beef leg bones, cut into 2- to 3-inch pieces

1 1/2 pounds boneless beef shank, halved crosswise

3/4 pound boneless pork leg with skin and fat

Salt

Black pepper

2 tablespoons canola or other neutral oil

2 yellow onions, cut into 1-inch chunks

1 tablespoon annatto seeds

5 quarts water

1 1/2 pounds pork hock, cut into 1/2-inch-thick pieces (8 pieces)

3 tablespoons fish sauce

1-inch chunk yellow rock sugar (about 1 ounce)

4 hefty stalks lemongrass, trimmed, cut into 3-inch lengths, and bruised

2 tablespoons fine shrimp sauce

CHILE-LEMONGRASS MIX

5 tablespoons canola or other neutral oil

3 tablespoons dried red chile flakes

3 cloves garlic, minced

1 stalk lemongrass, trimmed and minced

1 teaspoon sugar

2 1/2 teaspoons fish sauce

BOWLS

Cooked beef and pork from the broth

2 packages (14 ounces each) large or extralarge dried round rice noodles, cooked in boiling water for 10 to 15 minutes, drained, and flushed with cold water

1 yellow onion, sliced paper-thin, soaked in cold water to cover for 30 minutes, and drained

2 or 3 scallions, green parts only, thinly sliced

1/3 cup chopped fresh Vietnamese coriander or cilantro leaves

GARNISHES

2 or 3 limes, cut into wedges

12 sprigs mint

2 or 3 Thai or serrano chiles, thinly sliced

Leaves from 1 head romaine lettuce, halved lengthwise and cut crosswise into 1/4-inch-wide ribbons (optional)

3 cups bean sprouts (about 1/2 pound) (optional)

1 cup thinly sliced banana blossom bract (leaf), soaked in acidulated water, massaged with warm water, and drained well (optional; see Note)

Spoonful of fine shrimp sauce (optional)

MAKE THE BROTH

1   To achieve a clear broth, first parboil and rinse the beef bones. Put them in a stockpot (about 12-quart capacity) and add cold water to cover. Bring to a boil over high heat and boil for 2 to 3 minutes to release the impurities. Dump the bones and water into the sink, and then rinse the bones with water to wash off any residue. Set the bones aside. Scrub the stockpot, dry it, and set aside.

2   Lightly season the beef shank and the pork leg with salt and pepper and set aside. Add the oil to the stockpot and heat over medium-high heat. Add the onions and cook, until fragrant, about 1 minute. Add the annatto and stir to release its color. When the onion is yellow-orange, push it to the side and add the beef shank and pork leg. Briefly sear the meat to lightly brown.

3   Pour in the water and add the reserved bones and the pork hock. Bring to a boil over high heat and lower the heat to a gentle simmer. Use a ladle or large, shallow spoon to skim off any scum that rises to the top. Add 1 1/2 tablespoons salt, the fish sauce, rock sugar, and lemongrass. Simmer gently, uncovered, for 1 hour.

4   Transfer the pork leg and hock to a bowl of cold water to cover. Let soak for 10 minutes to prevent it from drying out and turning dark. Drain the meat, set aside on a plate to cool completely, then cover with plastic wrap and refrigerate. Meanwhile, simmer the broth for 1 hour longer after removing the pork, for a total of 2 hours.

5   When the broth is done, remove the beef shank, soak it in cold water as you did the leg and hock, and then drain, cool, and store with the pork. Strain the broth through a fine-mesh sieve (or a coarse-mesh sieve lined with cheesecloth) positioned over a pot. Discard the solids. Use a ladle to skim as much fat from the top of the broth as you like. (Or, let cool, refrigerate overnight, lift off the solidified fat, and reheat before continuing.)

6   To make the chile-lemongrass mix, put the oil, chile flakes, garlic, and lemongrass in a small saucepan and bring to a gentle simmer over low heat. Let bubble and sizzle for 5 minutes, swirling or stirring occasionally. Remove from the heat and stir in the sugar and fish sauce. Transfer to a small serving bowl and let cool.

7   To finish the broth, scoop out a little into a cup, stir the shrimp sauce into the cup, and pour the mixture through a fine-mesh sieve into the broth. Depending on your taste, stir in one-fourth to one-half of the chile-lemongrass mix, saving the rest for serving at the table. Taste and adjust the flavor with additional salt, if necessary. There should be about 4 quarts (16 cups) broth.

ASSEMBLE THE BOWLS

8   To reheat the noodles, fill a large pot with water and bring to a rolling boil. Meanwhile, cut the beef and pork leg across the grain into slices about 1/16 inch thick. For the best results, make sure they are cold. Set the beef and leg pork aside. Put the pork hock pieces in the broth. Have ready the noodles, yellow onion, scallions, and Vietnamese coriander. Arrange the garnishes on a plate or put them in small dishes and put on the table. To ensure good timing, bring the broth to a simmer over medium heat while you are assembling the bowls.

When the water has reached a boil, place a portion of the noodles on a vertical-handle strainer (or mesh sieve) and dunk the noodles in the water. After 5 to 10 seconds, pull the strainer from the water, letting the water drain back into the pot. Empty the noodles into a bowl and repeat with the remaining portions, while proceeding to assemble each bowl as the noodles are added.

9   Top each bowl of noodles with the beef and pork, arranging the slices flat. Place a mound of yellow onion in the center and then shower some scallion and Vietnamese coriander on top. Bring the broth to a rolling boil. Ladle 2 cups broth into each bowl, distributing evenly to warm the ingredients and including a piece of pork hock with each portion. Serve immediately with the garnishes and the remaining chile-lemongrass mix.

NOTE

For information on banana blossoms, see page 52. Simply remove some of the bracts, stack them, and then slice them. Soak for 10 minutes in 1 tablespoon distilled white vinegar and water to cover. Then massage and drain them.

CRAB AND SHRIMP RICE NOODLE SOUP

Bún Riêu Cua

THIS HEADY COMBINATION of seafood and tomato comes from the north, where it is traditionally made from small rice-field crabs called *cua đồng*. To extract enough flavor, cooks use many crabs, removing their back shells and pounding their bodies. The crushed crab is combined with water, carefully filtered, and finally mixed with fermented shrimp sauce (*mắm tôm*) to create a broth base. When heated, the crab solids rise to the top, forming a rich, seafood-laden floater that is the signature of the soup. Sections of the floater are carefully spooned atop round rice noodles (*bún*) before the broth is ladled into each bowl. A garnish plate of raw vegetables, limes, and fresh herbs accompanies the soup.

When I was a child, our family re-created this soup by using the tiny rock crabs foraged among the rocks at the local harbor. Nowadays, I make this more convenient and equally tasty version. Unlike many Vietnamese Americans (including my mom), I don't use canned *bún riêu cua* soup base. Rather, I start with a live Dungeness crab and mix its meat and tomalley with ground shrimp and egg for the floater.

Since Dungeness crab season (November through May) doesn't coincide with tomato season, I use premium canned tomatoes instead of fresh ones. If you are substituting other types of crab, you will need enough to yield 6 ounces of meat.

Serves 6

BROTH

3 1/2 quarts (14 cups) plus
    1 1/4 cups water
1 live Dungeness crab,
    1 1/2 pounds
2/3 cup dried shrimp
1 3/4 teaspoons salt
2 tablespoons fish sauce
8 egg whites, lightly beaten
3 tablespoons canola or other
    neutral oil
1 yellow onion, finely chopped
1 can (28 ounces) whole
    tomatoes, coarsely chopped
    with juices reserved
3 tablespoons fine shrimp sauce

BOWLS

1 pound small dried round rice
    noodles, cooked in boiling
    water for 3 to 5 minutes,
    drained, and flushed with
    cold water
2 or 3 scallions, green part only,
    thinly sliced
1/4 cup chopped fresh cilantro,
    leafy tops only

GARNISHES

1/4 to 1/3 pound water spinach
    stems, split into fine shreds,
    soaked in water to curl, and
    drained (see Note), or leaves
    from 1 small head romaine
    lettuce, halved lengthwise
    and cut crosswise into
    1/4-inch-wide ribbons
3 cups bean sprouts (about
    1/2 pound)

3/4 cup thinly sliced banana
    blossom bract (leaf),
    soaked in acidulated water,
    massaged with warm water,
    and drained well (optional;
    see Note)
2 or 3 limes, cut into wedges
12 to 20 sprigs Vietnamese
    balm and/or Thai basil
    (optional)
Spoonful of fine shrimp sauce
    (optional)
Mellow Chile-Garlic Mix
    (page 315), optional

1 Pour the 3½ quarts water into a 5- or 6-quart Dutch oven and bring to a rolling boil over high heat. Add the crab and cook, clean, and pick it as directed on page 322. Set the meat and the tomalley and fat aside. If you don't like the tomalley and fat, discard them along with the shell bits. Reserve 3 quarts (12 cups) of the cooking liquid for the broth.

2 To rehydrate the dried shrimp, put them in a small saucepan with the 1¼ cups water, bring to a simmer over medium heat, and cook for 10 minutes, or until slightly soft. Drain the shrimp into a sieve placed over a bowl and let cool completely. Add the cooking liquid to the reserved crab cooking liquid.

3 Put the cooled shrimp in a food processor and process to grind to a coarse texture. Add the crabmeat and tomalley and fat. Pulse 3 times to combine but not pulverize the crabmeat. Transfer to a bowl and mix in ½ teaspoon of the salt, 1 tablespoon of the fish sauce, and the egg whites. Set aside.

4 In a large, wide pot, heat the oil over medium-high heat. Add the onion and cook, stirring occasionally, for about 3 minutes, or until fragrant and a bit soft. Add the tomatoes and their juices and the remaining 1¼ teaspoons salt and bring to a vigorous simmer. Cook, stirring frequently, for 10 to 12 minutes, or until most of the liquid has evaporated and the mixture is thick.

5 Add the shrimp sauce, the remaining 1 tablespoon fish sauce, and the reserved cooking liquid. Bring to a boil over high heat, lower the heat to a gentle simmer, and cook for 30 minutes.

6 Meanwhile, bring a large pot of water to a rolling boil, for reheating the noodles; ready the scallions and cilantro for assembling the bowls; and arrange the garnishes on a plate or put them in small dishes and put on the table.

7 Keeping the broth at a gentle simmer, use a large spoon to slowly stir it in one direction, scraping the bottom of the pot. As you stir with one hand, use the other to pour in the egg mixture. Keep stirring, and as soon as the egg mixture floats to the top, remove the spoon. Let the broth cook undisturbed for

5 minutes. When small bubbles break the surface, the soup is done. The broth underneath will be golden and clear with some solids at the bottom. Lower the heat so the broth stays warm while you assemble the bowls.

8 When the water has reached a boil, place a portion of the noodles on a vertical-handle strainer (or mesh sieve) and dunk the noodles in the boiling water. After 5 to 10 seconds, pull the strainer from the water, letting the water drain back into the pot. Empty the noodles into a bowl and repeat with the remaining portions, while proceeding to assemble each bowl.

9 Use a slotted spoon to transfer an equal portion of the floater to each bowl, on top of the noodles. Bring the broth to a rolling boil, taste, and salt, if necessary. Ladle 2 cups broth into each bowl, distributing the hot liquid evenly. Top with the scallions and cilantro. Serve immediately with the garnishes. It is customary for diners to add some vegetables, torn herb leaves, and squeezes of fresh lime. Anyone wanting a brinier bowl should mix in a dab of shrimp sauce, while heat seekers should add a little of the chile-garlic mix.

NOTE

To split and curl water spinach stems, use only the hollow portion of the stems, removing all leaves and tender stems (save those for a stir-fry, page 178). Soak the stems in water for 5 minutes to make them easier to split. A knife is traditionally used to split the stems, but a water spinach splitter (*dao chẻ rau muống*, literally "knife for splitting water spinach"), available at Vietnamese markets, works much better. The thin metal rod attached to the round plastic top contains a set of sharp blades arranged like wheel spokes. Slide the splitter into the stem and then push the stem through the blades until about 4 inches of split stem protrudes. Grab the split portion and pull on it to drag the remaining stem portion through the blades. Deposit the shreds in a bowl of cold water and let soak for 15 minutes to curl. Drain before using.

For information on banana blossoms, see page 52. Simply remove some of the bracts, stack them, and then slice them. Soak for 10 minutes in 1 tablespoon of distilled white vinegar and water to cover. Then massage and drain them.

HANOI SPECIAL RICE NOODLE SOUP

Bún Thang

BÚN THANG is one of the most complex expressions of Vietnamese culinary prowess. Requiring many ingredients and much time, this popular Hanoi soup is traditionally reserved for special events and holidays such as Tet. The golden broth contains chicken, pork, and dried squid or shrimp. The toppings may include those items, too, in addition to egg shreds, *giò lụa* (sausage), and salted duck egg yolk. At the table, shrimp sauce gives the broth extra depth, and if it is affordable, male belostomatid beetle extract (*cà cuống*) is added from the tip of a toothpick, imparting a mesmerizing fragrance.

Aficionados of the soup can be particular. In a 1996 essay, food writer Bang Son asserts that its refinement is not for merely appeasing hunger, insisting that it be served in fine china on a joyous occasion to cherished loved ones. While my mom isn't that fanatical, she is a stickler for certain traditional notions, such as serving *bún thang* piping hot.

In my kitchen, I omit the beetle juice because the chemical version sold in the United States overwhelms the delicate flavors of the soup. Also, though *bún thang* is often savored in smallish bowls as part of a multicourse meal, I prefer to serve it in big ones.

Serves 6

BROTH

1 chicken, 3 1/2 pounds, excess fat and tail removed, cut into serving pieces

1 tablespoon salt

4 quarts plus 1 1/2 cups water

1 large yellow onion, sliced

2 pounds meaty pork neck or spine bones, cut into 2-inch pieces

3 dried squid (about 2 ounces total), briefly rinsed

2 tablespoons fish sauce

3/4 cup dried shrimp

BOWLS

Cooked chicken, shrimp, and pork from the broth, at room temperature

2 or 3 thin Egg Sheets (page 320), quartered and cut into fine strips, at room temperature

1/3 pound Classic Silky Sausage (page 160), cut into fine matchsticks, at room temperature

1/4 cup chopped fresh Vietnamese coriander or cilantro leaves

Black pepper

Spoonful of fine shrimp sauce

1/4 cup chopped Sweet and Salty Preserved Radish (page 196), optional

2 or 3 Thai or serrano chiles, thinly sliced (optional)

1 pound small dried round rice noodles, cooked in boiling water for 3 to 5 minutes, drained, and flushed with cold water

MAKE THE BROTH

1 Put the chicken pieces, salt, and the 4 quarts water into a stockpot (about 12-quart capacity) and bring to a boil over high heat. Lower the heat to a gentle simmer and then use a ladle or large, shallow spoon to skim off any scum that rises to the top. Add the onion and continue to simmer for 10 minutes.

2 Remove the breast from the pot and set aside in a bowl of cold water for 5 minutes to prevent it from drying out. Add the pork bones, squid, and fish sauce to the pot. Raise the heat to high to return to a boil and then lower the heat to simmer gently. Again, skim off any scum. Simmer, uncovered, for 2 hours.

3 When the breast has finished soaking, drain the water and set the breast aside. Allow it to cool completely, then shred the meat with your fingers into fine pieces about 1/8 inch wide, pulling it along its natural grain and discarding the bones and skin. Put the chicken shreds in a small container, cover, and refrigerate.

4 To rehydrate the dried shrimp, put them in a small saucepan with the 1 1/2 cups water, bring to a simmer over medium heat, and cook for 10 minutes, or until slightly soft. Drain the shrimp into a sieve placed over a bowl. Add the cooking liquid to the simmering broth. Let the shrimp cool completely, then put it into a food processor or electric mini-chopper and process to grind to a fine texture. Transfer to a small container, cover, and refrigerate.

5 When the broth is ready, use tongs to transfer the pork bones to a large bowl filled with cold water. Let them soak for 5 minutes to prevent them from drying out and turning dark. Drain the pork bones, let cool until they can be handled, and then remove the meat, discarding the bones and any odd bits. Use your fingers to break the meat into pea-sized pieces or tear it into fine shreds. Put in a small container, cover, and refrigerate.

6 Position a fine-mesh sieve (or a coarse-mesh sieve lined with cheesecloth) over a pot and gently ladle the broth into the sieve. Discard the solids, including the chicken parts. (This seems

wasteful, but these parts are spent.) Use a ladle to skim as much fat from the top of the broth as you like. (To make this task easier, you can cool the broth, refrigerate overnight, lift off the solidified fat, and then reheat before continuing.) There should be about 3 quarts (12 cups) broth.

ASSEMBLE THE BOWLS

7 Bring the broth to a simmer over medium heat while you are assembling the bowls. At the same time, bring a large pot of water to a rolling boil, for reheating the noodles. Make sure the chicken, shrimp, pork, egg, and sausage are at room temperature; ready the Vietnamese coriander and pepper for assembling the bowls; and put the shrimp sauce, preserved radish, and chiles on the table.

8 Place a portion of the noodles on a large vertical-handle strainer (or mesh sieve) and dunk the noodles in the boiling water. After 5 to 10 seconds, pull the strainer from the water, letting the water drain back into the pot. Empty the noodles into a bowl and repeat with the remaining portions, while proceeding to assemble each bowl as the noodles are reheating and draining.

Visually divide up each bowl into quadrants. Cover 1 quadrant with chicken, the next quadrant with egg, and the third one with sausage. If you have less shrimp and pork than the other ingredients, fill the remaining quadrant with half of each; if you have lots of pork, cover the quadrant with it, and put the shrimp in the center. Put some Vietnamese coriander in the middle, and then sprinkle with pepper.

9 Raise the heat on the broth and bring to a rolling boil. Do a final taste test, adding more salt, if necessary. Ladle about 2 cups broth into each bowl, distributing the hot liquid evenly to warm all the ingredients. Serve immediately with the fine shrimp sauce, preserved radish, and chiles. Diners should stir in about 1/4 teaspoon shrimp sauce to finish their bowls. The radish and chiles add crunch and heat.

NOODLE SOUP BROTH

Nước Dùng

ROUGHLY TRANSLATED AS "USEFUL WATER," this versatile broth serves as the basis for many of my Chinese-style noodle soups, including duck soup (page 220) and wonton soup (page 222). While you can use all pork bones, I prefer to combine pork and chicken for a more delicate flavor.

1 Remove and discard any loose pieces of fat from the chicken parts. Wielding a heavy cleaver designed for chopping bones, whack the bones to break them partway or all the way through, making the cuts at 1- to 2-inch intervals, depending on the size of the part. This exposes the marrow, which enriches the broth.

2 Put the chicken, pork bones, and water in a stockpot (about 12-quart capacity) and bring to a boil over high heat. Lower the heat to a gentle simmer and then use a ladle or large, shallow spoon to skim off any scum that rises to the top. Add the onion, ginger, rock sugar, and salt. Simmer gently, uncovered, for 2 hours.

3 Turn off the heat and let the broth sit undisturbed for 30 minutes to allow the impurities to settle and congeal. Position a fine-mesh sieve (or a coarse-mesh sieve lined with cheesecloth) over a pot and gently ladle the broth into the sieve. Discard the solids. Use a ladle to skim as much fat from the top of the broth as you like. (To make this task easier, you can cool the broth, refrigerate overnight, and then lift off the solidified fat.) The broth is ready to use. Or, store it in a tightly covered container in the refrigerator for up to 1 week or in the freezer for up to 3 months.

Makes about 3 quarts (12 cups)

2 pounds chicken backs, necks, or other bony chicken parts

3 pounds pork neck, spine, and/or leg bones, cut into 2-inch pieces

4 quarts water

1 large yellow onion, quartered

Chubby 3-inch piece fresh ginger, unpeeled and smashed with the broad side of a cleaver or chef's knife

1-inch chunk yellow rock sugar (about 1 ounce)

1 1/2 tablespoons salt

DUCK AND CHINESE EGG NOODLE SOUP

Mì Vịt Tiềm

THIS SOUP BORROWS HEAVILY from Vietnam's northern neighbor. *Mì vịt tiềm* is one of my mom's favorites, and she is partial to a version made by her friend Mrs. Tan, who, along with her husband, once owned a Chinese barbecue restaurant in San Diego.

Unlike *phở*, which most Viet home cooks know how to make, *mì vịt tiềm* is usually left to the pros. The trick is cooking the duck legs until tender (but not mushy), mahogany brown, and deeply seasoned. The traditional approach is to marinate them, flash fry them for color, and then simmer them in the broth. Some cooks even refry the legs right before serving. When my mom finally asked Mrs. Tan for her secret, she divulged that she roasted and then steamed the duck legs, instead of frying and simmering them. Her method evenly colors the duck, seals in the seasonings, preserves the integrity of the meat, and easily removes much of the fat.

I developed this recipe using Mrs. Tan's method. Traditionally, the duck leg is served whole on the side for diners to attack with chopsticks and spoons. Since that is hard to do, even for a native chopstick user like me, I slice the meat and serve it in the bowl.

Serves 6

6 duck legs, trimmed of excess fat and skin and backbone removed, if necessary (see Note)

MARINADE

1 teaspoon Chinese five-spice powder

1/2 teaspoon salt

1 tablespoon sugar

1 tablespoon oyster sauce

1 1/2 tablespoons dark (black) soy sauce

1 tablespoon Shaoxing rice wine or dry sherry

2 teaspoons peeled and grated fresh ginger, pressed through a fine-mesh sieve to extract 1 teaspoon juice

1 teaspoon sesame oil

3 quarts (12 cups) Noodle Soup Broth (page 219), with 1 star anise (8 robust points total) added during simmering

6 dried shiitake mushrooms, reconstituted (page 332), stemmed, and quartered

1 pound thin Chinese egg noodles, cooked in boiling water for 2 to 3 minutes until tender yet chewy, drained, and flushed with cold water

3/4 pound baby bok choy, sliced on the diagonal into 3/4-inch-wide pieces, cooked in boiling water for 1 minute, or until tender and bright green, and drained

Sesame oil

2 or 3 scallions, green part only, thinly sliced

1/4 cup chopped fresh cilantro, leafy tops only

White pepper

Mellow Chile-Garlic Mix (page 315), optional

1 1/2 cups Everyday Daikon and Carrot Pickle (page 192), optional

1 Use a toothpick or skewer to poke about 12 holes all over each duck leg. To make the marinade, mix together the five-spice powder, salt, sugar, oyster sauce, soy sauce, wine, ginger juice, and sesame oil in a bowl large enough to accommodate the duck legs. Add the duck legs and use your fingers to massage the marinade evenly into the legs, slipping some between the flesh and skin when possible. Cover and marinate in the refrigerator for at least 2 hours or up to 24 hours for the best flavor. Turn the legs 3 times during marination.

2 About 45 minutes before roasting, remove the duck legs from the refrigerator to bring them to room temperature. Line a baking sheet with aluminum foil, and place the legs, skin side up, on the prepared baking sheet. Add any leftover marinade to the broth. Position a rack in the upper third of the oven and preheat to 475°F.

3 Roast the duck for 18 to 20 minutes, or until sizzling and deep mahogany. Flip each leg over and roast for 3 to 5 minutes longer, or until the second side is browned. Transfer to a shallow bowl that will fit into your steamer tray and place the bowl in the steamer tray.

4 Fill the steamer pan halfway with water and bring to a rolling boil over high heat. Place the tray in the steamer, cover, and steam for about 45 minutes, or until tender and a knife easily pierces the thickest part of a leg.

5 When the legs are ready, transfer them to a plate. Use a spoon to skim off and discard the clear fat in the bowl and then add the dark cooking juices to the broth. (The duck legs may be cooked 2 days in advance, cooled, covered, and refrigerated. Bring to room temperature before serving.)

6 Pour the broth into a saucepan and add the mushrooms. Bring to a simmer over medium heat, and then lower the heat to keep the broth hot. At the same time, fill a large pot with water and bring to a rolling boil, for reheating the noodles.

7 Cut the duck meat off the bones, discarding the bones, and slice into bite-sized pieces. To reheat the noodles, place a portion on a large vertical-handle strainer (or mesh sieve) and dunk the noodles in the boiling water. After 5 to 10 seconds, pull the strainer from the water, letting the water drain back into the pot. Empty the noodles into a bowl and repeat with the remaining portions, while proceeding to assemble each bowl as the noodles are reheated and drained.

Position some bok choy to the side of each noodle mound, and then prominently display slices of duck on top. Garnish with a light drizzle of sesame oil, sprinkle with the scallion and cilantro, and add a pinch of white pepper.

8 Raise the heat on the broth and bring to a rolling boil. Do a final taste test, adding more salt, if necessary. Ladle about 2 cups broth into each bowl, distributing the hot liquid evenly to warm all the ingredients and including some mushroom wedges with each portion. Serve immediately with the chile-garlic mix and pickled vegetables for diners who want some chile and crunch.

NOTE

If a section of the backbone remains attached to a duck leg, use a boning knife to separate the backbone from the duck leg. At the hip joint, firmly bend the leg away from the backbone to pop the ball of the thighbone from the socket. Cut between the ball and socket to free the leg. Discard the backbone, freeze it, or add it to the simmering broth.

WONTON NOODLE SOUP

Mì Hoành Thánh

WONTON NOODLE SOUPS are often on the menus of Vietnamese noodle shops, but they are seldom as nuanced as those prepared by Chinese cooks. Years ago, while living in Southern California, I wanted to find out the Chinese secret to good wonton noodle soup, so I asked my friend Victor Fong. Born and raised in Chinatown, Los Angeles, he took me to the local Mayflower Restaurant, a tiny locals-only establishment on a side street. The noodles had a perfect chewy-tender texture, the crinkly wontons encased a toothsome pork and shrimp filling, and the golden broth was complex and not darkened by too much soy sauce.

The owners and their chef turned out to be ethnic Chinese from Vietnam, and though friendly, there were coy about what went into their noodle soup. After eating many bowls at Mayflower and some trial and error at home, I came up with my own version of this noodle soup classic.

Serves 6

WONTON FILLING

1/2 pound boneless pork shoulder, chopped by hand or machine to a coarse texture (page 69)

1/2 pound medium shrimp, peeled, deveined, and cut into pea-sized pieces

1 teaspoon cornstarch

3/4 teaspoon salt

1/4 teaspoon black pepper

2 scallions, white part only, finely chopped

1 teaspoon sesame oil

48 square wonton skins (1-pound package)

3 quarts (12 cups) Noodle Soup Broth (page 219), with 1/4 cup dried shrimp added during simmering

1 tablespoon light (regular) soy sauce

Salt

1 pound thin Chinese egg noodles, cooked in boiling water for 2 to 3 minutes until tender yet chewy, drained, and flushed with cold water

3/4 pound baby bok choy, sliced on the diagonal into 3/4-inch-wide pieces, cooked in boiling water for about 1 minute, or until tender and bright green, and drained

Sesame oil

2 or 3 scallions, green part only, thinly sliced

White pepper

Mellow Chile-Garlic Mix (page 315), optional

1 To make the filling, in a bowl, combine the pork, shrimp, cornstarch, salt, pepper, scallions, and sesame oil and use chopsticks or your fingers to mix well.

2 To shape the wontons, use your favorite method or use these instructions to guide you. Work in batches of 6 to 8 wonton skins. Place them on a work surface, such as large cutting board, inverted baking sheet, or tray. Using 2 teaspoons or demitasse spoons, place a scant teaspoon of filling (about the size of a 1/2-inch marble) in the center of a wonton skin. Dip a pastry brush in water and lightly brush the entire edge of the skin. Pick up a corner of the wonton skin and fold it over, enclosing the filling and forming a triangle. Press the edges of the triangle firmly with your finger to seal. Fold one of the outside tips of the triangle back over the filling, dab with water, and overlap with the opposing tip, pressing lightly to seal. Place the finished wonton on a large plate or tray. Repeat until all the filling is used up. Cover with a light dish towel to prevent drying while you ready the other ingredients.

3 Pour the broth into a large saucepan, add the soy sauce, and bring to a simmer over medium heat. Taste and season with enough salt to create a strong savory flavor. Lower the heat to keep the broth hot while you ready the bowls.

4 To cook the wontons, fill a large pot half full with water and bring to a rolling boil. At the same time, fill another large pot with water and bring to a rolling boil, for reheating the noodles.

5 Cook the wontons in 3 or 4 batches, dropping each batch into the pot of boiling water and stirring to separate them with a slotted spoon or wire skimmer. As soon as the wontons float to the top, let them cook for 2 to 3 minutes longer, or until the skins are translucent.

As each batch of wontons finishes, reheat the noodles for a couple of bowls by placing a portion on a large vertical-handle strainer (or mesh sieve) and dunking the noodles in the boiling water. After 5 to 10 seconds, pull the strainer from the water, letting the water drain back into the pot. Empty the noodles into a bowl and position some bok choy to the side of the noodle mound.

Scoop the cooked wontons up with the slotted spoon or wire skimmer, pausing briefly above the pot to allow excess water to drain. Divide the wontons among the noodle-filled bowls. Repeat for the remaining wontons, noodles, and bok choy.

6 Top each bowl with a light drizzle of sesame oil, a sprinkle of scallion, and a pinch of pepper. Raise the heat and bring the broth to a rolling boil. Do a final taste test of the broth, adding more salt, if necessary. Ladle about 2 cups broth into each bowl, distributing the hot liquid evenly to warm all the ingredients. Serve immediately with the chile-garlic mix for diners who want some heat.

NOTE

To keep uncooked wontons overnight, line a baking sheet with parchment paper and cover with a light dusting of flour. Lay the wontons on the prepared baking sheet, making sure that they don't touch. Cover tightly with plastic wrap and refrigerate. To prevent the wontons from getting sticky, be ready to boil them immediately when you remove them from the refrigerator. Or, freeze the wontons on the baking sheet until frozen solid and transfer them to an airtight plastic container. Store in the freezer for up to 1 month and thaw halfway at room temperature (lay them out flat on a baking sheet) before cooking.

If you want to dress up the bowl, add bite-sized slices of Char Siu Pork (page 142) when you add the bok choy.

RICE NOODLE BOWL WITH STIR-FRIED BEEF

Bún Thịt Bò Xào

MY MOM OFTEN PREPARED this southern noodle bowl for weekend lunches. It is remarkably easy to make, and with the exception of the beef topping, all of the ingredients are at room temperature and can be readied ahead of time.

Noodle dishes like this one are popular at Vietnamese American restaurants, where the topping options usually include grilled pork, grilled pork and shrimp, or grilled chicken. The stir-fried beef version is homey fare that rarely appears on menus. I have provided directions for four other versions of this rice noodle bowl at the end of the recipe, for anyone who wants to replicate his or her favorite restaurant dish.

Serves 4 as a one-dish meal

MARINADE

1 teaspoon cornstarch

3/4 teaspoon sugar

1/4 teaspoon salt

1/2 teaspoon black pepper

1 teaspoon fish sauce

2 tablespoons light (regular) soy sauce

1 pound flank steak, cut across the grain into strips about 3 inches long, 3/4 inch wide, and a scant 1/4 inch thick

SALAD MIX

Leaves from 1/2 small head red or green leaf lettuce, cut crosswise into 1/4-inch wide ribbons

1 pickling (Kirby) cucumber or 1/2 small English cucumber, halved lengthwise, seeded, and cut into matchsticks

2 cups bean sprouts (about 1/3 pound)

1/3 cup roughly chopped assorted fresh herb leaves such as cilantro, mint, red perilla, Thai basil, and Vietnamese balm

2/3 pound small dried round rice noodles, cooked in boiling water for 3 to 5 minutes, drained, and flushed with cold water

3 tablespoons canola or other neutral oil

1 small yellow onion, halved and sliced lengthwise 1/4 inch thick

3 cloves garlic, finely chopped

GARNISHES AND DRESSING

1/2 cup unsalted roasted peanuts, coarsely chopped

1/4 cup Crispy Caramelized Shallot (page 314), optional

1 1/2 cups Basic Dipping Sauce made without garlic (page 308)

1 To make the marinade, in a shallow bowl large enough to accommodate the beef, combine the cornstarch, sugar, salt, pepper, fish sauce, and soy sauce and mix well. Add the beef and use chopsticks or your fingers to coat evenly. Set aside to marinate while you ready the bowls.

2 To make the salad mix, in a large bowl, combine the lettuce, cucumber, bean sprouts, and herbs and toss well. Divide the salad among 4 noodle soup–sized bowls and top with a layer of noodles. Put the bowls near the stove. Place a plate nearby for holding the elements of the stir-fry as you cook them.

3 To stir-fry a large quantity of meat successfully on a home kitchen stove, it is best to work in batches and then bring them together at the end. In a wok or large skillet, heat 1 tablespoon of the oil over medium-high heat. Add the onion and stir-fry for about 1 minute, or until slightly soft and fragrant. Add the garlic and stir-fry for about 15 seconds, or until aromatic. Transfer to the plate with a slotted spoon.

4 Raise the heat to high and add another tablespoon of oil. Add half the beef, spreading it out into a single layer. Let it cook, undisturbed, for about 1 minute. When the beef begins to brown, use a spatula to flip and stir-fry it for another 1 to 2 minutes, or until it is still slightly rare. Transfer to the plate holding the onions and garlic. Repeat with the remaining 1 tablespoon oil and the second half of the beef. When the second batch is just about done, return the onion and garlic, first batch of beef, and any accumulated juices to the pan. Stir-fry for about 2 minutes to heat through and finish cooking the beef.

5 Remove from the heat and divide evenly among the bowls. Top with the peanuts and shallot. Serve immediately with the sauce for diners to dress and toss their own bowls.

NOTE

The base of raw vegetables, herbs, and noodles may be crowned with many other bold-flavored toppings. Here are my favorite variations:

Rice Noodle Bowl with Grilled Chicken (*Bún Gà Nướng*): Omit the marinade and the stir-fried beef. Prepare ½ recipe of the marinade used for Grilled Garlicky Five-Spice Pork Steaks (page 143), add 1 pound boneless, skinless chicken thighs, cover, and marinate in the refrigerator for 1 to 2 hours. Grill the thighs over a medium fire on a charcoal grill or a gas grill. Let cool briefly, then slice and divide evenly among the bowls. Garnish and serve as directed.

Rice Noodle Bowl with Grilled Pork (*Bún Thịt Nướng*): Omit the marinade and stir-fried beef. Prepare ½ recipe of the marinade used for Grilled Garlicky Five-Spice Pork Steak (page 143). Cut 1 pound pork shoulder across the grain into strips about 3 inches long, 1 inch wide, and a scant ¼ inch thick, add to the marinade, cover, and marinate in the refrigerator for 1 to 2 hours. Grill the pork strips over a medium-hot fire on a charcoal or gas grill. Divide evenly among the bowls. Garnish and serve as directed.

Rice Noodle Bowl with Grilled Pork and Shrimp (*Bún Thịt Tôm Nướng*): Proceed as directed for Rice Noodle Bowl with Grilled Pork (above), but add 12 large shrimp, peeled, deveined, and coated with oil, salt, and black pepper to the grill with the pork. Divide the pork and shrimp evenly among the bowls. Garnish and serve as directed.

Rice Noodle Bowl with Grilled Lemongrass Beef (*Bún Thịt Bò Nướng Xả*): Omit the marinade and stir-fried beef. Prepare Grilled Lemongrass Beef Skewers (page 28) and divide evenly among the bowls. Garnish and serve as directed.

TURMERIC CATFISH WITH RICE NOODLES, SCALLION, AND DILL

Chả Cá

THIS NORTHERN VIETNAMESE NOODLE DISH hits all five major taste sensations: salty, sour, sweet, bitter, and umami (savory). The unusual ingredient combination includes galangal, shrimp sauce, sesame rice crackers, and sour cream, the last standing in for *mẻ*, the same mash of fermented cooked rice traditionally used in mock turtle stew (page 153).

For many Vietnamese, the definitive *chả cá* is the rather complicated version served at the landmark Hanoi restaurant Chả Cá Lã Vọng. There, the fish is cooked partially on a grill and then finished at the table in a skillet of oil, scallion, and dill. While that restaurant rendition is delicious, my family takes an easier path to making the dish. We broil the fish and then enrich it with scallion and dill seared in hot oil. The fish can also be grilled over a medium-hot fire, but the small pieces can be difficult to manage on a grill.

Serves 4 generously as a one-dish meal

2 pounds catfish fillets

MARINADE

1/3 cup sour cream, preferably full fat

1 1/2 teaspoons ground turmeric

1 tablespoon fresh galangal juice (see Note) or 1 1/4 teaspoons dried galangal powder

1 1/2 tablespoons fine shrimp sauce

ACCOMPANIMENTS

2/3 pound small dried round rice noodles, cooked in boiling water for 3 to 5 minutes, drained, and flushed with cold water

Vegetable Garnish Plate (page 313), preferably with the addition of Vietnamese balm, fish mint, and sorrel

1/2 cup unsalted roasted peanuts

1 cup Tangy-Sweet Shrimp Sauce (page 310)

2 Toasted Sesame Rice Crackers (page 320)

GARNISHES

1/2 cup chopped fresh dill, feathery tops only

3 scallions, white and green parts, thinly sliced (about 3/4 cup)

1/4 cup canola or other neutral oil

1 Rinse the catfish fillets and pat dry with paper towels. Cut each fillet into index finger–sized pieces about 3 inches long and 3/4 inch thick. (To arrive at pieces that are long enough, you may need to angle the knife so that you cut on the diagonal.)

2 To make the marinade, in a shallow bowl large enough to accommodate the catfish, combine the sour cream, turmeric, galangal juice, and shrimp sauce and mix well. Add the catfish and use a rubber spatula to coat the fish evenly. Cover and refrigerate for 2 hours or up to overnight.

3 Thirty minutes before broiling, remove the catfish from the refrigerator. To prepare the accompaniments, arrange the noodles on 2 plates in 2-inch mounds for easy serving. Place the noodles, vegetable garnish plate, peanuts, dipping sauce, and rice crackers on the table.

4 Position a rack about 3 inches from the heat source and preheat the broiler for 20 minutes to get it nice and hot. Arrange the catfish pieces on an aluminum foil–lined baking sheet, spreading them out flat like a jigsaw puzzle. Broil for 8 to 10 minutes, or until the fish is sizzling and a little brown. Remove from the broiler, make a spout in one corner of the foil, and pour off the accumulated liquid. Use chopsticks or a spatula to flip the fish pieces over. Broil for another 5 to 8 minutes, or until browned on the second side. Transfer to a serving plate.

5 To garnish the fish, blanket it with the dill and scallions. Then, in a small saucepan, heat the oil until faint wisps of smoke start rising. Pour the hot oil over the scallion and dill to wilt them. Use 2 spoons to mix the fish and garnishes and then place on the table.

6 To eat this dish, each diner combines all the various ingredients in a small bowl (such as a rice bowl), tearing the lettuce and herbs into pieces and breaking up the rice cracker. He or she then drizzles a little sauce on top, mixes the contents of the bowl, and eats.

NOTE

To extract galangal juice, first reduce the knobby rhizome to a fine texture by either grating it with a Microplane or Japanese grater, or by thinly slicing it and then pounding the slices in a mortar to a mush. Press the solids through a fine-mesh sieve to obtain the milky liquid. For 1 tablespoon juice, you will need a 1 1/2-inch chunk of galangal.

Some people don't care for the taste of Tangy-Sweet Shrimp Sauce, finding it too strongly flavored. Include an alternative of Basic Dipping Sauce (page 308), made without garlic, on the table.

GRILLED PORK WITH RICE NOODLES AND HERBS

Bún Chả

> **THE INGREDIENTS FOR THIS RECIPE** resemble those for rice noodle bowl with beef (page 224). But instead of having big assembled bowls, diners compose their own small bowls, soaking the tender, sweet, salty pork in sauce, tearing up lettuce and herbs, adding some noodles, and then nibbling on their creations. Traditionally, a meal of *bún chả* is unhurried and encourages long conversation. A famous Hanoi rendition of this northern Viet specialty combines sliced pork belly and pork patties made from chopped shoulder, but I prefer a less complicated and healthier version that uses marinated pork slices.
>
> A grill best mimics the traditional brazier used in Vietnam, but the pork slices can also be roasted in the top third of a 475°F oven until nicely browned (about 9 minutes on each side).

1 To make the marinade, in a mortar, combine the shallot, sugar, and pepper and pound with a pestle until a rough paste forms that is slightly liquid. (Or, use an electric mini-chopper.) Transfer to a bowl and mix in the caramel sauce, fish sauce, and oil. Add the pork and coat evenly. Cover and refrigerate for at least 2 hours or up to 24 hours.

2 Thirty minutes before cooking the pork, remove it from the refrigerator. Arrange the noodles on 2 plates for serving. Place on the table with the dipping sauce and the vegetable garnish plate.

3 Prepare a medium-hot charcoal fire (you can hold your hand over the rack for only 3 to 4 seconds) or preheat a gas grill to medium-high. Grill the pork slices, turning once, for about 4 minutes on each side, or until nicely browned, a little charred, and sizzling. Transfer the pork to a plate and place on the table.

4 Each person needs 2 bowls, a small, shallow one and a larger, deeper one. In the small bowl, diners soak a few pieces of the grilled pork in some dipping sauce. They tear lettuce leaves and herbs into small pieces, put them in the large bowl, toss to distribute, and then top with a mound of noodles and the pieces of pork and some of the sauce they soaked in.

Serves 4 as a one-dish meal, or 6 to 8 with 2 or 3 other dishes

MARINADE

1 large shallot, chopped

2 1/2 teaspoons sugar

3/4 teaspoon black pepper

1 tablespoon Caramel Sauce (page 316) or honey

2 1/2 tablespoons fish sauce

3 tablespoons canola or other neutral oil

2 1/3 pounds boneless pork shoulder, well trimmed (about 2 pounds after trimming) and cut across the grain into strips about 3 inches long, 1 inch wide, and a scant 1/4 inch thick

2/3 pound small dried round rice noodles, cooked in boiling water for 3 to 5 minutes, drained, and flushed with cold water

1 1/2 cups Basic Dipping Sauce made without garlic (page 308)

Vegetable Garnish Plate (page 313), preferably with the addition of red perilla and Vietnamese balm

PANFRIED RICE NOODLES WITH BEEF AND VEGETABLES

Phở Xào Dòn

THIS CLASSIC VIETNAMESE NOODLE DISH features a lightly crispy bed of panfried rice noodles topped with a slightly tangy, saucy stir-fry of beef and vegetables. It is among my favorites. For this preparation, I usually start with dried noodles the size of *pappardelle* (or wide egg noodles), mostly as a matter of convenience because soft, room-temperature fresh rice noodles are hard to come by. If you should find good fresh rice noodles, use them the day you buy them. You will need to buy a pound for this recipe, and you don't have to boil them. They are already cooked and coated with oil, so just toss them with salt and panfry.

Serves 2 as a main dish, or 4 to 6 with 2 or 3 other dishes

1/3 pound wide dried flat rice noodles

Salt

6 tablespoons canola or other neutral oil

MARINADE

1 teaspoon cornstarch

1/4 teaspoon sugar

3/4 teaspoon fish sauce

1 1/2 teaspoons light (regular) soy sauce

1/2 pound flank steak, cut across the grain into strips about 3 inches long, 3/4 inch wide, and a scant 1/4 inch thick

FLAVORING SAUCE

1/2 teaspoon sugar

1 1/2 tablespoons oyster sauce

2 teaspoons fish sauce

1 teaspoon light (regular) soy sauce

3/4 cup warm water

1 tomato

1 1/2 cups small broccoli florets, about 2 inches long and 1 inch wide at the bud end

1 small carrot, peeled, halved lengthwise, and cut on the diagonal into 1/8-inch-thick slices

1/2 red bell pepper, seeded and cut into 3/4-inch squares

2 tablespoons water

1/2 small yellow onion, sliced lengthwise 1/4 inch thick

2 1/2 teaspoons cornstarch dissolved in 1 1/2 tablespoons water

Black pepper

1 Cook the rice noodles in a large pot of boiling water for 3 to 4 minutes, or until cooked but still firm. Drain, flush with cold water, and drain again. Transfer to a large plate or baking dish. Gently toss with a scant 1/2 teaspoon salt and 1 1/2 teaspoons of the oil, and then spread the noodles out to dry and cool. Once the noodles are cool, they are ready for panfrying. Or, you may put them in an airtight container or zip-top plastic bag and refrigerate them overnight; bring them to room temperature before panfrying.

2 To make the marinade, in a shallow bowl large enough to accommodate the beef, combine the cornstarch, sugar, fish sauce, and soy sauce and mix well. Add the beef and use chopsticks or your fingers to coat the beef evenly. Set near the stove.

3 To make the flavoring sauce, in a small bowl, combine the sugar, oyster sauce, fish sauce, soy sauce, and water and stir well to dissolve the sugar. Set near the stove.

4 Bring a saucepan filled with salted water to a rolling boil. Cut a small, shallow X in the blossom end of the tomato. Drop the tomato into the boiling water for about 30 seconds, or until the skin shows signs of loosening from the flesh. Remove the tomato from the pan with a slotted spoon. When cool enough to handle, peel, core, and cut the tomato into 1/2-inch-thick wedges. Put the wedges in a small bowl and set near the stove.

5 Return the water to a rolling boil. Add the broccoli, carrot, and bell pepper and cook for about 2 minutes, or until crisp tender. Drain the vegetables and quickly flush them with cold water. Drain well again and set near the stove. Place a plate near the stove for the holding the elements of the stir-fry as you cook them.

6 To panfry the noodles, heat 1 1/2 tablespoons of the oil in a 10-inch nonstick skillet over medium heat. Add the noodles and spread them out into a large, flat pancake. Add the water, cover, and cook for 1 to 2 minutes, or until the noodles have softened. Uncover and panfry the noodles, undisturbed, for

2 to 3 minutes, or until slightly crispy and barely golden. Don't let them cook until they turn gold, or they will be too chewy and hard. As the noodles crisp, they will move in a solid mass when you shake the skillet handle. Use a wide spatula to turn the noodles over, or flip them over with a confident sharp jerk of the skillet handle. Dribble 1 1/2 tablespoons of the oil into the pan, adding it at the rim. Fry the second side for 3 to 4 minutes. Slide the finished noodle pancake out onto a large serving plate. Use kitchen scissors to cut it into 6 to 8 wedges. If you like, put the plate of noodles in a warm oven while you stir-fry the topping.

7 In a wok or large skillet, heat 2 tablespoons of the oil over medium-high heat. Add the onion and stir-fry for about 30 seconds, or until fragrant. Bank the onion on one side of the pan, increase the heat to high and add the beef, spreading it out into a single layer. Let it cook, undisturbed, for about 1 minute. When the beef begins to brown, use a spatula to flip and stir-fry it, incorporating the onion, for another 1 to 2 minutes, or until the beef is still slightly rare. Transfer the beef and onion to the plate.

8 Lower the heat to medium-high and add the remaining 1 1/2 teaspoons oil to the pan. Add the broccoli, carrot, and bell pepper and stir-fry for about 1 minute, or until heated through. Add the tomato and stir-fry for 30 seconds, or until heated through. Give the flavoring sauce a stir and add it to the pan. When it begins to bubble, return the beef to the pan and stir-fry for 1 minute to combine everything and finish cooking the beef. Give the cornstarch mixture a stir, add to the pan, and stir for about 30 seconds, or until the sauce is smooth and thick. Pour the topping over the noodles and sprinkle with lots of pepper. Serve at once.

PANFRIED EGG NOODLES WITH CHICKEN, SHRIMP, AND VEGETABLES

Mì Xào Dòn Thập Cẩm

THE VIETNAMESE REPERTOIRE also includes panfried Chinese egg noodles, which are cooked just like rice noodles and crowned with a delicious stir-fry. Full of varied flavors, textures, and color, this stir-fry pairs exceptionally well with the egg noodles. I use fresh noodles about 1/8 inch thick. Their texture is superior to dried noodles, and they offer more body than thin ones.

Serves 2 as a main dish, or 4 to 6 with 2 or 3 other dishes

1/2 pound medium Chinese egg noodles, fresh or thawed

Salt

1 1/2 teaspoons sesame oil

MARINADE

1/4 teaspoon sugar

1 teaspoon cornstarch

1/8 teaspoon white pepper

2 teaspoons light (regular) soy sauce

1/2 teaspoon sesame oil

1/4 pound boneless, skinless chicken breast, cut across the grain into slices 2 inches long and a scant 1/4 inch thick

1/3 pound medium or large shrimp, peeled and deveined

FLAVORING SAUCE

1/2 teaspoon sugar

1/4 teaspoon salt

1 1/2 teaspoons fish sauce

1 tablespoon light (regular) soy sauce

1 teaspoon sesame oil

3/4 cup warm water

1 carrot, peeled, halved lengthwise, and cut on the diagonal into 1/8-inch-thick slices

1/2 pound baby bok choy, cut on the diagonal into 3/4-inch-wide pieces

3 dried wood ear mushrooms, reconstituted (page 334), trimmed, and cut into 1/4-inch-wide strips (about 1/4 cup)

5 1/2 tablespoons canola or other neutral oil

2 tablespoons water

2 scallions, white and green parts, cut into 1 1/2-inch lengths and white part bruised with the broad side of a cleaver or chef's knife

1 tablespoon peeled and finely shredded fresh ginger (page 51)

2 teaspoons cornstarch dissolved in 1 tablespoon water

1 Cook the egg noodles in a large pot of boiling water for 3 to 4 minutes, or until cooked but still firm. Drain, flush with cold water, and drain again. Transfer to a large plate or baking dish. Gently toss with a scant 1/2 teaspoon salt and the sesame oil, and then spread the noodles out to dry and cool. Once the noodles are cool, they are ready for panfrying. Or, you may put them in an airtight container or zip-top plastic bag and refrigerate them overnight; bring them to room temperature before panfrying.

2 To make the marinade, in a shallow bowl large enough to accommodate the chicken and shrimp, combine the sugar, cornstarch, white pepper, soy sauce, and sesame oil and mix well. Add the chicken and shrimp and use chopsticks to coat evenly. Set near the stove.

3 To make the flavoring sauce, in a small bowl, combine the sugar, salt, fish sauce, soy sauce, sesame oil, and water and stir to dissolve the sugar. Set near the stove.

4 Bring a pot of salted water to a rolling boil. Drop in the carrot. When the water returns to a boil, add the bok choy and cook for about 1 minute, or until the bok choy is tender and bright green. Drain the vegetables, flush with cold water, and drain again. Add the wood ear mushrooms and set near the stove. Place a plate near the stove for the holding the elements of the stir-fry as you cook them.

5 To panfry the noodles, heat 1 1/2 tablespoons of the canola oil in a 10-inch nonstick skillet over medium heat. Add the noodles and spread them out into a large, flat pancake. Add the water, cover, and cook for 1 to 2 minutes, or until the noodles have softened. Uncover and panfry the noodles, undisturbed, for 4 to 6 minutes, or until they are a nice crunchy brown on the bottom. As the noodles crisp, they will move in a solid mass when you shake the skillet handle. Use a wide spatula to turn the noodles over, or flip them over with a confident sharp jerk of the skillet handle. Dribble 1 1/2 tablespoons of the oil into the pan, adding it at the rim. Fry the second side for 5 to 7 minutes. Slide the finished noodle pancake out onto a large serving plate. Use kitchen scissors to cut it into 6 to 8 wedges. If you like, put the plate of noodles in a warm oven while you stir-fry the topping.

6 In a wok or large skillet, heat 2 tablespoons of the oil over medium-high heat. Add the scallions and ginger and stir-fry for about 15 seconds, or until fragrant. Bank the scallions and ginger on one side of the pan, and then add the chicken and shrimp, spreading them out into a single layer. Let cook, undisturbed, for about 1 minute. When they start to brown, use a spatula to flip and stir-fry them, incorporating the scallions and ginger, for another 1 to 2 minutes, or until the chicken and shrimp have turned color but are still undercooked. Transfer to the plate.

7 Add the remaining 1 1/2 teaspoons oil to the pan. Add the vegetables and stir-fry for about 1 minute, or until heated through. Give the flavoring sauce a stir and add it to the pan. When it begins to bubble, return the chicken and shrimp to the pan and move them around for about 1 minute to combine everything and finish cooking the chicken and shrimp. Give the cornstarch mixture a stir, add to the pan, and stir for about 30 seconds, or until the sauce is smooth and thick. Pour the topping over the noodles and serve at once.

GARLICKY NOODLES WITH MAGGI AND BUTTER

Nui Xào Maggi

WHEN MY FAMILY LIVED IN VIETNAM, these noodles were considered special because Western noodles (called *nui*, the Viet phonetic equivalent of the French *nouilles*) and butter were expensive imports. Once we arrived in the United States, we indulged in them to the point that they were no longer dear. In fact, I forgot about them for years, only to rediscover their garlicky, buttery, nutty goodness at a Vietnamese French restaurant in Westminster, California. Nowadays, I prepare these noodles not just because they are a comfort food from my youth, but also because they are good.

The unusually savory quality of the dish is due to Maggi Seasoning, a soy sauce–like condiment and Vietnamese staple that was most likely introduced to Vietnam by the French. It is fine to use dried pasta for this recipe, though fresh fettuccine or even flat Chinese egg noodles yield a superior dish.

1 Bring a large pot of water to a boil and add about ¹/₂ teaspoon salt. Add the pasta and cook until al dente. While the pasta cooks, put the Maggi sauce in a bowl large enough to accommodate the pasta once it is cooked and set the bowl near the sink.

2 Drain the pasta in a colander and give it a shake to remove excess water. Don't flush it with cold or hot water, however. You want to retain some of the starch, which will help the pasta soak up the seasonings. Immediately put the noodles into the bowl with the Maggi sauce. Use tongs to toss the pasta with the sauce. As the noodles absorb the sauce, they will darken. Keep tossing until they absorb all the sauce.

3 In a 12-inch nonstick skillet, melt the butter over medium heat. When it foams, add the garlic and sauté for about 30 seconds, or until fragrant. Add the noodles and use chopsticks to combine them with the butter and garlic. At first, the noodles will clump and stick together. Keep moving them around and they will eventually separate and spread out in the skillet. Increase the heat to medium-high and let the noodles cook, undisturbed, for

Serves 4 as a side dish

¹/₂ pound fettuccine,
   preferably fresh
Salt
2¹/₂ tablespoons Maggi
   Seasoning sauce,
   preferably Chinese made

2 tablespoons unsalted butter
2 or 3 cloves garlic, minced

30 seconds to 1 minute. This helps bring out the nutty, savory caramel qualities of the Maggi sauce. Give the noodles a good stir and let them sear again briefly. Repeat the searing and stirring several more times until the noodles have absorbed the rich, meaty, garlicky flavors; taste some to make sure. A few noodles may brown, but most of them should remain supple. Sautéing the pasta takes about 5 minutes from beginning to end.

4 Transfer the noodles to a serving bowl or divide them among individual dinner plates. Serve immediately.

RICE NOODLES WITH CHINESE CHIVES, SHRIMP, AND PORK

Bánh Phở Xào Hẹ

ONE SUMMER when I was child, a family friend regularly gave us grocery bags full of Chinese chives (*hẹ*) from her garden. The grassy foot-long chives are easy to grow from seed, and this woman must have had a bumper crop that year. We put the bounty to good use in this delicious noodle dish. No matter how many times it appeared on the dinner table, I never tired of the soft chives, hints of garlic, bits of shrimp and pork, and tart lime finish.

Chinese chives are significantly larger than Western chives, and their flat leaves have a delicate garlic, rather than onion, flavor. In Chinese and Southeast Asian markets, they are typically sold in one-pound bundles. Vietnamese cooks treat them like a green vegetable, often cooking them with noodles. Here, their flat shape mixes perfectly with *bánh phở*. For a light meal, serve the noodles as the main course, pairing it with one of the special-event salads in chapter 1.

1 Place the noodles in a bowl and cover with hot tap water. Let soak for 15 to 20 minutes, until they are pliable and opaque. Drain and use scissors to cut them into 3- to 4-inch lengths.

2 To make the flavoring sauce, in a small bowl, combine the sugar, fish sauce, and water and stir to dissolve the sugar. Set aside.

3 In a wok or large skillet, heat the oil over medium-high heat. Add the garlic and stir-fry for 15 seconds, or until fragrant. Add the shrimp and pork and stir briefly to break up the meat. Sprinkle in the salt and sugar. Keep stirring, and when the shrimp and pork have turned color, after about 2 minutes, add the Chinese chives. Because there is so much food in the pan now, use 2 cooking utensils to stir and toss the ingredients, ensuring even exposure to the heat. (Think of tossing a big salad.) When the chives have collapsed by one-third of their original volume, after about 3 minutes, add the noodles and combine well. When all of the ingredients are well combined, give the flavoring sauce a stir and pour over the mixture. Continue stirring and tossing for 2 to 3 minutes longer, or until the noodles and chives are soft and cooked.

Serves 2 or 3 as a main course, or 4 to 6 with 2 or 3 other dishes

1/2 pound medium dried flat
    rice noodles

FLAVORING SAUCE
1 1/4 teaspoons sugar
3 tablespoons fish sauce
3 tablespoons water

2 tablespoons canola or other
    neutral oil
3 cloves garlic, finely chopped
1/2 pound shrimp, peeled,
    deveined, and chopped
    into pea-sized pieces

1/3 pound ground pork,
    coarsely chopped to
    loosen
1/4 teaspoon salt
1/4 teaspoon sugar
1 pound Chinese chives,
    bottom 1/2 inch trimmed
    and cut into 3-inch lengths
2 or 3 limes, quartered

4 Remove from the heat, squeeze 4 lime wedges (1 lime) over the noodles, and mix well to distribute the flavors. Transfer to a serving plate and serve with the remaining lime wedges.

CELLOPHANE NOODLES WITH CRAB AND BLACK PEPPER

Miến Xào Cua

WHEN IT IS DUNGENESS CRAB SEASON (November through May on the West Coast), one of my favorite ways to capture the essence of *Cancer magister* is to make these golden noodles. Cellophane noodles absorb whatever flavors they are combined with, in this case the sweet brininess of crabmeat and tomalley.

This dish is best when it is made with a live crab that you cook yourself. If you are too squeamish to cook crab at home, buy a precooked crab the day it is cooked. But don't have the crab cracked, as you want all the delicious juices to stay inside. See page 322 for directions on cooking and cleaning the crab and picking the crabmeat.

1 In a bowl, combine the tomalley and fat, egg, water, fish sauce, pepper, and chopped cilantro and mix well. Measure the mixture; you want about 3/4 cup total. Add water if needed.

2 In a wok or large skillet, heat the oil over medium heat. Add the shallot and stir-fry for about 2 minutes, or until soft. Add the crabmeat and mushrooms and stir-fry for about 1 minute, or until aromatic. Add the noodles and continue to stir-fry for about 2 minutes, or until they begin to soften. They noodles will look a bit dry.

3 Give the tomalley mixture a good stir and pour over the noodles. Quickly work the mixture into the noodles to ensure an even distribution of flavors, lowering the heat if the noodles begin to clump. In about 2 minutes, the noodles will become translucent and lightly golden.

4 Remove from the heat and taste and adjust with extra sprinkles of fish sauce and/or pepper. Transfer to a serving plate and serve immediately.

Serves 2 as a main course, or 4 to 6 with 2 or 3 other dishes

Cooked meat and tomalley and fat from a 2-pound Dungeness crab (about 1/2 pound crabmeat and 1/4 cup tomalley and fat)

1 egg

1 tablespoon water

1 1/2 tablespoons fish sauce

1/2 to 3/4 teaspoon black pepper, preferably freshly ground

2 tablespoons finely chopped fresh cilantro

2 tablespoons canola or other neutral oil

1 large shallot or small yellow onion, thinly sliced

3 dried wood ear mushrooms, reconstituted (page 334), stemmed, and cut into 1/8-inch-wide strips (about 1/4 cup)

1/4 pound cellophane noodles, soaked in hot water until pliable, drained, and cut into 10-inch lengths

NOTE

If only blue crabs are available, substitute 9 or 10 crabs (3 1/3 pounds total) for the Dungeness. If you prefer not to use the tomalley and fat, or if there isn't any, use 2 eggs instead of 1 egg and increase the fish sauce in step 1 to 2 tablespoons.

9. INDISPENSABLE RICE

We were in the middle of making spaghetti with meat sauce for dinner when my mother started the electric rice cooker. "Why do we need rice when we have spaghetti?" one of us kids asked her. "Because I must eat rice every day," she replied. On the traditional Vietnamese table, rice is always present even if a noodle dish is on the menu.

To put me on the path to culinary competency, the first thing my mother taught me to prepare was rice. Every night, I scooped the kernels from a bin, rinsed them well, leveled them, and then added water, making sure the amount was correct by resting the tip of my index finger on the uppermost grains. Because my father likes his rice cooked "dry," so that each grain retains its individuality (think al dente rice), I was cautious, adding enough water just to graze my first knuckle joint. When I flubbed, we discussed it at the table, but no one ever got upset. Frankly, you can't cook perfect rice every time, and there is always another batch to be made.

When you eat rice daily, you learn to appreciate its nuances: how perfectly cooked rice is chewy and faintly sweet from the natural starch in each grain, and how the nutty brown crust that forms at the bottom of the pot is wonderful dipped into heady sauces. At its most commonplace, boiled rice is an accompaniment to other foods, but the versatile grains are also steamed, ground into flour, and fermented into wine and vinegar. Although rice is mostly used for savory foods, it is also featured in some sweets.

Yet the importance of rice reaches beyond the table. It is a symbol of well-being, sustenance, and hospitality to Vietnamese, just as it is to other Asians, and its presence in everyday language reflects its centrality to the culture. For example, the term *cơm*, or "cooked rice," is used throughout the day. "Ăn cơm chưa?" (Have you eaten rice?) is a common casual greeting. All the activities involved in preparing a meal are described as *nấu cơm* or "cooking rice," and when you call dinner guests to the table, you say, "Ăn cơm!" (It's time to eat rice!).

Because rice is such an integral part of Vietnamese cuisine, it turns up in various forms in all kinds of dishes. In this chapter, you will find recipes in which long-grain rice and sticky rice star, while the majority of recipes in the following chapter call for rice flour and sticky rice flour. Elsewhere in the book, rice appears in a variety of other guises, such as creamy soups, noodles, rice paper, batters, and even a dessert.

LONG-GRAIN RICE BASICS

Whether you cook long-grain rice in an electric rice cooker or a saucepan, practice and consistency are the keys to doing it well. The following tips will help you cook a good pot of rice every time. For information on shopping for long-grain rice, see page 15.

The pan: If you elect to cook rice on the stove top, choose a heavy-bottomed saucepan with a tight-fitting lid. Since rice more than triples in volume during cooking, the amount of raw rice should fill no more than one-fourth of the pan. For example, use a 1 1/2- or 2-quart pan for 1 1/2 cups of rice, and a 2- or 3-quart pan for 2 cups of rice.

continued

Amount to cook: One cup raw rice yields 3½ cups cooked rice, or enough for 3 light eaters. To be sure you have enough rice, prepare 1½ cups raw rice for 3 or 4 people and 2 cups raw rice for 4 to 6 people.

Rinsing: Don't worry that you are washing away precious nutrients when you rinse rice. The amount lost is minimal. Rinsing rice rids the grains of surface starches, prevents clumping, and yields a clean, fresh taste. Whether you are rinsing the rice in a pan, a rice cooker insert, or a bowl, use plenty of water and always start by stirring the rice in circles with your fingers or by rubbing it gently between your palms to loosen the starches. Repeatedly rinse the rice with fresh water until the water is nearly clear. If you use a precise water-to-rice ratio, drain the rice in a sieve before putting it in the pan or rice cooker insert.

Water-to-rice ratio: There is no set rule on how much water to use. The proportions depend on the amount of rice you are cooking, the type of rice, and how you like your rice cooked. In general, I find that 1¼ cups water for each cup of long-grain rice yields firm, chewy, dry rice. Rice labeled new crop is from a fairly recent harvest, which means that it has not had as much time to dry. Because of its relatively high moisture content, it typically requires slightly less water. If the packaging provides a ratio, try it. Continue to experiment with your favorite pan or rice cooker insert until you arrive at a formula that works for you.

The process: Rice is typically cooked by first boiling with the pan uncovered, and then lowering the heat, covering the pan, and simmering. During the initial boiling, I employ the northern Viet technique of stirring the rice several times to ensure even cooking. To cook a pot of rice, bring the rice and water to a boil (or near boil) over medium-high or high heat. (Salt isn't traditionally added to plain boiled rice because other foods will season it at the table.) Give the rice a stir with chopsticks to loosen the grains sticking to the bottom. Lower the heat to medium so the rice simmers vigorously. Cook the rice, stirring 2 or 3 times, for a few minutes, or until most of the water appears to have been absorbed and the surface looks glossy and thick. You may also see small craters in the surface. Decrease the heat to low, cover, and cook for 10 minutes. Turn off the heat and let the rice sit for 10 minutes to firm up and finish cooking. Uncover, fluff with chopsticks or a fork, and then re-cover and wait for 5 minutes before serving. The rice will stay warm for 30 minutes.

PRESSED RICE LOGS

Cơm Nắm

A BATCH OF RICE in which the grains remain distinct is called *cơm rời* (separated rice), while rice that has been compacted by hand into dense balls or logs is called *cơm nắm* (pressed rice). Like Japanese *onigiri* (rice balls), *cơm nắm* is both shaped and eaten by hand. You simply pick up a piece, press it against a boldly flavored food like Caramelized Minced Pork (page 131), Cotton Pork (page 134), or sesame salt (see Note), and pop the morsel into your mouth.

For many Vietnamese of my parents' generation, *cơm nắm* is an old-fashioned food that conjures up memories of home, perhaps because it was a creative way for moms to get their kids to eat more rice, the main source of sustenance. As a reminder of such times, my dad regularly prepared *cơm nắm* and then presliced it for family road trips, picnics, and whenever we wanted a fun alternative to eating rice from a bowl.

1   Following the directions in Long-Grain Rice Basics (page 238), cook the rice so the grains are on the soft side, rather than dry or firm. You may have to use extra water. This is the one time when mushy rice is good.

2   Wet a lint-free, nonterry dish towel, wring it out, and spread it out on a work surface. Fluff the hot rice and then place half of it on the center of the towel. Gather up the towel and start vigorously kneading the rice as if it were a ball of bread dough. When the rice is compact and malleable, 1 to 2 minutes later, open up the towel and shape the rice into a log 2 inches in diameter. Wrap the log in the dish towel and roll it back and forth to smooth the surface. Put the log on a plate and repeat with the remaining rice.

3   Allow the logs to cool until they are dry to the touch, about 1 hour. Rotate the logs after 30 minutes, so the wetter underside dries out, too. To serve, use a knife to slice the logs into $1/4$- to $1/2$-inch-thick pieces, dipping the blade in cold water before each cut.

Serves 4 to 6 as a side dish

2 cups long-grain rice

NOTE

When making rice logs in advance, loosely cover them with plastic wrap and keep at room temperature. They are best when eaten within 2 hours.

To make sesame salt (*muối mè*), toast 3 tablespoons sesame seeds (page 332) and transfer to a mortar. Add $1/2$ teaspoon kosher or sea salt and crush with a pestle to a fine, sandy texture. Alternatively, use an electric mini-chopper and process for 12 to 15 seconds.

CHICKEN AND VEGETABLE CLAY POT RICE

Cơm Gà

> DEEPLY SEASONED and studded with chicken and colorful vegetables, this special-occasion rice is traditionally cooked in a clay pot and presented at the table in the cooking vessel. Many Vietnamese American cooks, my mother included, switched to preparing this dish in large, heavy Western pots, such as Dutch ovens, which conduct heat well and don't break like clay pots sometimes do. Their easier and more convenient approach doesn't compromise flavor, and sometimes a wonderful golden crust forms at the bottom. However, if you would like to cook the rice in a clay pot, see the Note following the method.
>
> For this recipe, you want to use long-grain rice that will cook up to a chewy firmness. If you happen to have new-crop rice, which tends to cook up more sticky than firm, reduce the quantity of stock slightly, or purchase regular long-grain rice.

1 In a bowl, stir together the salt, white pepper, sugar, soy sauce, and oyster sauce. Add the chicken and use chopsticks to mix well. Set aside.

2 In a large skillet, heat 2 tablespoons of the oil over medium heat. Add the onion and sauté for about 1 minute, or until fragrant. Add the celery, carrot, and mushrooms and continue to sauté for about 3 minutes, or until half cooked. Add the chicken and sauté gently for 3 to 4 minutes, or until the chicken is cooked through. Remove from the heat, stir in the peas, and set the pan aside.

3 Rinse the rice and let it drain for 10 minutes in a sieve positioned over a bowl. Meanwhile, bring the stock to a near simmer in a small saucepan and then cover to keep it hot.

4 In a heavy-bottomed 5-quart Dutch oven or similar pot, heat the remaining 3 tablespoons oil over medium-high heat. Firmly shake the sieve holding the rice to expel any hidden water, and then add the rice to the pot. Stir constantly with a large spoon

continued

Serves 3 or 4 as a light main dish, or 6 with 2 or 3 other dishes

1/2 teaspoon salt

1/4 teaspoon white pepper

1/2 teaspoon sugar

2 teaspoons light (regular) soy sauce

2 tablespoons oyster sauce

3/4 pound boneless, skinless chicken thighs, cut into 1/2-inch cubes

5 tablespoons canola or other neutral oil

1 small yellow onion, finely chopped

2/3 cup chopped celery (pea-sized pieces)

2/3 cup chopped carrot (pea-sized pieces)

5 or 6 dried shiitake mushrooms, reconstituted (page 332), trimmed, and chopped into pea-sized pieces

1/2 cup frozen peas, preferably petite peas, thawed

2 cups long-grain rice

2 2/3 cups chicken stock, homemade or quick version (page 317)

for about 3 minutes, or until the grains are opaque and feel light. Add the stock and expect dramatic boiling. Immediately give the rice and stock a big stir, then lower the heat to medium so the contents simmer and cover the pot. Put your ear by the pot and you will hear gentle bubbling.

5   During the next 5 minutes, encourage the grains to absorb the stock and cook evenly. To do this, periodically remove the lid, give the rice a big, quick stir, and then replace the lid. I typically stir the rice 3 times, usually about 30 seconds after the steam plumes begin shooting from under the lid. The rice will first swim in stock and then progressively become less easy to move. Small craters will form on the surface, too. When you stir the third time, the rice should stick a bit to the pan and most of the stock will have been absorbed. (If it has not reached this point, continue cooking for a minute or so and check again.) At this point, level the rice and turn the heat to low. Cover and cook for 10 minutes.

6   Uncover and add the vegetables and chicken and any juices from the skillet, distributing them evenly over the rice. Replace the lid and continue cooking for 10 minutes longer. Uncover and stir the contents, scraping the bottom to combine all the ingredients. Replace the lid, remove from the heat, and let the rice sit for 10 minutes to allow the flavors to meld.

7   Fluff the rice with chopsticks or a fork and then spoon it into 1 or 2 serving bowls or platters. If a little crust has formed on the bottom of the pot, scoop it out and serve the shards separately for anyone who enjoys their crisp, nutty taste.

NOTE

To cook this rice dish in a clay pot, you will need a 4- to 5-quart pot. A Chinese sand pot of this size is more affordable than a Japanese *donabe*. Marinate the chicken and sauté it with the vegetables as directed. Rinse the rice, and while it is draining, bring the chicken stock to a boil in the clay pot over medium heat. Lower the heat to a simmer and cover to keep the stock hot. Wipe out the skillet used to sauté the chicken and vegetables and follow step 4 to sauté the rice in the oil. When the rice is almost ready, bring the stock to a vigorous simmer. Add the sautéed rice to the hot stock, bring back to a boil, lower the heat to a simmer, and continue as directed in step 5. At the end of step 5, when you lower the heat to cook the rice, it should be between medium-low and low, as opposed to the low heat used for the Dutch oven. Also, listen for a very gentle hiss, rather than gentle bubbling. Proceed as directed in steps 6 and 7. A plastic dough scraper is perfect for removing the rice crust that may form at the bottom of the clay pot. For more on clay pot cooking, see page 108.

MIXED RICE

Cơm Trộn

ANYONE WHO HAS TRIED to cook Chinese fried rice knows how challenging it can be to do it well. While the Vietnamese repertoire has a number of fried rice dishes, it also includes an easier alternative called *cơm trộn*, freshly cooked rice tossed with a handful of ingredients. In this recipe, you can use whatever meats or seafood you have on hand, such as Char Siu Pork (page 142), any Vietnamese sausage (see chapter 6), roast chicken, grilled pork, or shrimp, along with bell pepper, egg strips, and scallion to create a beautiful mixture of colors, shapes, and textures.

1 To marinate the bell pepper, in a small bowl, combine the water and vinegar. Add the bell pepper and set aside while the rice cooks.

2 Following the directions in Long-Grain Rice Basics (page 238), cook the rice so that grains are chewy, firm, and dry. You want the grains to mix well with the other ingredients, so the rice must not be too soft or gummy.

3 Meanwhile, heat the oil in a large skillet over medium heat. Add the scallions and sauté for about 15 seconds, or until fragrant and soft. Add the meat and continue cooking for a few minutes just to combine the flavors and warm up all the ingredients. Season to taste with salt, and then transfer to a large bowl. Add the egg strips and set aside.

4 To serve, drain the bell pepper and add to the bowl of meat and egg strips. Use chopsticks or a fork to fluff the rice and then add it to the bowl and mix all the ingredients together well. Transfer the rice to a serving bowl or platter and place on the table. Since the rice is lightly seasoned, invite diners to season their own servings with the condiments.

Serves 3 or 4 as a light main course, or 6 with 2 or 3 other dishes

MARINATED BELL PEPPER
1/4 cup water
1/4 cup distilled white vinegar
1 red bell pepper, seeded and cut into 1-inch matchsticks (1 cup)

2 cups long-grain rice
1 tablespoon canola or other neutral oil
2 scallions, white and green parts, chopped

2 cups chopped cooked meat and/or shrimp (pea-sized pieces)
Salt
2 or 3 thin Egg Sheets (page 320), quartered and cut into fine strips
Fish sauce, light (regular) soy sauce, and/or Maggi Seasoning sauce

STICKY RICE WITH ROAST CHICKEN AND SCALLION OIL

Xôi Gà

WHENEVER WE HAVE leftover garlicky roast chicken, my family prepares this simple sticky rice dish, which we typically eat for breakfast, though it would be fine for lunch, too. If you don't have time to roast your own chicken, you can use store-bought rotisserie chicken. Try to shred the chicken into bite-sized pieces as thick as a chopstick.

1 Put the rice in a bowl and add water to cover by 1 inch. Let stand for at least 2 hours (or even overnight).

2 Dump the rice into a colander and rinse under cold running water. Give the colander a few shakes to expel extra water and then return the rice to the bowl. Toss the rice with the salt.

3 Fill the steamer pan halfway with water and bring to a rolling boil over high heat. If you are concerned about cleanup and/or the rice falling through the holes of the steamer tray, line the tray with a piece of parchment paper or banana leaf, leaving a few holes uncovered for heat circulation. Pour the rice into the tray, keeping it 1 inch away from the edge where condensation will collect.

4 Place the tray in the steamer, cover, and steam the rice for 20 minutes, or until the grains are shiny, tender, and slightly chewy. To ensure even cooking, give the rice a big stir with chopsticks or a spatula 2 or 3 times during steaming. Take care when lifting the lid that you don't allow any condensation to drip onto the rice and that you are not burned by the steam. After each stirring, gather the grains back into a mound in the center, leaving a 1-inch border between the rice and the edge of the steamer tray. When the rice is done, lower the heat to keep it hot. (The rice may be steamed up to 2 hours in advance and left at room temperature. Before serving, resteam it until hot.)

Serves 2 or 3 as a light main course, or 4 to 6 as a side dish

2 cups short-grain sticky rice
1/2 teaspoon salt
2 cups hand-shredded Garlicky Oven-Roasted Chicken (page 80), preferably leg or thigh pieces with the skin removed

1/4 cup Scallion Oil Garnish (page 314)
Fish sauce, light (regular) soy sauce, and/or Maggi Seasoning sauce

5 To serve, warm the chicken in the microwave oven or in a nonstick skillet over medium heat. It doesn't need to be piping hot, just soft and juicy. Turn off the steamer, fluff the rice with chopsticks or a large spoon, and then spoon it onto a platter or 2 plates, spreading it out into a 1-inch-thick layer. Arrange the chicken on top and then distribute the scallion oil evenly over the chicken. Serve with the condiments. Eat with chopsticks or a fork.

STICKY RICE WITH HOMINY, MUNG BEAN, AND CRISPY SHALLOTS

Xôi Bắp

IMAGINE MY MOM'S DELIGHT when she first spotted canned hominy at American markets (and later, hulled mung beans). Gone were the days when she had to soak and treat dried corn kernels with slaked lime before cooking them to prepare this treat. She also had to soak and skin unhulled mung beans before she could steam and grind them. By the time this dish appeared at the table, nearly two days had passed. But it was all worth it: the rice and hominy formed a chewy, soft base for the buttery yellow mung beans, toasted sesame seeds, and fried shallots.

Serve this sticky rice dish alone or with slices of Viet sausages or roasted chicken, duck, or pork.

1 Put the rice in a bowl and add water to cover by 1 inch. Let stand for at least 2 hours (or even overnight).

2 Dump the rice into a colander and rinse under cold running water. Shake the colander to expel extra water and then return the rice to the bowl. Add the hominy, breaking it up into individual kernels. Toss the rice and hominy with 1/4 teaspoon of the salt.

3 Fill the steamer pan halfway with water and bring to a rolling boil over high heat. If you are concerned about cleanup and/or the rice falling through the holes of the steamer tray, line the tray with a piece of parchment paper or banana leaf, leaving a few holes uncovered for heat circulation. Pour the rice and hominy into the tray, keeping the mixture 1 inch away from the edge where condensation will collect.

4 Place the tray in the steamer, cover, and steam the rice for 20 minutes, or until the rice is shiny, tender, and slightly chewy; the hominy is already cooked. To ensure even cooking, give the rice a big stir with chopsticks or a spatula 2 or 3 times during steaming. Take care when lifting the lid that you don't allow any condensation to drip onto the rice and hominy and that you are not burned by the steam. At the end of each stirring, gather the grains back into a mound in the center, leaving a 1-inch border

between the rice and the edge of the steamer tray. When the rice is done, lower the heat to keep it hot.

5 While the rice and hominy steam, put the sesame seeds, the remaining 1/2 teaspoon salt, and the 1 tablespoon sugar in a mortar and crush with a pestle to a fine, sandy texture. (Or, use an electric mini-chopper and process for 10 seconds.) Set aside.

6 To serve, turn off the steamer, fluff the rice and hominy, and transfer to a platter, spreading it out into a 1-inch-thick layer. Sprinkle the mung bean on top and then follow with the sesame mixture and finish with the shallot. Serve with a small bowl of sugar for anyone who wants a little extra sweetness.

Serves 3 or 4 as a light main course, or 6 as a side dish or snack

1 1/2 cups short-grain sticky rice

1 can (15 ounces) white hominy, drained

3/4 teaspoon salt

2 tablespoons sesame seeds, toasted (page 332)

1 tablespoon sugar, plus sugar for serving

1 cup Ground Steamed Mung Bean (page 322), at room temperature

1/3 cup Crispy Caramelized Shallot (page 314)

STICKY RICE AND CHESTNUT DRESSING

Nhân Gà Nhồi Hạt Dẻ

WHEN VIETNAMESE COOKS stuff fowl for roasting, the dressing is often made with sticky rice. These preparations, which bridge Vietnamese and French culinary traditions, commonly include lotus seeds, too. My family prefers the flavor of chestnuts, however, which we simmer in chicken stock, butter, and cilantro. The presence of shiitake mushrooms and Cognac in this recipe illustrates yet another marriage of East and West.

This dressing is good with roast turkey, chicken, game hens, and goose. While you may stuff the birds, I find baking the dressing separately is easier, plus the grains on the bottom form a tasty crust. Shelling and peeling chestnuts is time-consuming, but this recipe doesn't require many of them. For guidance on buying and peeling the nuts, see the accompanying Note.

1 Put the rice in a bowl and add water to cover by 1 inch. Let stand for at least 2 hours (or even overnight).

2 To prepare the chestnuts, place them in a small saucepan in which they will fit in a single layer. Add the butter, cilantro, and broth to cover by 1/2 inch. Bring to a simmer, cover partially, and simmer gently for about 20 minutes, or until the nuts are tender yet firm and still hold their shape. Do not allow the nuts to boil, or they will disintegrate. When they are ready, some pieces will be intact and others will have broken apart. Set aside.

3 Dump the rice into a colander and rinse under cold running water. Shake the colander to expel extra water and then return the rice to the bowl. Toss with 1/2 teaspoon of the salt.

4 Fill the steamer pan halfway with water and bring to a rolling boil over high heat. If you are concerned about cleanup and/or the rice falling through the holes of the steamer tray, line the tray with a piece of parchment paper or banana leaf, leaving a few holes uncovered for heat circulation. Pour the rice into the tray, keeping it 1 inch away from the edge where condensation will collect.

Makes about 8 cups, to serve 6 to 8 as a side dish

1 1/2 cups short-grain sticky rice

FOR THE CHESTNUTS
1 1/2 cups shelled and peeled chestnuts (3/4 pound unpeeled), halved lengthwise (see Note)
1 tablespoon unsalted butter
5 sprigs cilantro
2 cups canned low-sodium chicken broth, or as needed

1 teaspoon salt
4 tablespoons unsalted butter
1 small yellow onion, finely chopped

1 clove garlic, minced
Liver from the bird, yellowish membranes trimmed and chopped (optional)
1/2 pound ground pork, coarsely chopped to loosen
8 dried shiitake mushrooms, reconstituted (page 332), trimmed, and chopped
1/2 teaspoon black pepper
1 teaspoon chopped fresh thyme or generous 1/4 teaspoon dried thyme
3 tablespoons Cognac
2 tablespoons finely chopped fresh cilantro

5 Place the tray in the steamer, cover, and steam the rice for 20 minutes, or until the grains are shiny, tender, and slightly chewy. To ensure even cooking, give the rice a big stir with chopsticks or a spatula 2 or 3 times during steaming. Take care when lifting the lid that you don't allow any condensation to drip onto the rice and that you are not burned by the steam. At the end of each stirring, gather the grains back into a mound in the center, leaving a 1-inch border between the rice and the edge of the steamer tray. When the rice is done, turn off the heat and leave the rice in the steamer while you ready the other ingredients.

6 In a large skillet, melt 2 tablespoons of the butter over medium heat. Add the onion and garlic and sauté for about 2 minutes, or until fragrant and soft. Add the liver and sauté for less than 1 minute, or just until cooked through. Add the pork, pressing and poking it to break it up into small pieces, and cook and stir for about 2 minutes, or until half done. Add the mushrooms, pepper, thyme, and remaining 1/2 teaspoon salt and continue to cook, stirring often, for 2 minutes, or until the pork is cooked through. Remove from the heat.

7 Position a rack in the middle of the oven and preheat to 400°F. Butter the bottom and sides of a 9-by-13-inch baking dish (or baking dish of similar size) with 1 tablespoon of the butter. Transfer the pork mixture and any juices to a large bowl and add the rice and Cognac. Use a rubber spatula or 2 spoons to combine the ingredients well, breaking apart any large clumps of rice. Discard the cilantro sprigs from the chestnuts and drain the chestnuts, reserving the liquid for a sauce or a soup if desired. Add the chestnuts to the rice mixture along with the chopped cilantro and mix together gently. Taste and adjust with more salt, if necessary. (The dressing may be prepared to this point up to 1 day in advance. Cover partially to prevent drying and let cool completely, then transfer to an airtight container and refrigerate. Bring to room temperature before baking.) Transfer the dressing to the prepared baking dish. Cut the remaining 1 tablespoon butter into bits and use to dot the top evenly. Cover the dish with aluminum foil.

8 Bake the dressing for 35 to 40 minutes, or until heated through and the bottom browns. Although the top will not brown, some grains at the edge will brown. Remove from the oven and let cool for 5 to 10 minutes before serving.

NOTE

Chestnuts are in season in the late fall and early winter. Select shiny nuts that feel heavy for their size and store them in a cool, dry place. Be sure to use them while they still feel full and heavy. Or, freeze them unshelled for up to a year and thaw in the refrigerator before using.

To shell and peel chestnuts, first cut a cross on the flat side of each nut with a sharp paring knife. To do this, place the nuts on a dish towel so they don't roll away. Preheat a toaster oven or a regular oven to 400°F and place the nuts, cut side up, directly on the rack (use the middle rack of a regular oven) or in a shallow pan. Bake them for about 5 minutes in a toaster oven or 10 to 15 minutes in a regular oven, or until the chestnuts feel hot and the cut on each shell opens and curls.

Carefully transfer the hot nuts to a dish towel, wrap them up, and squeeze the bundle to crack their shells. Working with 1 nut at a time and using the paring knife, remove the smooth outer shell and then peel, scrape, and/or cut off the papery inner brown skin. Use the knife tip to pry out skin bits stuck in the crevices. It is okay if a nut breaks during peeling. As you work, keep the unpeeled nuts warm in the dish towel, so the shells remain pliable and easier to remove. You can shell and peel chestnuts up to 3 days in advance of using and keep them tightly covered in the refrigerator, or you can freeze them for up to 6 months.

FESTIVE ORANGE-RED STICKY RICE

Xôi Gấc

A HARBINGER OF GOOD FORTUNE, *xôi gấc* is traditionally served at Viet weddings and Tet celebrations, paired with roast pork or sausages. As my mom says, "Red is a lucky color and the sticky rice helps the luck stay with you."

This sticky rice is named after the *gấc* fruit (*Momordica cochinchinensis*) whose cockscomb red pulp and seed membranes stain the grains with brilliant color and impart a light fruity fragrance and flavor. Rough skinned and cantaloupe sized, the fruit is believed to promote health and energy. (In fact, it is full of antioxidants.) Because this exotic fruit is not yet widely available in the United States, Vietnamese American cooks often substitute food coloring when they make this dish. I prefer a combination of tomato paste and ground annatto seeds, which better mimics the real thing. If you travel to Vietnam, buy some *gấc* powder from one of the spice vendors at Ben Thanh Market in Saigon, and use 2 tablespoons of the powder in place of the tomato paste and annatto.

1 Put the rice in a bowl and add water to cover by 1 inch. Let stand for at least 2 hours (or even overnight).

2 Dump the rice into a colander and rinse under cold running water. Give the colander a few shakes to expel extra water and set aside to drain. In the bowl used for soaking the rice, combine the tomato paste, annatto, salt, and wine and mix to create a thick red paste. Add the rice and mix well to coat the grains evenly, breaking up any clumps of red paste.

3 Fill the steamer pan halfway with water and bring to a rolling boil over high heat. If you are concerned about cleanup and/or the rice falling through the holes of the steamer tray, line the tray with a piece of parchment paper or banana leaf, leaving a few holes uncovered for heat circulation. Pour the rice into the tray, keeping it 1 inch away from the edge where condensation will collect.

4 Place the tray in the steamer, cover, steam the rice for 5 minutes, and then give it a good stir with a large metal spoon. Take care when lifting the lid that you don't allow any

Serves 4 to 6 as a side dish

2 cups short-grain sticky rice
2 tablespoons tomato paste
1 teaspoon annatto seeds, finely ground
Generous 1/2 teaspoon salt
1 tablespoon Shaoxing rice wine or dry sherry
1/4 cup sugar
2 tablespoons canola or other neutral oil

Slices of Classic Silky Sausage; Beef, Dill, and Peppercorn Sausage; Roasted Cinnamon Sausage (pictured); or Headcheese (pages 160 to 170); or 1 to 2 pounds roast pork purchased at a Chinese barbecue shop or restaurant

condensation to drip onto the rice and that you are not burned by the steam. After stirring, gather the grains back into a mound in the center, leaving a 1-inch border between the rice and the edge of the steamer tray. Steam for another 5 minutes, turn the heat down to low, remove the lid, and repeat the stirring. This second time, sprinkle in the sugar as you stir, and then stir in the oil. Increase the heat to high, mound the rice, and replace

the lid. After the water returns to a rolling boil, steam for 10 to 15 minutes, or until the grains are chewy yet tender and orange-red. Turn off the heat. (The rice may be steamed up to 2 hours in advance and left at room temperature. Before serving, resteam the rice until it is hot.)

5 To serve, fluff the hot rice with chopsticks or the metal spoon and then transfer to a platter or 2 plates, shaping it into a mound. For a traditional presentation, press the hot rice into a mold (like a shallow bowl or other mold) and then invert the mold onto a plate. Serve with the meat of your choice.

10. THE WORLD OF BÁNH

The word *bánh* immediately conjures *bánh mì* (baguette sandwiches), but it actually describes much more. It is the generic term for a savory or sweet made primarily of starchy ingredients, including various flours and legumes, and it embraces breads, buns, cakes, cookies, crepes, dumplings, fritters, and noodles. This wildly diverse group employs a wide range of ingredients and techniques and is made up of foods that are both simple and sophisticated, national and foreign, modern and ancient.

Two of the most beloved *bánh*, *bánh dầy* and *bánh chưng*, share a mythical beginning. According to legend, the savory cakes were created during the earliest years of Vietnamese civilization, the golden era of the Hong Bang dynasty. To pick his successor, Hung Vuong VI held a food contest among his many sons in the days leading up to Tet, challenging them to find the tastiest dishes unknown to him. Most of the princes ventured long distances to procure exotic and extravagant foods. The winner stayed at the palace and cleverly used common, locally available ingredients to create *bánh dầy*, made round like the sky, and *bánh chưng*, made square to symbolize the earth. The former consisted of sticky rice dough steamed on banana leaf, while the latter was a mixture of sticky rice, mung bean, and pork wrapped in banana leaf and boiled. The ideas and cooking instructions for the dishes came from a genie that appeared to the prince in a dream. The king, on trying them and learning of the divine inspiration, was so impressed that he had recipes for the modest preparations distributed throughout his kingdom.

Today, these two *bánh* are deeply ingrained in Vietnamese culinary lore. It is traditional to prepare *bánh chưng* for Tet, and many cooks also make *bánh dầy* for the festivities, which are a celebration of good luck and good fortune. The simple cakes are served as humble expressions of gratitude for life's blessings.

Other *bánh* are illustrations of the unique character of Vietnamese cooking. An obvious example is *bánh tráng*, or rice paper, a staple that completes many signature dishes. Equally important are *bánh phở*, the emblematic rice noodles used in *phở*, the national noodle soup.

Vietnamese cooks have also manipulated rice and other grains and starches into more complex *bánh*, many of which street vendors, restaurants, and home cooks build their reputations on. Each region specializes in certain preparations, and people are proud of their distinctive contributions. Whenever I travel in Vietnam, I make sure to sample crispy *bánh tôm* (shrimp and sweet potato fritters) in Hanoi, rich *bánh khoái* (small rice crepes) in Hue, and sizzling *bánh xèo* (large rice crepes) in Saigon.

But *bánh* is not only about preserving ancient ideas and culinary pride. The category is so broad in part because the Vietnamese are open to assimilating new ideas. A number of foreign foods have *bánh* status, and they are often identified by partially transliterated names. French *choux à la crème* (cream puffs) are known as *bánh su*, a French *gâteau* (cake) is *bánh ga-tô*, and Chinese *bao* (buns) are called *bánh bao*. *Bánh mì*, which indicates a *bánh* made from wheat (*mì*), means Western-style baked bread and is also the colloquial term for sandwich.

This chapter focuses on the classic savory *bánh* that our family particularly enjoys. The following chapter contains a number of sweet *bánh*. Together, the recipes offer a glimpse into a remarkably varied Vietnamese food category.

RECIPES

CAKES AND DUMPLINGS

SPECIAL EVENT

BUNS

PANCAKES, CREPES, AND FRITTERS

STICKY RICE CAKES

Bánh Dầy

HERE, SIMPLE DOUGH made of glutinous rice flour, water, and salt is shaped into small, round disks and steamed on banana leaf circles, which impart fragrance and prevent sticking. The result is *bánh dầy*, eggshell-white cakes that are eaten in pairs with slices of Viet sausage slipped between them. The cakes are sweet and chewy, while the sausage provides a savory counterpoint. If you don't have time to make the sausage at home, pick some up at a Viet market or deli.

1   In a bowl, stir together the 2 rice flours and the salt. Make a well in the center, pour in the water, and stir with a spatula until a clumpy dough forms. Then, use your hand to knead the dough into a rough mass. Turn out the dough and all the unincorporated bits onto a work surface and knead with both hands into a soft, smooth ball that feels like modeling clay. If necessary, add water by the teaspoon or a bit of rice flour (either kind is fine) to achieve the correct consistency. To test if the dough is ready, pinch it; it should barely stick to your fingers. Shape the dough into a log and cut it into 8 equal pieces. Set aside for a moment.

2   Fill the steamer pan halfway with water and bring to a rolling boil over high heat. Lower the heat until you are ready to steam.

3   Have ready a shallow bowl of water for moistening your hands. Spread out the banana leaf circles on the work surface, and very lightly brush the top of each circle with oil (this prevents the cakes from sticking to the leaf). To form each cake, lightly moisten your hands and roll a piece of dough between your palms into a smooth ball. Center the ball atop a banana leaf circle. Repeat with the remaining dough, remoistening your hands as needed. Finish by moistening the heel of your hand and gently flattening each ball of dough into a 1/2-inch-thick disk.

Makes eight 2 1/2-inch cakes, to serve 4 as a light breakfast or snack

1 cup Mochiko Blue Star brand glutinous (sweet) rice flour

1/2 cup glutinous (sweet) rice flour, any Thai brand

1/4 teaspoon salt

3/4 cup water

8 circles, each 3 1/2 inches in diameter, cut from fresh or thawed, frozen banana leaf, rinsed and wiped dry

Canola or other neutral oil

Classic Silky Sausage; Beef, Dill, and Peppercorn Sausage; Roasted Cinnamon Sausage; or Rich and Crisp Sausage (pages 160 to 165), sliced

Place the cakes in steamer trays, spacing them 1 inch apart and keeping them 1 inch away from the edge where condensation will collect.

4 Return the water in the steamer pan to a rolling boil. Loosely cover 1 tray with parchment or waxed paper to prevent drying. Place the other tray in the steamer, cover, and steam the cakes for 6 minutes, or until they have expanded and no longer look chalky. Turn off the heat and wait for the steam to subside before lifting the lid, and then lift it away from you carefully to avoid condensation dripping onto the cakes. Remove the tray and use a metal spatula to transfer the cakes, still on the banana leaf, to a wire rack. Steam the second tray the same way. Let the cakes cool for about 1 hour, or until they are at room temperature. A shiny skin forms on top to make them easier to handle.

5 Arrange the cakes, still on the banana leaf, on 1 or more platters and place on the table with the sausages. To eat, peel off the banana leaf from the bottom of a cake. Lay 1 or 2 sausage slices on the bottom, or stickier side, of the cake. Remove the banana leaf from another cake and place it, shiny side up, on top to create a sandwich.

NOTE

These cakes taste best the day you prepare them. If you have to store them, keep the cakes in pairs. Invert one on top of another, with a piece of banana leaf between the top sides to prevent them from sticking. Put the cakes in an airtight container and refrigerate. Refresh the cakes in the steamer or microwave oven until hot, letting them cool before eating.

This sticky rice dough can be used to encase a savory filling of shrimp, pork, and mushroom for steamed dumplings called *bánh ít tôm thịt*, a traditional breakfast treat that is also great for brunch, lunch, or a snack. Make a batch of the filling used for steamed rice crepe rolls (page 270). Then prepare 1½ recipes of the sticky rice dough, shaping the finished dough into a log and cutting it into 12 equal pieces.

To form the dumplings, have ready a shallow bowl of water for moistening your hands. Spread out 12 banana leaf circles (each 3½ inches in diameter) on your work surface, and very lightly brush the top of each circle with oil (this prevents the dumplings from sticking to the leaf). Lightly moisten your hands, pick up a piece of dough, and roll it into a ball. Holding it with one hand, use the fingers of your other hand to press the dough gently from the center toward the rim to create a 3-inch circle slightly thinner at the center than at the rim. As you press, rotate the dough to make an even circle. (It is like shaping a tiny pizza.)

Gently cup one hand and put the dough circle in that hand, placing it toward the fingertips, which will cradle the dumpling as you shape it. Place a heaping tablespoon of the filling in the center of the circle. Lightly press on the filling with the back of the spoon to create a shallow well; your hand will naturally cup a little tighter as you do this. Now, use your free hand to push and pinch the dough together to enclose the filling completely. You will end up with a ball about 2 inches in diameter. Pass the ball between your hands a few times to smooth the surface, and then center it on a banana leaf circle. Repeat with the remaining dough and filling. Place the dumplings in steamer trays, spacing them 1 inch apart and 1 inch away from the edge where condensation will collect.

Steam the dumplings, one tray at a time, for 15 minutes, or until they have expanded and no longer look chalky. Turn off the heat and wait for the steam to subside before lifting the lid, and then lift it away from you carefully to avoid condensation dripping onto the dumplings. Remove the tray and use a metal spatula to transfer the dumplings, still on the banana leaf, to a wire rack or serving plate. Let them firm and cool for 5 to 10 minutes before serving. Diners can use chopsticks or forks to lift them from the banana leaf (they come off easily). They are good as they are, but they are even better dipped into a mixture of soy sauce and black pepper.

SPINACH DUMPLINGS WITH MUNG BEAN AND SHALLOT

Bánh Khúc

IN THE WINTER MONTHS, when *khúc*, a green that looks like edible chrysanthemum leaves but tastes like spinach, is in season, cooks in northern Vietnam pound the leaves and use the juice to color the dough for these dumplings, which are filled with buttery mung bean and caramelized shallot. Sticky rice appears twice in the recipe, as the flour in the dough and as pearly grains covering the dumplings, making them look like snowballs.

My mother remembers these jade green dumplings as the perfect antidote to the north's cold, dreary winters. Well-positioned street vendors would lure customers with steamers full of piping-hot *bánh khúc*, which were piled on top of one another in the tray and had to be carefully pried apart before the exchange of money and food could occur.

This is her recipe, which substitutes spinach for the *khúc*. For convenience, I use prewashed baby spinach leaves and purée them in a food processor. Measure the spinach carefully to ensure the dough won't be too soft or mushy. Regular oil and ground pork stand in for the traditional filling enrichment of freshly rendered pork fat and hand-chopped pork belly. To yield nice round dumplings, I stray from tradition and steam them in a single layer, rather than piling them up.

1 Put the rice in a bowl and add water to cover by 1 inch. Let stand for at least 2 hours (or even overnight).

2 To make the filling, in a saucepan, combine the oil and shallot over medium heat and fry gently, stirring occasionally, for 7 to 8 minutes, or until golden brown. Add the pork, stirring and pressing it to break it up into small pieces, and cook for about 1 minute, or until it is just cooked through. Remove from the heat and stir in the mung bean, salt, and pepper. If the filling feels stiff, add water by the teaspoon. You want a texture like that of dry mashed potatoes. To test, press some between your fingers; it should stick together and leave your fingers slightly oily. Set aside for 5 to 10 minutes to cool, then shape into 12 balls, each about 1½ inches in diameter, or about the size of a golf ball.

continued

Makes twelve 2½-inch dumplings, to serve 6 as a light main course

1 cup short-grain sticky rice

FILLING

1/3 cup canola or other neutral oil

1/2 cup chopped shallot

1/4 pound ground pork, coarsely chopped to loosen

2 cups Ground Steamed Mung Bean (page 322)

Generous 1/2 teaspoon salt

1/2 teaspoon black pepper

1/4 teaspoon salt

DOUGH

2 cups (3½ ounces) packed baby spinach leaves

1/4 cup water

1²/3 cups Mochiko Blue Star brand glutinous (sweet) rice flour

1/2 cup glutinous (sweet) rice flour, any Thai brand

1/2 teaspoon salt

Fresh or thawed, frozen banana leaf, rinsed and wiped dry, or parchment paper for lining steamer trays

3 Dump the rice into a colander and rinse briefly under running water. Give the colander a few shakes to expel extra water. Return the rice to the bowl and toss with the 1/4 teaspoon salt. Set aside.

4 To make the dough, combine the spinach and water in a food processor and purée until smooth. Transfer to a measuring cup and add water as needed to total 1 1/3 cups.

5 In a bowl, stir together the 2 rice flours and the salt. Make a well in the center, pour in the spinach purée, and stir with a rubber spatula until a clumpy dough forms. Then, use your hand to knead the dough into a rough mass. Turn out the dough and all the unincorporated bits onto a work surface and knead with both hands into a soft, smooth ball that feels like very soft modeling clay. If necessary, add water by the teaspoon or a bit of rice flour (either kind is fine) to achieve the correct consistency, but err on the firmer, drier side because this dough softens as it sits. To test if the dough is ready, pinch it; it should barely stick to your fingers. Shape the dough into a log and cut it into 12 equal pieces, which will each be slightly larger than the balls of filling. Set aside for a moment.

6 Fill the steamer pan halfway with water and bring to a rolling boil over high heat. Lower the heat until you are ready to steam. To prevent the dumplings from sticking to the steamer trays, line them with banana leaf, leaving a few holes uncovered for heat circulation.

7 Have ready a shallow bowl of water for moistening your hands. To form a dumpling, lightly moisten your hands. Your hands must not be too wet, or this very soft dough will be difficult to manage, so wipe off excess water before you handle the dough. Pick up a piece of dough and roll it into a ball. Holding it with one hand, use the fingers of your other hand to press the dough gently from the center toward the rim to create a 3-inch circle slightly thinner at the center than at the rim. As you press, rotate the dough to make an even circle. (It is like shaping a tiny pizza.)

Place the dough in the palm of one hand and use your other hand to place a ball of filling on the center of the circle. Now, use your free hand to push and pinch the dough together to enclose the filling completely. (If the dough is loose and fails to grip onto the filling, quickly remove the dough, knead it, and start over. This dough is very forgiving.) Pass the dumpling between your hands a few times to smooth the outside, and then roll it around in the grains of sticky rice to coat well. Place the dumpling in a prepared steamer tray. Use the heel of your hand to flatten it lightly to a thickness of 1 to 1 1/4 inches. Repeat with the remaining dough and filling, arranging the dumplings about 1 inch apart in the trays and 1 inch away from the edge where condensation will collect.

8 Distribute the leftover sticky rice evenly on top of the dumplings. Return the water in the steamer pan to a rolling boil. Loosely cover 1 tray with parchment or waxed paper to prevent drying. Place the other tray in the steamer, cover, and steam the dumplings for 15 minutes, or until the dough is a dark green and the sticky rice is shiny and tender. Turn off the heat and wait for the steam to subside before lifting the lid, and then lift it away from you carefully to avoid condensation dripping onto the dumplings. Remove the tray and set it aside for 5 to 10 minutes, or until the dumplings cool a bit and firm up. They are too hot to eat straight from the steamer and will stay warm for about 30 minutes. Steam the second tray the same way.

9 Have the table set with salad plates and chopsticks or forks. Use a metal spatula to transfer the dumplings to a platter or 2 serving plates and serve.

NOTE

Leftover dumplings may be stored in an airtight container and refrigerated for about 5 days or frozen for up to 1 month. Return them to room temperature before reheating in the steamer or microwave oven.

FEASTS FOR THE NEW YEAR

When the Vietnamese celebrate Tet, they say "*ăn Tết*," literally "eat the Lunar New Year." During the festivities, which traditionally last a full month in Vietnam, food is a primary focus. But people actually take in the holiday with all their being. Tet is the most important event of the year, symbolizing rebirth, family, and relaxation. It is like Christmas, New Year, Easter, Thanksgiving, and Yom Kippur all bundled together.

Many overseas Vietnamese, nostalgic for days gone by, return to Vietnam to spend Tet with family and to pay respect to elders and ancestors. People are busy in the days before the first day of the New Year, known as Tết Nguyên Đán. They clean their homes and then decorate them, particularly with flowering branches of yellow *hoa mai* or pink *hoa đào* (similar to apricot, peach, and quince blossoms). Everyone shops for specialty items wrapped in auspicious red and gold packaging. Superstitions abound as people try to ensure good luck, prosperity, and happiness for the future. Among them is the belief that the first person to offer Tet greetings at your home will share his or her good fortune with you in the coming year.

At the center of the hubbub is the food, most of which is prepared in advance to allow people plenty of time for fun once the holiday begins. While regional differences exist, typical dishes include such rich meats as long-simmered *kho* made with pork or beef (chapter 5) and various *giò* and *chả* sausages (chapter 6); pickled and preserved vegetables (chapter 7) to cut their richness; and candies and sweetmeats (chapter 11) to refresh the palate.

But regardless of the region, *bánh chưng* (page 261) are always on the menu. The square sticky rice cakes are wrapped in banana leaf and boiled for up to twelve hours, depending on their size. Small ones measure four to five inches wide and larger ones are the size of adobe bricks. The outer layer of rice becomes perfumed and tinted by the green leaf. Inside, the grains remain white and encase a buttery bean filling streaked with pepper and studded with chunks of lean pork and bits of its opaline fat. *Bánh chưng* may be eaten warm or at room temperature; they may also be fried up as crispy pancakes. (When the same ingredients are wrapped as cylindrical cakes, they are called *bánh tét*.) Because they are inexpensive to prepare and they keep for a long time, Vietnamese families traditionally cooked up dozens of them.

My parents revel in describing the sequence of events that went into making the cakes when they lived in Vietnam. Two days before Tet, the ingredients were gathered and readied. The next day, everybody from young to old got involved in wrapping and boiling the cakes, which lasted from early morning to late at night. The boiling was done outdoors in huge pots set over a wood, coal, or rice-straw fire. Since the moon barely shone on New Year's Eve, the pitch black night was lit by people's *bánh chưng* fires. Everyone eagerly anticipated their first tastes of the cakes, especially the children, some of whom slept by the fire. By the time the cakes were done, it was already the first day of the New Year, and the leaf-wrapped *bánh chưng* were quickly carried into the house, where they were prominently displayed to signal the start of the feast.

TET STICKY RICE CAKES

Bánh Chưng

> BÁNH CHƯNG ARE SOLD at Viet markets and delis, but making them yourself guarantees high quality and is a great way to take part in an ancient Vietnamese tradition. An intersection of cooking, art, and engineering, the cakes come together in an ingenious way, and it is remarkable how so few ingredients create such meaningful and tasty food. See Feasts for the New Year, page 259, for more information on the tradition surrounding the cakes.
>
> While some people wrap the cakes free-form, I prefer using a simple homemade wooden mold (see Note for details) to produce beautiful cakes with straight edges, believing that since the ingredients are modest, the presentation matters. The process is surprisingly easy: the mold is lined with bamboo leaves and then banana leaves, the edible ingredients are added, the package is closed up, and the mold is removed, so the cake looks a little box. The cake is then securely wrapped in foil and boiled for several hours.
>
> The instructions for these cakes come from my mother and her friend Mr. Lung, who decades ago wrote an extensive article on the subject. When we left Vietnam, Mom carried the piece with her so she could replicate *bánh chưng* here. The ingredients are available at Chinese and Vietnamese markets. Dried bamboo leaves are bundled up in plastic and are usually near the dried mushrooms. Be sure to select a fatty piece of pork for the best flavor, and bright green banana leaves for beautiful color.

READY THE INGREDIENTS

1 The night before, soak the rice and bamboo leaves. Put the rice in a large bowl and add water to cover by 2 inches. Place the bamboo leaves in a large roasting pan and add water to cover. Put a plate on top of the leaves to keep them submerged.

2 The next morning, drain the rice in a colander and then return it to the bowl. (It will have swollen to more than 8 cups.) Gradually mix in the salt, sprinkling it over the rice and using your hands to distribute it well.

continued

Tet Sticky Rice Cake, pictured with Classic Silky Sausage (page 160) and Pickled Shallots (page 195)

Makes four 5-inch-square cakes; each cake serves 4 as a main course for breakfast or lunch, or 6 to 8 as part of an elaborate meal

5¼ cups long-grain sticky rice

16 dried bamboo leaves

1½ tablespoons salt

1¼ pounds boneless pork leg with skin and fat or pork shoulder

3 tablespoons fish sauce

2½ teaspoons black pepper, preferably freshly ground

12 pieces fresh or thawed, frozen banana leaf, each 5 by 10 inches, trimmed, rinsed, and wiped dry

1 tablespoon canola or other neutral oil

4 cups lightly packed Ground Steamed Mung Bean (page 322)

Sugar

Canola or other neutral oil if frying cakes

3 Cut the pork into pieces the size of a deck of cards, about 3 inches long, 2 inches wide, and 1/2 inch thick. If you are using pork leg, each piece should have some fat and skin. Add the fish sauce, pepper, and pork to a bowl and mix well. Let marinate for 30 minutes.

4 Meanwhile, drain the bamboo leaves. Follow these directions, which will make sense when you assemble the cakes: Take each leaf and fold it lengthwise along the spine (dull side out) and then in half crosswise. Measuring from the center fold, use scissors to cut the leaf to measure 4³/₄ inches; unfolded, the trimmed leaf is 9¹/₂ inches long. Use a ruler or one of the inner edges of the wooden mold (which is 5 inches long) as your guide. Rinse the trimmed leaves and set aside with the banana leaves.

5 To cook the pork, in a large skillet, heat the oil over medium heat. Add the meat in a single layer and all the marinade. Cook, turning once, for about 2 minutes on each side, or until the pork is just cooked through. Transfer to a plate. Divide it into 4 equal portions and set aside.

ASSEMBLE AND BOIL THE CAKES

6 Fill a 12-quart stockpot half full with water and bring to a boil over high heat. Lower the heat and cover to keep hot.

7 To make each cake, put a 12-by-18-inch piece of heavy-duty aluminum foil on your work surface, with a short side closest to you. Place the mold on the center of the foil. You will need 4 bamboo leaves to form the frame—corners and edges—for the cake. Working on one corner at a time, fold a bamboo leaf lengthwise (dull side out) along the spine and then in half crosswise. Crease the center fold. To form a 90-degree corner, simply unwrap the leaf and bring the lower center crease up to meet the spine. The leaf now looks like an upright corner of a paper box. Place the folded bamboo leaf into one of the corners of the mold, with the ends pointing toward (or touching) two of the walls. Repeat with the remaining 3 bamboo leaves, going in one direction around the mold and overlapping the leaves as you go. When you are done, the leaves will look like a picture frame.

Push the leaves down into the corners to make sure they are snug and flush. Straighten any slouching leaf.

8 Next, line the mold with banana leaf. Place a piece of banana leaf so that one of its short sides is flush with the inner wall of the mold that is closest to you; the banana leaf should cover the bottom and extend above the mold on the far wall. Place a second piece of leaf in the reverse direction. The 2 pieces will overlap each other on the bottom. Equal lengths of leaf should extend above the mold on the far and near walls. Then arrange a third piece of leaf, with a long side closest to you, evenly across the bottom of the mold, so that short lengths of leaf extend above the right and left walls. All 4 walls of the mold are now lined. Use your fingers to tuck the leaves into the mold.

9 To add the edible ingredients, first scoop up 1 cup of the rice and pour it into the mold. Use your fingers to push some rice toward the outer edges. Add 1/2 cup lightly packed mung bean, pouring it into the center. Center a portion of pork on top. (If you are using pork leg, position the fat and skin in the center, so that at serving time, everyone gets an equal amount. You may need to tear or cut some of the fat from the meat to create an equal distribution.) Top with another 1/2 cup lightly packed mung bean. Finish with 1 cup rice. The mold will look very full. Push some of the rice to the sides and corners.

10 Cover the top of the cake by folding in the side flaps of banana leaf, then fold the side farthest from you down, and finally fold over the side nearest you. Press down firmly on the cake with your hand to distribute and compact the ingredients. Once the top is relatively flat, put one hand on top of the cake to hold it in place while you gently pull off the mold with the other hand. Temporarily keep the mold on your lower arm while you fold the top flap of foil down, and then fold the bottom flap up and over. This should keep the cake in place enough for you to remove the mold from your arm. Then, as if wrapping a gift, fold in the sides to form a foiled-covered square box. Pick up the cake and gently tap the sides against your work surface to make sure the elements are set. Put the cake aside. Repeat to make the remaining 3 cakes. Save or discard leftover rice.

11 Tie each cake together with kitchen string. Since the rice expands during cooking, don't tie too tightly. The string should not make an impression in the foil. (See illustration, page 264.)

12 Return the stockpot of water to a boil. Add the cakes, stacking and/or standing them up. To keep the cakes from floating, place an empty saucepan on top to weight them down gently. Return the water to a boil and cook, uncovered, for 7 hours. To maintain the boil, keep a kettle of boiled water on the stove to replenish the water as needed; it is okay if the water occasionally simmers. As the cakes cook, they will expand and gain weight. Every 2 hours, rotate the cakes so they will cook evenly. When the cakes no longer float, about midway through the full cooking time, remove the saucepan and continue boiling.

13 Use tongs to transfer the cooked cakes to a baking sheet, placing the best-looking square side down. Put another baking sheet on top and center a 14- or 15-ounce food can on each cake to weight it down. (Eager people let the cakes cool for only 1 to 2 hours before unwrapping and eating.)

14 The next morning, remove the foil, wipe off stray bits of rice, and then wrap each cake in plastic wrap. For display purposes, you may tie colorful ribbon (red symbolizes good luck) around each cake. The cakes may be kept at room temperature for 3 days, beyond which they should be stored in the refrigerator, where they will last for a week. They may also be frozen for up to 3 months (see Note for information on how to refresh frozen cakes).

SERVE THE CAKES

15 There are two ways to enjoy *bánh chưng*: soft, which allows you to appreciate fully the pale green color and ethereal flavor of the banana leaf, or fried into a delicious crispy pancake. Regardless of which method you use, serve the cake with sugar for lightly dipping the pieces. It sounds odd but is quite nice.

To cut and serve a cake soft: Cut the cake into 8 equal triangular wedges (think of an asterisk). Because it is hard to

cut through the sticky rice with a knife, Vietnamese cooks use a type of fibrous string. I substitute unflavored dental floss or linen kitchen string. (If the cake is firm from refrigeration, unwrap and cut with a knife. Reheat the pieces in a microwave oven until soft before serving.) To cut with floss or twine: Undo the plastic wrap, keeping it spread out underneath the cake. Remove and discard the bamboo leaves. Return the cake to the plastic wrap, open side up (as it was when you were assembling the cake). Peel off the top and side flaps of banana leaf, leaving them on the plastic wrap.

Cut 4 lengths of floss or string each about 20 inches long and arrange them on the cake in the pattern of an 8-spoked asterisk: position 2 strands on the diagonals, 1 strand horizontally across the middle, and 1 strand vertically down the middle. One at a time, grab the ends of each strand and pull the strand down about $1/4$ inch into the cake to secure it in place.

Invert the cake onto a serving plate. (Use the plastic wrap to pick up the cake.) Peel off the plastic wrap and banana leaves. One at a time, grab each strand by its ends and pull it up through the cake toward the center, crossing in the middle and lifting it out of the cake. (You may have to pause midway to pull on other strands as you make the cuts.) When all the strands are removed, the cake will be cut into perfect wedges.

To fry and serve a cake: Nicely cut wedges are not necessary if you are frying the cake. Use a knife to quarter the cake and then cut each quarter into $1/2$-inch-thick slices. In a 10-inch nonstick skillet, heat 1 tablespoon oil over medium heat. Add half of the slices and fry, undisturbed, for about 6 minutes, or until the rice has softened. Use a spatula to press and mash the chunks to form a pancake and continue to fry for 5 to 6 minutes, or until the underside is crispy and golden. Flip the pancake with a quick and confident jerk of the skillet handle (or slide the pancake onto a plate and then invert it into the skillet). Increase the heat to medium-high and fry the second side for about 4 minutes, or until crispy and golden. Slide the pancake onto a plate, cut into wedges, and serve. Repeat with the remaining slices to make a second pancake.

continued

The wooden mold for these cakes is not commercially produced because people typically make the molds themselves. If you are not good at woodworking, do as I did and ask someone for help. The mold should have a 5-inch-square opening and stand 1½ inches high. (For my mold, I bought a 30-inch-long piece of ¾-inch-thick unfinished oak from a spare wood bin at a lumberyard.) My friend Mike Crane cut the wood into 4 pieces, 2 pieces that were 5 inches long and 1½ inches wide and 2 pieces that were 6½ inches long and 1½ inches wide.

Although nails would have held the pieces together, he used screws, drilling 2 holes at the end of each of the longer pieces. When he screwed the pieces together, he added a little glue for extra security. To finish the mold, he lightly sanded the edges.

To refresh a thawed *bánh chưng*, bring it to room temperature. Rewrap it in foil and tie it with cotton string as you originally did. Boil the cake in a large pot of water for 1 hour, adding water as needed to keep the cake submerged. Remove the cake and let cool for 1 to 2 hours before eating.

VEGETABLE AND PORK STEAMED BUNS

Bánh Bao

RICE IS KING in the Vietnamese kitchen, but wheat also plays a role in foods such as these steamed buns. A classic Viet riff on Chinese *bao*, the buns encase a hearty vegetable-and-meat mixture, with a creamy wedge of hard-boiled egg in the center.

Traditional *bao* are made from a yeast-leavened dough, but many Vietnamese Americans leaven the dough with baking powder. This New World innovation is faster and the dough is easier to manipulate. The buns are also more stable in the steamer than the yeasted version, which can sometimes deflate during cooking. Viet delis sell softball-sized *bánh bao*, but I prefer more manageable baseball-sized ones. I use bleached all-purpose flour, which yields slightly lighter-colored buns than unbleached flour.

Like all *bao*, these buns are great for breakfast, lunch, or a snack. They will keep in the refrigerator (stored in an airtight container) for a few days and are easily reheated, making them a great homemade fast food. For additional flavor, serve them with a simple dipping sauce of soy sauce and freshly cracked black pepper.

Makes sixteen 3-inch buns, to serve 8 generously

FILLING

- 1 tablespoon light (regular) soy sauce
- 1¹/2 tablespoons oyster sauce
- 1 teaspoon sugar
- ¹/4 teaspoon salt
- ¹/2 teaspoon white pepper
- 3 tablespoons water
- 2 tablespoons canola or other neutral oil
- ¹/4 cup finely chopped yellow onion
- ¹/2 pound ground pork, coarsely chopped to loosen
- 3 or 4 dried shiitake mushrooms, reconstituted (page 332), stemmed, and chopped
- 2 cups packed thinly sliced green cabbage
- ¹/2 cup finely diced carrot
- ¹/3 cup frozen peas, preferably petite peas, thawed
- 1 Chinese sweet sausage, halved lengthwise and thinly sliced crosswise
- ¹/2 cup matchstick-cut Char Siu Pork (page 142)
- 1 tablespoon cornstarch dissolved in 1¹/2 tablespoons water

DOUGH

- 4¹/2 cups all-purpose flour, preferably bleached
- ³/4 cup sugar
- 1 tablespoon baking powder
- 3 tablespoons canola or other neutral oil
- 1¹/2 cups whole milk

- 2 eggs, hard boiled, peeled, halved lengthwise, and each half quartered lengthwise (16 wedges total)

1 To make the filling, in a small bowl, combine the soy sauce, oyster sauce, sugar, salt, white pepper, and water and stir to dissolve the sugar. Set this flavoring sauce aside. In a large skillet, heat the oil over medium heat. Add the onion and sauté for 1 to 2 minutes, or until soft and fragrant. Add the pork, breaking it into small pieces, and cook and stir for about 2 minutes, or until half done. Add the mushrooms, cabbage, carrot, and peas, stir to combine, and then pour in the flavoring sauce. Sauté for 5 to 6 minutes, or until the vegetables are cooked and only a little liquid remains. Add the Chinese sausage and Char Siu Pork and stir to combine. Add the cornstarch and stir for 1 minute to bind the filling. Transfer to a bowl and set aside, uncovered, to cool completely.

2 To make the dough, in a bowl, stir together the flour, sugar, and baking powder. Make a well in the center, pour the oil and milk into the well, and use a rubber spatula to stir the ingredients to form a soft, ragged mass. Turn out the dough onto a lightly floured work surface and knead for 1 to 2 minutes, or until it is a relatively smooth, yet slightly sticky ball. Transfer to a lightly oiled bowl and cover with plastic wrap. Let rest for 1 hour.

3 Fill the steamer pan halfway with water and bring to a rolling boil over high heat. Lower the heat until you are ready to steam.

4 Have ready sixteen 3-inch squares of parchment paper. Remove the dough from the bowl, cut it in half, and then re-cover one-half with the inverted bowl while you work with other half. On your work surface, shape the dough into a log and cut into 8 equal pieces. Loosely cover 7 of the pieces with a dish towel to prevent drying. To make a bun, place a piece of dough, cut side down, on a lightly floured work surface and shape it into a disk. Imagine a quarter-sized circle in the center, what the Chinese call the belly of the wrapper. You want to roll out the disk into a flat, round wrapper that retains a thick belly, so that there won't be more dough on the bottom of the bun than on the top.

With this in mind, start rolling out the disk from the center to the rim, keeping the belly 1/4 inch thick. (An Asian-style rolling pin, which is essentially a 1-inch wooden dowel, is ideal for this job.) Lift and rotate the dough frequently to make sure it doesn't stick to your work surface. Aim for a wrapper about 5 inches in diameter and 1/8 inch thick at the edge.

5 Pick up the wrapper and hold it in a slightly cupped hand. Use your free hand to spoon a heaping tablespoon of the filling into the center of the wrapper. Gently press on the filling with the back of the spoon to create a well. Add a wedge of egg, curved white side up. Mound another tablespoon of filling on top. The wrapper will seem very full; your cupped hand should naturally close a little more to keep the bun's shape.

6 To enclose the filling, use your free hand to pleat the rim of the wrapper. Pick up the rim of the dough circle between the tips of your thumb and index finger, stretching it a bit and pinching the dough together to form 1/4- to 1/2-inch pleats. Keep gathering and pleating the rim in an accordion pattern. As you pleat, use the thumb of your cupped hand to tuck the filling inside the wrapper. After you have pleated all around the rim, there will be a small fluted hole at the top. Twist and pinch it closed; if there is an excessive amount of dough, pinch some off and discard. Place the bun, pleated side down, on a parchment square. Repeat with the other dough pieces. Then cut and shape the remaining half of the dough for 8 more buns. Place as many buns in the steamer trays as possible, spaced 1 inch apart and 1 inch away from the edge where condensation collects. Leave the remaining buns out, covered, until a tray is available.

7 Return the water in the steamer pan to a rolling boil. Loosely cover 1 of the filled trays with parchment or waxed paper to prevent drying. Place the other tray in the steamer, cover, and steam the buns for 20 minutes, or until they have puffed up and look dry. Turn off the heat and wait for the steam to subside before lifting the lid, and then lift it away from you carefully to avoid condensation dripping onto the buns. Remove the tray and use a metal spatula to transfer the buns, on the parchment, to a wire rack to cool for 5 minutes. Steam the second tray the same way. Put the remaining buns in the empty tray and repeat.

8 Arrange the buns, still on the parchment, on a platter and serve. Remove the parchment before eating the buns out of hand.

SHORTCUT PLAIN STEAMED BUNS

Bánh Bao Chay

AT VIET PARTIES OR SPECIAL EVENTS, Chinese-style roasted meats accompanied by small steamed buns are usually on the menu. Shaped like half-moons, the plain buns are used like rolls: they are split open, a morsel of roast pork, duck, or *char siu* (barbecued pork) is tucked inside, and if there is a sauce, a little is drizzled over the meat. The resulting tiny sandwich is a great hors d'oeuvre or starter course.

Steamed buns made from scratch take time. It is worth the effort to make your own dough for filled buns, such as the ones on page 265. But when you want the buns only as a small side dish, a shortcut may be in order. I learned a trick from my Chinese American friend Victor Fong, who revealed that his mom always used refrigerated biscuit dough to make the plain steamed buns she served at home. (In their 1976 book *The Gourmet Chinese Regional Cookbook*, Calvin and Audrey Lee mentioned a similar practice, describing it as a "guiltily traded secret in America's Chinatowns.") The shortcut buns are surprisingly light and spongy, a perfect counterpoint to the rich meats. Serve them with slices of Honey-Roasted Duck Legs (page 94), Char Siu Pork (page 142), or roast pork or duck bought in a Chinese barbecue shop.

1 Fill the steamer pan halfway with water and bring to a rolling boil over high heat. Line the steamer tray with parchment paper, leaving a few holes uncovered for heat circulation.

2 Unwrap the package of biscuit dough. Take 1 round of dough and use your fingers to stretch it gently until the center is about half of its original thickness. Fold the dough in half and place in the steamer tray. It will look like giant smiling lips. Repeat with the remaining dough rounds, spacing them a generous 1/2 inch apart and 1 inch away from the edge of the tray where condensation collects.

3 Place the tray in the steamer, cover, and steam the buns for 10 minutes, or until they have nearly doubled in size and look dry. Turn off the heat and wait for the steam to subside before lifting the lid, and then lift it away from you carefully to avoid condensation dripping onto the buns. Remove the tray and use a metal spatula to transfer the buns to a wire rack. If the buns

Makes ten 3-inch buns, to serve 3 or 4 as an accompaniment to roasted meats

1 package (7 1/2 ounces) refrigerated buttermilk biscuit dough (use regular, *not* jumbo size)

are left to cool completely, transfer them to a plate and cover with plastic wrap to prevent them from drying out. (The buns may be steamed up to 4 hours in advance of serving and kept at room temperature. To serve warm, reheat in the steamer or microwave oven.)

4 Serve the buns warm or at room temperature. They are not served hot because the meats that they accompany are not served hot.

RICE PANCAKES WITH SHRIMP AND SCALLION OIL

Bánh Bèo Mặn

MADE OF A SIMPLE RICE FLOUR BATTER, these dainty and rich rice pancakes are akin to blini. *Bánh bèo* are eaten all over Vietnam and boast a number of regional variations. They come in sweet (*ngọt*) and savory (*mặn*) varieties, and in sizes ranging from 1½ to 3 inches in diameter. They may be served directly from the small ceramic dish in which they are steamed or transferred to a serving platter.

This recipe for savory *bánh bèo* features a classic topping of fragrant bits of briny shrimp, rich scallion oil, and mildly sweet chile sauce. I use small, inexpensive dipping sauce dishes for the molds. Look for them at Asian housewares and restaurant-supply stores and at some Asian markets.

1 To make the batter, in a bowl, stir together the rice flour, cornstarch, and salt. Make a well in the center, pour the oil and water into the well, and whisk together all the ingredients to produce a thin, smooth batter. You should have about 2 cups. Let the batter rest for 30 minutes.

2 To make the topping, in a small saucepan, combine the shrimp and salt with water just to cover and bring to a boil over medium heat. Cook for about 8 minutes, or until the water has evaporated. (This intensifies the flavor of the shrimp.) Transfer the shrimp to a small bowl and let cool for 10 minutes. Transfer the shrimp to an electric mini-chopper and process to a minced, fluffy texture. Return the shrimp to the bowl.

3 In a small nonstick skillet, heat the oil over medium heat. Add the shallot and sauté for about 1 minute, or until fragrant. Add the shrimp and stir to combine. Sprinkle in the sugar, white pepper, and fish sauce. Continue to cook, stirring, for 3 to 4 minutes to dry the shrimp, lowering the heat when bits of shrimp pop. The shrimp are done when they look crumbly and are brilliant orange. Transfer to a bowl and set aside until ready to use. (The shrimp may be prepared up 3 days in advance,

Makes about thirty-two 2-inch pancakes, to serve 4 to 6 as a starter

BATTER

1 cup rice flour, any Thai brand

3 tablespoons cornstarch

3/4 teaspoon salt

1½ tablespoons canola or other neutral oil

1¾ cups water

SHRIMP TOPPING

1/3 pound medium shrimp, peeled and deveined

2 pinches of salt

1 tablespoon canola or other neutral oil

1 tablespoon minced shallot

Pinch of sugar

2 pinches of white pepper

1/2 teaspoon fish sauce

SAUCE

2 tablespoons sugar

1½ tablespoons unseasoned Japanese rice vinegar

1/3 cup water

2 tablespoons fish sauce

1 Thai or serrano chile, thinly sliced (optional)

1/4 cup Scallion Oil Garnish (page 314)

cooled, covered, and refrigerated. Bring to room temperature before using.)

4 To make the sauce, in a small bowl, combine the sugar, vinegar, water, and fish sauce and stir to dissolve the sugar. Taste and make any adjustments to create a light, slightly sweet sauce. Add the chile and set aside until serving time.

5 Fill the steamer pan halfway with water and place a steamer tray on top. Bring the steamer to a rolling boil over high heat. Nearby have the batter, a ladle, a small knife or metal spatula, and serving plates for holding the pancakes.

6 Make the pancakes in batches. Have ready about 8 small dishes, each about 2 1/2 inches wide and at least 1/2 inch deep. Put the dishes into the steamer tray, placing them away from the edge where condensation collects. To set the batter quickly, cover the steamer and let the dishes preheat for 2 minutes. Carefully remove the lid to avoid condensation dripping into the dishes. Give the batter a good stir and ladle it to a depth of 1/4 inch into each dish (about 1 tablespoon batter). Replace the lid and steam for 3 minutes, or until the pancakes are shiny and firm and have a shallow indentation in the center. Reduce the heat to low and wait for the steam to subside before lifting the lid, and then lift it away from you carefully to avoid condensation dripping onto the pancakes. Use metal tongs to transfer the dishes to the counter. Let the pancakes cool for 2 minutes. They will firm up slightly.

7 To unmold, dip the tip of the knife (or spatula) in water and run it along the edge of a pancake to loosen it. Use your fingers to pry the pancake gently from the dish, and then place it on a serving plate. Repeat until you have unmolded all the pancakes. The finished pancakes resemble tiny white plates.

8 Return the steamer to a boil over high heat. Give the dishes a quick rinse and wipe before returning them to the steamer tray for another batch. Repeat until all the batter is used. When you have filled up 1 serving plate with pancakes, begin with another plate. (The cooled pancakes may be covered with plastic wrap and kept at room temperature for up to 8 hours.)

9 To serve, fill the indentation of each pancake with a generous 1/2 teaspoon of the shrimp topping and dot with a generous 1/4 teaspoon of the scallion oil garnish. Serve with the sauce. The best strategy for eating the pancakes is to use chopsticks to scoot one onto a soupspoon and then drizzle on some sauce.

NOTE

For an extra layer of flavor and texture, scatter some Ground Steamed Mung Bean (page 322) or pork cracklings over the shrimp topping.

RICE CREPE ROLLS WITH SHRIMP, PORK, AND MUSHROOM

Bánh Cuốn

THESE NEARLY TRANSLUCENT, soft steamed rice crepes are served plain with slices of *giò lụa* (sausage), or they are filled and shaped into small rolls, as they are here. Finished with cilantro, shallots, *thịt ruốc bông* (cotton pork), and a little sauce, these rolls were one of my father's favorite foods to prepare for our family when I was growing up.

In Vietnam, making *bánh cuốn* was usually left to professional cooks who had mastered the technique of steaming a thin rice batter on fabric stretched over a pot of boiling water. In the 1970s, Vietnamese expatriates devised an easier method of making the crepes in a nonstick skillet. For the batter, they blended cake flour (very fine, soft Thai rice flour was not readily available then) with tapioca starch and cornstarch. While that approach works fine, I prefer to use Thai rice flour in place of the cake flour because it yields a more delicate result that is closer to the original version. The tapioca starch and cornstarch help the batter set up nicely and contribute to achieving the tender yet chewy texture of the traditional crepes.

Makes about twenty-four 3¹/2-inch rolls, to serve 4 as a light breakfast or lunch main course

FILLING

1 tablespoon canola or other neutral oil

¹/4 cup finely chopped yellow onion

¹/4 pound ground pork, coarsely chopped to loosen

1 dried wood ear mushroom, reconstituted (page 334), trimmed, and finely chopped (about 1¹/2 tablespoons)

2 dried shiitake mushrooms, reconstituted (page 332), stemmed, and chopped

¹/4 pound medium shrimp, peeled, deveined, and cut into pea-sized pieces

1 teaspoon fish sauce

¹/4 teaspoon salt

¹/2 teaspoon black pepper

BATTER

¹/2 cup cornstarch

¹/2 cup tapioca starch

¹/2 cup rice flour, any Thai brand

¹/2 teaspoon salt

2 teaspoons canola or other neutral oil

3 cups water

2 tablespoons canola or other neutral oil

¹/3 cup Cotton Pork (page 134), optional

2 tablespoons chopped fresh cilantro, leafy tops only

¹/3 cup Crispy Caramelized Shallot (page 314)

³/4 cup Basic Dipping Sauce made without garlic (page 308)

1 To make the filling, in a skillet, heat the oil over medium heat. Add the onion and sauté for 1 to 2 minutes, or until soft and fragrant. Add the pork, pressing and poking it to break it up into small pieces, and sauté for about 1 minute, or until half cooked. Add the wood ear mushroom, shiitake mushrooms, and shrimp, stir to combine, and then sprinkle in the fish sauce, salt, and pepper. Continue to sauté for 2 to 3 minutes, or until the shrimp turn pink. Transfer to a bowl and set aside for about 45 minutes, or until completely cooled. (The filling may be prepared up to 1 day in advance and stored in an airtight container in the refrigerator. Bring to room temperature before using.)

2 To make the batter, in a bowl, stir together the cornstarch, tapioca starch, rice flour, and salt. Make a well in the center, pour in the oil and water, and whisk together all the ingredients to make a thin, smooth batter. There should be about $3\frac{3}{4}$ cups. Let the batter rest for 30 minutes.

3 Organize your cooking station before you begin making the rolls. Set the batter and oil on one side of the stove and the filling on the other side. Nearby, spread out a dish towel on a countertop and invert a baking sheet on top of it, close to the edge of the counter. You need to use a sturdy baking sheet because you will be banging the skillet against it. Lightly brush the baking sheet with oil. Have ready a platter for holding the finished rolls.

4 For each crepe, brush an 8-inch nonstick skillet with $\frac{1}{4}$ teaspoon of the oil and place over medium-low heat. The skillet is ready when a bit of batter flicked onto it gently sizzles.

Give the batter a good stir and ladle $2\frac{1}{2}$ tablespoons into the skillet, quickly swirling the pan to coat the bottom evenly. Cover and allow the crepe to steam for about 45 seconds and then uncover. The crepe should be translucent, bubbling (or even ballooning), and gently sizzling. (Replace the lid if it is not.) Cook for 30 to 60 seconds more to dry the crepe slightly and help it release. A longer cooking time yields a firmer crepe that releases nice and flat. For a slightly softer crepe, use a shorter cooking time, but keep in mind that it may fall out slightly wrinkled and need to be straightened out before filling and rolling.

When the edges have pulled away from the skillet—the crepe will still look wet—pick up the skillet and quickly invert it onto the baking sheet, banging it to release the crepe. Return the empty skillet to the burner to reheat, adjusting the heat as needed. At the beginning, expect to tinker with the heat, the level of which depends on the skillet and the stove. Lower the heat slightly if huge craters form when the batter hits the skillet. Aim for crepes that look like relatively smooth white sheets.

5 Once you have banged the crepe out of the pan, immediately turn your attention to filling and rolling it while it is still a bit slippery and easier to manipulate. The slight stickiness helps the crepe to seal. If it didn't fall out flat, do your best to straighten out any wrinkles with your fingers. (It is not that hot.) Fold up the bottom inch of the crepe. At the top edge of that flap, center 1 tablespoon filling, spreading it out horizontally and leaving 1 inch of space on both sides. Fold in the side flaps to cover the filling partially. Lift the bottom edge over the filling, and then roll it up to seal. The finished roll is shaped like a stubby $3\frac{1}{2}$-inch-long cigar, with the filling visible on top. Place the roll on a plate or platter. Before making another roll, brush more oil on the skillet and on the baking sheet.

Once you have made a few rolls, you will establish a rhythm for steaming, filling, and rolling. Remember that imperfections are hidden once the crepe is rolled; if one side got bunched up or is particularly wrinkly, fill and roll from that direction. Hide ragged edges by folding them inward.

6 To serve, divide the rolls among 4 plates. (You may reheat them in a microwave oven until just warm, not hot.) Garnish with a sprinkling of the pork, followed by the cilantro, and then the shallot. Instruct diners to drizzle the dipping sauce directly onto the rolls. Use chopsticks or a fork and knife for eating.

NOTE

These rolls are at their best when freshly made, but they may be prepared in advance and refrigerated in an airtight container for 2 days. Bring to room temperature and then reheat in a microwave oven just until they soften and are warm.

SHRIMP AND SWEET POTATO FRITTERS

Bánh Tôm

GOLDEN ORANGE AND CRISPY, this Hanoi specialty blends the fragrance and crunch of sweet potatoes with the brininess of shrimp. The fritters, which look like roughly formed nests on which whole shrimp rest, are cut into bite-sized pieces and bundled in lettuce with fresh herbs and cucumber.

My mother taught me to soak the potatoes with a bit of slaked lime (calcium hydroxide), which Southeast Asian and Indian cooks use to crisp ingredients for frying and pickling. It is basically moistened food-grade slaked lime powder, the same compound used to treat corn for making Mexican masa. The Vietnamese call it *vôi* and it is sold in small, round plastic containers in Chinese, Thai, and Viet markets, usually stocked in the flour aisle. Two varieties are available, red and white. I prefer the white one, though the red one, which has been colored by the heartwood of the cutch tree and is traditionally chewed with betel leaf, may also be used. A small container of slaked lime lasts for a long time because only a little is needed.

1 Peel the sweet potato and cut it into flat, skinny sticks about 2 inches long, 1/4 inch wide, and 1/8 inch thick. (Think of them as short lengths of very thick fettuccine.) It is okay if the sticks are not all the same length, or if they come out a little rough looking.

2 In a large bowl, dissolve the slaked lime paste in the water. Add the sweet potato sticks and set aside to soak for 4 hours.

3 Pour oil to a depth of 1 1/2 inches into a wok or a 5-quart Dutch oven and heat over medium-high heat to 350°F on a deep-frying thermometer. (If you don't have a thermometer, stand a dry bamboo chopstick in the oil; if small bubbles immediately gather on the surface around the chopstick, the oil is ready.) Put a wire rack on a baking sheet and place the baking sheet next to the stove.

4 While the oil is heating, make the batter. In a bowl, stir together the all-purpose flour, rice flour, salt, and turmeric. Use a rubber spatula to gradually stir in the water to make a smooth,

Makes 12 fritters, to serve 2 or 3 as a one-dish meal, or 4 as a light main course

1 large Garnet sweet potato, 3/4 pound
1/4 teaspoon slaked lime paste, preferably white variety
3 cups water
Corn or canola oil for deep-frying

BATTER
3/4 cup all-purpose flour
1/2 cup rice flour, any Thai brand
1/4 teaspoon salt
2 pinches of ground turmeric
3/4 cup plus 1 tablespoon water

1/2 pound small white shrimp in their shells (see opposite), legs and tails trimmed
Vegetable Garnish Plate (page 313), preferably with the addition of red perilla and Vietnamese balm
3/4 cup Basic Dipping Sauce made with garlic (page 308)

thick batter. Drain the sweet potato and add to the batter, mixing to coat well. The batter will seem gluey.

5 Fry the fritters in batches to avoid crowding them in the pan. Using 2 large metal spoons, scoop up about 1/4 cup of the batter into 1 spoon and flatten it with the back of the second spoon. Arrange 3 shrimp on top, pressing them gently into the batter to ensure they stick. Lower the spoon just to touch the oil, and then use the second spoon to slide the fritter gently into the hot oil. Fry the fritters, turning once, for 5 to 6 minutes, or until they are crisp and golden orange and the potatoes are cooked through. Use a skimmer or slotted spoon to transfer the fritters to the rack to drain.

6 Before serving, use kitchen scissors to cut the fritters into quarters, making sure that each piece gets some shrimp. Serve with the vegetable garnish plate and dipping sauce. To eat, tear a piece of lettuce roughly the size of your palm, top with a piece of fritter, add cucumber slices and a few herb leaves, shape into a bundle, and dunk into the dipping sauce.

SMALL WHITE SHRIMP

Vietnamese cooks often use shell-on small shrimp in foods because the shells contribute fragrance and crunch. Small white shrimp (61 to 70 shrimp per pound), which have very thin shells, are ideal. You will find them at Asian and Latin markets. For the crepe recipes on pages 274 and 277, you may peel the shrimp first if you don't like the idea of chewing on the shells. Be sure to leave the shells on when making these sweet potato fritters, however, or they will dry out. For details on trimming the feet and tail, see page 115.

SIZZLING CREPES

Bánh Xèo

NAMED FOR THE SSSSSEH-AO SOUND that the batter makes when it hits the hot skillet, these turmeric yellow rice crepes are irresistible. Fragrant with a touch of coconut milk, they are filled with pork, shrimp, and vegetables and eaten with lettuce, herbs, and a mildly garlicky dipping sauce.

Most Viet cooks make sizzling crepes with a rice flour batter, but the results fall short of the nearly translucent ones made by pros in Vietnam. To reproduce the traditional version, which captures the alluring toastiness of rice, I soak and grind raw rice for the batter. It is not as daunting as it sounds. You just need a powerful blender to emulsify the batter to a wonderful silkiness. Adding leftover cooked rice and mung bean, a technique I found buried in a book on Viet foodways, gives the crepes a wonderful chewy crispiness.

Make your crepes as large as you like. These instructions are for moderately sized eight-inch ones. In Saigon, the same crepes are typically as big as twelve inches, but in the central region, they are as small as tacos. At my house, we serve and eat these crepes as fast as we can make them.

Makes eight 8-inch crepes, to serve 4 to 6 as a one-dish meal

BATTER

1 cup raw jasmine or regular long-grain rice

2 tablespoons firmly packed leftover cooked rice

1 tablespoon firmly packed Ground Steamed Mung Bean (page 322)

3/4 teaspoon salt

1/2 teaspoon ground turmeric

1/4 cup coconut milk, canned or freshly made (page 318)

13/4 cups plus 2 tablespoons water

1 scallion, white and green parts, thinly sliced

FILLING

3/4 pound ground pork or thinly sliced boneless pork shoulder

1/2 pound small white shrimp in their shells (page 273), legs and tails trimmed

1 can (15 ounces) whole or broken straw mushrooms, drained and cut lengthwise if whole

1 small yellow onion, thinly sliced (3/4 cup)

1 cup Ground Steamed Mung Bean (page 322)

4 cups bean sprouts (about 2/3 pound)

1/2 cup canola or other neutral oil

Vegetable Garnish Plate (page 313), preferably with the addition of red perilla

11/2 cups Basic Dipping Sauce made with garlic (page 308)

1   To make the batter, put the raw rice in a bowl and add water to cover by 1 inch. Let soak for 3 to 4 hours.

2   Drain the rice and transfer to a blender. Add the cooked rice, mung bean, salt, turmeric, coconut milk, and water. Blend for about 3 minutes, or until very smooth and lemony yellow. Pour the batter through a fine-mesh sieve positioned over a bowl and discard the solids. Stir in the scallion and set the batter aside for 1 hour. It will thicken to the consistency of heavy cream. There should be about 3 cups batter.

3   To make the filling, roughly divide the pork, shrimp, mushrooms, and onion into 8 portions. (Dividing the ingredients now will ensure less frantic frying and avoid overstuffing.) Put these ingredients along with the mung bean, bean sprouts, batter, and oil next to the stove.

4   For each crepe, heat 2 teaspoons of the oil in a 10-inch nonstick skillet over medium-high heat. Add a portion each of the pork, shrimp, mushrooms, and onion and sauté, breaking up the meat, for about 45 seconds, or until seared and aromatic. Visualize a line down the middle of the skillet and roughly arrange the ingredients on either side of the line. Anything in the middle would make it hard to fold the crepe neatly later.

5   Because the rice will have settled at the bottom of the bowl, give the batter a good stir with a ladle. Pour 1/3 cup of the batter into the skillet and swirl the skillet to cover the bottom; a bit going up the side forms a lovely lacy edge. The batter should dramatically sizzle (making that *xèo* noise!) and bubble. When it settles down, sprinkle on 1 1/2 tablespoons of the mung bean, and then pile 1/2 cup of the bean sprouts on one side. Lower the heat to medium, cover, and cook until the bean sprouts have wilted slightly, about 3 minutes.

6   Remove the lid and drizzle in 1 teaspoon of the oil around the rim of the pan. Lower the heat slightly and continue to cook, uncovered, for 3 to 4 minutes to crisp the crepe. The edge will have pulled away from the skillet and turned golden brown. At this point, use a spatula to check underneath for a crispy bottom. From the center to the edge, the crepe should go from being soft to crispy. Lower the heat if you need to cook it longer. When you are satisfied, use a spatula to fold the half without the bean sprouts over the other half. Use the spatula to transfer the crepe to a serving dish, or simply slide it out of the pan onto the dish.

Increase the heat to medium-high and repeat with the remaining batter and filling ingredients to make 8 crepes in all. Use any leftover batter to make a poor man's crepe without filling. When you are comfortable with the technique, you can try frying the crepes in 2 skillets at the same time. These crepes taste best straight from the skillet, so have diners at the ready.

7   Serve the crepes with the vegetable garnish plate and dipping sauce. Pass around 1 or 2 pairs of kitchen scissors for diners to cut their crepes into manageably sized pieces. To eat, tear a piece of lettuce roughly the size of your palm, place a piece of the crepe on it, add cucumber slices and a few herb leaves, shape into a bundle, and dunk into the dipping sauce.

NOTE

To prepare a shortcut rice flour batter, in a bowl, stir together 2 cups rice flour, 1 1/2 tablespoons cornstarch, 3/4 teaspoon salt, and 1/2 teaspoon ground turmeric. Make a well in the center, pour in 1/3 cup coconut milk and 2 cups water, and whisk to create a silky batter. Add 1 scallion (white and green parts), thinly sliced, and set aside for 1 hour. Cook this batter in the same way.

For these crepes and the ones on page 277, buy a pork shoulder steak, debone it, and slice the meat. You do not need to invest in a whole roast.

DELIGHTFUL CREPES

Bánh Khoái

AT A GLANCE, this recipe may look like the one for Sizzling Crepes (page 274), and in fact these crepes from the central region begot sizzling crepes. But the popularity of the child has eclipsed that of the parent, and nowadays it is hard to get *bánh khoái* unless you make them yourself or go to the source, Hue, where delightful crepes live up to their name. They are crunchy, rich from being cooked in a fair amount of oil, and full of toasty rice flavor.

Bánh khoái are traditionally fried in special small cast-iron skillets (five to six inches in diameter) with long handles (so you can avoid the splattering hot oil). They are difficult to find, however, so I use an eight-inch cast-iron or heavy nonstick skillet.

1　To make the batter, put the rice in a bowl and add water to cover by 1 inch. Let soak for 3 to 4 hours.

2　Drain the rice and transfer to a blender. Add the salt, turmeric, and water and blend for about 3 minutes, or until very smooth and lemony yellow. Pour the batter through a fine-mesh sieve positioned over a bowl and discard the solids. Set the batter aside for 1 hour to thicken; it should be the consistency of heavy cream. There should be about 4 cups.

3　Meanwhile, make the filling. In a bowl, combine the pork, fish sauce, pepper, and 1/4 teaspoon each of the sugar and salt and use chopsticks to mix well. In another bowl, combine the shrimp with the remaining 1/4 teaspoon each sugar and salt and mix well. In a skillet, heat 2 teaspoons of the oil medium heat. Add the pork and sauté for about 2 minutes, or until aromatic and just cooked through. Transfer to a small plate or bowl. Add the remaining 1 teaspoon oil to the skillet over medium heat, add the shrimp, and sauté for 1 to 2 minutes, or until the shells are pink. Transfer to another small plate or bowl.

continued

Makes twelve 6-inch crepes, to serve 4 to 6 as a one-dish meal

BATTER

1 3/4 cups jasmine or regular long-grain rice

3/4 teaspoon salt

3/4 teaspoon ground turmeric

2 1/2 cups water

FILLING

1/2 pound boneless pork shoulder, thinly sliced into small strips

2 teaspoons fish sauce

1/8 teaspoon black pepper

1/2 teaspoon sugar

1/2 teaspoon salt

1/2 pound small white shrimp in their shells (page 273), legs and tails trimmed

1 tablespoon canola or other neutral oil

3 eggs, lightly beaten

4 scallions, green part only, cut into 1-inch lengths (brimming 1/3 cup)

3 cups bean sprouts (about 1/2 pound)

1 1/2 cups canola or other neutral oil

Vegetable Garnish Plate (page 313), preferably with the addition of red perilla

1 1/2 cups Spicy Hoisin-Garlic Sauce (page 310)

4 Put the pork, shrimp, and other filling ingredients; the batter; and the oil next to one side of the stove. Put a wire rack on a baking sheet and place the sheet on the other side of the stove.

5 For each crepe, heat 1 1/2 to 2 tablespoons of the oil in an 8-inch cast iron or heavy nonstick skillet over medium heat. Because the rice will have settled at the bottom of the bowl, give the batter a good stir with a ladle. Pour 1/3 cup of the batter into the skillet and swirl the pan to film the bottom thickly. The batter should sizzle, seize, and bubble. Visualize a line down the middle of the skillet and roughly arrange about 2 tablespoons pork and 3 shrimp on either side of the line. Drizzle a scant tablespoon of beaten egg evenly over the crepe, scatter 1 1/2 teaspoons of the scallions on top, and then place 1/4 cup of the bean sprouts on one-half. Cover and cook until the bean sprouts have wilted slightly, about 2 minutes.

6 Remove the lid and continue to cook for 3 to 4 minutes to crisp the crepe. The edge will have pulled away from the skillet and be lifting upward. At this point, use a spatula to check underneath. It should be pockmarked, crispy, and without soft spots. If the crepe needs to cook a little longer, lower the heat and add more oil if necessary to prevent sticking. When the crepe is ready, use the spatula to fold it in half and transfer it to the rack to drain. (If the crepe is hard to fold, transfer it to the rack and fold it after it has cooled; it is okay if the spine breaks.)

Adjust the heat as needed to ensure a hot, but not smoking, skillet. Repeat with the remaining batter and filling ingredients to make 12 crepes in all. When you are comfortable with the technique, you can try frying the crepes in 2 skillets at the same time. The crepes taste best straight from the skillet, but they will stay crunchy and tasty for 2 hours. Keep them on the rack until serving.

7 Arrange the crepes on platters and serve with the vegetable garnish plate and dipping sauce. Pass around 1 or 2 pairs of kitchen scissors for diners to cut their crepes into manageably sized pieces. To eat, tear a piece of lettuce roughly the size of your palm, place a piece of the crepe on it, add cucumber slices and a few herb leaves, drizzle on a little sauce, and shape into a bundle.

NOTE

To make a shortcut rice flour batter, in a bowl, stir together 2 1/2 cups rice flour, 2 1/2 tablespoons cornstarch, 3/4 teaspoon salt, and 3/4 teaspoon ground turmeric. Make a well in the center, pour in 3 1/4 cups water, and whisk to create a silky batter. Set aside for 1 hour. Cook this batter in the same way.

Dried white tree fungus, soaking (see page 76)

11. SWEETS AND PALATE REFRESHERS

Vietnamese sweets are a juxtaposition of Eastern and Western culinary traditions. At a Vietnamese American bakery, colorful molded desserts, sweet soups, and tropical fruit candies vie with frosted layer cakes, éclairs, and butter cookies for every customer's attention. To the uninitiated, the diverse array may seem bewildering, but to a Vietnamese, it is simply a reflection of the multicultural nature of the cuisine.

Called *món tráng miệng* (palate cleansers), Vietnamese sweets are meant to refresh, rather than satiate. Some are French in origin, but most of them have Asian roots and utilize the local bounty of fruits, vegetables, legumes, and rice. They are generally light and not cloying, though as you move from north to south, the preparations become progressively sweeter due to regional preferences. Many include an interplay between sweet and savory, and all portions tend to be small or snack sized. People enjoy nibbling on sweets throughout the day, which is easy to do in Vietnam, with its countless specialty shops and street vendors.

Both the number of categories and the variety of Vietnamese sweets are nearly staggering. *Bánh* covers cakes, cookies, crepes, dumplings, and pastries made from wheat flour, rice flour, tapioca starch, mung bean, and similar ingredients. (See chapter 10 for savory *bánh* recipes.) It includes Southeast Asian, Chinese, and French preparations; ingredients that range from cassava, coconut milk, and salted eggs to butter; and cooking techniques that vary from baking, boiling, and steaming to deep-frying.

In contrast, *chè*, or sweet soups, are far less complicated. They don't require fancy equipment or expensive ingredients, generally take little time, and keep for days, making them one of the most commonly prepared categories of sweets in the Vietnamese kitchen. Viet cooks simmer beans, fruits, seeds, rice, or vegetables with sugar to create *chè* that are thick and creamy like a pudding, light and delicate like a consommé, or cool and layered with other ingredients like a parfait. Some sweet soups are eaten alone, while others are paired with *xôi* (sticky rice dishes).

In Vietnam's generally hot and humid climate, pleasantly cooling *thạch*, jellied desserts based on agar-agar, are welcome treats. Agar-agar, a pure vegetable gelatin made from seaweed, sets quickly without refrigeration and doesn't melt in tropical heat. Western-style frozen desserts, called *kem* (an abbreviated phonetic adaptation of the French *crème glacée*), are special because they are difficult for most people to prepare at home. Not everyone has a refrigerator, and dairy products like milk and cream are luxury goods. Despite such obstacles, Vietnamese cooks have concocted countless frozen treats over the years, and in Saigon, ice cream cafés are popular hangouts.

Tasty sweetmeats, or *mứt*, are also well liked, and both fruits and vegetables—coconut, sweet potato, winter melon rind, star fruit, kumquat, ginger—are candied. Fruits are also turned into *kẹo*, or confections, that are savored alongside wonderful candies made of peanuts, cashews, and sesame seeds. Tart-sweet-spicy-salty *ô mai* are a confection that most likely originated in China. Resembling small truffles, they are made from a mixture of dried fruits, such as tamarind, apricot, and plum, and flavored with ginger and dried licorice root. Sweetmeats and confections are ubiquitous at Tet, which is why people are busy either making or shopping for these sweets during the days leading up to the holiday.

continued

RECIPES

This chapter offers a broad sampling that ranges from simple preparations, like banana cake and coconut sorbet, to more challenging sweets, like moon cakes. Many of the recipes can be made in advance, which allows you to eat sweets in the Vietnamese way, with great variety, in small doses, and whenever you crave them.

A dessert course can simply be the best fruit of the season, peeled (if needed) and cut into serving pieces. But you can also follow the fruit with one, two, or a few more treats. At my mom's house, she pulls out a myriad of sweets that may include cake, a sweet soup, cookies, candied fruits, chocolates—whatever she has on hand that she thinks will delight her guests. Feel free to supplement your homemade sweets with store-bought ones. The point is to graze, linger, and talk. Serve tea or liqueur for a marvelous ending to a memorable meal.

COCONUT SORBET

Kem Nước Cốt Dừa

THIS EASY SORBET captures the essence of coconut in frozen form. Vanilla amplifies the alluring fragrance of coconut, while salt underscores the sorbet's delicate sweetness. High-quality canned coconut milk works fine, but freshly made coconut milk yields the best results, with wonderfully delicate and complex flavors.

1 In a saucepan, combine the coconut milk, sugar, salt, and corn syrup and place over medium heat. Cook, stirring or whisking gently, until the sugar dissolves. Remove from the heat and whisk in the vanilla. Transfer to a bowl and set aside to cool. Cover with plastic wrap and refrigerate for at least 24 hours to chill well and develop the flavor.

2 The mixture separates as it sits, so whisk to reblend, and then freeze in an ice-cream maker according to the manufacturer's directions.

Makes about 3 cups, to serve 6

2½ cups coconut milk, canned or freshly made (page 318)

½ cup sugar

Generous pinch of salt

2½ tablespoons light corn syrup

½ teaspoon vanilla extract

LEMONGRASS ICE CREAM

Kem Xả

MADE WITH MILK, rather than cream and eggs, this ice cream is thickened with cornstarch, which Vietnamese cooks use to yield a smooth texture. The result is a lighter-than-usual ice cream that allows the lemongrass to shine.

When preparing the lemongrass, you need to remove only the dry outer leaves and trim any dry edges at the very top. You can then use as much of the stalk as you like, as it is discarded after the milk is infused. In fact, sometimes when I trim lemongrass for other recipes, I freeze the tough top sections for making this ice cream.

1 In a saucepan, combine 2 cups of the milk and the lemongrass and bring to a simmer over medium heat. Cover, remove from the heat, and let steep for 30 minutes.

2 In a bowl, whisk together the remaining 1 cup milk, the sugar, and the cornstarch until the sugar and cornstarch are dissolved. Position a fine-mesh sieve over the bowl and pour in the lemongrass-infused milk, pressing on the solids to extract as much liquid as possible. Discard the solids.

3 Rinse and dry the saucepan, pour in the milk mixture, and place over medium heat. Bring to a simmer and cook, stirring constantly with a wooden spoon, for 4 to 5 minutes, or until thick enough to coat the back of the spoon. To test, run your finger along the back of the spoon; it should leave a trail that does not fill in.

4 Strain the base one last time through the sieve to remove any bits, and then set aside to cool completely. Cover with plastic wrap and refrigerate for at least 24 hours to chill well and develop the flavor.

5 Freeze the mixture in an ice-cream maker according to the manufacturer's directions.

Makes about 3 1/2 cups, to serve 6

3 cups whole milk

1 1/2 cups coarsely chopped lemongrass (3 to 4 stalks)

3/4 cup sugar

2 1/2 tablespoons cornstarch

SORBET AND ICE CREAM TIPS

• Prepare the base a day or two in advance of churning and let it chill and develop flavor in the refrigerator.

• Churn the sorbet or ice cream at least 2 hours before serving, pack tightly into a container to prevent crystallization, and place in the freezer to firm up and smooth.

• Let the sorbet or ice cream stand at room temperature for about 15 minutes to soften before serving.

• The flavor of a sorbet or ice cream fades after 3 or 4 days. To revive it, thaw it until it is once again a liquid, make any flavor adjustments, and refreeze in an ice-cream maker.

MANDARIN SORBET

Kem Trái Quít

> SWEET, LOOSE-SKINNED, AND WITH FEW SEEDS, mandarin oranges are more popular in Vietnam than regular oranges. The small fruits are commonly eaten as a peel-and-eat snack, but may they also be juiced and frozen for sorbet. Served alone or with a cookie, the sorbet is an elegant conclusion to a meal.
>
> Find the best tangerines, clementines, or satsumas in your area and juice them yourself. Avoid pasteurized juice, which can have an unpleasant cooked flavor.

1 To make a sugar syrup, whisk together the sugar and water in a small saucepan, place over medium heat, and bring to a boil. Boil for about 30 seconds, or until the sugar dissolves and the mixture is clear. Remove from the heat and let cool completely before using. (This syrup may be made days, or even weeks, in advance and stored in a tightly covered jar in the refrigerator.)

2 In a bowl, stir together the sugar syrup, tangerine juice, and 6 tablespoons lime juice. Taste and add more lime juice if needed to create a strong sweet-tart balance. Strain through a fine-mesh sieve positioned over a bowl. Cover with plastic wrap and refrigerate for at least 24 hours to chill well and develop the flavor.

3 Freeze the mixture in an ice-cream maker according to the manufacturer's directions.

Makes a scant 4 cups, to serve 6 to 8

3/4 cup sugar

1 cup water

2 1/2 cups fresh tangerine, clementine, or satsuma juice (from 12 to 14 fruits)

6 tablespoons fresh lime juice, or as needed

Mandarin Sorbet, pictured with Currant Cookies (page 291)

BANANA, TAPIOCA PEARL, AND COCONUT SWEET SOUP

Chè Chuối

IF YOU HAVE NEVER TRIED a Vietnamese *chè* (sweet soup), this one is a good place to start. The perfume of the banana comes through wonderfully, and the tapioca pearls, enrobed in coconut milk, cook up to resemble large orbs of clear caviar. Once the tapioca pearls have fully expanded and set, the texture of this mildly sweet treat is like that of a thick Western-style tapioca pudding.

Small, creamy bananas, such as the Nino variety, also known as Finger or Baby, are traditionally simmered for this sweet soup. They are sold at Asian and Latin markets. If they are unavailable, substitute regular bananas. Regardless of the variety, use ripe but firm, blemish-free fruits.

1 In a saucepan, bring the water to a boil over high heat. Add the tapioca pearls, stirring to prevent them from sticking together. Boil, stirring occasionally, for 12 to 14 minutes, or until the tapioca pearls are halfway clear. Look for a tiny white dot in the center of each pearl. The water will be thick and viscous.

2 Meanwhile, peel the bananas, discarding any strings. If using small bananas, cut on a slight diagonal into pieces a scant 3/4 inch thick. Or, halve regular bananas lengthwise and then cut the same way. Set aside for a moment.

3 When the tapioca pearls are ready, add the coconut milk, sugar, and salt and stir to dissolve the sugar. When the mixture comes to a near boil, add the bananas. Lower the heat to a simmer and cook for about 2 minutes, or until the bananas are slightly soft and the flavors are blended. Remove from the heat and stir in the vanilla. Allow the soup to cool and thicken for about 15 minutes. Taste and adjust with more sugar and salt, if necessary. (The soup may be prepared up to 2 days in advance, tightly covered, and refrigerated. Warm over low heat, adding a splash of water to thin and prevent scorching, before serving.)

Serves 4 to 6

3 cups water
1/4 cup small tapioca pearls (about 1/8 inch in diameter)
1 to 1 1/4 pounds ripe but firm bananas, preferably small
2/3 cup coconut milk, canned or freshly made (page 318)
3 1/2 tablespoons sugar
1/8 teaspoon salt
1/2 teaspoon vanilla extract
2 tablespoons chopped unsalted roasted peanuts (optional)

4 To serve, ladle the soup into small bowls and top with a sprinkle of peanuts.

LOTUS SEED AND LONGAN SWEET SOUP

Chè Hạt Sen Long Nhãn

WARM VIETNAMESE SWEET SOUPS may be rich and thick, like the preceding recipe, or light and clear, like this one. Here, buttery lotus seeds are paired with longans, a Southeast Asian fruit similar to lychees. During cooking, the dried longans give off a slightly smoky vanilla scent, which is underscored by the vanilla extract. My father swears that this soothing soup helps him sleep soundly. For me, the draw is the interplay among texture, taste, and fragrance.

Lotus seeds normally require long simmering, but they quickly reconstitute when boiled with baking soda, as is done here. (The alkalinity and salt content of baking soda speeds the cooking.) When shopping for the lotus seeds, choose slightly opened ones that have had their bitter green centers removed. If you can't tell from the packages whether they have been removed, choose one of the higher-priced brands. Dried longans resemble giant raisins and are often shelved near the lotus seeds in Chinese and Vietnamese markets. Look for both of them in the same aisle where you find dried mushrooms and beans.

1 Put the baking soda in a medium saucepan and add water to fill the pan halfway. Bring to a boil over high heat and add the lotus seeds. When the water returns to a rolling boil and threatens to rise over the sides of the pan, remove the pan from the heat but don't turn off the burner. When the boiling subsides, after about 20 seconds, return the pan to the heat. Bring it back to a vigorous, threatening boil and remove from the heat again until the boiling subsides. Repeating the boiling one more time, and then pour the lotus seeds into a colander to drain. They will have expanded and be tender yet still firm.

2 Transfer the seeds to a bowl. Rinse them in several changes of water, swirling the seeds gently to coax any leftover pearly skins to float upward and then pouring out the water. After removing most of the skin bits, drain the seeds. Inspect each seed to ensure the bitter green centers have been removed. As needed, gently pry open the seed and extract the center.

3 Return the lotus seeds to the saucepan and add the water. Bring to a boil over medium heat, lower the heat to a very gentle simmer, and cook for 10 to 15 minutes, or until the seeds are

Serves 6

1 teaspoon baking soda

1 package (5 or 6 ounces) dried white lotus seeds, rinsed and drained

5 cups water

3 ounces (about 3/4 cup) dried longans, rinsed and drained

1/3 cup plus 1 tablespoon sugar

1/2 teaspoon vanilla extract

tender but not mushy. Use a large spoon to skim and discard any scum that floats to the top. Add the longans and continue cooking for another 5 minutes, or until the longans have expanded and softened. Expect the water to cloud slightly. It will settle later.

4 Add the sugar and stir gently to dissolve. Remove from the heat, stir in the vanilla, and set aside to cool for about 15 minutes. (The soup may be prepared up to 3 days in advance, tightly covered, and refrigerated. Warm before serving.) To serve, ladle into small bowls.

ADZUKI BEAN, TAPIOCA NOODLE, AND COCONUT SWEET SOUP

Chè Đậu Đỏ Bánh Lọt

IN THIS CLASSIC cold sweet soup, maroon adzuki beans and chewy clear tapioca noodles, jokingly called worms in Vietnamese because they are slippery and sticky, swim in rich coconut milk. I usually prepare all the ingredients in advance and then bring everything together at the last minute. The beans and coconut milk base may be prepared a few days ahead and refrigerated until serving time, and the sugar syrup keeps in a jar in the refrigerator indefinitely. The noodles, however, are best if readied only a few hours ahead.

Adzuki beans are sold at Asian markets and health-food stores. Once you have made this version, you may substitute other beans, such as black beans, hulled mung beans, or black-eyed peas. You may also blend the beans for a mixture of colors and flavors.

1 Rinse the beans in several changes of water. Drain the beans and put them into a bowl. Add enough water to cover by 1 inch. Set aside to soak for 6 to 9 hours.

2 Drain the beans and rinse them again. Put them into a saucepan with water to cover by 1 inch. Bring to a near boil over medium heat, and then lower the heat to a gentle simmer. Cover partially and cook for about 45 minutes, or until the beans are tender but not mushy. Let cool before using. Or, you may refrigerate them in their cooking liquid in a tightly covered container for up to 3 days.

3 To make the sugar syrup, in a small saucepan, whisk together the sugar and 2/3 cup of the water until combined. Bring to a boil over medium heat and boil for about 1 minute, or until the sugar dissolves and the mixture is clear. Let cool before using. There will be 3/4 cup. Or, refrigerate in a tightly covered jar until needed.

4 Put the tapioca starch in a large bowl and make a well in the center. Bring the remaining 1/3 cup water to a boil, immediately

Serves 6

1/2 cup dried adzuki beans, picked over well
1/2 cup sugar
1 cup water
1 cup tapioca starch
1 1/4 cups Coconut Dessert Sauce (page 313), cold or at room temperature
Crushed ice

pour it into the well, and stir with a wooden spoon or sturdy rubber spatula until the mixture is lumpy. Use your hand (it is not that hot) or a plastic dough scraper to gather the mixture into a rough mass. Turn it out, along with all the unincorporated bits, onto a large cutting board. Knead the dough vigorously for 2 to 3 minutes, pushing it with the heel of one hand and folding it over, to create a smooth, dense dough. The dough will seem dry at first, but as the water is absorbed throughout the mass, the dough becomes malleable like modeling clay. Work in a little more tapioca starch if the dough is sticky, or a few drops of water at a time if the dough is too firm. The finished dough will be slightly warm.

5 Cut the dough into 3 equal pieces. Roll out each piece into a strip 2 to 2 1/2 inches wide and a scant 1/4 inch thick. Allow the strips to cool, firm, and dry for 6 to 8 minutes, so they are easier to work with, flipping them midway so they dry evenly on both sides. Use a knife to cut the strips crosswise into short noodles a generous 1/8 inch thick. Pause occasionally to separate them with your fingers. They will be dry, which means they won't stick together during cooking.

6 Set a bowl of cold water large enough to accommodate the noodles near the sink. Fill a 5-quart pot half full with water and bring to a rolling boil over high heat. Pick up the cutting board and scoot the noodles into the pot. Stir the noodles to prevent sticking. After the water returns to a boil, cook the noodles for about 5 minutes, or until they are coated with a clear layer of cooked tapioca. (They will look white in the pot, so use a slotted spoon to examine one.) Drain the noodles in a colander and immediately transfer them to the cold water bowl, where they will turn clear. Let the noodles cool before pouring off the water. (The noodles can be covered and kept at room temperature for about 4 hours. They lose their springiness if they are refrigerated. Cooled noodles stick together, so loosen and separate them with warm water before using.)

7 To serve, have ready 6 glasses; each should hold 1 to 1 1/4 cups. Drain the beans and divide them and the noodles evenly among the glasses. Add 2 tablespoons sugar syrup and about 3 tablespoons coconut sauce to each glass. Top with 2 to 4 tablespoons crushed ice, depending on everyone's sweet tooth. Serve with spoons for stirring up the contents and eating.

ALMOND COOKIES

Bánh Hạnh Nhân

HEAVILY INFLUENCED BY THE CUISINE and culture of the Middle Kingdom, Viet cooks prepare many classic Chinese sweets, including these cookies. Although Chinese almond cookies are available at Asian bakeries and markets, I prefer to make them myself to ensure that they are full of real almond flavor. The cookies are slightly crispy at the edges and tender in the middle, and have a nice rich color from the glaze.

I often make a double batch of this dough and freeze the extra, along with some whole blanched almonds, so that I can simply thaw the dough and bake it up when I crave the cookies.

1 Position a rack in the middle of the oven and preheat to 350°F. Spread the slivered almonds on a baking sheet and toast, stirring every 3 to 4 minutes, for about 10 minutes, or until fragrant and light brown. Remove from the oven, let cool, and then transfer to a food processor or electric mini-chopper. Add 1 tablespoon of the sugar and process to a fine, sandy texture. Set aside.

2 In a bowl, using an electric mixer, beat the butter until soft and creamy. Gradually add the remaining sugar and beat until well blended, about 2 minutes. Add the whole egg and almond extract and beat until smooth.

3 In another bowl, sift together the flour, baking soda, and salt. Add the dry ingredients to the butter mixture and mix with a rubber spatula until smooth. Add the ground almonds and mix well until a soft dough forms. Cover with plastic wrap and refrigerate for about 30 minutes, or until the dough has firmed up. (The dough may also be transferred to an airtight container and frozen for up to 1 month. Thaw before continuing.)

4 Reheat the oven to 350°F. Line 2 baking sheets with parchment paper. Pinch off 1-inch chunks of dough and lightly roll them between your palms into smooth balls. Place the balls on the prepared baking sheets, spacing them 2 inches apart. Use

Makes 30 to 36 cookies

1 cup slivered blanched almonds	1 tablespoon almond extract
3/4 cup sugar	1¼ cups all-purpose flour
1/2 cup (1 stick) unsalted butter, at room temperature	1/2 teaspoon baking soda
	1/4 teaspoon salt
	1/4 teaspoon Caramel Sauce (page 316), optional
1 whole egg plus 1 egg yolk	36 whole blanched almonds

your thumb to make an indentation in the middle of each ball, reducing it to about half of its original thickness.

5 To make the glaze, in a small bowl, lightly beat the egg yolk with the caramel sauce. Brush a little of the glaze on each cookie, and then place a whole blanched almond in the center of each indentation. Bake the cookies, 1 sheet at a time, for 10 to 11 minutes, or until they have spread out, cracked on top, and the glaze is golden brown. The cookies themselves will have just a touch of color. Remove from the oven and let cool on the pan for 10 minutes. Transfer the cookies to racks to finish cooling before serving. Store any leftover cookies in an airtight container at room temperature for up to 3 days.

CURRANT COOKIES

Bánh Bơ Nho

THESE BUTTER COOKIES are one of my favorite French sweets in the Vietnamese repertoire. With just a few good ingredients, you can quickly bake a batch to serve alone or with ice cream, sorbet, or fresh fruit.

When Vietnamese bakers make these cookies, they don't normally include currants in the batter because the dried fruit is not readily available in Vietnam. They top each cookie with a raisin instead. Although currants are widely sold in the United States, Vietnamese American bakers still use raisins. I prefer to stir currants into the batter to distribute their chewy sweetness, and the results are closer to the original French version.

Illustrated on page 285

Makes about 40 small cookies

4 tablespoons unsalted butter, at room temperature	2 egg whites, lightly beaten
1/3 cup sugar	1/2 cup minus 1 tablespoon all-purpose flour, sifted
1/4 teaspoon salt	2 tablespoons currants tossed with 1/4 teaspoon all-purpose flour
1/2 teaspoon vanilla extract	

1 In a bowl, combine the butter and sugar. Use a wooden spoon or rubber spatula to beat together until light and fluffy. Beat in the salt and vanilla until well mixed. Add the egg whites gradually, beating thoroughly after each addition to incorporate fully. Gently mix in the flour to create a smooth batter. Stir in the currants, distributing them evenly. Cover with plastic wrap and refrigerate for 30 minutes, or until the batter has firmed up and is easier to manipulate.

2 Position a rack in the middle of the oven and preheat to 375°F. Line 2 baking sheets with parchment paper.

3 Use 2 demitasse spoons (or other small spoons) to shape the cookies. Scoop up about 1 teaspoon of batter with 1 spoon and slide it off with the other spoon onto the baking sheet. As you work, space the cookies about 2 inches apart. Do your best to create marble-sized mounds.

4 Bake the cookies, 1 sheet at a time, for 12 to 13 minutes, or until the edges are brown and the centers are pale yellow. Remove from the oven and let cool on the pan for 5 minutes. Transfer the cookies to racks to finish cooling and crisping before serving. Store any leftover cookies in an airtight container at room temperature for up to 3 days, or freeze for up to 2 months.

BANANA CAKE

Bánh Chuối

THE VIETNAMESE ADORE BANANAS, arguably the country's national fruit. Many kinds—small, large, stubby, sweet, starchy—are available, and people know the seasonal and regional differences. A giant herb related to lilies and orchids, the entire banana plant (leaves, fruits, blossoms, trunk, and roots) is used in cooking. In Vietnam, my mother regularly bought a full bunch (about a hundred fruits) from a vendor. After we arrived in America, bananas continued to be one of our favorite fruits, but we ate fewer of them since they are costlier here.

Whenever we had overripe bananas, we made this easy and delicious cake, which is among the most popular sweet *bánh* preparations. Thin banana slices decorate the slightly caramelized top, and the cake itself has a puddinglike texture because of the large number of bananas in the batter. For the best flavor, use fragrant, extremely ripe fruit with deep yellow skin marked with lots of brown spots.

1 Position a rack in the middle of the oven and preheat to 375°F. Oil an 8-inch round cake pan and line the bottom with parchment paper.

2 Select the firmest, bruise-free banana. Set aside half of it for decorating the top of the cake. Peel the remaining half and all the remaining bananas and cut them into 1/8-inch-thick slices. Put the slices in a bowl.

3 In another bowl, lightly beat the egg to break it up. Beat in the butter and milk, and then pour over the bananas. Add the 1/2 cup sugar and stir gently with a spatula or wooden spoon to mix. Sift the flour directly into the bowl and continue stirring to incorporate all the flour. Pour the batter into the prepared pan. Give the pan a few shakes to level the batter.

4 Peel and cut the reserved banana half into slices about 1/16 inch thick. Arrange the slices in a decorative pattern on top of the cake. Create a wide circle of overlapping slices, or place the slices randomly. This is your artwork. Sprinkle the top with the remaining 1 teaspoon sugar.

Serves 6

1 1/2 pounds extremely ripe
    bananas
1 egg
1/4 cup unsalted butter,
    melted and cooled

1/4 cup whole milk
1/2 cup plus 1 teaspoon sugar
3/4 cup all-purpose flour

5 Bake for 1 1/4 to 1 1/2 hours, or until a toothpick inserted into the center comes out clean and the top is golden brown. Remove from the oven and put on a rack to cool completely. The cake will puff up slightly during baking and then deflate as it cools.

6 Run a knife around the pan sides to loosen the cake and unmold the cake onto a serving plate. Cut into wedges to serve.

CASSAVA COCONUT CAKE

Bánh Khoai Mì

IF YOU ARE UNFAMILIAR with Asian sweets, this delicious cake may surprise you. There is no flour in the batter, and the cassava (the source of tapioca starch) makes the texture slightly gelatinous but firm. The mung beans function like ground nuts do in Western cakes, lending richness and body to the batter. While the cake bakes, the kitchen is filled with the aroma of coconut, and when it is served, the result is pleasingly soft, chewy, and sweet. I'm grateful to Mrs. Oanh, a friend of my mother's, for sharing this recipe. A similar preparation in the Filipino repertoire is called *cassava bibingka*.

Look for grated cassava (usually imported from the Philippines) in the frozen-food section of Southeast Asian and Chinese markets. Because coconut is the primary flavor in this recipe, it is especially important to use thick, rich, flavorful milk, whether it comes from a can or is freshly made. For a special treat, serve a wedge of this cake with a scoop of Coconut Sorbet (page 282).

1 Position a rack in the middle of the oven and preheat to 375°F. Oil a 9- or 10-inch round cake pan with at least 2-inch sides and line the bottom with parchment paper.

2 Pick through the cassava, discarding any large chunks or stringy pieces. Set aside.

3 To make the batter, in a bowl, stir together the sugar and cornstarch. In another bowl, whisk together the water, coconut milk, and egg until blended. Add the wet ingredients to the dry ingredients and mix well. Add the mung bean and cassava and whisk gently until fully incorporated. Pour the batter into the prepared pan.

4 Bake for about 1 1/4 hours, or until a toothpick inserted into the center comes out clean and the top is yellow with patches tinged golden brown. Remove from the oven and put on a rack to cool completely. The cake will rise slightly and then fall during baking.

Serves 8

1 package (1 pound) frozen grated cassava, thawed and well drained in a sieve
1 1/2 cups sugar
2 1/2 tablespoons cornstarch
1/3 cup water
1 2/3 cups coconut milk, canned or freshly made (page 318)
1 egg, lightly beaten
1 cup lightly packed Ground Steamed Mung Bean (page 322)

5 Run a knife around the pan sides to loosen the cake and unmold the cake onto a serving plate. Cut into wedges to serve.

CANDIED ORANGE PEELS

Mứt Vỏ Cam

THESE SWEETMEATS are not traditional New Year fare, but since navel oranges are at their peak in California during Tet, the peels have found a place in my annual candy-making production. I use blemish-free organic oranges because the peel is what matters in this recipe. (Scrub the oranges well if they have a waxy coating.) The pith is included, but all the bitterness is removed in the candying process. For a touch of decadence, dip the peels in melted dark chocolate.

1 Use a small, sharp knife to trim $1/4$ to $1/2$ inch from both ends of each orange. Reveal some flesh to make removing the peel easier. Then make cuts, from top to bottom and at 1-inch intervals, around each orange. Make sure the knife goes through the peel and pith down to the flesh. Use your fingers to remove the peel from the orange in beautiful, discrete sections. Cut the each section lengthwise into $1/3$-inch-wide strips.

2 Put the peels into a saucepan and add enough water so that they float. Cover with a lid or plastic wrap and refrigerate overnight.

3 Uncover and drain the peels. Return them to the saucepan and again add enough water so the peels float. Bring to a boil over medium heat and then drain. This mellows the harsh flavor of the peels.

4 To candy the peels, use a wide, high-sided skillet (like a chicken fryer) that can accommodate them in a single layer. Put a wire rack on a baking sheet and place the baking sheet nearby for drying the finished strips. Put the $12/3$ cups sugar and all the water into the skillet. Bring to a boil over medium heat, stirring to dissolve the sugar. Add the peels, lower the heat to a simmer, and cook for 25 to 30 minutes, or until they look glazed and shiny. Occasionally stir the peels or swirl the pan to ensure even cooking, and lower the heat as needed to prevent scorching.

Makes 60 to 70 candied peels, each 2 to 3 inches long

6 small or 5 medium blemish-free, thick-skinned oranges, preferably California navels

1 2/3 cups plus 1/4 cup sugar
3/4 cup plus 2 tablespoons water

During candying, the plump peels will shrink, straighten out, and soften. The white pith will turn golden and somewhat translucent. Use tongs to transfer each strip to the rack, placing them orange side up and not touching. Discard the sugar syrup. Allow the peels to dry for about 1 hour, or until they feel tacky.

5 To coat the peels, put the $1/4$ cup sugar into a small bowl. Drop in a few strips at a time and shake the bowl back and forth to coat them well. Transfer to a plate and then repeat with the remaining peels. When all the strips are coated, put them into an airtight container and store at room temperature for up to a week.

CANDIED COCONUT RIBBONS

Mứt Dừa

NUTTY, RICH, AND JUST A TOUCH SWEET, these candied coconut ribbons are part of the regular assortment of sweets offered to guests during Tet. When I was growing up, the holiday was filled with visits to the homes of relatives and close friends. While the adults chatted and wished one another well for the year, I satiated myself with the sweetmeats and confections. These candied coconut ribbons were my favorites.

Several years ago, I decided to make my own from a loosely written recipe found in an old Vietnamese cookbook. I mailed batches to my mother (a coconut lover) and invited her criticisms. After several rounds, I arrived at this recipe. Don't be daunted by the need to crack open a coconut, as it is much easier than it sounds. In the end, you will be rewarded by the sweet coconut aroma that fills your kitchen and by a big batch of tasty candied coconut.

1 Position a rack in the middle of the oven and preheat to 400°F. Locate the 3 black spots, or "eyes," at the top of coconut. Using a Phillips screwdriver or a hammer and large nail, pierce holes in 2 of the eyes and pour out the liquid, capturing it and reserving it to drink or discarding it. (Make sure the holes are good sized, or the water will dribble out slowly.) Put the coconut on a baking sheet and bake for 15 minutes. The heat will loosen the meat from the shell. The coconut may crack in the oven, which is fine.

2 Remove the coconut from the oven. Holding it with a dish towel, firmly tap it around the equator with a hammer until it has cracked around the entire circumference and broken apart. Try to keep the pieces as large as possible. Use a dinner knife to pry the coconut meat from the shell. Discard the shell.

3 Using a vegetable peeler, shave off the papery brown skin from the white coconut meat. Rinse the meat to remove any excess bits of brown skin. Then, using a sharp knife, cut the meat into ribbons about 2 inches long and 1/16 to 1/8 inch wide. Some

Makes about 4 cups

1 mature (brown) coconut, 1¾ to 2 pounds	1 cup sugar
	¼ cup water

continued

ribbons will be very short because the pieces of coconut meat are not all the same size.

4 Fill a 5-quart Dutch oven or other large pot half full with water and bring to a rolling boil. Add the coconut ribbons and parboil for 1 minute to remove some of the oil. Drain in a colander and rinse under lots of cold running water.

5 Wash the pot and add the sugar and water to it. Place over medium-high heat and heat, stirring, until the sugar melts, forming a thick syrup. Add the ribbons and lower the heat to a simmer. Cook, stirring frequently with a metal spoon to expose the ribbons evenly to the syrup. They will gradually become silvery and soften.

After about 30 minutes, when the sugar syrup is as thick as corn syrup, lower the heat further to slow the cooking and start stirring constantly with the spoon. The ribbons will soon turn white, become dry looking, and stiffen. To dry the ribbons thoroughly without browning them, keep stirring. The sugar will first cling to the ribbons and then flake off in white, sandy bits. When the ribbons are opaque and covered by a dry, sandy sugar film, they are done. This second cooking stage, which began when you lowered the heat, should take about 2 minutes.

6 Pour the ribbons onto a baking sheet and spread them into a single layer to cool completely. Transfer the cooled ribbons to an airtight container, discarding the powdery sugar. They will keep at room temperature for about 2 weeks.

COFFEE AND CONDENSED MILK

An opened can of sweetened condensed milk is a great excuse to indulge in Vietnamese coffee, called *cà-phê sữa*. To create this jolting beverage, brew an inky-strong cup of coffee. Any full-bodied, dark roast will work, although a perennial favorite of Vietnamese Americans is Café Du Monde from New Orleans, which contains chicory. Regardless of the coffee, brew it in a regular electric coffeemaker or a stove-top espresso maker. (The small Vietnamese stainless-steel presses are slow and often don't work well.) If you are starting from beans, grind them extrafine to extract the maximum flavor.

Now, put about 1 tablespoon sweetened condensed milk in a cup. Add about 3/4 cup of your hot, heady brew and stir to combine. Taste and adjust with more milk to your liking, then drink as is or pour into an ice-filled glass for a cold version.

ALMOND JELLY WITH LYCHEES, JACKFRUIT, AND STRAWBERRIES

Thạch Hạnh Nhân

VIETNAMESE COOKS, like many other Asian cooks, make jellied treats from agar-agar. When a particularly grand presentation is on the menu, they use intricate molds to create multicolored desserts that look like elaborately decorated Western cakes.

This simple almond jelly and fruit combo is a summertime favorite in my home. Originally prepared in China, the mildly sweet chunks of firm white jelly may be eaten alone, but they are more festive when accompanied with fruits. I use lychees and jackfruit, both of which are surprisingly good canned, along with fresh strawberries for contrast, but you may use any macerated or poached fruit you like.

Twenty-five-gram packets of agar-agar powder (*bột rau câu*, or seaweed powder) are sold at Chinese and Southeast Asian markets. If the powder is not shelved with the agar-agar sticks or strands, ask for it; it is sometimes kept at the cash registers. Telephone brand from Thailand is popular. If you cannot find agar-agar, use unflavored gelatin.

1 Put the water in a saucepan, sprinkle the agar-agar (or gelatin) onto the surface, and stir to mix well. If using agar-agar, bring to a boil over medium heat, stirring constantly, until the agar-agar dissolves. If using gelatin, heat over low heat, stirring constantly, until the gelatin dissolves. Remove from the heat, add the sugar, condensed milk, and almond extract, and stir until the sugar dissolves.

2 Pour into an 8-inch square or 9-inch round cake pan or shallow dish; the jelly should fill to a depth of 1/2 to 3/4 inch. Push any surface bubbles to the side, so they won't mar the top. Let stand for about 1 hour, or until cooled completely and set. If you are using gelatin, let it cool for 15 minutes and then refrigerate for about 3 hours, or until well chilled and firm. (The jelly may be prepared up to 2 days in advance, covered with plastic wrap, and refrigerated until serving.)

3 About 1 hour before serving, drain the jackfruit in a sieve placed over a serving bowl. Cut the jackfruit into 1-inch pieces and add to the bowl with the syrup. Add the lychees, with

Serves 6 to 8

3 cups warm water

1 tablespoon agar-agar powder, or 2 1/2 tablespoons unflavored gelatin

1/4 cup sugar

1/2 cup sweetened condensed milk

2 teaspoons almond extract

1 can (20 ounces) jackfruit

1 can (20 ounces) lychees

2 cups ripe strawberries, hulled and halved lengthwise if small or quartered lengthwise if large

all their syrup, and the strawberries to the bowl. Cover and refrigerate to chill until serving.

4 Just before serving, cut the jelly into 1-inch squares or diamonds and add them to the fruit bowl. To serve, spoon the mixture into individual dessert bowls. Include as much syrup with each serving as you like.

GRILLED BANANAS WITH COCONUT STICKY RICE

Chuối Nướng

> **IN THIS CAMBODIAN TREAT** that is also a favorite in Vietnam, bananas are covered with coconut-infused sticky rice, wrapped in banana leaf, and grilled. As the leaf chars, the ingredients inside steam and meld, picking up a hint of the leaf's tealike fragrance. The bit of the rice that gets crusty and smoky from the grilling is nicely balanced by a drizzle of lightly sweetened coconut sauce.
>
> Creamy, sweet three- to four-inch-long Nino bananas, also known as Finger or Baby bananas, are best for these rolls, though you can use regular bananas cut to size in a pinch. For easy wrapping, use thin banana leaves and cut the rectangles so that the long side runs parallel with the leaf veins. Unsweetened dried coconut is sold at Asian markets (you will find the bananas there, too, or at Latin groceries) and health-food stores.

1 Rinse the rice, drain in a sieve, and put into a small, heavy saucepan. Add the water, coconut milk, and salt and bring to a near boil over medium-high heat. Give the rice a stir to loosen the grains on the bottom, and then lower the heat to medium. Let cook, stirring occasionally, for 1 to 2 minutes, or until most of the liquid has been absorbed. Decrease the heat to low, cover, and cook for 10 minutes. Remove from the heat and let stand, covered, for 10 minutes to finish cooking.

2 Uncover the rice, fluff it with chopsticks or a fork, and transfer it to a bowl. Add the grated coconut and sugar and mix well. Set aside until cool enough to handle.

3 For each packet, put a banana leaf rectangle, with the smoother side up and a short side closest to you, on a work surface. Tear off a long, narrow strip, about 1/3 inch wide, and set aside to use later to secure the packet. Put 1/3 cup of the rice on the center of the leaf. Moisten your fingers with water to prevent the rice from sticking to them and then press the rice into a 5-inch circle. Vertically center a banana on top of the rice.

Makes 6 rolls

1 cup long-grain or short-grain sticky rice

3/4 cup water

2 tablespoons coconut milk, canned or freshly made (page 318)

1/4 teaspoon salt

1/2 cup unsweetened finely grated dried coconut

2 teaspoons sugar

6 pieces fresh or thawed, frozen banana leaf, each 9 by 12 inches, trimmed of browned edges, rinsed, and wiped dry

6 small bananas, peeled, or 3 sections from regular bananas, each 3 1/2 inches long, peeled and halved lengthwise

1 1/4 cups Coconut Dessert Sauce (page 313), warm or at room temperature

Pull up the long sides of the leaf so that they meet in the middle, pressing gently on the rice so it covers the top of the banana. To encase the banana fully, use your fingers to push and pinch the rice at the ends. You may find it easier to do this if you hold the packet in one hand. Do your best to cover the banana in rice, although thinly covered spots are okay. Once you are satisfied the banana is covered as well as possible, roll up the banana in the leaf, cigar style, to create a 12-inch-long, open-ended tube. Fold the ends of the leaf under to close the packet (they will partially overlap), and then tie the ends down securely with the reserved leaf strip. Repeat to make 5 more packets.

4   Prepare a medium-hot charcoal fire (you can hold your hand over the rack for only 3 to 4 seconds) or preheat a gas grill to medium-high. Grill the packets, fold side down, for 6 to 8 minutes, or until deeply charred on the underside. Flip each packet over and grill for about 4 minutes longer, or until the second side is lightly charred.

   Alternatively, position a rack in the upper third of the oven and preheat to 500°F. Arrange the packets on a baking sheet and roast, turning once, for 7 to 8 minutes on each side, or until the packets are gently hissing and the leaves are tinged brown and crispy. (The banana leaf packets may be grilled or roasted about 2 hours in advance and kept at room temperature. Reheat in a 350°F oven for about 10 minutes, or until warm, before serving.)

5   Let the packets cool for 5 to 10 minutes before serving. If the packets are blackened and unsightly, open them and transfer the rice-coated bananas to dessert plates. Otherwise, enjoy the bananas directly from the packets. Drizzle about 3 tablespoons coconut sauce over each banana and eat with a fork or spoon.

MOON CAKES

Bánh Nướng

EVERY LATE JULY, I look up the solar calendar dates of Tết Trung Thu (Autumn Moon Festival), which is celebrated on the fifteenth day of the eighth lunar month and usually falls mid- to late September. An ancient Chinese harvest festival akin to Thanksgiving, it is a time for family and togetherness. The culinary focus of the celebration is the moon cake, a small baked pastry shaped in a hand-carved wooden mold. Thin, pliable dough encases a dense, sweet filling, at the center of which sits a salted egg yolk, symbolizing the moon. In between nibbling thin wedges of cake and sipping fragrant tea, you gaze at the largest and brightest moon of the year and reflect on your good fortune.

Making moon cakes requires lots of ingredients and time, so most people buy them from bakeries and markets. But the culinary process is remarkable, requiring both precision and artistry, and the results are splendidly beautiful and delicious, making store-bought cakes pale imitations of homemade.

Moon cakes are often filled with a paste of red beans or lotus seeds, but my family prefers an aromatic mixture of nuts and sweetmeats. My mother used this recipe in Vietnam, where she and her friend Mrs. Ly mastered the techniques. Some minor changes were made over time. For example, Mom substituted canned cooked chicken to mimic the luxurious texture of shark fin, and I added corn syrup to prevent the filling from drying and hardening. For decades, I watched and assisted my mother with the annual ritual. A few years ago, she handed me the molds, asking me to carry on the tradition.

You must plan well in advance to make these cakes. The eggs need to stand in brine for four weeks, which is why I check the dates in July and work backward. While the eggs are curing, you can roast and freeze the pork at any point, and you can prepare the sugar syrup up to a few days in advance. The night before making the cakes, chop all the filling ingredients. The next day, forming and baking the cakes will be a pleasure. Moon cakes keep well in the refrigerator for a couple of weeks and will keep in the freezer for months, which means that you may make them way ahead of the celebration date or even enjoy them on other special occasions.

Before embarking on this recipe, read it carefully from beginning to end, including the Note, which provides information on where to find the molds and any unusual ingredients. Also, make sure you have all the special equipment you will need: one or two wooden molds, a scale, toothpicks (preferably flat ones), and a water spray bottle.

Makes 10 to 12 moon cakes, depending on mold size

SUGAR SYRUP

1¼ cups sugar

¼ plus ⅛ teaspoon citric acid (sour salt)

½ cup water

FILLING

12 Salted Preserved Eggs (page 101), unboiled

3 ounces pork fatback, blanched in boiling water for about 1 minute until firm, cooled, and finely diced (about ½ cup)

½ cup finely diced Char Siu Pork (page 142)

1 Chinese sweet sausage, finely chopped

½ cup powdered sugar

½ cup roasted sunflower seeds

⅔ cup chopped toasted walnuts, with any loose bits of skin removed

3 tablespoons chopped toasted cashews

2 tablespoons chopped toasted slivered blanched almonds

⅓ cup sesame seeds, toasted (page 332)

¼ cup chopped crystallized ginger

¾ cup chopped candied citron or fruitcake mix

¼ cup drained canned white chunk chicken, flaked

1 cup plus 1 tablespoon sugar

3 tablespoons light corn syrup

⅓ cup Chinese sorghum and rose petal liquor (mei kwei lu chiu)

3 tablespoons freshly grated lime zest, or 10 tender young lime leaves (any variety), minced

DOUGH

¼ cup canola or other neutral oil, plus extra for shaping

3 tablespoons Caramel Sauce (page 316), or as needed

¾ teaspoon potassium bicarbonate solution (lye water)

Sugar syrup

2¾ cups plus about 2 tablespoons all-purpose flour, plus extra for dusting

GLAZE

3 egg yolks

2½ teaspoons Caramel Sauce (page 316)

MAKE THE SUGAR SYRUP

1 In a small saucepan, combine the sugar, citric acid, and water and let stand for 30 minutes. Then bring the mixture to a boil over medium heat and cook for 2 to 3 minutes, or until the syrup turns pale yellow (the color of canola oil). If the citric acid turns dark yellow during boiling, swirl the pan or stir the contents to distribute. Remove from the heat and pour into a large measuring cup or heatproof bowl.

2 Set the syrup aside for about 4 hours to cool completely. It will thicken and darken a bit as it cools. Then cover with plastic wrap and keep at room temperature. There should be a scant 1 cup syrup. (The syrup can be made up to 3 days in advance and kept at room temperature until using.)

COOK AND SHAPE THE FILLING

3 Position a rack in the middle of the oven and preheat to 250°F. Line a baking sheet with parchment paper. Crack each salted egg and separate the yolk from the white, discarding the white and depositing the yolk on the prepared baking sheet. Discard yolks that are liquid, but keep yolks that hold their shape, even if they are partial ones; you can make a double-yolk cake. Once you have enough yolks (either 10 or 12, whole and partial ones combined), stop; the number of yolks needed depends on the size of your mold. Save any leftover salted eggs for another use.

4 Bake the egg yolks for 12 to 15 minutes, or until they have lost most of their sheen. You want the yolks to cook sufficiently to hold their shape in the cakes. If the surfaces crack, they have baked a little too long but will be okay in the cakes. Remove the yolks from the oven and let cool. When cool enough to handle, use your fingers or a paring knife to pry the yolks from the baking sheet. Trim each yolk so that it is as round as possible and place on a plate or in a plastic container. Cover and set aside.

5 Put the pork fatback, Char Siu Pork, and sausage in a bowl and use a fork to combine well. Add the powdered sugar and toss to coat the pork and sausage thoroughly. Set aside for at least

30 minutes or up to 1 hour to marinate. The meat will look wet as it absorbs the sugar.

6 Put the marinated meats and the sunflower seeds, walnuts, cashews, almonds, sesame seeds, crystallized ginger, candied citron, chicken, sugar, and corn syrup into a 12-inch nonstick skillet. Place over medium heat and sauté gently for about 10 minutes, or until the pieces of fatback are clear and the sugar has melted. (If you taste some, you should detect just a bit of graininess from the sugar.) Turn off the heat and wait for the bubbling sugar to subside before stirring in the liquor and lime zest. Let cool for 30 minutes before continuing.

7 To shape the filling into balls, line the baking sheet with fresh parchment paper and gather the following: the filling, plastic wrap, the baked yolks, and a scale. Tear off 4 pieces of plastic wrap each about 20 inches long, and fold each piece in half. Put a folded sheet on the scale. Scoop up 1/3 cup of the filling and deposit it on the plastic wrap. Make a depression in the middle, and put an egg yolk in the depression. Top with 1 to 2 tablespoons of the filling to achieve the total weight you want: 3 ounces for a 1/2-cup mold, or 3 1/2 ounces for a 2/3-cup mold.

Gather up the edges of the plastic wrap and pick up the bundle in one hand. With the other hand, twist and squeeze the plastic to compress the filling into a ball the size of a tangerine (about 2 1/4 inches in diameter). Use some pressure to make sure the elements have stuck together. Undo the plastic and roll the filling onto the prepared baking sheet. The ball should hold together as it sits. If it falls apart, squeeze it back into shape. Repeat with the remaining filling, using new pieces of plastic wrap as the old ones get too tacky to release the balls easily once they are shaped. (If lots of clear, thickish liquid remains toward the end, don't try to use it all, or the filling will be too wet.) Set the balls of filling aside.

MAKE THE DOUGH

8 Add the 1/4 cup oil, 3 tablespoons caramel sauce, and potassium bicarbonate solution to the sugar syrup. Use a rubber spatula to stir for about 1 minute, or until the mixture has increased in volume, is opaque, and is a rich caramel color. If necessary, add caramel sauce, 1/4 teaspoon at a time, to darken.

9 Put the 2 3/4 cups flour into a large bowl and make a well in the center. Pour the sugar syrup mixture into the well and use the spatula to stir until you have a soft dough with the texture of marzipan. Turn the dough out onto a lightly floured work surface and knead in about 2 tablespoons flour to create a smooth, very malleable, slightly tacky dough. It may spread a bit when left to sit.

10 Shape the dough into a log 2 inches in diameter. For 1/2-cup molds, cut the log at scant 1-inch intervals to yield 2-ounce pieces; for 2/3-cup molds, cut at 1-inch intervals to yield 2 1/2-ounce pieces. Weigh each piece for accuracy, pinching off or adding on dough as necessary. Save extra dough for emergency patching up. Cover the dough pieces loosely with plastic wrap and set aside. (The dough may be prepared 1 hour in advance of shaping the cakes.)

SHAPE THE CAKES

11 Set up a station that allows you to whack the wooden mold firmly against a hard surface. Kitchen counters are *not* good. I typically put a piece of plywood and a section of a two-by-four on a dining room chair. Both pieces of wood should roughly span the width of the chair. The plywood does not have to match the depth of the chair. Position the wood pieces at the edge of the chair. The thin, wide plywood acts as a stabilizer, while the thicker two-by-four takes the pressure. (If you want to protect the floor, fold a towel or blanket to create a double or triple thickness and put it under the chair's feet.) When you are satisfied with the setup, take the mold by the handle and practice the whacking sequence outlined in step 17. Strike with confidence and strength to get a loud whack. If your arrangement seems sufficiently sturdy, continue to the next step.

continued

12 Set up a station for shaping the moon cakes near the "whacking station," outfitting it with the following: a large work surface (such as a cutting board), flour for dusting, a small bowl of oil, a pastry brush, a rolling pin (preferably an Asian-style pin, which is essentially a 1-inch wood dowel), the dough pieces, the balls of filling, and the mold(s). Line 2 baking sheets with parchment paper, oil the paper, and place them with the other tools.

13 To shape each moon cake, first oil and flour the mold. Use a pastry brush dipped in oil to coat the carved surfaces lightly. Sprinkle in some flour and tap the mold against your hand to spread the flour evenly over the entire interior surface. Invert and tap the mold against the sink to remove excess flour. Set the prepared mold by your work area.

14 Lightly flour the work surface and place a piece of dough on top of it. With a lightly floured hand, smack the dough to flatten it to a 1/4-inch-thick disk. Flip it over. Quickly dip 2 fingers into the oil and very lightly oil the rolling pin; this tiny bit of oil makes the dough easier to manipulate. With short, fast strokes, roll the dough away from its center, leaving a plump, roughly 1-inch-wide "belly" in the middle. With each roll, pick up the dough and give it a quarter turn to prevent sticking. When it is about 4 inches in diameter, stop turning the dough and make the final passes to create a circle 5 to 5 1/2 inches in diameter and a generous 1/8 inch thick at the edge. This Chinese method of rolling dough ensures an even thickness all around the cake. (If the dough sticks or breaks, scrape it up with a plastic dough scraper or knife, knead it back into a ball, and start over. It is a forgiving dough.)

15 Pick up the dough circle and put it in one hand. Place a ball of filling in the center of the circle, and then invert the entire thing into the other hand; the dough will naturally droop over the filling. (The dough side that now faces you will be the pretty top of the cake.) Pass the ball back to the other hand so that the bottom of the cake now faces upward. Cupping the cake in one hand, use the fingers of your other hand to seal the dough, completely encasing the filling. Gently press, nudge, and mold the dough as

needed. Once sealed, cup the ball in both hands and gently roll and pat it smooth. The pastry will take on a slight sheen.

16 Place the ball, top side down, into the mold. Using the fleshy part of your hand between the base of your thumb and wrist, press the ball into the mold. Try to apply even pressure. Once the cake has filled the mold, go around the edge to press the pastry inward gently and away from the side walls of the mold. This helps the cake to release.

17 To loosen the cake from the mold, step over to your whacking station. Take the handle of the mold and firmly whack it against the wood in this precise order: The first 4 whacks are applied to each side of the mold (left, top, right, and bottom). For the dramatic fifth and final whack, turn the mold so that the cake faces down and place your hand underneath to catch the cake as it falls out. Place the cake on the baking sheet. Repeat with the remaining dough and filling, spacing the cakes about 2 inches apart on the baking sheets. As you work, take note of the following: If the cake threatens to jump out of the mold while you are whacking, immediately reduce the amount of pressure and continue through the entire sequence. If you have to set the ball of filling and dough down at any time, place it on a floured surface to prevent sticking. Because the carved impressions dull as oil and flour accumulate in the mold, occasionally pause between shaping the cakes to clean out the mold. (Use 2 molds and you will clean less often.) For cleaning, use a toothpick, skewer, or the tip of a paring knife to dislodge bits. A hard spray of water from the sink faucet also helps. After spraying, dry the mold with paper towels before oiling and flouring it for the next cake.

BAKE AND GLAZE THE CAKES

18 Position a rack in the lower third of the oven and preheat to 250°F. Meanwhile, make the glaze by combining the egg yolks and caramel sauce in a small bowl and mixing with a fork until well blended. Pass the glaze through a fine-mesh sieve into another small bowl. Discard the solids and set the bowl aside. Fill the spray bottle halfway with water and set aside.

19 Use a toothpick to poke 3 or 4 air vents into the top of each cake, about 1/4 inch deep. (This helps the cakes bake more evenly.) Flat toothpicks make less conspicuous holes than round ones.

20 Baking moon cakes is a three-step process, and you must bake only 1 sheet at a time. Loosely cover the unbaked cakes on 1 sheet with parchment paper. Slip the other sheet into the oven and bake for 22 to 25 minutes, or until the cakes look dull and a little puffed. Remove from the oven, and immediately spray the cakes with water to soften the dough. Wait for about 2 minutes, or until the water is absorbed, and then use your fingers to push and straighten up the cakes. (They are not that hot.) This "cosmetic surgery" helps to produce prettier cakes. Ideally, the sides should be straight, not flared. The cakes should retain most of their out-of-the-mold appearance but be slightly puffed.

21 Once you are satisfied with how the cakes look, brush the tops with the glaze and return the cakes to the oven. Bake this second time for 10 minutes. Remove the cakes from the oven, brush again with the glaze, and return to the oven. Bake for a final 10 minutes, or until the tops are richly colored and shiny. Remove from the oven and put on a rack to cool. When the cakes are cool enough to handle, after about 30 minutes, you may straighten any lopsided, unsightly cakes. While the first baking sheet cools, bake the second sheet.

22 As the moon cakes cool, they darken from the caramel sauce in the dough and glaze. When they are completely cool, store them in an airtight plastic container. Before eating them, allow them to age for 1 to 2 days to soften the pastry and develop the flavors. They will keep at room temperature for up to 5 days and in the refrigerator for up to 2 weeks. Enjoy them at room temperature, cut into small wedges.

To freeze, wrap each cake in plastic wrap and place the cakes on a baking sheet. Put the baking sheet in the freezer for several hours, or until the cakes are hard. Transfer the cakes to zip-top plastic bags and freeze for up to 6 months. To thaw, remove the plastic wrap from the still-frozen cakes, put the cakes in an airtight plastic container, and let stand at room temperature for 1 to 2 days before cutting and eating.

NOTE

Wooden moon cake molds are typically sold at Chinese and Vietnamese cookware stores, especially as the holiday nears. Or, check the Resources section (page 335) for an online vendor. Look for molds with holes pierced on the sides; they provide handy drainage and air vents. Moon cake molds hold either 1/2 cup or 2/3 cup and are sometimes marked 150 or 200 grams, respectively. If you are unsure, fill the mold with water to determine the size. For your first time making moon cakes, use the larger mold (about 2 3/4 inches in diameter and 1 1/4 inches deep), which is easier to work with. Molds from Vietnam are for making either baked moon cakes (this recipe) or for chewy unbaked cakes called *bánh dẻo* (also eaten on this holiday). In general, molds for the former are carved with small, delicate scalloped edges, while molds for the latter have much bigger, robust edges. Although I have made this recipe with both kinds of molds, the cakes are prettiest when made with the proper mold.

Here are some tips for locating ingredients:

- Citric acid, sold in crystallized form as sour salt (also called citric salt), is usually stocked in the kosher-food section of mainstream supermarkets.

- Potassium bicarbonate solution (lye water) is sold at Chinese markets in glass bottles shelved near the vinegars.

- Sorghum and rose petal liquor (*mei kwei lu chiu*) is available at Chinese markets, too. Look for the Chinese name on the bottles or boxes. It is also great for sipping.

- Health-food stores with a bulk section are great places to buy small quantities of nuts.

- Candied citron and fruitcake mix are seasonal ingredients that may be stored for several years. Buy a small supply in November, when they are sold for holiday baking.

- See page 169 for tips on finding pork fatback.

BASICS

BASIC DIPPING SAUCE
Nước Chấm

EVERY VIETNAMESE COOK makes this dipping sauce, with the differences among them reflecting personal preferences and regional variations. In general, as you move south the sauce gets sweeter, hotter, and more garlicky. Yet no matter exactly how it is made, its role is always the same: to enhance and unify all the elements of a dish.

As with much of Viet cooking, parameters apply more than rules. This recipe will help you develop your own version. Sensing subtle distinctions between sour, sweet, salty, and spicy requires practice. Plus, fish sauces differ, and even lime juice can be inconsistent. To deal with these variables, I don't mix everything together at once, but rather break up the process to simplify matters for the taste buds. This allows for adjustments along the way. While you may omit the rice vinegar, it actually brightens the flavors and softens any harsh or bitter edges contributed by the lime juice. The garlic is optional; some recipes will suggest including or excluding it.

Makes about 1½ cups

⅓ cup fresh lime juice (2 or 3 limes)
1 tablespoon unseasoned Japanese rice vinegar (optional)
3 tablespoons sugar
⅔ cup lukewarm water
5 to 6 tablespoons fish sauce
2 or 3 Thai or serrano chiles, thinly sliced
2 cloves garlic, minced (optional)

1 In a small bowl, combine the lime juice, vinegar, sugar, and water and stir to dissolve the sugar. Taste and adjust the flavors to balance the sweet and sour as needed.

2 Add the fish sauce, starting out with 5 tablespoons and then adding more as your palate dictates, balancing the sour, sweet, and salty. How much fish sauce you use depends on the brand and your own taste. Aim for a light honey or amber color and a bold, forward finish. Keep in mind that this sauce is typically used to dress dishes that include unsalted ingredients like lettuce and herbs—ingredients that will need an extra flavor lift. When you're satisfied, add the chiles and garlic. (If diners are sensitive to chile heat, serve the chiles on the side.)

3 Put the sauce on the table so that diners can serve themselves, or portion it out in advance for serving. It may be prepared early in the day and left at room temperature until serving.

NOTE

When using both garlic and chiles in the sauce, try pounding them together with a pinch of sugar in a mortar. This quickly releases their oils (helpful if you are in a hurry) and gives the sauce an appealing orange cast.

SIZING UP DIPPING SAUCE DISHES

Small, cute dishes are good for plunging little morsels of food into sauce. But if you are dunking a bundle of food wrapped in lettuce or a hand roll, you need shallow bowls three to four inches in diameter.

BUYING AND JUICING LIMES

Look for limes with smooth skins. They are juicier and easier to work with than fruits with dimpled, tough skins. Before juicing, use your palm to roll the limes back and forth on a firm work surface. This breaks down the membranes, which allows you to extract the maximum amount of juice from the fruit. Because I like pulp in my sauces, I use an old-fashioned handheld reamer for juicing. If your juicer filters out the pulp, start with a scant measurement of what is called for in a recipe, as you won't be working with the extra bulk contributed by the pulp. You can always add more juice when making final adjustments.

SIMPLE DIPPING SAUCE
Nước Mắm Ớt

NOT EVERY VIET MEAL requires assembling a nuanced tart-sweet-salty-spicy dipping sauce. Sometimes, the food just needs a light dip in something straightforward. This sauce is basically diluted fish sauce emboldened by thin rings of fiery chiles. With only three ingredients, it is important to use high-quality fish sauce and chiles with fragrance and heat.

Makes about 1/3 cup

2 tablespoons fish sauce

3 tablespoons water

1 or 2 Thai or serrano chiles, thinly sliced

1 In a small bowl, combine the fish sauce and water. Taste and adjust the level of saltiness with more fish sauce or water as needed. Add the chiles and set aside for at least 15 minutes for the flavors to develop.

2 Put the sauce on the table so that diners can serve themselves, or divide among individual dipping sauce bowls.

GINGER-LIME DIPPING SAUCE
Nước Mắm Gừng

USED SPARINGLY to coat food lightly, this sublime sauce goes well with seafood, chicken, and even boiled green vegetables. If you are portioning it for your guests, serve it in small, shallow dishes, as a little of it goes a long way. This sauce is so good that a family friend drank his serving.

While an electric mini-chopper makes quick work of mincing ginger (cut it into 1/2-inch chunks and use a little lime juice to move things along), a sharp knife will allow you to hone your knife skills. For the best flavor, select a heavy knob of ginger with smooth, thin skin.

Makes 2/3 cup

Chubby 2-inch piece fresh ginger, peeled and minced

5 tablespoons fresh lime juice (2 or 3 limes)

2 1/2 tablespoons sugar

2 to 3 tablespoons fish sauce

1 In a small bowl, combine the ginger, lime juice, and sugar and stir to dissolve the sugar. Taste and adjust the flavors with more lime juice or sugar as needed. The ginger and lime should both be prominent, but not to the point that they make you wince and pucker. Add the fish sauce, starting out with 2 tablespoons and adding more as your palate dictates. Set aside for 30 minutes to let the ginger bloom before serving.

2 Put the sauce on the table so that diners can serve themselves, or divide among individual dipping sauce bowls. It may be prepared 2 to 3 hours in advance and left at room temperature until serving.

TANGY-SWEET SHRIMP SAUCE
Mắm Tôm Chấm

THIS SAUCE is intensely flavored by lots of lime juice, which rounds out the edges of the shrimp sauce (*mắm tôm*), a salty, pungent fermented staple of the Viet kitchen. The fish sauce lends savoriness, the chiles add heat, and the sugar softens everything. Although the rice vinegar is optional, it helps smooth out all the flavors. This sauce is the traditional condiment with turmeric catfish with rice noodles (page 226).

Makes about 1 cup

6 tablespoons fresh lime juice (3 limes)
1 tablespoon unseasoned Japanese rice vinegar (optional)
1 tablespoon fine shrimp sauce
3 tablespoons fish sauce
2¹/2 tablespoons sugar
¹/4 cup water
2 or 3 Thai or serrano chiles, thinly sliced (optional)

1   In a small bowl, combine the lime juice and vinegar. Whisk in the shrimp sauce, blending well. Add the fish sauce, sugar, and water and whisk to dissolve the sugar. Taste and adjust as needed to arrive at a pleasantly tangy, sweet, salty, pungent sauce. A little more lime (up to 1 tablespoon) will tame the pungency and sweetness. If the overall flavors are too intense, add water by the teaspoonful. If you like shrimp sauce, whisk in more. When you are satisfied with the balance, add the chiles and set aside for 30 minutes to let the flavors develop before serving.

2   Put the sauce on the table so that diners can serve themselves, or divide among individual dipping sauce bowls. It may be prepared 2 to 3 hours in advance and left at room temperature until serving.

SPICY HOISIN-GARLIC SAUCE
Tương

IN THE VIET KITCHEN, *tương* refers to various heady sauces made from fermented beans. It might be thin like soy sauce, which some folks call *nước tương* (*tương* water), or thick like this sauce, which accompanies Southern Salad Rolls (page 32), Beef and Jicama Hand Rolls (page 30), chicken meatballs (page 86), and Delightful Crepes (page 277).

There are several ways to prepare this sauce, and my family's version is based on *nước lèo*, a sweet and earthy sauce from central Vietnam made with pork liver. We substitute lighter-tasting chicken livers, which are saved from whole chickens used for other dishes. Sweet hoisin sauce tempers the chile and garlic, while tomato paste brightens the sauce, which otherwise would be dull brown.

At Vietnamese restaurants, this sauce is often called peanut sauce and made with peanut butter, a nontraditional ingredient. It is convenient and tasty, but not as complex and deeply flavored as this liver version. If you do not like liver or are a vegetarian, make the version in the Note that follows.

Makes about 1¹/2 cups

2 fat chicken livers
2 tablespoons plus 1 cup water
1 tablespoon canola or other neutral oil
1 large clove garlic, finely minced
¹/4 to ¹/2 teaspoon dried red chile flakes
1 teaspoon tomato paste
6 to 8 tablespoons hoisin sauce
1 teaspoon fish sauce (optional)
1¹/2 teaspoons cornstarch dissolved in 1¹/2 teaspoons water
2 tablespoons unsalted roasted peanuts, finely chopped
1 teaspoon sesame seeds, toasted (page 332)

1   Rinse the chicken livers and trim away any visible membrane. In an electric mini-chopper, combine the liver and the 2 tablespoons water and process until smooth. (Or, mince the livers by hand, flipping them over occasionally with the knife blade to ensure that you are reducing them to a shapeless mass.

Use the knife blade to transfer the minced livers to a small bowl and combine with the 2 tablespoons water.)

2   In a small saucepan, combine the oil, garlic, and chile flakes over medium-low heat. When the oil is sizzling and pale yellow, add the tomato paste, breaking it up with a whisk or fork. When the oil is a bright yellow-orange, immediately pour in the 1 cup water to stop the cooking. Increase the heat to medium and whisk in the liver mixture. Discard the larger liver pieces that eventually cling to the whisk. As the sauce cooks and changes color, the liver will appear as brown bits.

3   When the sauce begins to boil, whisk in 6 tablespoons hoisin sauce. Let the sauce cook for 1 minute and taste, adding more hoisin sauce, if necessary. The amount you use depends on the brand and your own taste. Aim for a sweet, tangy, spicy balance. For extra depth, add the fish sauce. Bring the sauce to a simmer, whisk in the cornstarch mixture, and then cook for about 30 seconds, or until thickened. Remove from the heat and let cool, uncovered, to concentrate the flavors and thicken further. (The sauce may be prepared ahead and refrigerated for up to 1 day or frozen for up to 1 month. Return to room temperature or warm slightly before serving.)

4   Transfer the sauce to a bowl and sprinkle the peanuts and sesame seeds on top. Put the sauce on the table so that diners can serve themselves. (Or, divide the sauce among individual dipping sauce bowls and then sprinkle with peanuts and sesame seeds before serving.)

NOTE

For a vegetarian version, substitute 2 tablespoons creamy salted peanut butter (preferably an all-natural brand) for the liver. Whisk together the peanut butter and the 2 tablespoons water and proceed as directed. The sauce may be quite thick, in which case you can omit the cornstarch binder.

SALT, PEPPER, AND LIME DIPPING SAUCE
Muối Tiêu Chanh

EVERY TIME I make this easy dipping sauce, I am amazed at how good it is, especially when paired with such simple dishes as grilled chicken, fish, squid, shrimp, or summer squash or with Poached Chicken with Lime Leaves (page 84). Depending on how you tilt its balance, the sauce may hit your palate with pungency, saltiness, tartness, and/or heat.

Kosher salt is the best type to use for this recipe. It is coarse, less assertive than iodized salt, and a little sweet. Assembling this sauce is fun, fast, and up to each individual. As the cook, all you have to do is set out individual dishes filled with the ingredients.

Kosher or other coarse salt
White pepper
Lime wedges
Thinly sliced Thai or serrano chiles

Place each of the ingredients in a separate shallow dish, put the dishes on the table, and provide diners with individual dipping sauce dishes. Then, tell them how to go about assembling the sauce: First, put some salt and white pepper into the dish (2 parts salt to 1 part pepper is a good balance). Next, add a squeeze of lime. Finally, if heat is desired, use chopsticks to muddle some chile slices in the mixture to release their oils. That's it. Diners should dip each bite of food into the sauce right before eating. They can make flavor adjustments and extra sauce as the meal progresses.

For a more elegant—and perhaps easier—assembly, set up a dipping sauce dish with mounds of salt and white pepper for each diner, and then let them add their own lime juice and chile.

SWEET-AND-SOUR SAUCE
Nước Xốt Chua Ngọt

OUR FAMILY'S Viet recipe for sweet-and-sour sauce is lighter and more nuanced than traditional Chinese versions. There is no pineapple or tomato ketchup to give it heavy-duty weight and color. Instead, finely chopped vegetables are added at the end, delivering a delicate finish and a colorful confetti-like appearance. Use fish sauce for a lighter color and a slightly briny flavor. Use soy sauce for a darker color and a bolder flavor.

Makes about 1¹/₂ cups

1¹/₂ cups water
1 tablespoon finely chopped yellow onion
1 small clove garlic, finely minced
3¹/₂ tablespoons sugar
2 tablespoons distilled white vinegar
1¹/₂ tablespoons fish sauce or 2 tablespoons light (regular) soy sauce
¹/₄ teaspoon salt
¹/₈ teaspoon white pepper
1¹/₂ tablespoons cornstarch dissolved in 2 tablespoons water
1 tablespoon chopped scallion, green part only
1 tablespoon finely chopped carrot
1¹/₂ tablespoons finely chopped red bell pepper

1 In a saucepan, combine the water, onion, garlic, sugar, vinegar, fish sauce, salt, and white pepper and bring to a boil over medium heat, stirring to dissolve the sugar. Lower the heat and simmer for 5 minutes.

2 Give the cornstarch mixture a stir, add it to the pan, and continue to cook, stirring, for about 30 seconds, or until the sauce thickens. Remove from the heat and stir in the scallion, carrot, and bell pepper. Let the sauce stand for 5 to 10 minutes.

3 Taste and adjust the flavors. Transfer to a bowl or divide among dipping sauce bowls, and serve warm or at room temperature.

TAMARIND-GINGER DIPPING SAUCE
Nước Mắm Me

THE UNUSUALLY TART flavor and slightly thick texture of this sauce is great with a simple grilled fish or boiled green vegetable. It is easy to make when you have frozen cubes of tamarind liquid on hand, and can be prepared hours in advance of the meal and left at room temperature.

Makes about 1¹/₂ cups

1 tablespoon canola or other neutral oil
2 tablespoons peeled and minced fresh ginger
1 large clove garlic, finely minced
6 tablespoons Tamarind Liquid (page 319)
²/₃ cup water
3 to 4 tablespoons sugar
4 to 5 tablespoons fish sauce
2 or 3 Thai or serrano chiles, thinly sliced (optional)

1 In a small saucepan, heat the oil over medium heat. Add the ginger and garlic and cook, stirring, until fragrant, about 30 seconds. Whisk in the tamarind liquid and water. When the mixture comes to a boil, remove from the heat.

2 Whisk in the sugar and fish sauce, starting out with the smaller amounts. Taste and add additional sugar or fish sauce to create a tart, spicy, sweet, savory sauce. Set aside, uncovered, to cool to room temperature and to let the flavors bloom.

3 Before serving, taste again and adjust the flavor balance a final time. Transfer to a serving bowl or divide the sauce among individual dipping sauce bowls. If all the diners like chile heat, add the chile slices to the bowl(s). If not, serve the chile slices on the side for diners to add as desired.

COCONUT DESSERT SAUCE

Nước Cốt Dừa Ngọt

SLIGHTLY SWEET, this simple, creamy sauce is used to finish various sweets in the Viet repertoire. Use it cold, warm, or at room temperature, depending on the preparation.

Makes 1¼ cups

1 cup coconut milk, canned or freshly made (page 318)
2 pinches of salt
1 tablespoon sugar
3 tablespoons water
1½ teaspoons cornstarch dissolved in 2 teaspoons water

1 In a small saucepan, whisk together the coconut milk, salt, sugar, and water. Place over medium heat and bring to a near simmer, lowering the heat if the coconut milk spews or pops. Give the cornstarch mixture a good stir and add it to the sauce, mixing well. Cook, stirring, for about 30 seconds, or until the sauce thickens, then remove from the heat.

2 Let the sauce cool, uncovered, to concentrate the flavors before serving. It will keep in a tightly capped container in the refrigerator for up to 3 days. If serving warm, reheat gently over low heat.

VEGETABLE GARNISH PLATE

Đĩa Rau Sống

ONE OF THE DISTINCTIVE aspects of eating Vietnamese food is the large plate of lettuce and herbs that accompanies many grilled and fried dishes. For example, Sizzling Crepes (page 274) would be incomplete without the texture, flavor, and color of the lettuce, herbs, and cucumber that arrive with them. It is this final layering of cooked and raw ingredients that contributes to the uniqueness of Vietnamese food.

Select lettuces with pliable leaves. Butter, red or green leaf, or soft varieties of romaine are ideal. Baby lettuces make a beautiful presentation and usually don't need to be torn into smaller pieces. Always avoid crisp lettuces and those without broad leaves, such as oak leaf. They don't wrap well.

This plate can accompany any Vietnamese dish that is typically eaten with vegetable and herb garnishes. In the case of the herbs, a minimum of cilantro and mint must be included. Some foods taste particularly good with certain herbs, however, so specific recipes may suggest including red perilla, Vietnamese balm, fish mint, or sorrel. For details on these herbs, see page 17.

Serves 4 to 6

1 large or 2 small heads soft-leaved leaf lettuce
2 pickling (Kirby) cucumbers or 1 small English cucumber, unpeeled, halved lengthwise, seeded, and thinly sliced
½ small bunch cilantro, leafy top portion only
½ small bunch mint
½ bunch red perilla, Vietnamese balm, fish mint, and/or sorrel (optional)

Arrange the ingredients on 2 large plates and place on the table. Invite diners to tear large lettuce leaves into palm-sized pieces and to pluck herb leaves from their stems. Big herb leaves may be torn into bite-sized pieces, while young, tender cilantro leaves and stems may be enjoyed together. There are few rules, only guidelines on how to incorporate these raw garnishes into meals.

CRISPY CARAMELIZED SHALLOT
Hành Phi

THESE TERRIFIC shallot slices are like bacon bits—a garnish for when you want to add final rich notes. For them to turn out well, you must first remove all the excess moisture from the fresh shallots. Many Viet cooks skip that step and fry up presliced dehydrated shallot. Sold at Chinese and Vietnamese markets, the time-saving alternative sadly lacks flavor and depth, much like the difference between onion soup made from scratch and a packaged mix. However, they are convenient and inexpensive, which perhaps explains why *hành phi* are sometimes overused to embellish food.

I am a traditionalist when it comes to this garnish. I prepare it the day I need it so that it stays crisp, and I always start with fresh shallots to capture their subtle sweetness. I especially like them sprinkled on *bánh cuốn* (steamed rice crepe rolls, page 270) and *xôi bắp* (sticky rice with hominy, page 247).

Makes about 1/3 cup

1/2 cup thinly sliced shallot (1 very large or 2 to 3 small shallots)
3 tablespoons canola or other neutral oil

1 To ensure that the shallot slices crisp up, you must first remove some excess moisture. Using your fingers, separate the slices into individual layers, depositing them on a paper towel. Gather up the paper towel and gently blot away the moisture. Set near the stove.

2 In a 10-inch skillet, heat the oil over medium-low heat. Add the shallot and fry gently, stirring occasionally to ensure even cooking. After 5 to 6 minutes, when the shallot is fragrant and lightly golden, watch the progress closely, moving the shallot slices frequently by stirring them or swirling the pan. During frying, the shallot will soften into a mass and then stiffen as it caramelizes and crisps. When most of the slices are a rich golden brown, remove the pan from the heat. The total cooking time should be about 10 minutes. Using a slotted spoon, transfer the shallot slices to a paper towel–lined plate, spreading them out in a single layer. Discard the fragrant oil or reserve it for other uses.

3 When the shallot slices have cooled, crisped, and darkened slightly, transfer them to a small bowl or plate. Left uncovered at room temperature, they will retain their crispiness for a good 8 hours. Even if they no longer rustle when you shake them, they are still tasty.

SCALLION OIL GARNISH
Mỡ Hành

THIS SIMPLE GARNISH is great way to finish dishes with a little richness and some bright green color. Small steamed rice pancakes (page 268), sticky rice with roast chicken (page 246), and trout hand rolls (page 110) are only a few of the dishes that benefit from scallion oil.

Makes about 1/2 cup

4 scallions, white and green parts, thinly sliced (1 cup)
1/4 cup canola or other neutral oil

1 Have the scallions ready in a small bowl so they may be quickly added to the oil. In a small saucepan, heat the oil over medium heat until hot. To test, drop in a scallion slice; it should sizzle on contact. Add the scallions and stir immediately to expose them quickly to the oil. When the scallions have collapsed and are soft, after about 30 seconds, remove from the heat. Transfer the scallion oil to a small heatproof bowl and let cool completely.

2 The garnish will keep for several hours at room temperature. Or, cover and refrigerate for up to 7 days, then bring to room temperature before using.

MELLOW CHILE-GARLIC MIX
Ớt Tỏi

WHEN DEFINITIVE HEAT is what you want in a dish, fresh chiles are what you add. But when you want to inject subtle spiciness and preserve the delicate nuances of a dish, this aromatic mixture is the solution. I grew up with this condiment on the family dinner table, where it sat in a small jar alongside dispensers of fish sauce, soy sauce, salt, and pepper. Its flavors are gentler than commercially produced chile sauces, which often overpower dishes with their vinegary taste.

Slowly frying the garlic and chile melds their individual flavors, so that when you add a bit of this mixture to food, it doesn't assault your palate with its boldness. It is particularly good with stir-fry dishes and certain noodle soups. There are different kinds of chile heat, and through practice and experimentation you will learn when to use them.

Makes ½ cup

6 tablespoons canola or other neutral oil
¼ cup finely chopped garlic
¼ teaspoon dried red chile flakes

1   In a small saucepan (a butter warmer is ideal), combine the oil, garlic, and chile flakes over medium-low or low heat. Bring to a gentle simmer and let the mixture bubble and sizzle for 5 minutes, occasionally swirling the pan or stirring the mixture to ensure even cooking and watching carefully that it does not burn. The finished mixture will be a rich orange-red and have a pleasant toasty fragrance. Remove from the heat and let cool completely. The mixture will darken to a reddish brown as it cools.

2   Transfer the mixture to a small jar and keep it on the table for frequent use, or in the refrigerator for occasional use.

CARAMEL SAUCE

Nước Màu

THIS IS A CORNERSTONE of Vietnamese cooking. The term *nước màu* was originally coined in southern Vietnam. Northerners know this same ingredient as *nước hàng* (merchandising water), probably because it was so often used by food hawkers to enhance the appearance of their wares. Its ability to impart incredibly savory-sweet flavors is the key to simmering meats, seafood, eggs, and/or tofu for everyday *kho* dishes. Some cooks substitute brown sugar, but the results tend to be too sweet. The inky sauce also lends rich brown color to grilled meats, much as molasses does in American barbecue.

Traditionally, the sauce is made by pouring boiling water into the caramelized sugar, a somewhat dangerous step that causes the mixture to bubble and spew dramatically. This method immediately arrests the cooking, so that the sugar doesn't burn to a bitter black stage. I find it easier to place the pan in a sink partially filled with water, which cools the caramelized sugar, halting the cooking, and then add the water to dilute the sugar. The result with both approaches is the same bittersweet, inky sauce that is a staple in every Vietnamese kitchen.

Makes about 1 cup

3/4 cup water
1 cup sugar

1 Select a small, heavy saucepan with a long handle. Use one with a light interior (such as stainless steel) to make monitoring the changing color of the caramel easier. Fill the sink with enough water to come halfway up the sides of the saucepan.

2 Put 1/4 cup of the water and all the sugar in the saucepan and place over medium-low heat. To ensure that the sugar melts evenly, stir with a metal spoon. After about 2 minutes, when the sugar is relatively smooth and opaque, stop stirring and let the mixture cook undisturbed. Small bubbles will form at the edge of the pan and gradually grow larger and move toward the center. A good 7 minutes into cooking, bubbles will cover the entire surface and the mixture will be at a vigorous simmer. As the sugar melts, the mixture will go from opaque to clear.

If a little sugar crystallizes on the sides of the pan, don't worry. After about 15 minutes, the sugar will begin to caramelize and deepen in color. You will see a progression from champagne yellow to light tea to dark tea. When smoke starts rising, around the 20-minute mark, remove the pan from the heat and slowly swirl it. Watch the sugar closely as it will turn darker by the second; a reddish cast will set in (think the color of a big, bold red wine) as the bubbles become a lovely burnt orange. Pay attention to the color of the caramel underneath the bubbles. When the caramel is the color of black coffee or molasses, place the pan in the sink to stop the cooking. The hot pan bottom will sizzle on contact. Add the remaining 1/2 cup water; don't worry, the sugar will seize up but later dissolve. After the dramatic bubble reaction ceases, return the pan to the stove over medium heat.

3 Heat the caramel, stirring until it dissolves into the water. Remove from the heat and let cool for 10 minutes before pouring into a small heatproof glass jar. Set aside to cool completely. The result will seem slightly viscous, while the flavor will be bittersweet. Cover and store the sauce indefinitely in your kitchen cupboard.

CHICKEN STOCK
Nước Dùng Gà

RAISED BY RESOURCEFUL and persnickety parents, I always cut and bone my own chickens because I know I will get the pieces the way I want them. Leftover bones and scraps are frozen in plastic bags for future stock-making sessions. When the bags are full, it is time to make stock. If you don't maintain a supply of bones in the freezer, you can buy necks, backs, and wings at the meat counter of the supermarket or at the butcher shop.

Many Asian cooks don't salt their stock, assuming that salt will be added later. I prefer to salt my stock lightly, which allows me to gauge its overall flavor better. If time is tight, make the quick version included in the Note that follows.

Makes about 3 quarts (about 12 cups)

4 1/2 to 5 pounds chicken parts or bones with some meat on them
4 quarts water
1 large yellow onion, quartered
Chubby 3-inch piece fresh ginger, unpeeled and smashed with the
　　flat side of a cleaver or chef's knife
2 1/2 teaspoons salt

1 Rinse the chicken under cool water to remove any bloody residue. Remove and discard any loose pieces of fat. Wielding a heavy cleaver designed for chopping bones, whack the bones to break them partway or all the way through, making the cuts at 1- to 2-inch intervals, depending on the size of the bone. This exposes the marrow, which enriches the stock.

2 Put the bones in a stockpot, add the water, and place over high heat. Bring almost to a boil and then lower the heat to a simmer. For the next few minutes, use a ladle or large, shallow spoon to skim off and discard the scum that rises to the top. Add the onion, ginger, and salt and adjust the heat to maintain a gentle simmer. Let the stock cook, uncovered, for 2 1/2 hours.

3 Remove the pot from the heat and let stand undisturbed for 30 minutes, to allow the impurities to settle and congeal. Position a fine-mesh sieve (or a coarse-mesh sieve lined with cheesecloth) over a large saucepan. Gently ladle the stock through the sieve. Remove and discard the bones as they get in your way. Tilt the stockpot to ladle out as much clear stock as possible, then discard the sediment-laden liquid and any remaining bits at the bottom of the pot.

4 Taste the stock. If it is not as flavorful as you would like, simmer it to reduce the liquid and concentrate the flavors. Once you are satisfied with the taste, let the stock cool completely, cover, and refrigerate for at least 8 hours, or until the fat solidifies on the surface. Remove and discard the fat. The stock is now ready to use. Or, store in a tightly capped container in the refrigerator for up to 1 week or in the freezer for up to 3 months.

NOTE

Like many cooks, I keep a supply of canned chicken broth in my cupboard for emergencies. (Choose a brand that tastes like chicken and not much else.) Before using it for Vietnamese dishes, I doctor it to give it an Asian flavor. In a pinch, here is how to mimic homemade stock closely.

In a saucepan, dilute the canned broth (use the full-sodium kind) with water in a ratio of 2 parts broth to 1 part water. For example, if you are starting with 3 cups broth, add 1 1/2 cups water. Start with between 5 and 10 percent more liquid than what you will actually need, as there will be some evaporation during the short simmering.

For every 4 cups liquid, you will need 2 quarter-sized slices ginger and 1 scallion, cut into 3-inch lengths. Lightly smash these ingredients with the broad side of a cleaver or chef's knife. Bring the broth and water to a simmer, add the ginger and scallion, and simmer gently, uncovered, for 20 minutes. Discard the scallion and ginger. The stock is now ready to use.

COCONUT MILK
Nước Cốt Dừa

I APPRECIATE the convenience of canned coconut milk, but I admit that freshly made coconut milk has a bright flavor and soft, luscious mouthfeel that no canned product can ever match. And although you may opt for the ease of canned coconut milk most of the time, making your own milk at least once will prove rewarding.

Coconut milk is extracted from the meat of mature coconuts, which have a dried brown husk (as opposed to the green husk of young coconuts). Look for one that is heavy for its size, an indication that it has lots of meat, the source of the rich milk. Give the coconut a shake to make sure there is liquid inside, a sign that the flesh has not fermented.

Traditionally, the meat is grated, steeped in hot water, and then strained to yield the milk. The grating is done with a special round serrated blade, or the cook grates the meat while seated on a squat wooden stool to which a blade is attached. The food processor method given here is a great time-saver and yields excellent results.

Makes about 2 cups

1 mature (brown) coconut, 1³/4 to 2 pounds

1 Position a rack in the middle of the oven and preheat to 400°F. Locate the 3 black spots, or "eyes," at the top of coconut. Using a Phillips screwdriver or a hammer and large nail, pierce holes in 2 of the eyes and pour out the liquid, capturing it and reserving it to drink or discarding it. (Make sure the holes are good sized, or the water will dribble out slowly.) Put the coconut on a baking sheet and bake for 15 minutes. The heat will loosen the meat from the shell. The coconut may crack in the oven, which is fine.

2 Remove the coconut from the oven. Holding it with a dish towel, firmly tap it around the equator with a hammer until it has cracked around the entire circumference and broken apart.

Try to keep the pieces as large as possible. Use a dinner knife to pry the coconut meat from the shell. Discard the shell.

3 Using a vegetable peeler, shave off the papery brown skin from the white coconut meat. Rinse the meat to remove any excess bits of brown skin, then coarsely chop into ¹/2-inch or smaller pieces. There should be about 2 cups.

4 To yield creamy milk, I grind the coconut in a ratio of 4 parts meat to 3 parts hot water, so 2 cups coconut meat requires 1¹/2 cups hot water. Put half of the meat (about 1 cup) into a food processor. Start the machine and slowly pour in half of the water through the feed tube. Once the water has been added, let the machine run for several minutes, stopping it occasionally to scrape down the sides, until the coconut meat is finely textured and resembles slushy snow.

5 Transfer the ground meat to a clean nonterry kitchen towel, piece of muslin, or several layers of cheesecloth and wring tightly over a bowl to extract the milk. Deposit the solids in a separate bowl. Repeat the grinding and extracting with the remaining coconut meat and water. The resulting coconut milk is ready to be used in recipes. This first extraction is the best and contains nearly all of the flavorful cream (about 1 cup for a normal coconut). Some cooks extract a second, thin coconut milk by combining the solids with more hot water (1 to 1¹/2 cups) and wringing again, but I find little use for it.

6 As the coconut milk sits, it will separate into a thick, opaque cream layer and a thin, cloudy "skim" layer. Always whisk the milk to recombine before measuring it for cooking. If just coconut cream is needed, allow the milk to separate (or refrigerate the milk to coagulate the cream) and then spoon off the cream. Fresh coconut milk is best if used within hours of being made. However, you may cover it tightly and refrigerate it for 1 to 2 days or freeze it for up to 2 months.

TAMARIND LIQUID
Nước Me

WITH MODERN REFRIGERATION, there is no need to make fresh tamarind liquid each time you need it. Just as some cooks freeze cubes of stock for when they need only a small amount, I keep a stash of frozen cubes of tamarind liquid on hand. They cut down on prep time and can be used whenever a dish needs some tartness. For information on buying tamarind pulp, see page 333.

Makes about 3 cups

1 package (14 or 16 ounces) seedless tamarind pulp,
    broken into 6 chunks
4 cups water

1 In a small saucepan, combine the tamarind pulp and water over medium heat. Bring to a simmer and cook, uncovered, for 10 minutes. Remove from the heat, cover, and set aside to steep and soften for about 30 minutes, or until you can easily press the pulp against the side of the pan with a fork.

2 Roughly break up the pulp to make it easier to strain. Position a coarse-mesh sieve over a bowl and pour in the tamarind. Using a rubber spatula or metal spoon, vigorously stir and press the solids against the mesh to force as much of the pulp through as possible. If necessary, return the pulp to the saucepan, add some of the already-strained liquid, stir to loosen up more of the pulp, and then work it through the sieve again. When the pulp is spent, discard the fibrous leftovers. The resulting liquid will resemble chocolate cake batter.

3 Use the liquid immediately, or pour into ice-cube trays and freeze. Note how much each tamarind cube contains; it is typically about 2 tablespoons. Once the cubes are frozen hard, transfer them to a zip-top plastic bag and store in the freezer for up to 6 months. To make sure you use the correct amount of the liquid in a recipe, always measure it again before adding it.

BEEF STIR-FRY MARINADE
Gia Vị Ướp Thịt Bò Xào

HERE IS A HANDY marinade that I use for beef stir-fries. The combination of fish sauce and soy sauce gives the meat a wonderful savoriness that is uniquely Vietnamese.

Enough for 3/4 pound beef

1 teaspoon cornstarch
3/4 teaspoon sugar
1/4 teaspoon black pepper
2 1/2 teaspoons fish sauce
1 1/2 teaspoons light (regular) soy sauce

In a shallow bowl, combine the cornstarch, sugar, pepper, fish sauce, and soy sauce and stir to mix. Add the beef called for in the recipe, turn to coat the meat evenly, and set aside to marinate while you ready the remaining ingredients for the stir-fry.

EGG SHEETS
Trứng Tráng

CUT INTO STRIPS, these sunny yellow sheets add splashes of color and flavor to foods. When thin and delicate like a crepe, they are perfect for mixing into rice and garnishing *bún thang* noodle soup (page 217). When thick and fluffy, they punctuate boldly flavored foods, such as Beef and Jicama Hand Rolls (page 30) and Headcheese (page 170). Regardless of thickness, egg sheets are made the same way, in a nonstick skillet and flipped over to cook both sides. Here, I have given you directions for preparing thin sheets, which are a little trickier to make. I have included instructions for thick sheets in the Note that follows.

Makes 2 or 3 thin egg sheets

2 eggs
1/2 to 1 teaspoon canola or other neutral oil

1 In a small bowl, beat the eggs until blended.

2 For each egg sheet, heat 1/4 to 1/2 teaspoon oil in an 8- or 10-inch nonstick skillet over medium-low heat until hot. To test, drop in a tiny bit of egg; it should sizzle on contact. Pour about half of the beaten egg into the pan and swirl to form a thin film in the bottom. Swiftly return any excess egg to the bowl. If the egg doesn't swirl and adhere to the skillet, the pan isn't hot enough. If the egg sticks in a thick film and immediately starts to brown, your skillet is too hot. Wait for the pan to heat up or lower the heat. You want the egg to adhere quickly yet cook gently.

When the edge of the sheet starts to pull away from the skillet, after about 1 minute, use your index fingers and thumbs to pull up the egg sheet and flip it over. (It is not that hot.) Cook for another 15 seconds to dry the second side. Lift and transfer the egg sheet to a plate to cool. Repeat with the remaining egg, stacking the sheets. The total number of egg sheets you make depends on the skillet size and how thin they are.

3 When the sheets are finished, cut them into whatever size you need. You can save time by preparing the egg sheets several hours in advance and keeping them at room temperature covered with plastic wrap.

NOTE

To make a thick egg sheet, use the same number of eggs but increase the oil to 2 teaspoons. You need the extra oil to yield a fluffy, thick texture. Pour the oil into the skillet and heat over medium heat until hot. Pour in all of the beaten egg and swirl to cover the pan bottom evenly. When the edge of the sheet begins to pull away from the skillet, flip the sheet over with a spatula (the extra oil and higher heat make the sheet too hot to handle with your fingers). Cook the second side for 15 to 20 seconds, or until it is dry, then transfer to the plate.

TOASTED SESAME RICE CRACKERS
Bánh Đa

THESE CRUNCHY, nutty rice crackers flecked with white or black sesame seeds turn up in a variety of roles on the Vietnamese table. They may be munched as a snack, used like a tortilla chip to scoop up food, or crumbled and mixed into dry noodle dishes. Although I prefer *bánh đa* crunchy, some folks add them to noodle soups, where they soften into chewy accents. They may even be soaked in water until pliable and then wrapped in rice paper with other ingredients to create hand rolls.

These unique crackers are mostly available at Viet markets and delis and at some Chinese markets with a large Vietnamese clientele. They are usually stocked near the rice paper. Dried and untoasted, the crackers look like translucent rounds of hard plastic. Eight-inch ones are easiest to work with. Look for them bundled in short stacks of six to eight, wrapped in plastic or packed in bags and sealed with staples (which means they are probably locally made and very good). Pretoasted crackers are often broken, so skip the convenience and buy them untoasted. Once toasted and cooled, the crackers are broken into lovely shards and served. Here are two options for toasting them.

Oven Toasting: Position a rack in the middle level of a conventional oven or toaster oven and preheat to 400°F. Place the rice cracker directly on the rack and bake for 3 to 4 minutes, or until golden. (Clear, shiny crackers don't color as much as the translucent ones.) Flip the cracker occasionally with tongs to ensure even cooking. The cracker may blister as it toasts. This method yields consistent, beautiful color and the cracker doesn't warp much.

Open-Fire Grilling: Toast the cracker on a charcoal grill over a medium fire (you can hold your hand over the rack for only 4 to 5 seconds) or on a gas grill preheated to medium, turning it over several times with tongs to expose both sides equally to the fire. You will get big bubbles (extra crunch), unusual warping, and a little char, all of which lend more character to the finished cracker. Plus, there is the thrill of watching it soften, blister, and then settle into a crisp finish. However, the color will not be as even as when oven toasting.

NOTE

In central and southern Vietnam, these crackers may be called *bánh tráng mè*, which is easily confused with the term for rice papers, *bánh tráng*; *mè* means "sesame seeds." I use *bánh đa* (the northern Vietnamese term) to avoid misunderstanding. Look for both terms when shopping.

You may toast the crackers 2 days in advance and store them in a zip-top plastic bag at room temperature. If you are making a recipe in this book that calls for the crackers and can't find them, substitute lightly salted tortilla chips.

GROUND TOASTED RICE
Thính

RICE THAT HAS BEEN slowly toasted and then ground is mixed into smooth meat pastes for added texture and depth or sprinkled onto foods as a garnish. It can be purchased, usually packed in small plastic bags, but it is more fragrant and flavorful when freshly made. Some cooks like to grind the rice in an old-fashioned hand-cranked coffee or spice grinder. I prefer the speed of an electric coffee grinder that I reserve exclusively for grinding spices.

Rice, in amount specified in recipe

1 Select a skillet in which the rice fits in a thin layer. Put the rice in the pan, place over medium-low heat, and toast the rice, shaking the pan occasionally. The grains will first turn opaque and then golden. When the rice starts to show color, monitor the skillet closely, shaking it more frequently so that each grain toasts evenly. The grains will give off a fragrant nuttiness and shrink a bit, and the small holes at the end of each grain will be dark and visible. In general, it takes about 15 minutes to toast rice properly. When the grains are golden and/or golden brown, they are ready. Remove from the heat and let cool.

2 When the grains are cool enough to handle, grind the rice in 1-tablespoon batches in a clean, dry electric coffee grinder. Pulse each batch about 8 times to achieve the texture of fine cornmeal. Do not grind to a fine powder. Put the ground rice through a coarse-mesh sieve, return the bits that didn't go through the sieve to the grinder, and add the next batch of whole toasted grains. Repeat, passing each batch through the sieve and returning any bits to the grinder. At the end, there will be some bits that will have to be discarded. You can save time by preparing the ground toasted rice several hours in advance and keeping it at room temperature covered with plastic wrap.

GROUND STEAMED MUNG BEAN
Đậu Xanh

GROUND COOKED MUNG BEANS are used as an ingredient and a garnish in Vietnamese cooking. In both roles, they contribute a buttery richness, a highly desirable characteristic known as *bùi*. You must steam the yellow hulled and split beans, as they easily turn mushy and lose their nuanced flavor if boiled. A stainless-steel Chinese steamer is ideal because the tray is easy to manage and clean. If the tray holes are larger than 3/16 inch in diameter, line the tray with parchment paper, leaving a few holes uncovered for heat circulation. This is particularly important if you are steaming a small quantity of beans and don't want to lose too many to the steamer bottom. It is not as crucial with a larger amount because the beans expand and stick together as they cook, forming a barrier of sorts.

Dried mung beans expand to about three times their original volume during cooking, so if you need 1 cup cooked, start with 1/3 cup raw dried beans.

Dried yellow hulled and split mung beans

1 Place the mung beans in a bowl and add water to cover by 1 inch. Let soak for 2 hours, or longer if you must. The beans absorb only a certain amount of water and can actually stand overnight. However, I typically soak them for 2 to 6 hours.

2 Drain the beans and put them in the steamer tray, spreading them out evenly. Fill the steamer bottom halfway with water and bring to a rolling boil over high heat. Place the tray in the steamer, cover, and steam for about 8 minutes, or until the mung beans are tender. Remove the tray from the steamer bottom and set aside until the beans cool completely. (Or, transfer the beans to a bowl to cool.)

3 Process the cooled beans in an electric mini-chopper or food processor to a fluffy consistency. It should look like fine cornmeal but hold together when a small bit is pinched between your fingers. The ground beans are now ready to use.

NOTE

Because ground mung beans are a mainstay of the Viet kitchen, I typically buy a 14- or 16-ounce bag of beans, steam and grind the whole bag, and then freeze the ground beans in 1-cup portions for later use. They may be frozen for up to 3 months. Each portion will thaw at room temperature in about 2 hours.

HOW TO COOK, CLEAN, AND PICK CRAB

COOKING LIVE CRABS and then picking their meat takes time, but you will be amply rewarded at the table. These instructions are for a Dungeness crab, which is what I use in my recipes, but they may be applied to other types of crab as well.

1. To cook the crab, fill a large pot two-thirds full with water. Add 1 tablespoon salt and bring to a rolling boil over high heat. Use tongs to grasp the crab firmly from the rear and then, holding it top side down, slide it head first into the pot. If the crab thrashes about, press down on it with the tongs until it is still; the legs will fold inward. Return the water to a gentle boil and cook for 8 minutes per pound. Transfer the crab to a plate or baking sheet for about 20 minutes, or until it is cool enough to handle.

2 Position yourself near the sink and have a plastic bag nearby to hold unwanted shell bits. Put the crab, top side down, on the work surface. Pull off the claws and legs and pile them nearby. Lift up and break off the triangular flap (the apron). Holding the crab down with one hand, pry off the body section with the other hand, lifting from the back hinge. Set the body section aside.

3 Discard the shell if you don't want the tomalley (liver) and fat. Otherwise, pour out the liquid inside the shell, stopping short of the more solid, thickish contents, which is the greenish gold tomalley and white fat. Use a teaspoon to scrape the tomalley and fat into a small bowl and discard the empty shell.

4 Discard the fang-shaped spongy gills on the body section. Snap off and discard the thin jaws. If present, discard the reddish membrane that covers the center and the squiggly white pieces underneath. Scrape out any additional tomalley from the body section with the spoon.

5 Break the body in half with your hands. Use your fingers to remove the meat from all the little channels, depositing it in another bowl. Then crack and remove the meat from the claws and legs, adding it to the bowl. (A metal nutcracker is handy for cracking, and the pointy tip of a crab leg is perfect for digging out the meat.)

6 A 2-pound Dungeness crab yields about 1/2 pound meat. To save time, cook, clean, and pick the crab a day or two in advance, then cover the bowls of meat and tomalley and fat and refrigerate.

HOW TO CLEAN SQUID

BUYING FRESH SQUID and cleaning it yourself guarantees the best flavor. Yes, it is a tedious job, but put on some music and follow these directions, which are adapted from Barbara Tropp's estimable *China Moon Cookbook*.

1 If you are a right-hander, position a cutting board on the left side of your kitchen sink. (Left-handers should reverse directions.) In the sink, directly beneath the edge of the cutting board, place a bowl or a plastic bag to catch the innards. Keep a colander in the sink for holding and rinsing the cleaned squid.

2 Place each squid on the board and chop off the tentacles just above the eyes. Put the tentacles in the colander.

3 Grab the head just below the eyes, pull out the insides, and drop into the trash bowl. Use your fingers to remove the swimming fins and add them to the trash bowl.

4 Turn your knife over and use the dull edge to scrape the squid from the pointy tip toward the head hole, forcing the slimy innards out and into the trash bowl. Repeat the scraping 3 or 4 times, turning the squid over at the midway point. Stop when you feel the squid tube is free of innards. The scraping will also have removed most or all of the mottled skin, leaving the tube white.

5 Locate the quill by reaching inside the cavity or looking for its protruding tip at the head hole. Pull out the quill and discard, making sure all of it has been removed.

6 Remove any remaining skin with your fingers and place the cleaned squid in the colander. When all of the squid are cleaned, rinse them under lots of cold running water, flushing out the insides as well as cleaning the outsides. Cut the squid as directed in individual recipes. You may clean the squid a day in advance and keep well covered in the refrigerator until you are ready to cook. The squid will weep water as they sit, so drain well before cooking.

GUIDE TO INGREDIENTS

Each entry includes both the common English term and the Vietnamese. When there are two Vietnamese terms separated by a slash, the first one is used by southern and central Viet speakers and the second is used by northerners.

Annatto seeds (*hạt điều*)
In many cuisines, these heart-shaped seeds (illustrated on page 12) from the evergreen annatto tree are used to impart orange-yellow brilliance to foods. It is no different in the Vietnamese kitchen, where cooks release the seeds' color by frying them in oil or grinding them to a powder; I grind the hard seeds in an electric spice grinder. Only a small amount is used, so their slightly musky flavor doesn't overwhelm. Rusty red seeds are fresh and flavorful; avoid brown ones. Purchase annatto seeds (a.k.a. achiote) at Asian or Latin markets. Regular supermarkets sometimes carry them where Mexican spices are stocked.

Banana leaves (*lá chuối*)
These large green leaves play an important role in traditional Vietnamese cooking. Sticky rice dumplings are often steamed on banana leaves to prevent sticking, and foods wrapped and cooked in them absorb their pale green color and mild tealike flavor and fragrance. The leaves also make beautiful plate

---

Dried shiitake mushrooms, soaking

liners and natural placemats. Frozen 1-pound packages are a convenient modern alternative to cutting a leaf from a nearby tree. Look for very flat packages in Chinese, Southeast Asian, and Latin markets. They contain thin, soft leaves that are easier to fold and manipulate.

When working with frozen banana leaves, partially thaw the package until you can gently pry the leaves open. Use scissors to cut off a tear-free section that meets your needs (torn leaves are hard to work with), then refold and refreeze the unused portion. As you trim the section to size, don't let the stiff ribs dictate your cut (or you will get a misshapen piece of leaf) and always remove any dark brown edge. Before using the leaf in cooking, rinse it and then wipe it dry with a paper towel to remove the white residue. If a leaf is particularly stiff, blanch it quickly or pass it over the flame of a gas stove or a hot electric burner.

Cellophane noodles (*bún tàu/miến*)
For a discussion of the types of noodles used by Vietnamese cooks, see page 200.

Chiles, fresh and dried (*ớt*)
Viet food is not nearly as hot as Thai food, but chiles are still important. They are traditionally enjoyed seeds and all so that you get their full effect. The fresh chile most commonly sold at

Asian and farmers' markets is the small, slender Thai or Thai bird chile called *ớt hiểm* (illustrated on page 174). I like to grow my own chiles and purchase several plants (Thai Dragon is a good performer) each spring. You can freeze your freshly harvested or purchased chiles in zip-top plastic bags. They will keep for up to a year and are easy to cut straight from the freezer.

Aim for a balance of fragrance and heat when picking potent peppers. Remember, you smell the perfume of the chile oil before you taste it. Despite what many people claim, the size and color of chiles are not always indicators of their potency. I have tasted largish orange, small yellow, purple-brown, and tiny purple-black chiles that pack a punch. If Thai chiles are unavailable, you may substitute serrano or Fresno chiles. Both offer heat but not much fragrance.

When I am working with hot chiles, I don't wear rubber gloves to protect my hands from their fiery oils. Instead, I minimize contact by using the stem of the chile to scoot cut-up pieces and seeds onto the knife blade, and then I use the stem again to push them off the blade to wherever they are needed. If I do end up touching the seeds or inner membranes, the source of most of the heat, I wash my hands promptly afterward.

Widely available dried red chile flakes (*ớt khô*) are used when subtle heat and/or a reddish cast is desired. Spicy Hue Beef and Rice Noodle Soup (page 212) and Mellow Chile-Garlic Mix (page 315) are good examples of dried chile flakes in action.

Chile sauce (*tương ớt*)

Two chile sauces have become synonymous with Vietnamese food in the United States: Huy Fong brand smooth Sriracha hot chile sauce (*tương ớt Sriracha*, illustrated on page 12) in the squirt bottle and coarse chile garlic sauce (*tương ớt tỏi Việt-Nam*) in the jar. The former is pleasantly hot and slightly sweet, while the latter is milder, more nuanced, and slightly tangy. Both sport Kelly green plastic tops and the proud rooster logo of their manufacturer. (The rooster is the astrological sign of the company's Chinese Vietnamese owner, David Tran, and the company is named after the boat in which he escaped from Vietnam, where he had enjoyed success making and selling sauces.) Compared to their counterparts in Vietnam, these

sauces are brighter in flavor and more versatile, working well as both an ingredient and a condiment in a variety of cuisines. Both are available at Asian markets and some mainstream markets.

Chinese egg noodles (*mì*)

For a discussion of the types of noodles used by Vietnamese cooks, see page 200.

Chinese five-spice powder (*bột ngũ vị hương*)

Originally named for the symbolic power of the number five (believed to ensure good health), this mixture today doesn't always have five spices. It typically includes star anise, fennel seeds or aniseeds, cinnamon, cloves, licorice root, Sichuan peppercorns, and sometimes ground ginger. Often added to heady meat marinades, a little bit of the powder goes a long way. The amber, brown, or tan mixture is sold in plastic bags and glass jars at Chinese and Vietnamese markets and some supermarkets. Use your nose to find a well-balanced, fragrant product. It should not be too medicinal or too sweet. At this writing, I am particularly fond of an elegant jarred blend that lists fennel as the first ingredient. Don't mistake this five-spice mixture for a spice mixture that contains white pepper and salt. Keep five-spice powder in an airtight jar in a cool, dark cupboard. It is good as long as it has a pronounced fragrance.

Chinese sweet sausages (*lạp xưởng*)

Available at Chinese and Vietnamese markets, these dried sausages look shriveled up and hard whether they are shrink-wrapped or are free of packaging and hung from strings at meat counters. Don't be put off by their appearance. *Lop chong* (the Cantonese name) are rich, savory, and absolutely delicious. They are made with pork, chicken, pork liver, or duck liver and are about six inches long. I prefer the standard pork sausages that taste sweet and have a nice amount of fat without the heaviness of liver; those made with rice wine taste even better. While these sausages can be diced and added to foods during cooking, they are generally steamed first and then thinly sliced for serving with rice (regular or sticky) or other foods. Refrigerated, the sausages will keep for weeks. Frozen, they will keep for months.

Cinnamon (*quế*)

Even though it is technically cassia bark, Vietnamese cinnamon is considered by some cooks to be the best cinnamon in the world. It is rich, dark, and offers a spicy, fragrant punch. Cinnamon is not heavily used in the Viet kitchen, though the broth for *phở* (beef noodle soup) would be lackluster without it. Ground cinnamon also figures prominently in *chả quế* (roasted cinnamon sausage). You don't have to use Vietnamese cassia cinnamon for these recipes. Just select what is most fragrant.

Coconut juice (*nước dừa*)

This slightly cloudy juice in young, green coconuts is often enjoyed as a refreshing drink, either straight from the coconut or canned. Mildly sweet, the juice (a.k.a. coconut water) is also a favorite ingredient in southern Viet cooking. Since good young coconuts are rarely available in the United States, I purchase canned juice at Asian and Mexican markets, where it is shelved with other canned juices. Mostly imported from Thailand, the cans contain chunks of white coconut meat to remind you of the experience of sipping juice from the nut itself. For the best flavor, choose the brand with the least amount of sugar. Coconut juice isn't the same as coconut milk.

Coconut milk (*nước cốt dừa*)

The sweet, creamy liquid pressed from the grated flesh of mature, brown coconuts enriches a number of Viet dishes, particularly those prepared in the more tropical south, where coconut palms flourish. Most people know that coconut milk is high in saturated fat and assume that it is unhealthy because of it. But a number of independent studies have shown that the saturated fat in coconut milk is a good one. It is not hydrogenated (in other words, it is not an unhealthy trans fatty acid) and its chief fatty acid, lauric acid, is easily metabolized, which means it doesn't hang around to become bad cholesterol.

Cooks in Vietnam typically use fresh coconut milk (page 318), but I rarely prepare it because it is time-consuming and good coconuts are hard to find in the United States. More important, great canned coconut milk is available. Chaokoh and Mae Ploy brands from Thailand offer excellent flavor and creaminess; both are sold at Asian markets and the former is stocked at some supermarkets. If you need the creamy plug on top, don't shake the can. Otherwise, shake or whisk the contents well before measuring the amount needed. Always use unsweetened coconut milk, not the stuff that goes into a piña colada. Also, avoid insipid "light" coconut milk.

Cornstarch (*bột bắp*)

The Vietnamese started using cornstarch only after they arrived in the United States. Traditionally, tapioca starch was used, but when it couldn't be found here, cooks switched to what was conveniently stocked at supermarkets, which was cornstarch. The two starches are similar. They both thicken with a clear sheen without influencing the taste of foods, and when used in batters for deep-frying, they yield a crunchy crust. However, when used in rice flour batters, there are subtle differences. In the shortcut batters for the crepes on pages 276 and 278, cornstarch produces a slightly crispier texture than tapioca starch. In the batter for *bánh cuốn* (steamed rice crepe rolls, page 270), the two starches are combined to create a texture that is tender yet chewy and slightly firm.

Culantro (*ngò gai*)

For a discussion of fresh herbs commonly eaten with Vietnamese food, see page 17.

Curry powder (*bột cà-ri*)

Several kinds of Indian-style curry powder are sold at Chinese and Vietnamese markets, but the most popular product among Viet cooks is a spicy-hot blend bottled by D&D Gold. It comes in a tall jar and is described as Madras curry powder. For decades, my mom has been a fan of Sun Brand's premium blend, which comes in a metal container and is available at gourmet markets and specialty grocers; few Asian markets stock it. Sun Brand curry powder smells of sweet coriander, while D&D Gold favors turmeric. Both curry powders are made in the United States and contain salt.

Dried shrimp (*tôm khô*)

For the most part, Viet cooks use dried shrimp like other Asian cooks do, to add an alluring sweet brininess to food. They are also snacked on like peanuts, usually with cold beer. Many kinds are available in Vietnam, but the huge *tôm he* are special. About 2 inches long, they are softened in water and then torn or pounded into shreds to be used as a salty, briny, orange garnish. Dried shrimp in the United States are not as spectacular. Sold in plastic packages labeled small, medium, or large, they are usually in the cold-food section at Asian markets. Buy whole shrimp (not shrimp powder) that are pinkish orange. Medium or large shrimp have more flavor than small ones. Refrigerate the package to prevent the shrimp from developing an off odor. When a recipe calls for chopping dried shrimp, I soften them first with a rinsing or soaking.

Fine shrimp sauce (*mắm ruốc/mắm tôm*)

Compelling, pungent, and stinky are commonly used to describe this sauce popular in southern China and Southeast Asia. Although made much like fish sauce, shrimp sauce is thick like toothpaste and purplish. For Western palates, it is probably the most difficult Asian fermented seafood product to accept. (But what about a ripe, room-temperature Camembert or Roquefort? They are quite heady, too.) Shrimp sauce is not eaten right out of the jar. A bit of it is blended into foods or dipping sauces, where it imparts an aroma and savoriness that deepen the overall flavor of a dish. Central and northern Viet cooks have a penchant for the sauce.

Sold in jars at Chinese and Southeast Asian markets, shrimp sauce may be smooth or coarse. I prefer the smooth version labeled fine shrimp sauce. Koon Chun and Lee Kum Kee are two good brands. After opening, refrigerate shrimp sauce to keep its smell at bay. When measuring it for recipes, use a small plastic spatula to push it out of the measuring spoon, so you won't have to touch it and later smell it on your finger.

Fish mint (*diếp cá*)

For a discussion of fresh herbs commonly eaten with Vietnamese food, see page 17.

Fish sauce (*nước mắm*)

For a lengthy discussion on Vietnam's national condiment, see page 13.

Flat rice noodles (*bánh phở*)

For a discussion of the types of noodles used by Vietnamese cooks, see page 200.

Galangal, fresh and dried (*riềng*)

A relative of ginger, galangal is spicy hot, pungent, and rather medicinal. Although the rhizome (illustrated on page 174) is popular throughout Southeast Asia, especially in Thailand, it is not a major ingredient in the Viet kitchen. Galangal is present in just a handful of robust dishes from the central and northern regions, including fish simmered in caramel sauce (page 109), turmeric catfish with rice noodles (page 226), pickled shrimp, and dog (or fake dog) stew.

When possible, use fresh galangal, particularly young pieces that are ivory or pale yellow. At about four dollars a pound, it is pricey, so I use what I need and cut the rest into 1-inch pieces and freeze them for up to several months. Unlike ginger, there is no need to peel galangal before using it. When fresh galangal is unavailable, buy a small plastic bag of sliced dried galangal (thin, smaller slices reconstitute faster), and use one-third to one-half the quantity of fresh galangal. Ground dried galangal (*bột riềng*) usually lacks flavor and fragrance, so use it only as a last resort. Don't confuse chunky galangal with fingerlike clusters of lesser galangal, which, as the name suggests, is less pungent.

Ginger, fresh (*gừng*)

Like its pungent cousin galangal, ginger is a rhizome, not a root. It is an indispensable ingredient in Vietnamese cooking, so I keep plenty on hand. When buying fresh ginger, select heavy, hard rhizomes with taut skin. Wrinkly ones are over the hill. Fibrous, more mature ginger (check where the knobs are broken) is hotter and more flavorful, but may be hard to cut finely or mince. Store ginger in a typical thin produce-section plastic bag in the vegetable crisper, where it will stay fresh for weeks.

Glutinous rice flour (*bột gạo nếp*)

Nothing more than ground grains of sticky rice, glutinous rice flour, also known as sweet rice flour, is mostly found in savory and sweet cakes and dumplings. I typically combine two brands to achieve dough with the ideal chewy-firm texture. Mochiko Blue Star brand by Koda Farms is a premium flour that cooks up to a nice firmness but is not chewy enough when used alone. Thai glutinous rice flour is too elastic to be used alone. But when mixed together, the two flours produce dough that is perfectly balanced. At Asian markets, Mochiko Blue Star flour (labeled sweet rice flour) is sold in boxes near the plastic bags of Thai glutinous flours, which are generally all of good quality. Don't confuse glutinous rice flour with regular rice flour (see the Rice Flour entry), or your recipe will fail.

Hoisin sauce (*tương hòi xìn*)

Measure how much hoisin sauce Viet cooks use and you will understand the extent of Chinese influence on the cuisine. The sweet-garlicky-spicy Chinese sauce made from soybeans is sold in industrial-sized cans at Vietnamese markets. *Phở* joints offer it as a standard ketchuplike condiment, a practice that I abhor because a squirt of it ruins a well-constructed broth. I use it sparingly and buy it in small jars (Koon Chun and Lee Kum Kee are good brands) to prepare a garlicky dipping sauce and to add to Chinese-style meat marinades. It is a wonderful ingredient when used judiciously. After opening, refrigerate hoisin sauce and it will keep indefinitely.

Lemongrass (*xả*)

Vietnamese food would be lackluster without this fragrant tropical grass (illustrated on page 174). A relative of citronella, the fibrous stalks impart a delicate perfume similar to lemon verbena. When selecting lemongrass, choose stalks that are rigid, tight, and 1/2 to 3/4 inch thick at the widest point. Avoid old ones that bend easily or have dry blades that have separated and curled. Slip the stalks into a plastic bag and store in the refrigerator in the vegetable crisper. They will keep for weeks.

To trim lemongrass before using, chop off and discard the tough bottom 1/2 inch of the base that contains a hard core.

Then chop off the green, woody top section and discard it or reserve it for another use. (For example, you can boil it in water for 15 minutes for a refreshing tea, or you can use it to make the ice cream on page 283.) Peel away any loose or dry outer layers to reveal a smooth and tight stalk. The usable section will be 3 to 8 inches long, depending on the size of the original stalk. (You can store trimmed lemongrass in a zip-top plastic bag in the freezer for up to 3 months. Thawed lemongrass retains most of its flavor and is easier to chop than fresh.)

To chop or mince lemongrass, first cut the trimmed stalk into 3- to 4-inch sections. Then halve each section lengthwise. Place each half cut side down and cut crosswise into very thin half-moons (the thinner the better). Finally, rocking the knife blade over the slices, chop the pieces to the size needed. Mincing may be done in an electric mini-chopper. A medium stalk yields about 3 tablespoons minced lemongrass. Expect twice as much from hefty stalks.

Grow lemongrass from starters sold at nurseries or farmers' markets. If you find stalks with their roots still intact, plant them in a pot or bed. Easier yet, purchase stalks with fat, pale green bases and remove any dry outer sheaths. If the bottoms are black from age, cut away a thin layer to reveal the light core. Put the stalks in water and place in a sunny location. Wait for a few weeks for roots to appear before planting. Lemongrass enjoys sun and good drainage. Harvest stalks by cutting each at its base.

Long-grain rice (*gạo tẻ*)

For a discussion of the types of rice used by Vietnamese cooks, see page 14.

Maggi Seasoning sauce (*Maggi*)

Invented in Switzerland in the late 1880s, this versatile sauce was most likely brought by French colonialists to Vietnam, where it became a staple and symbol of European sophistication. Languidly pronounced "mah-ji" by Vietnamese, the amazingly good and meaty-tasting brown liquid (despite the flavor, it is made from pure vegetable protein) is often sprinkled onto rice and into baguette sandwiches, used as a dipping sauce, added to marinades, and tossed with Western-style noodles. There are two varieties of Maggi, the more robust kind made in China and the delicately flavored European version produced in Germany. When I am cooking, I prefer the Chinese one, which is sold at Asian, Latin, and mainstream supermarkets; Viet markets also carry the pricier European version, which is great for table use. Maggi is made by the Nestlé company. Poor imitations abound, so make sure you have the real condiment in the unusual long-necked bottle.

Mung beans (*đậu xanh*)

After soybeans, the basis of tofu, mung beans are the next important legume in Vietnam. They grow into bean sprouts, and cellophane noodles are made from them. Unhulled mung beans, which means their green skins are intact, are used less often than hulled beans, which have their yellow flesh exposed. Before modernization, soaked unhulled beans were laboriously rubbed by hand to remove the green skins. Thank goodness the hulled ones are now available at reasonable prices at Asian, Indian, and Middle Eastern markets and health-food stores. Ground cooked mung beans (page 322) contribute rich, buttery goodness to savory and sweet foods.

Oyster sauce (*dầu hào*)

The widespread use of oyster sauce (also called oyster-flavored sauce) in the Viet kitchen reflects how Vietnamese cooks have embraced Cantonese ingredients and traditions. Whenever a little rich, briny, salty-sweet flavor is needed, oyster sauce is used. I like to combine oyster sauce with fish sauce to underscore the sealike character of the sauce. There are many brands and qualities of oyster sauce to choose from. At minimum, buy Lee Kum Kee's basic oyster sauce. Better yet, step up to their premium sauce, which has the woman and boy on the label; it has more oyster extractives and a richer flavor. After opening, store oyster sauce in the refrigerator, where it will keep indefinitely. Before using, let it stand at room temperature for several minutes, so it is easier to pour and measure.

Peanuts (*đậu phụng/đậu lạc*)

The peanut plays a key role in Vietnamese cooking, just as it does in the cuisines of other Southeast Asian countries and of China. It is unclear how the legume (yes, it is a bean) got from the American tropics to Asia, but people undoubtedly took to it with vigor. In Vietnam, peanuts are used to garnish food, made into candy, and added to vegetarian dishes for protein. Raw peanuts are treated like shell beans and may be boiled in the shell for a snack, simmered in stews, or steamed with sticky rice.

Roasted peanuts are used more often than raw peanuts. When my family first came to the United States, we toasted unskinned peanuts in a skillet and then rubbed the papery skins off with our hands. That old-fashioned, time-consuming method was all we knew, until we "discovered" unsalted roasted peanuts at specialty grocery stores and health-food markets. Freeze a supply so they are handy and remain fresh.

Red perilla (*tía tô*)

For a discussion of fresh herbs commonly eaten with Vietnamese food, see page 17.

Rice (*gạo*)

For a discussion of the types of rice used by Vietnamese cooks, see page 14.

Rice flour (*bột gạo tẻ*)

Milled from long-grain rice, rice flour is an essential ingredient in a host of Vietnamese specialties, such as Sizzling Crepes (page 274). Rice flour from Thailand works best. Sold in 1-pound plastic bags at Asian markets, it is fine and soft and cooks up light, without the graininess found in other rice flours. As David Thompson explains in his comprehensive *Thai Food*, Thai rice flour is made by soaking rice overnight and then grinding it the next day into a paste. Dried in the sun, the paste becomes flour. All Thai rice flours are generally of good quality; Erawan brand is popular. Don't mistakenly choose glutinous (sweet) rice flour (*bột gạo nếp*) when shopping for rice flour. Most manufacturers use different-colored lettering to distinguish the two flours.

Rice paddy herb (*rau om*)

For a discussion of fresh herbs commonly eaten with Vietnamese food, see page 17.

Rice paper (*bánh tráng*)

One of the unique aspects of Vietnamese cooking and dining is wrapping food up in sheaths of translucent rice paper. Aside from looking pretty and holding a bunch of goodies together, they contribute chewy texture and a slight tang to whatever they encase. Extremely hard to make at home, rice papers are traditionally purchased. They are widely available at Asian markets, as well as some gourmet groceries and health-food stores. Rice papers used for wrapping food are called *bánh tráng*. Don't confuse them with *bánh tráng mè* (known as *bánh da* in northern Vietnam), which are thicker rice crackers that contain sesame seeds and require toasting before eating.

When selecting rice paper, choose a comfortable size, such as the 8½-inch round (about the size of a regular flour tortilla). It is the easiest to manipulate, and all the recipes in this book use that size. Skilled cooks use the smaller rounds and triangles for making thumb-sized rolls.

Also look for rice papers made of all rice or a combination of rice and tapioca starch. The more rice in the papers, the more opaque and the thicker they are. Papers made with rice and tapioca starch are somewhat translucent and appear loftier in their packaging. Because they are thinner, they conveniently soften in warm or lukewarm water, as opposed to the hotter water demanded by the thicker papers. Avoid the superthin, see-through all–tapioca starch papers, which lack the tang of rice, go limp in a flash, and tear easily. They are often labeled *bánh tráng dẻo* (soft and pliable rice paper) or *bánh tráng mỏng* (thin rice paper). Despite what the ingredients listing may say, rice paper doesn't contain wheat flour; it is a translation problem. The reliable Red Rose brand is borrowed by many producers as a symbol of quality. The imposters are often quite good, so don't shy away from them. Three Ladies is another good brand. Rice paper can be stored indefinitely in the cupboard.

USING RICE PAPER

To make rice paper pliable so you can use it, fill a wide, shallow bowl or baking dish partway with water. The water temperature must be right for your rice papers, so do a test dip; thicker rice papers need hotter water. If you are serving hand rolls at the table, set out one or two communal dipping bowls for diners. If the papers require hot water, consider using a portable electric burner. Preheat the burner in advance and boil the water on the stove first. Then pour the hot water into a wide, shallow pan and set it on the burner.

When dipping rice paper in water, try to get it only moderately wet on both sides, rather than soften it completely. Horizontally slide or rotate it in the water, and do not let it linger too long or it will go limp, collapse on itself, and stick together. Once it is damp and has softened slightly, put it on a flat work surface. If you're making a bunch of rolls in advance of serving, work in batches and use a large work surface like a cutting board, inverted baking sheet, or dish towel. For do-it-yourself hand rolls that are part of a meal, have diners put their wet rice papers on their dinner plates.

After it is dipped, the rice paper takes a minute or two to soften fully and become usable. It is ready for wrapping and rolling when it is pliable and slightly tacky.

To wrap with a rice paper round, mentally divide it into three horizontal sections and center the filling in the bottom third, near the edge closest to you. Bring the lower edge up over the filling, then fold in the two sides, and finally roll the entire thing up. With triangles, position the curved edge closest to you and follow the same guidelines for positioning your filling and for wrapping. If you mess up, remember that rice paper is forgiving. Plus, most packages contain plenty of papers for beginners to practice.

Round rice noodles (*bún*)
For a discussion of the types of noodles used by Vietnamese cooks, see page 200.

Sesame oil (*dầu mè*)
This rich, nutty, amber-colored oil made from roasted sesame seeds is usually added to Chinese-style dishes in the Viet kitchen. Sesame oil burns easily, so it is used as a flavorful seasoning oil, rather than for cooking. Japanese toasted sesame oils are excellent, particularly Kadoya brand.

Sesame seeds (*mè/vừng*)
Although sesame seeds are commonly associated with Asian food, they are thought to be native to Africa, or perhaps to Iran or India, since they have been cultivated there for millennia. They were probably introduced to China by Persian traders in the earlier part of the Christian era, making them a Chinese food ingredient for more than two thousand years. Vietnamese cooks don't use sesame seeds to the extent that Chinese, Japanese, and Korean cooks do, but they are still a staple. The tiny seeds are always toasted in a dry skillet before they are used, with the exception of the raw seeds added to sesame seed crackers. Toast sesame seeds in a skillet over medium heat, stirring frequently until they are lightly golden (about 8 minutes for 1 cup toasted in a large skillet, 3 minutes for 2 tablespoons toasted in a medium skillet); let the seeds cool before using. Toasted sesame seeds are used as a garnish, are made into candies, and are pounded with sugar and/or salt for sprinkling on rice.

Hulled white sesame seeds are used more often than black ones. They can be found priced inexpensively at Asian markets and in the bulk section of health-food stores. Select the palest golden seeds and sniff (if you can) to ensure freshness. To save time, keep a small stash of toasted sesame seeds in the freezer.

Shaoxing rice wine (*rượu đế/rượu trắng*)
Aromatic and pleasantly nutty tasting, this rice wine is the standard spirit in Chinese cooking. It adds an unmistakable flavor and fragrance to food. I exclusively use Pagoda brand, which is actually made in Shaoxing, in Zhejiang Province. The tall 750-milliliter bottles are sold at Chinese markets. Substitute a good dry sherry when Shaoxing rice wine is unavailable. Avoid Shaoxing "cooking wine" and "cooking sherry," which are salted.

Shiitake mushrooms, dried (*nấm đông cô khô/nấm hương khô*)
The popularity of Asian cooking has made these mushrooms, also known as Chinese black mushrooms, widely available both fresh and dried. Vietnamese cooks, like their Chinese brethren, prefer the intensity of the dried ones. Their musty fragrance, meaty texture, and deep flavor contribute unrivaled sumptuousness to dishes. Buy whole mushrooms, not presliced ones, which are of questionable quality. Look for thick mushrooms with deep white fissures on the caps. They may be labeled *hana*, or "flower" mushroom, a term Japanese packagers use to signal the highest grade. Second-grade mushrooms, labeled superior, are also thick but have fewer fissures.

Asian markets and herbal shops are the best places to look for these mushrooms (premium mushrooms make great gifts). Beware of cheap deals on packages with beautiful big ones. Too often a bunch of scrawny mushrooms of lesser quality are hidden underneath. I keep dried shiitake mushrooms in a plastic container at room temperature; others prefer to freeze them.

To reconstitute dried shiitake mushrooms, soak them for at least 8 hours or overnight in water to cover; the temperature of the water doesn't matter. Follow this instruction and the rehydrated mushrooms will be deeply flavored and amazingly firm and velvety when cut. A rushed soaking in hot water won't yield the same superior results. Before using the mushrooms, rinse out any particles of sand or dirt trapped under the gills, give each a gentle squeeze to expel excess water, and slice off the knobby stem. Reconstituted shiitake mushrooms, drained of their soaking water, can be refrigerated for several days.

Sorrel (*rau chua*)
For a discussion of fresh herbs commonly eaten with Vietnamese food, see page 17.

Soy sauce (*nước tương/xì dầu*)

Soy sauces are not all the same. There are many kinds and they all taste different. Chinese soy sauces, the light (regular) and dark kinds, are what Viet cooks use. Light soy sauce, sometimes called thin soy sauce, is not low in sodium. It is merely light in color. By comparison, dark (black) soy sauce is a touch sweet and deeper in flavor and color. It is great for heady, robust dishes and yields a lovely mahogany color in roasted meats. Pearl River Bridge makes excellent soy sauces. The superior is good, but for pennies more, the golden label superior, which is fermented longer, is more complex and nuanced.

Pay attention to the sodium content (around 900 milligrams per tablespoon) when buying soy sauces. Some are saltier, but you may prefer their taste. To compensate, just reduce the amount used in the recipes. At regular supermarkets, choose Kikkoman soy sauce. Pearl River Bridge is slowly gaining shelf space at mainstream markets. You can always find it at Chinese and Vietnamese markets.

Star anise (*đại hồi/hồi hương* **or** *tai hồi*)

This beautiful star-shaped pod (illustrated on page 12) grows on small evergreen trees (or shrubs) in southwestern China and northern Vietnam. No wonder its smoky licorice flavor is present in *phở*, which originated around Hanoi. Each pod has eight pointed segments radiating from the center, with a light brown seed in each segment. Despite the name, these aromatic pods are not related to aniseed. Star anise is sold in small plastic bags in the spice aisle at Chinese and Southeast Asian markets. Select packages in which the pods look unbroken. Health-food stores with bulk spice sections are another good source.

Sticky rice (*gạo nếp*)

For a discussion of the types of rice used by Vietnamese cooks, see page 14.

Straw mushrooms, canned (*nấm rơm*)

For centuries, straw mushrooms, also known as paddy straw mushrooms, have been grown in China and Southeast Asia. Cute, bite sized, and a good source of protein, they take their name from the fact that they were traditionally cultivated on rice straw. Although they are the most important fresh mushroom in southern Asia, abroad they are only available canned, and the flavor is very mild. Canned straw mushrooms add their charming, diminutive appearance and slightly slippery texture to dishes. When harvested young, before the caps have burst open, the mushrooms are considered "unpeeled" and look like tan quail eggs. "Peeled" ones have had their edible shroud removed and are prettier and less slippery. Canned straw mushrooms are labeled peeled or unpeeled. It is your choice of which to buy. Whole, not broken, mushrooms are best.

Tamarind (*me*)

Native to tropical Africa, tamarind is one of the primary sour ingredients in Vietnamese cooking, much like it is throughout Southeast Asia. The pulp of the brown, curved seedpods varies from very sweet to very sour. The fresh pods in Southeast Asian markets are usually sweet, and you can peel and eat them. For cooking purposes, use sour tamarind pulp available in 5-inch square slabs resembling thick slices of pumpernickel bread. The double-wrapped packages (the pulp is very sticky), which weigh 14 to 16 ounces, are sold in Chinese and Southeast Asian markets. To use the pulp, you must first transform it into liquid (page 319). Look for seedless, relatively soft, dark reddish brown slabs and store them in the cupboard for up to 6 months. Avoid the weak-tasting concentrated tamarind liquid sold at Indian and Middle Eastern markets.

Tapioca starch (*bột năng*)

Also called tapioca flour, this is the starch of the cassava root (a.k.a. yuca or manioc), a native of South America. In Viet kitchens, tapioca starch, like cornstarch (see entry), is used to thicken soups and sauces. (I mostly use the more readily available cornstarch.) It is also blended into rice flour batter to produce savory foods that are slightly chewy and shiny, and some rice papers contain the starch. Dumplings or noodles made from tapioca-starch dough are translucent and elastic. The starch also produces a crispy result when added to batters or used to coat foods for deep-frying. Compared with cornstarch, tapioca starch is finer and denser; it easily becomes airborne. Tapioca pearls (*bột bán*) are tapioca starch rolled into small balls.

Tapioca starch is inexpensively sold at Asian markets. It is also available at Latin, African, Caribbean, and health-food stores. Tapioca pearls are sold in various sizes at Asian markets. I mostly use the small ones, about 1/8 inch in diameter.

Thai basil (*húng quế*)
For a discussion of fresh herbs commonly eaten with Vietnamese food, see page 17.

Turmeric, fresh and ground (*nghệ*)
This relative of ginger is used throughout Southeast Asia to color and flavor food. Long recognized for its medicinal qualities, the fresh rhizome is traditionally rubbed on cuts or bruises to promote healing. When employed in cooking, fresh turmeric is pounded and then mixed with water. The resulting bright yellow liquid is then added to foods. Ground turmeric (*bột nghệ*) is integral to Indian curry powder, a staple in the Vietnamese kitchen. Since fresh turmeric is relatively expensive and not substantially better than ground, I chiefly rely on ground turmeric for my cooking needs. If you do buy fresh turmeric, store it in a plastic bag in the vegetable crisper like you would fresh ginger.

Vietnamese balm (*kinh giới*)
For a discussion of fresh herbs commonly eaten with Vietnamese food, see page 17.

Vietnamese coriander (*rau răm*)
For a discussion of fresh herbs commonly eaten with Vietnamese food, see page 17.

Wood ear mushrooms, dried (*nấm mèo khô/mộc nhĩ khô*)
Black-gray, crunchy, and flavorless, wood ear mushrooms add terrific texture to foods. Also called black fungus, these mushrooms grow on rotting wood and are mostly sold dried. They are available fresh too, but I don't use them since they are rare; if you happen upon fresh ones, store them as you would any

fresh mushroom, and trim and cut them up for cooking. The dried mushrooms range from tiny ones that must be measured in a spoon to huge, tough ones. I buy the small to midsized ones because they are tender yet crunchy, can be cut into strips or finely chopped, and neither disappear nor overwhelm. Small, flakelike ones are so delicate that they tend to get lost in food. No matter how the big ones are cut, they are unpleasant to chew. Dried wood ear mushrooms are sold at Asian markets in plastic packages. They keep indefinitely in the cupboard.

To reconstitute dried wood ear mushrooms, soak them in hot water to cover for about 15 minutes, or until they are pliable. If the tough "eye" remains at the center of the mushroom, remove it before cutting up the mushroom for a recipe. Because these mushrooms vary in size, gauge how much to use for a recipe by looking at the count and corresponding measurement.

Yellow rock sugar (*đường phèn*)
Mildly sweet, golden chunks of rock sugar (illustrated on page ii) are what give many Vietnamese noodle soup broths their nuanced sweetness and soft roundness. While some cooks substitute granulated white sugar, its use produces a flat, cloying result. (In Chinese cooking, yellow rock sugar is used in certain braised dishes and sweet soups. Food stewed with yellow rock sugar develops an interesting sheen in addition to a unique flavor.)

A combination of white sugar, unrefined brown sugar, and honey, yellow rock sugar is sold at Chinese and Viet markets. The 1-pound boxes or plastic bags are often labeled yellow rock sugar or yellow lump sugar. Don't confuse it with white rock sugar, which is often stocked nearby and is not as flavorful. With every new package, you will need to break up large chunks by wrapping them in a lint-free cloth and banging away with a hammer. Store the small chunks and bits in an airtight container at room temperature and they will last practically forever.

RESOURCES

MARKETS AND OTHER RETAILERS

A list of specific stores is certain to be incomplete and go out of date, so here are tips for locating businesses that carry Vietnamese ingredients and equipment.

- Find a Vietnamese enclave nearby and check the yellow pages for grocers and markets. According to the 2000 U.S. Census, Vietnamese Americans are the fourth largest Asian ethnic group in America. While the biggest concentrations are in California and Texas, the cities of Atlanta, Boston, New Orleans, New York City, Seattle, and Washington, D.C., boast good-sized communities, too. Even Wichita, Kansas, and Grand Rapids, Michigan, have burgeoning populations. If you don't already know where to find a Vietnamese community, try using the Internet to search for one in your area.

  If you are in Orange County, California, home to the largest concentration of Vietnamese outside of Vietnam, visit the granddaddy of Little Saigons, the oldest and best-established shopping-and-business district of its kind. Don't expect an urban enclave. Located off the 405 freeway in the cities of Westminster and Garden Grove, it is a suburban scene crisscrossed by wide streets and dotted with strip malls. Most of the action is on the stretch of Bolsa Avenue between Brookhurst and Magnolia, particularly at the two-story Asian Garden Mall. From there it radiates outward to adjacent neighborhoods and cities. For more information on Little Saigons in America, see the Little Saigon entry at en.wikipedia.org.

- Don't limit yourself to Vietnamese markets. Chinese, Thai, Cambodian, Laotian, and Filipino markets also sell ingredients for Vietnamese cooking. The herbs may not be available, but other essentials, like fish sauce, will be on the shelves. Also, where there is a substantial community of Asian people, there are generally big markets that cater to its cooking needs. Ranch 99 Market (99ranch.com) is a great pan-Asian chain of big grocery stores with locations in California, Washington, Arizona, Hawaii, and Nevada. Other notable chains include Hong Kong Supermarket and Shun Fat Supermarket. For a listing of Southeast Asian markets in America, visit thaifoodandtravel.com.

- Explore Chinatowns. Chinese influences in Vietnamese cooking run deep, and many of the ingredients are the same. A number of the grocery stores are operated by ethnic Chinese from Vietnam. Chinatown housewares and restaurant-supply shops stock steamers, dishware, and other cooking tools.

- Ask Viet people "in the know." For example, the owner of your favorite Vietnamese restaurant or a member of a local university's Vietnamese Student Association (VSA) will likely have a bundle of sound advice on where to shop for food and specialty equipment. (VSA is an international organization with numerous chapters in the United States. The students sponsor cultural events and food festivals and know their community's culinary resources.)

- Go beyond Asian markets. Visit Latin, Middle Eastern, Caribbean, and other ethnic markets; health-food stores; and the international or Asian food section of mainstream supermarkets. Good butcher counters in Mexican groceries and *carnicerias* (meat markets) are treasures.

- Shop farmers' markets. In a number of places in the country, Hmong, Laotian, and Vietnamese farmers are trucking loads of fresh Asian produce to weekly markets. Non–Southeast Asian farmers are increasingly growing Asian vegetables and herbs. Check Web sites such as localharvest.org for local markets and farms.

- Use culinary message boards such as egullet.com. The virtual community of cooks is full of insights.

SHOPPING STRATEGIES

If you are new to Vietnamese food, trying to decipher what various products are is challenging. The English names and other labeling on Asian food packaging are confusing and inconsistent; imitations of the best brands abound; and new brands and sale items contribute to the confusion. These are obstacles for Vietnamese and non-Vietnamese speakers alike. For your shopping trip, remember to do the following:

- Copy down the Vietnamese terms for the ingredients and look for them on the labels.

- Buy at the middle- or high-price range. Asian food producers are fiercely competitive. Pay a little more and generally you get higher quality.

- Stick with a good thing. The leading brand manufacturers keep tabs on the marketplace. It is rare for a newer or cheaper product to replace a reliable one.

- Ask fellow shoppers or the store staff for help. Be reluctant to chat and you will stay in the dark.

- Walk every aisle. Familiarize yourself with the inventory and where it is located.

- Stock up. If you live far from a decent Asian market, buy extra bottles and jars of condiments and other hard-to-find frozen, canned, or dried ingredients.

- As a last resort, purchase ingredients and equipment online or by mail order. Because inventories and service fluctuate, check to see what is currently available and reliable. Among the online and mail-order sources worth exploring are:

The Oriental Pantry (Acton, MA)
(978) 264-4576, orientalpantry.com
Offers a broad selection of Asian ingredients.

Pacific Rim Gourmet (San Diego, CA)
pacificrimgourmet.com
Inventory is organized by cuisine and ingredient category.

The Wok Shop (San Francisco, CA)
(415) 989-3797, wokshop.com
Excellent selection of equipment, including moon cake molds.

GARDENING SOURCES

If you cannot buy an herb or a vegetable, try growing it. Here are some helpful resources:

Baker Creek Heirloom Seeds (Mansfield, MO)
(417) 924-8917, rareseeds.com
Carries an amazing variety of seeds from all over the world.

Evergreen Y.H. Enterprises (Anaheim, CA)
(714) 637-5769, evergreenseeds.com
Specializes in Asian vegetables and herbs.

Kitazawa Seed Company (Oakland, CA)
(510) 595-1188, kitazawaseed.com
Specializes in Asian vegetables and herbs. The catalog and Web site offer interesting cross-cultural information.

Richters Herbs (Goodwood, ON, Canada)
(905) 640-6677, richters.com
Offers an extensive selection of seeds and plants. The engaging catalog and the Web site are chock-full of information.

BIBLIOGRAPHY

IN ENGLISH

Anderson, E.N. *The Food of China*. New Haven: Yale University Press, 1988.

Brillat-Savarin, Jean Anthelme. *The Physiology of Taste*. Translated by M.F.K. Fisher. San Francisco: North Point Press, 1986.

Carmack, Robert, Didier Corlou, and Nguyen Thanh Van. *Vietnamese Home Cooking*. Boston: Periplus Editions, 2003.

Chang, K. C., ed. *Food in Chinese Culture: Anthropological and Historical Perspectives*. New Haven: Yale University Press, 1977.

Child, Julia. *From Julia Child's Kitchen*. New York: Alfred A. Knopf, 1975.

Chute, David. "Fire in the Bowl." *Los Angeles*, April 2001, 72–75, 171–72.

Cooks Illustrated. *The New Best Recipe*. Brookline, MA: America's Test Kitchen, 2004.

Cost, Bruce. *Asian Ingredients*. New York: Quill, 2000.

Davidson, Alan. *The Oxford Companion to Food*. Oxford: Oxford University Press, 1999.

———. *Seafood of South-East Asia*. Singapore: Federal, 1977.

Duong, Binh, and Marcia Kiesel. *Simple Art of Vietnamese Cooking*. New York: Prentice Hall Press, 1991.

Foo, Susana. *Susana Foo Chinese Cuisine*. Shelburne, VT: Chapters, 1995.

Fletcher, Janet. "Secret Ingredient: Fish Sauce Adds Distinction to Cuisines Far Beyond Southeast Asia." *San Francisco Chronicle*, 27 April 2005, sec. F.

Freeman, Meera, and Le Van Nhan. *The Flavours of Vietnam*. Melbourne: Black Inc., 2002.

Goldberg, Shoshana. "Move Over, Ketchup." *Saveur*, October 2005, 22–23.

Kuo, Irene. *The Key to Chinese Cooking*. New York: Alfred A. Knopf, 1977.

Lang, Jennifer Harvey, ed. *Larousse Gastronomique*. New York: Crown, 1988.

Lee, Calvin B. T., and Audrey Evans Lee. *The Gourmet Chinese Regional Cookbook*. Secaucus, NJ: Castle Books, 1976.

Loha-unchit, Kasma. *Dancing Shrimp*. New York: Simon & Schuster, 2000.

McGee, Harold. *On Food and Cooking: The Science and Lore of the Kitchen*. New York: Scribner, 1984, 2004.

Miller, Jill Nhu Huong. *Vietnamese Cookery*. Rutland, VT: Charles E. Tuttle, 1968.

Ngo, Bach, and Gloria Zimmerman. *The Classic Cuisine of Vietnam*. New York: Plume, 1986.

Parsons, Russ. *How to Read a French Fry and Other Stories of Intriguing Kitchen Science*. New York: Houghton Mifflin, 2001.

Pham, Mai. *Pleasures of the Vietnamese Table*. New York: HarperCollins, 2001.

Reeves, Terrance J., and Claudette E. Bennett. "We the People: Asians in the United States." *Census 2000 Special Reports*. Washington, D.C.: U.S. Census Bureau, December 2004. http://www.census.gov/prod/2004pubs/censr-17.pdf.

Routhier, Nicole. *The Foods of Vietnam*. New York: Stewart, Tabori & Chang, 1989.

Saville, Carole. *Exotic Herbs: A Compendium of Exceptional Culinary Herbs*. New York: Henry Holt, 1997.

Schneider, Elizabeth. *Uncommon Fruits & Vegetables: A Commonsense Guide*. New York: William Morrow, 1986.

Solomon, Charmaine. *Encyclopedia of Asian Food*. Boston: Periplus Editions, 1996.

Taylor, Keith Weller. *The Birth of Vietnam*. Berkeley: University of California Press, 1983.

Templer, Robert. *Shadows and Wind: A View of Modern Vietnam*. New York: Penguin Books, 1999.

Thompson, David. *Thai Food*. Berkeley: Ten Speed Press, 2002.

Thorne, John, and Matt Lewis Thorne. *Pot on the Fire: Further Exploits of a Renegade Cook*. New York: North Point Press, 2000.

Trieu, Thi Choi, and Marcel Isaak. *The Food of Vietnam: Authentic Recipes from the Heart of Indochina*. Singapore: Periplus Editions, 1997.

Tropp, Barbara. *China Moon Cookbook*. New York: Workman, 1992.

———. *The Modern Art of Chinese Cooking*. New York: Hearst Books, 1982.

Wikipedia. "Little Saigon." *Wikipedia*. http://en.wikipedia.org/wiki/Little_Saigon.

Xuan, Phuong, and Daniele Mazingarbe. *Ao Dai: My War, My Country, My Vietnam*. Great Neck, NY: EMQUAD International, 2004.

Young, Grace, and Alan Richardson. *The Breath of Wok: Unlocking the Spirit of Chinese Wok Cooking through Recipes and Lore*. New York: Simon & Schuster, 2004.

IN VIETNAMESE

Vietnamese names are presented in an inverted format (surname, middle name, first name). Some authors, however, exclude their surname or use pen names that do not include surnames. To simplify matters, the works below are listed alphabetically according to how the authors' names appear in the publications. Older works (pre-1975 and perhaps even pre-1954) were brought to the United States and printed here. Due to a lack of copyright laws and guidelines at that time, those works do not have publication years.

Đỗ Kim Trung. *Nấu Ăn Gia Đình: Miền Nam*. Hà Nội: Nhà Xuất Bản Phụ Nữ, 2003.

———. *Nấu Ăn Gia Đình: Miền Bắc*. Hà Nội: Nhà Xuất Bản Phụ Nữ, 2003.

Hoàng Thị Kim-Cúc. *Những Món Ăn Nấu Lối Huế*. Los Alamitos, CA: Xuân Thu.

Lệ Hoa. *Cách Làm Những Món Ăn Đặc Biệt Ba Miền*. Glendale, CA: Dainamco.

———. *Nghệ Thuật Làm Các Món Nhậu*. Los Alamitos, CA: Xuân Thu.

Mai Khôi. *Văn Hóa Ẩm Thực Việt Nam: Các Món Ăn Miền Trung*. Hà Nội: Nhà Xuất Bản Thanh Niên, 2002.

Mai Khôi, Vũ Bằng, and Thượng Hồng. *Văn Hóa Ẩm Thực Việt Nam: Các Món Ăn Miền Nam*. Hà Nội: Nhà Xuất Bản Thanh Niên, 2002.

Nguyễn Dzoãn Cẩm Vân. *100 Món Ăn Ngày Thường*. Hà Nội: Nhà Xuất Bản Phụ Nữ, 2002.

———. *Những Món Ăn Đãi Tiệc và Gia Đình*. Hà Nội: Nhà Xuất Bản Phụ Nữ, 1999.

Nguyễn Thu Hà and Huỳnh Thị Dung. *Bí Quyết Chế Biến Bánh, Mứt, Kẹo, Ô Mai*. Hà Nội: Nhà Xuất Bản Văn Hóa Thông Tin, 2001.

———. *Các Món Ăn Chay*. Hà Nội: Nhà Xuất Bản Văn Hóa Thông Tin, 2001.

Nhiều Tác Giả. *Văn Hóa Ẩm Thực Việt Nam: Các Món Ăn Miền Bắc*. Hà Nội: Nhà Xuất Bản Thanh Niên, 2001.

Quốc Việt. *Nghệ Thuật Nấu Ăn Toàn Tập*. Thành Phố Hồ Chí Minh: Nhà Xuất Bản Văn Nghệ Thành Phố Hồ Chí Minh, 2001.

Quỳnh Hương. *Xôi Chè Việt Nam*. Hà Nội: Nhà Xuất Bản Phụ Nữ, 2003.

Trần Văn Lùng. "Gói Bánh Chưng." *Khoa Học Phổ Thông*.

Triệu Thị Chơi, and others. *Kỹ Thuật Nấu Ăn Toàn Tập*. Thành Phố Hồ Chí Minh: Nhà Xuất Bản Tổng Hợp, 2004.

Trường Đại Học Thương Mại Hà Nội. *555 Món Ăn Việt Nam: Kỹ Thuật Chế Biến và Giá Trị Dinh Dưỡng*. Hà Nội: Nhà Xuất Bản Thống Kê, 2000.

Vân Đài. *Làm Bếp Giỏi*. Los Alamitos, CA: Xuân Thu.

Võ Thị Hòa. *Nghệ Thuật Làm Bếp: 252 Món Ăn Ba Miền*. Hà Nội: Nhà Xuất Bản Phụ Nữ, 2001.

INDEX